THE USSR AND IRAQ

The Soviet Quest for Influence

Oles M. Smolansky with Bettie M. Smolansky

DUKE UNIVERSITY PRESS *Durham and London*

© 1991 Duke University Press
All rights reserved.
Printed in the United States of America
on acid-free paper ∞
Library of Congress Cataloging-in-Publication Data
appear on the last printed page of this book

To Our Children

Contents

■ Preface

My interest in Soviet-Iraqi relations was first aroused in the course of research for an earlier work, *The Soviet Union and the Arab East under Khrushchev* (1974). It was rekindled in the early 1980s when Alvin Z. Rubinstein of the University of Pennsylvania suggested that I prepare a study on the USSR and Iraq for the series on influence relationships in international politics which he was then editing. For a variety of reasons, the most important of which was the outbreak of the Iran-Iraq war, this project took much longer than I had originally anticipated. The manuscript also turned out to be much larger than the parameters set out by Rubinstein had allowed, and thus it now appears as an independent study, although it has an intellectual affinity to Rubinstein's series.

Put differently, rather than a diplomatic history of Soviet-Iraqi relations, this volume examines how and under what circumstances the USSR and Ba'thist Iraq interacted with each other in situations where their respective interests were involved, occasionally in a complementary but more often in a conflicting fashion. Specifically, such major domestic problems as the nationalization of the oil industry, the Kurdish demands for autonomy and ultimately independence, and the role to be assigned to the Communist party in the political life of Iraq represented issues on which both Moscow and Baghdad had reasonably coherent positions. In the area of foreign relations, the Iraqi and Soviet policies in the Persian/Arabian Gulf—the main focus of Baghdad's foreign political and economic activity—have also been scrutinized to determine areas of conflicting or complementary interests.

Having established their respective positions, an attempt was made to follow through separately on their development and on Moscow's and Baghdad's interaction with respect to the issues at hand. The chronological approach used in the individual chapters enables a demonstration of how the positions of the respective protagonists changed over time. This type of exercise was concluded by posing and by trying to answer the questions of who influenced whom, under what circumstances did the interaction occur, and why—in those particular situations—one side seemingly succeeded in influencing the other. It is apparent that in most situations where Iraq's vital national interests were at stake, its wishes prevailed over Moscow's preferences. For the Kremlin, this was not a novel experience. In the late 1950s and the 1960s the Soviets had learned the hard way that most of the leading neutralist (later nonaligned) states were using the USSR for their own purposes and refused to pursue policies which contradicted their perceived vital interests.

Indeed, in light of the restructuring of the world order now taking place this conclusion may strike even the casual observer as less than startling. However, it is an issue that continues to bear careful empirical analysis for, even in the post-glasnost world, states will continue to assert their national interests and in the process will attempt to influence each other's policies and actions. While some of the specific sources of leverage will no doubt continue to change, the resource-dependence balancing nature of such relationships will remain an essential part of the game. Case studies of the unfolding of such relationships can therefore teach us valuable lessons for the future.

The time frame chosen for this study was the twenty-year period between 1968 and 1988. The logical starting point was the second, and this time successful, seizure of power in Iraq by the military, members of the Ba'th party. (The first, abortive attempt was made in 1963 and collapsed in a few months' time.) The organization has remained in power ever since. Since the late 1970s it has been dominated by its erstwhile civilian leader Saddam Hussein. The year 1988 has been selected as the end point. It was then that Ayatollah Khomeini finally decided to terminate the bloodiest conflict of the post-World War II period which Saddam Hussein had unleashed in 1980. The end of the Iran-Iraq war and the subsequent death of Ayatollah Khomeini thus represent the end of an epoch in Gulf politics. From then on, Iraq's designs on the Gulf shifted from the defeated and exhausted Islamic Republic to the region's oil-rich, politically conservative, and militarily weak states.

Since access to relevant Soviet and Iraqi source material remains closed—a standard time restriction is imposed by virtually all governments—and since official functionaries of both states are not in the habit of discussing such matters beyond the accepted line of the day, research had to be conducted primarily in Soviet and Iraqi (as well as general Arab) public sources. These included official government statements as well as pronouncements of their respective leaders and officials. This material has been widely supplemented by articles and other pertinent information appearing in the Soviet and Iraqi press, journals, and magazines. Since, for much of the period under discussion, Moscow's and Baghdad's publications had operated under strict government supervision, their pronouncements usually reflected the current party line. Glasnost under Gorbachev has brought sweeping changes to Soviet publications; however, relative freedom of expression has been confined mainly to internal developments. With the major exception of Afghanistan, foreign policy issues have not, until recently, attracted the attention of Soviet investigative journalists. Informal discussions with Soviet academic specialists, in contrast, proved to be very helpful.

The Ford Foundation and the Earhart Foundation generously provided financial assistance that enabled me to undertake the early stages of research on this project. Thanks are also due to Lehigh University for a sabbatical leave to finish the first draft of the manuscript as well as for financial support in typing its various versions. Anonymous reviewers for the Duke University Press made many helpful suggestions and comments, and Richard Rowson, its chief editor, guided the manuscript through its initial stages at the Press with great skill and patience. Marcia Mierzwa, Doris Wilkinson, Jean Schiffert, and Shirley Sutton typed the various drafts of the manuscript's components.

Numerous friends at Lehigh University and elsewhere sustained me in the moments when the problems at hand appeared insurmountable. They know that their moral support has been invaluable. Finally, the manuscript would not have been completed without the constant support, encouragement, and, in later stages, the collaboration of my wife, Bettie M. Smolansky, who has contributed the Introduction and Conclusion to this study. I owe her an enormous debt.

■ Introduction: The Nature of Influence Relationships

The analysis that follows focuses on the meshing of three topics: Iraq, the Soviet Union, and influence relationships. All three share at least two implicit characteristics. They are believed by the American public to have international significance (albeit not equal in weight), and they are but vaguely understood by most educated Americans, who know little of the history, geography, or culture of Iraq, and are only slightly more familiar with the Soviet Union. Yet there existed until recently a widespread lingering impression, occasionally fostered by both policy-makers and the press, that Moscow has exercised undue influence over Baghdad and that Iraq has been a significant ally, if not indeed a puppet, of the USSR.

The purpose of this volume is to examine in detail the recent history of what is in fact a very complex, bi-directional relationship between Iraq and the USSR and to dispel some of the widely held misconceptions about it. At the same time, the study attempts to use the Soviet-Iraqi case to further understanding of the nature of influence relationships.

The Nature of Influence

Since the advent of nation-state societies, nations have sought to influence the policies and actions of other states in a variety of different ways. In a sense, that is what both war and diplomacy are all about. Thus, analysts of international affairs have long discussed, both implicitly and explicitly, the quest for influence in interstate relations. Unfortunately, more often than not, such discussions have been based on ill-defined concepts and unarticulated assumptions. Indeed, few terms in the literature of international affairs are so widely but loosely used as the concept of influence. Far too often, analysts assume that everyone knows what influence is, and, therefore, give little if any attention to a careful definition of the concept. To avoid the same trap, this analysis will begin with an attempt to answer the basic question, What is influence?

What Is Influence? Although many analysts adopt a blithe, common-sensical approach to the issue of influence, some scholars have given the matter careful attention. While each writer is likely to prefer his or her own unique phraseology, the definitional disagreements among them tend to devolve to differences over two main issues: whether or not to include the use of military force and the pursuit of mutual interests as part of an influence process.

The work of Alvin Z. Rubinstein, who has written extensively on the topic, provides an excellent example of the school of thought which excludes the use of military force.[1] Otherwise, however, his definition is quite broad: "Influence is manifested when A affects *through non-military means*, directly or indirectly, the behavior of B so that it rebounds to the policy advantage of A."[2] (It is not entirely clear in this definition what role a credible threat of military action may play in the influence process, but it is presumably not excluded. Indeed, it seems likely that the existence of such a threat alters the balance of interstate relationships dramatically.) While the actual use of military force is ruled out by this definition, the pursuit of mutual interests is included. Analysts at the Center for Defense Information, in contrast, provide an example of the approach which adopts a more limiting definition of the mutual interest issue. They describe influence as "the ability of one nation to have another do something that it otherwise would not do."[3]

In the hope of formulating a more encompassing definition of influence, and at the risk of complicating the issue further, it was initially decided to consider the issue at a somewhat higher level of abstraction. Borrowing some useful formulations from sociological theory, it could be argued that influence is ultimately an interactive process, albeit one enacted between and among nation-states rather than individuals or simple groups. In their most basic terms, influence relationships among states can be seen as a special subset of what the sociologist Richard Emerson has called "power-dependence relations."[4]

Emerson claims that all power-dependence relationships are mutual, but that they are not generally symmetrical. In its simplest terms, influence (like power, of which it is one manifestation) resides in the dependency of one actor on another. Emerson goes on to claim that the specific nature of any such relationship must always be seen as an empirical question; the same can be said of influence relationships.

Thus, to say that "A has influence over B" is an essentially vacuous statement.

Indeed, in Emerson's view, the primary origin of power (and thus influence) is control by one actor over resources that another actor needs or wants: "The dependence of actor A upon actor B is (1) directly proportional to A's *motivational investment* in goals mediated by B and (2) inversely proportional to the *availability* of those goals to A outside the A–B relationship."[5]

Also involved in assessing the nature as well as the degree of A's dependence (and thus B's influence) is an understanding of A's will to resist doing what B wishes A to do. That is to say, if A wants to do what B wishes anyway, then Emerson contends that A's actions should not be seen as a function of A's dependence; it is not, in Emerson's terms, an example of influence. Here, I contend that Emerson is framing the issue too narrowly. Specifically, even if A wishes to undertake an action also urged by B but can do so only if B provides the necessary resources, that situation constitutes a form of dependence by A upon B (and, by extension, comprises a form of influence by B over A).

Extending Emerson's definition in this fashion, however, in no way obviates another important insight developed as part of his analysis. Specifically, since the exercise of power involves A doing something at the behest of B that A otherwise would not do because B controls scarce resources that A wants or needs to accomplish his goals, such processes are inevitably embedded in an unstable equilibrium. The resultant balancing act comprises the essence of influence relationships.

As Emerson makes clear, power-dependence relationships are inherently unstable because they encourage "balancing operations" and "cost reduction" by the participants. Thus, the exclusiveness of B's control over the relevant resources is a key issue in the relationship. That is, A can reduce dependence upon B by finding (an) alternative source(s) of the necessary resources. For example, in the international arena, a client can sometimes either find or threaten to find another patron. Conversely, A can lessen dependence on B by reducing the commitment to those goals that require the resources controlled by B. In the case of interstate relations, commitment to less than vital interests can sometimes be redefined or scaled down as a client nation seeks to reduce its dependence on a patron.

Moreover, as time passes and B commits resources to A, resulting in A's transitory needs being partially or fully met, A's dependence on B will automatically lessen. Such a situation comprises, in other words, an instance where success breeds its own failure, becoming a kind of classic dialectical contradiction. Concomitantly, A's leverage (and thus the ability to resist B's wishes) is increased as B's interest in maintaining the A–B relationship increases, and B's expenditure of resources on A's behalf inevitably gives B a vested interest in maintaining the link. Such a situation leads to a reduction in A's dependence on B and an increase in B's dependence on A. That is, A, having the ability to continue to enhance, to reduce, or to sever the relationship, has acquired control over a resource that B desires. [6]

These descriptions of balancing or cost-reduction operations suggest implicitly that there are many types of goals and policy options with which a putatively dependent actor in an influence relationship may be confronted:

1. A strives for a valued goal for which indigenous resources are lacking (e.g., enhancement of its industrial base or military power) and thus turns to B for those resources;
2. A tries to avoid a negative contingency (e.g., loss of territory and/or defeat in a military conflict) which it lacks the resources to confound;
3. A uses B's resources to achieve a goal or enact a policy about which A is essentially neutral, thus incurring little or no cost to A, but winning for A the continued good will of B and/or other tangible benefits (e.g., A voting in bloc or siding with B in international disputes which do not affect A directly);
4. A initially rejects a policy urged upon it by B, but in response to some explicit or implicit quid pro quo or threat from B acquiesces to B's wishes in the matter.

This latter category of interaction is likely if, and only if, the policy or action toward which A had originally been negative does not touch what A construes to be a vital national interest and the attendant benefits to be gained from B are substantial or if the threat is credible and is aimed at a vital interest of A.

This broad and deliberately abstract analysis of the nature of power-dependence relationships leads inevitably to a definition which recognizes that influence is not a singular but rather a multifaceted phenomenon. Thus, it is preferable to use Rubinstein's general approach with its implicit inclusion of the pursuit of mutual interests under the influence rubric. This stance has been adopted because, in practical terms, it is virtually impossible for the external analyst to understand whether and to what extent the perception of some level of mutual interest played a role in the specific policy decisions of a given client in regard to the wishes of a patron state.[7]

Viewed from this angle, influence should be seen as any activity by one state (B) which causes or helps to cause the actions of another state (A) to conform to B's wishes. Having so defined the term, however, it is important to acknowledge that there are two major types of influence, facilitative and instigative, and each is further divisible into subtypes.

Specifically, facilitative influence involves the provision by a great power to a lesser power of resources which allow the latter to pursue policies deemed to be in the interests of both (albeit sometimes for differing reasons and at different levels of significance). Furthermore, some such instances can be seen as constructive while others might be labeled protective.

Instigative influence refers to the provision by a greater to a lesser power of resources in return for which the latter pursues policies which it would not otherwise have undertaken. The reader should not automatically infer, however, that in such cases the client state has been coerced into doing something which it finds repugnant, for here, too, a pair of subtypes are readily apparent. Specifically, such instances can be divided into those which are cooperative and those which are coercive.

In other words, constructive facilitative influence characterizes the first category of the "goals and policy options" enumerated above, while protective facilitative influence would more accurately describe the second. Cooperative instigative and coercive instigative influence are the more appropriate designations for the third and fourth of those categories, respectively.

This typology is not created simply for the pleasure of indulging in a symmetrical, abstract analysis. Rather, it seems likely that an understanding of a phenomenon as complex as influence will be best served by breaking the analysis down into meaningful subsets. This is especially true when, as seems probable with the concept of influence, the activities and processes which achieve success for an influence-seeker in one situation will be unproductive or counterproductive in another. Thus, the search for patterns is likely to be more fruitful when guided by a useful typology.

Two further explanatory comments need to be added to the typology proposed above: (1) the credible threat of the use of military force, either against the lesser power or on its behalf, cannot be excluded from the resources potentially involved in influence processes (the necessity for their actual use, however, does represent, by definition, a failure of influence); and (2) "provision of resources" can include the process of buffering the less powerful nation from negative responses to its actions by other nations.

In sum, when great powers set out to acquire influence, they commit some of their resources, directly or indirectly, to the use or control of a lesser power. They do so presumably, despite their frequently contrary rhetoric, in a self-interested rather than in an altruistic spirit. That leads us then to inquire about their specific motives in undertaking such a process.

Why Do Great Powers Seek Influence? Nations have historically engaged in informal cost-benefit analysis, long before anyone thought to use the term. Nowhere is this more obvious but less amenable to definitive measurement than in the influence-building process. Based both upon the *post factum* analysis of the actions of states over the long term and of the retrospective firsthand accounts of diplomats from many nations, one can readily discern in general terms the kinds of benefits that states hope will result from their quests for influence. For analytical convenience, these possible benefits may be subsumed under three headings: military, economic, and political.

Militarily, states seek such benefits as bases or access to support facilities for their forces, the strategic guarantee that "friendly" nations will buffer their borders, and sometimes formal alliances against common enemies. Pursuit of such objectives is not without costs even when successfully achieved. The use of bases or facilities generally involves substantial monetary fees and often harbors a potential for political problems, given the widespread sensitivity to perceived encroachment upon national autonomy in less powerful nations. The buffering effect of "friendly" border states can prove illusory (especially in the missile age), and such "friendships" almost always also have substantial economic costs. Finally, alliances, by definition, incur reciprocal obligations for their participants, that create a situation in which the great power patron inherits some of the military liabilities of the less powerful client.

Economically, an influence relationship can lead to relatively stable, favorable trade arrangements, can provide ready access to needed raw materials, and, in the case of economically well-off clients, can provide a source of hard currency for goods sold (civilian or military). Unfortunately, for great powers, most lesser powers are not so economically advantaged that they can be hard currency-paying customers. Most Third World clients require foreign aid or loans for their external purchases. Even in dealing with states such as oil-rich Iraq, which do not require financial subsidies, a great power must be careful to avoid driving too hard a bargain, lest the asymmetrical nature of the transaction come to breed resentment in the client state and produce a festering political problem.

The political fruits which powerful nations can expect from sowing the seeds of influence among client states are even more perishable. In return for the provision of resources to a lesser power, a great power can generally expect public support for, or at least acquiescence to, its basic domestic and international policies but only insofar as they do not come into direct conflict with a perceived important national interest of the client state. This means that a patron should be able to call upon a client to use its influence with third parties in negotiations of interest to the former, to count on its clients' support in the United Nations and other formal international forums on most issues, and generally to expect a client to favor its views in the "court of world opinion." While one should not make a sweeping negative generalization, it is difficult to think of instances where such political advantages have been so substantial as to have justified significant resource expenditure exclusively for the purpose of their accrual.

Indeed, the barely hidden agenda in most of these processes is not some direct positive benefit to the patron state but is instead the effort to deny such benefits to one's adversaries. In sum, the most significant political motivator of the influence-seeking process, especially for the two superpowers, is the very fact of competition with their adversaries. "If they have clients in Region X, then we must have some, too." The quest for influence is, in part, a status contest, and the putative direct, cost-effective benefits to be gained often pale into insignificance when compared to the motivational force of that competition.

Therein, of course, also lies the primary latent cost of the process. In a world riddled with cross-cutting currents of multiple sets of international rivalries, the courting of favor in one nation, with its own tangled network of relationships with other states, brings with it an incredibly complex array of choices to be made. It is much like the thankless and endless task of parenting a large, contentious group of siblings. If you satisfy the one, others will be miffed; alas, shifting your attention to the aggrieved party (or parties) will only undo the good originally engendered with the first.

How Can We Know When Influence-Seekers Succeed or Fail? From the analyst's viewpoint this question might better be rephrased, How can influence be measured?; because the success or failure of an influence-building process will always be, in one sense, relative. In other words, a satisfactory level of success is always a perceptual, eye-of-the-beholder matter. Nevertheless, coherent analysis requires operational-izing the concept, that is, devising at least some meaningful indicators of influence and procedures for their discovery and measurement.

Useful clues are provided by earlier analysts, but their discussions also make it plain how difficult it is to link the conceptual and opera-tional definitions of a term like influence. Thus, authors at the Center for Defense Information, after having produced the rather limiting con-ceptual definition cited earlier, go on to acknowledge that the direct measurement of such a concept is virtually impossible. They suggest instead the use of indicators of "level of involvement" or patron "pres-ence" as surrogates for direct measurement even though they admit overtly that "Presence does not equal influence."[8]

Among the specific indicators which they enumerate are such items as treaty relationships, access to military facilities, presence of troops or military advisers, large-scale arms transfers, economic aid level, significant bilateral trade, common UN voting patterns, exchanges of high-level state visits, and appropriately worded joint communiqués. They also suggest augmenting firsthand analysis of such data with a summary assessment of available evaluations by "knowledgeable ana-lysts." In their own subsequent analysis of the level of Soviet influence in a large number of nations, the Center analysts search for periods during which there was a high level of Soviet involvement with each specific nation, looking apparently for some vaguely discernible differ-ences in the level of policy coincidence or congeniality in periods of intense involvement as compared to those of lesser involvement.

In fact, the Center's so-called "indicators of influence" are actually those of the quest for influence, and the relative success or failure of that quest is almost impossible to measure over the short term. In sum, without some dramatic evidence, such as an eviction or a public sever-ing of ties,[9] the analyst is left to use as evidence data that are once removed and to make the implicit assumption that, all else being equal, greater efforts to acquire influence yield greater influence. Alas, "other things" are never equal.

Rubinstein's discussion of measurement procedures is more elabo-rate than that of the Center analysts. He enumerates five different categories of measurement techniques: "(1) measures of direct interac-tion; (2) measures of perceptual and attitudinal change; (3) measures of attributed influence; (4) case studies, and (5) impressionistic and idio-syncratic commentary."[10]

Direct interaction measures include such quantifiable data as pat-terns of aid and trade and coincidence of UN voting patterns as well as

publicly verifiable matters such as exchanges of missions and the existence of treaty arrangements. He is emphatic, however, in cautioning
that such data must be examined contextually; simplistic quantitative
approaches are likely to obscure rather than illuminate the nature of an
influence relationship.

In Rubinstein's view, perceptual or attitudinal change is best measured by careful thematic analysis of joint communiqués, speeches of
key officials, and the editorials and commentaries in newspapers and
other periodicals known to be tied to the governments in question. His
subsequent detailed description of the specific processes involved in
such analysis suggests that it is virtually an art form, one necessarily
undertaken by a scholar familiar not only with generic diplomatic
conventions but also with the fine points of linguistic practice in the
languages of both parties.

What Rubinstein labels "attributed influence" requires "polling the
experts," presumably both by careful review of their written commentaries and by personal interviews (both formal and informal). His "impressionistic and idiosyncratic material" constitutes a kind of residual
category of all other potentially useful information (e.g., accounts by
journalists and third-party diplomats). In sum, both of these categories
imply that the scholar should be acquainted with the perceptions of all
available, well-placed observers on the state of the influence relationship in question. How to weigh and assess conflicting perceptions is, of
course, case-specific and inevitably somewhat problematic.

Finally, Rubinstein suggests heavy reliance on case studies. While, as
he notes, some of the relevant information is almost always missing,
the process of "trac[ing] the unfolding of influence on significant issues"[11] allows for the synthetic and contextual analysis of all the categories of data mentioned above and should be seen as the preferred
omnibus approach to the measurement of influence. Thus, it is the
primary approach of this volume.

The Plan of the Book

Although this volume is not a standard chronological account of Soviet-
Iraqi relations, the first substantive chapter does give an overview of the
evolution of that relationship. In addition to setting the general context
for the case studies which follow, chapter 1 integrates much of the
available information of the type which Rubinstein has called "measures of direct influence" for the period from 1958, when the modern era
of Soviet-Iraqi relations begins, until 1980. (These include the quanti-

fiable patterns of reciprocal trade and of economic and military aid.)
After the outbreak of the Iran-Iraq war in September of 1980, these
patterns were essentially "driven" by the war; thus comparable data for
that later period are presented in the chapter on that conflict.

The context-setting chapter on the general patterns of relationship
between Baghdad and Moscow is followed by a series of detailed case
studies of the primary issues and problems that have been the focuses of
Soviet-Iraqi relations in the modern era. This connected series of case
analyses is divided into two categories, those that primarily affect Iraq's
domestic policies and those focused on its foreign affairs.

In the domestic arena, chapter 2 examines the Soviet contribution to
the nationalization of the Iraqi oil industry, an issue on which the two
regimes were in virtually full agreement. A second concern, how to deal
with the "Kurdish Question" (examined at length in chapter 3), pro-
duces a more complex and turbulent picture, one in which Moscow and
its putative client were often in disagreement. Finally, chapter 4 is
devoted to an analysis of the tortured history of the Iraqi Communist
party, whose eventual destruction by the Ba'th stands as a stark lesson
on the limits of great power influence.

In foreign affairs, the primary focal point of Baghdad's interest has
been the Persian/Arabian Gulf region. Because it sees itself as a major
player in Gulf affairs, and because both states actually aspire to regional
dominance, Iraq's natural primary rival is Iran. (Current geopolitical
realities are augmented in this regard by a long history of strife between
the two.) However, modern Iraq also has a complex set of relationships
with such other Gulf states as Kuwait, Saudi Arabia, Bahrain, Qatar, the
United Arab Emirates, and Oman. Given Soviet aspirations to become a
leading actor in Gulf affairs, it has had more than a passing interest in
Iraq's attempts to assume a central place in the regional network. The
relative lack of success for either of these two nations in realizing their
ambitions in the Gulf and their often conflicting, counterproductive
efforts to use each other to further their own goals and objectives in the
region are the focus of chapters 5 and 6.

The culmination of Moscow's frustration over its inability to reap
tangible rewards commensurate with its "investment" in the quest for
influence in Iraq came in September 1980. Hard on the heels of joining
the international chorus of condemnation of the Soviet invasion of
Afghanistan, Saddam Hussein sent his armed forces surging across the
Iranian border in an apparent belief that they would score a swift,
decisive military victory over a supposedly disintegrating Iran, wrecked
by the domestic chaos attendant to the Khomeini regime's revolution-

ary excesses. An obviously alarmed Kremlin, whose position in the region depends on the continued precarious balance of contending forces, immediately cut off the flow of military supplies to Baghdad and pressed for an early cessation of hostilities and the withdrawal of Iraqi forces. Indeed, substantial resupply of Saddam Hussein's forces by the USSR resumed only when the magnitude of his miscalculation became apparent in 1982, as the tide of battle had turned in Tehran's favor. (An Iranian victory was even less appetizing a prospect for the Kremlin than an Iraqi one.) Some of the details of the relatively impotent Soviet role in this long and bloody struggle are examined in chapter 7.

Finally, the general lessons to be learned from these separate analyses of specific cases for our understanding of the nature of influence relationships between great and lesser powers are discussed in the conclusion.

One parenthetical note should be added here about what analysts interested in the Middle East may regard as a peculiar omission, a lack of systematic consideration of the Soviet role in Iraqi-Syrian relations. Geography has made Iraq and Syria neighbors, and history has provided an additional bond in that both are ruled by what are supposed to be two branches of the same party (the Ba'th). However, the relationship between these two "fraternal" states has occasionally bordered on the fratricidal, and even in calmer periods can be described as at best "sibling tolerance." Thus, the Kremlin apparently recognized early on that any effort to involve itself directly in the continuing disputatious relationship between two nations in which it sought influence was a no-win situation. Therefore, it has generally tended to maintain a prudent distance from their conflicts with each other.

In other words, the USSR has attempted to foster good relations with Syria for whatever entry and leverage such a link might provide for Moscow in the Arab-Israeli sector[12] and to focus its ties to Iraq upon its concern with Gulf affairs. While Iraq has had some long-term involvement in the Arab-Israeli dispute, the Soviet leadership apparently concluded that Baghdad will inevitably play a secondary role in that arena. Thus, although Iraq assigns considerable importance to its role in Pan-Arab affairs (as a matter of national pride) and, therefore, to its relationship with Syria, Moscow has remained ostentatiously aloof from the intervening squabbles between Baghdad and Damascus. That being the case, an early decision was made not to devote separate attention to the minor Soviet role in Iraqi-Syrian affairs, but instead to focus southward to the primary object of Soviet interest with regard to Iraq's foreign policy, the Persian/Arabian Gulf.[13]

When a military coup overthrew the pro-Western monarchy in Baghdad in July 1958, the Kremlin, led by irrepressible Nikita Khrushchev, expressed a great deal of interest in the newly created republic. This was not surprising. Iraq had by then emerged as an important Arab state whose population base and economic potential (above all its huge oil reserves) propelled it into a position of leadership in a region engaged in shaking off the colonial tutelage and in asserting its political and, eventually, economic independence from the Western "imperialist" powers.

The aspirations and the actions of the Iraqi military corresponded closely—or so it seemed to the Kremlin—to the analysis of the situation in the Third World which Khrushchev developed in the mid-1950s. Specifically, the Soviet leader rejected the ideological precept which Stalin adhered to in the post-World War II period. It will be recalled that, according to Stalin's "two camp" view of the world, "those who are not with us, are against us." Since only the communists were working for "proletarian" revolutions and since the native leaders of the emerging Third World countries were not communists, they were automatically relegated to the enemy camp. This narrow definition, explained by Stalin's preoccupation with more pressing problems (such as postwar reconstruction and absorption of Eastern Europe into the communist system, to name but the most obvious ones), deprived the USSR of an opportunity to cooperate with the national liberation movements which were sweeping across Asia (and, later, Africa) and to benefit directly from the breakup of the colonial empires which began after the end of World War II.

In contrast to Stalin, Khrushchev recognized that the policies and actions of many national liberation movements were complementary to the objectives which the Soviet government was pursuing in the international arena. Specifically, the "national bourgeoisie" of the "colonial and dependent" Third World countries were bent on securing the political and economic independence of their respective states. In the process, the newly independent countries as well as those struggling to achieve their independence were undermining the entire "capitalist" system which, according to Marx and Lenin, had thrived on economic exploitation and politico-military control of the "colonial hinterland." Adopting this Leninist interpretation to current conditions, Khrushchev argued that "those who are not against us, are with us (at least for the time being)." In line with this approach, he extended superpower competition to the Third World and offered military, economic, and technical support to any anti-Western developing country that asked for Soviet assistance. The results of the change in Soviet policy were outwardly impressive: a number of important Third World countries—among them India, Indonesia, Burma, Egypt, Syria, Ghana, and, subsequently, Iraq—declared their friendship for and improved relations with the USSR and sided with it on a number of international problems in which Moscow was directly involved. In no instance, however, did the leaders of the "positive neutralist" (later nonaligned) states compromise their own national interests or become Soviet stooges. In any event, in pursuing his grandiose scheme of attacking the colonial empires through their Asian and African "backyards" regardless of the costs involved, Khrushchev strained Soviet resources. He was ultimately accused in the Politburo of "hare-brained schemes," and the task of introducing some rationality into Moscow's relations with its Third World clients was left to Leonid Brezhnev, who assumed power in 1964.

As a result of the reappraisal of Soviet policies in the Third World, the Kremlin's ambitions were scaled down significantly. Military, economic, and technical assistance were still made available to important clients, but the overriding factor was no longer their abstract "contribution" to the "struggle against capitalism" but some practical advantage which they offered the USSR in its quest to protect and advance its national interests. In addition, Moscow endeavored also to woo some openly pro-Western Third World states, such as Mohammed Reza Shah's Iran and Turkey and Pakistan. Thus, Brezhnev's Kremlin continued to adhere to the bipolar view of the world and remained committed to the concept of global competition, which it pursued vigorously, with the "capitalist" West and its leading exponent, the United States. In this sense, Brezhnev did not differ from Khrushchev. Brezhnev also shared his predecessor's view that the newly independent states had an important role to play in the worldwide competition between the two antagonistic systems. However, although agreeing on principle, the two leaders disagreed on the question of benefits which the USSR should be deriving from an association with a Third World client. Although Khrushchev did not view utility as an important issue, to Brezhnev, it became a major consideration. A closer look at the countries which, in the 1970s, emerged as Moscow's main Third World clients supports this proposition.

Geopolitically, Vietnam, Somalia (later Ethiopia), South Yemen (the PDRY), Egypt, Syria, Angola, and Cuba were all important regional actors which also, at one time or another, had made some of their naval and air facilities available to the Soviet navy and air force. Iraq, too, fell into this category, but its importance to the USSR was enhanced by its location in the Persian Gulf, a region which, because of its enormous oil resources, had attracted a great deal of Western attention. Baghdad's anti-Western credentials and policies, directed at undermining "imperialist" positions and influence, were in harmony with Moscow's own position. Last but not least, Iraq belonged to a small group of Third World clients which, because of their economic wealth, were able to secure Soviet military and industrial equipment in exchange for hard currency or oil. All of these considerations made Iraq a particularly important and attractive client, explaining the relative benevolence with which it was treated by Brezhnev's Kremlin in spite of occasionally grave provocations.

Background

Diplomatic relations between Iraq and the Soviet Union were first established in 1944, during the latter stages of World War II. They were broken off in 1955 by Prime Minister Nuri al-Said after Moscow criticized his government's decision to join the Baghdad Pact.[1] In July 1958, following the coup that brought Colonel Abd al-Kerim Kassem to power, the USSR promptly recognized the Iraqi Republic. This initiative and the subsequent improvement in Moscow-Baghdad relations were based, above all, on the Kremlin's appreciation of the anti-Western stance adopted by the republican regime. In late 1958 Iraq and the USSR signed their first trade and military assistance agreements. In addition to East-West competition, Moscow's support of Kassem coincided with, and was influenced by, the deterioration of relations between Baghdad and Cairo. As the crisis unfolded, the Soviets sided with Iraq. They did so, in part, because of the Kremlin's growing disenchantment with

Gamal Abd al-Nasser and because, initially, Kassem had initiated a number of "progressive" reforms. (Among other things, the Iraqi Communist party was allowed, for the first time, to operate openly and in relative freedom from government persecution.)[2]

In March 1959 Baghdad and Moscow signed another agreement pledging $137 million for Iraq's economic development. In late spring and summer Iraq's formal withdrawal from the Baghdad Pact was followed by increased bilateral cooperation in economic as well as military spheres.[3] Relations cooled considerably in the period between 1960 and 1962, in part as a result of Kassem's crackdown on the Iraqi Communist party.[4] Nevertheless, in spite of disenchantment with Kassem, the USSR did not curtail its economic and military assistance programs to Iraq.[5]

The Arab Socialist Renaissance party—the Ba'th (*Renaissance* in Arabic)—staged its first coup in Iraq in February 1963.[6] Following the atrocities which the government committed against the Iraqi Communist organization, relations between Baghdad and Moscow deteriorated sharply, and the Kremlin was pleased when the ruling Ba'th party was overthrown in November 1963.[7] In July 1964 the USSR resumed arms shipments to Iraq, then headed by Colonel Abd al-Salam Aref, who had discontinued government persecution of the Communist party as well as military operations against the Kurdish nationalists in the northern part of the country. In December 1967, the Soviet Union undertook to assist Iraq in developing its oil resources (chapter 2).

Relations from 1968–1975

In July 1968, the Ba'th returned to power in Iraq, an occasion that Moscow did not seem to mind. The ruling Ba'th and the Iraqi Communist party had, in the meantime, reached a tentative understanding not to return to the bloody confrontation of 1963 (chapter 4). Moreover, the Ba'th was well known for its strong anti-Western, and particularly anti-U.S., views. One of the early manifestations of Moscow-Baghdad rapprochement was the Kremlin's consent, given in 1969, to provide Iraq with sizable quantities of modern arms, followed by economic and technical aid agreements.[8]

In the late 1960s and early 1970s the Ba'th made a major effort to consolidate its power in Iraq and to propel Baghdad into a position of regional leadership in the Persian Gulf as well as in the wider Arab East. The party leaders recognized early on that Soviet support was indispensable for the attainment of many of their political and economic objectives. Leading among the domestic problems were the Kurdish question and, above all, the quest to nationalize the assets of the Western oil companies operating in Iraq. Because resolution of these issues depended on Soviet cooperation, the political role of the Communist party, in which Moscow was displaying an interest, became another sensitive problem for the Ba'th to tackle (chapters 2, 3, and 4).

In general, in the period between 1968 and 1975, the Ba'th pursued policies which conformed to its leaders' perceptions of Iraq's national interests. At the same time, however, the ruling party went out of its way in an effort not to antagonize the USSR. For example, in 1970 Baghdad accepted the principle of Kurdish autonomy, a move long favored by Moscow. In 1971, the Ba'th promulgated the draft National Action Charter, intended to secure the political backing of the Kurdistan Democratic party and of the Iraqi Communist party. The latter supported the Ba'thi initiative, but the former did not. As a result, when relations between the Kurds and the central government deteriorated in 1972 and 1973, the Communists as well as the USSR sided with the ruling Ba'th. Moreover, as already noted, the authorities were determined to nationalize the country's petroleum industry, an ambition which was fully backed by Moscow as well as by the Iraqi Communist party.

In addition to domestic considerations, Baghdad also needed Soviet support on the regional as well as on the wider international scenes. Due to the militant radicalism of its ideology, Iraq was generally isolated in the Persian Gulf. Nevertheless, as will be shown in chapter 5, Baghdad's attention was focused largely on its rivalry with neighboring Iran. Because its ruler, Mohammed Reza Shah, was also driven by an ambition to play a dominant regional role, and because relations between the two states were usually tense, Baghdad felt the need to expand and modernize its armed forces. Given the Ba'th's strong anti-Western bent, sophisticated military equipment could have been obtained initially only from the USSR. (Of course, Soviet arms could have been used for other purposes, such as wars against Israel or, more to the point, in the fighting against the Kurds.)

Moscow's political backing was secured in April 1972, when the two states signed a fifteen-year Treaty of Friendship and Cooperation. Based on the Egyptian model of 1971, the accord provided for "comprehensive cooperation" in the political, economic, cultural, and "other fields." The only direct references to military cooperation were contained in Article 8 (the signatories agreed to "coordinate their positions" in case of a threat to peace) and in Article 9 (the parties undertook to assist each other in strengthening their "defense capabilities").[9] In retrospect, it would appear that the initiative for the 1972 treaty emanated from Baghdad. Although Iraq's immediate objective was to nationalize its oil industry, the accord was also intended generally to strengthen the domestic and international positions of the Ba'th.

As it turned out, the USSR proved willing to accommodate another important Third World nation. (Similar treaties had already been signed with India and Egypt.) Strategically, Iraq as well as the People's Democratic Republic of Yemen (PDRY)—the only Persian Gulf-Arabian peninsula countries to have developed close relations with the Soviet Union—were situated on the western fringes of the Indian Ocean in which the Kremlin had developed an interest in the late 1960s and early 1970s. Politically, in the Gulf and elsewhere in the Middle East, Iraq had emerged as a staunch opponent of "imperialism, colonialism, and Zionism," a line which, in the main, corresponded with the Soviet position. To be sure, Moscow and Baghdad differed on the problem of Israel's existence, with the Ba'th, but not the Kremlin, demanding the destruction of the "Zionist entity." More often than not, however, this particular issue was of little practical significance and was submerged in the vociferous "anti-imperialist" and "anti-Zionist" propaganda emanating from both capitals. Domestically, as noted, the USSR favored autonomy for the Kurds as well as political freedom for the Iraqi Communist party, issues on which the Ba'th was initially prepared to give some ground. Organizationally, the Ba'th had expressed an interest in establishing a relatively close working relationship with the Soviet Communist party (CPSU)—the Iraqis wished to draw on its long experience in such matters as imposing party control on the executive branch of the government as well as on the military. Although not widely publicized in either capital, the CPSU was not averse to maintaining a party-to-party relationship with the Ba'th. Economically, the Kremlin wholeheartedly approved of Baghdad's determination to nationalize the Iraq Petroleum Company and its affiliates. In addition to obvious political advantages, the move against major Western oil interests also promised significant economic gains. In return for Soviet goods and services, required in the initial stages to keep the petroleum industry going, the USSR expected to be paid in hard currency or in oil. (Precedents for such exchanges had been established before 1972.) Militarily, in contrast, the Soviets gained less than was commonly assumed in the West. Contrary to reports circulating in the early 1970s, no Iraqi bases were placed at the USSR's disposal. In retrospect, it appears that the Soviet air force and the navy were given limited access to some Iraqi military facilities. However, as subsequently became apparent, both Soviet use of the Iraqi airfields and Soviet naval visits to the Persian Gulf port of Umm Qasr proved to be limited as well as rare.

Thus, in entering the 1972 treaty, Iraq and the USSR were motivated by enlightened self-interest—both endeavored to promote their respective interests and were prepared to make some concessions to achieve their goals. The Soviets extended Baghdad important military aid and lent their political and economic support to Iraq's drive to nationalize the Western oil companies. In return, the ruling Ba'th eased its stance on the Kurdish and communist problems, offered limited use of its naval and air facilities, and, above all, provided the USSR with important economic opportunities in Iraq. The bilateral cooperation served their interests well. Both countries derived important benefits from it, explaining why, in the first half of the 1970s, the USSR and Iraq maintained a relatively close military, political, and economic relationship.

It bears repeating that the initial delivery of Soviet weapons to Iraq occurred in late 1958, the year of the overthrow of the pro-Western monarchy. Another infusion of arms was made in the late 1960s. As a result, by mid-1971, the USSR had supplied Iraq with "110 MIG-21 and SU-7 fighters, over 20 helicopters and trainers, 100–150 tanks, some 300 armored personnel carriers, and about 500 field guns and artillery rockets."[10] After the signing of the 1972 Treaty of Friendship and Cooperation, Baghdad also took delivery of SA-3 surface-to-air (SAM) missiles; TU-22 medium-range bombers ("the first and [at the time] only deployment of this type of aircraft outside the Soviet Union or Eastern Europe"); Scud surface-to-surface missiles armed with conventional warheads; and MIG-23 fighters, then the most advanced model available to the USSR. The arrival of TU-22s and MIG-23s significantly improved the effectiveness of the Iraqi air force. Finally, in January 1975 Moscow undertook to supply an unspecified number of armored personnel carriers, artillery, missiles, Osa patrol boats, and P-6 torpedo boats.[11]

Concurrently, the USSR was making an important contribution to the economic development of Iraq. Shortly after the nationalization of the Iraq Petroleum Company on June 1, 1972, Minister of Industry Taha al-Jazrawi visited Moscow and signed a number of agreements. One, in particular, provided for the repayment of all Soviet loans in oil "instead of only 70 percent as stipulated previously." As a result, in 1973 the USSR imported 4 million tons of Iraqi crude.[12]

Nevertheless, in spite of the growing military and economic cooperation between the two states, in 1973 and 1974, the Kremlin encountered a major problem in dealing with Baghdad. Economic in origin, it soon acquired pronounced political overtones. This, from Moscow's view-point, deplorable situation was a product of developments outside of Soviet control as well as of the USSR's own initiatives. In the former category belong the Arab oil embargo, instituted against some Western powers during the 1973 war, and the concurrent quadrupling of petroleum prices. This and subsequent price increases made available to Iraq and the other producers vast sums of hard currency which could be utilized to foster economic development. Faced with a choice between the Eastern and Western trading partners, Baghdad showed a marked preference for the latter. This decision, which manifested itself, in part, in insistence on cash as a basis for foreign trade, was generally thought to have been prompted by economic rather than political consider-ations. As noted by a high Iraqi official: "What we want is the best technology and the fastest possible fulfillment of orders and contracts. That is more important than the price."[13] Put differently, because West-ern expertise and technology were judged to be by and large superior to those from the Communist countries, Iraq opted to do more business with the members of the Western bloc. Nevertheless, this decision also reflected a degree of dissatisfaction with Soviet trading practices. As one Arab diplomat explained to C. L. Sulzberger of the *New York Times*: "When making a business deal an Iraqi always thinks of four things and in the following order: (1) time (how long it will take); (2) performance (efficiency); (3) cost; and finally (4) the nationality of the other partici-pant. Russia . . . has lost out here by trying to fix priorities in precisely the reverse order."[14]

Moreover, by 1974 Baghdad was also annoyed with some of Moscow's oil export practices. It will be recalled that, in the late 1960s and early 1970s, when continuous quarrels with the Iraq Petroleum Company had produced a slowdown in petroleum production and a decrease in government revenues, Iraq attempted to secure foreign credit and assist-ance in exchange for obligations of future deliveries of oil. As noted by Edith Penrose and E. F. Penrose, in 1970 the USSR consented "to in-crease its purchases of Iraqi crude, but reserved the right to export it if it so wished. . . ." One year later, the Soviets "finally agreed to accept payment in crude oil . . . [but at] almost 30 per cent below the posted price." In 1972, following the nationalization of the Iraq Petroleum Company which left Baghdad with "very large amounts" of unsold crude, the two states "signed . . . a more general agreement . . . which permitted all utilized credits to be repaid in crude oil and provided for a schedule of deliveries through 1980."[15]

What began as something of an economic burden, however, soon turned into a bonanza. After 1973 the USSR continued to receive Iraqi petroleum at the pre-increase price of below $3.00 per barrel and, given the oil shortages in the West, proceeded to make a killing. Specifically, the Soviets accelerated petroleum sales to the Western countries, charging them as much as $18 per barrel.[16] Moreover, in a calculated attempt to expand old and acquire new markets, the USSR undersold the OPEC producers by charging some customers as little as $8.00 per barrel. This amount was $3.65 less than the posted price for Gulf oil.[17]

These Soviet machinations offered an intriguing illustration of a conflict between economic and political interests: while increased sales of petroleum to the West made excellent economic sense, they also proved to be a source of considerable political embarrassment in the Middle East. (The Kremlin had long been at work in an effort to persuade the Arabs of the "unselfishness" of its assistance.) Once the USSR resolved the problem in the best tradition of what Marshall I. Goldmann described as "manipulating entrepreneur[ship],"[18] it was accused by the Arab press of making "massive profits" on the sale of the Iraqi petroleum and of helping to "destroy the Arab oil weapon."[19] Subsequent explanation by the *New Times* that "oil purchased in the Arab countries" was sent with the Arabs' consent only to "other socialist countries" sounded hollow in view of the fact that, in the last quarter of 1973, the Soviet Union sold petroleum not only to West Germany, Denmark, and Switzerland but also to the United States and the Netherlands—the primary targets of the Arab embargo. To add insult to injury, this was done at a time when "some Soviet officials actively sought to induce the Arab countries to withhold oil from the West."[20]

It is, of course, impossible to argue that Iraq's sharp economic swing to the West was due to Moscow's petroleum-selling practices in Western Europe at the time of the embargo. After all, Iraq refused to cut down its own production and sales, the only Arab country to do so. At the same time, the decision to expand economic cooperation with the West may well have been influenced by what Baghdad clearly perceived as Moscow's double-dealing. None of this is to say that Iraq had seriously considered breaking off with the USSR—the dependence on arms alone would have precluded that, no matter what the Ba'th's sentiments might have been. But unsuccessful efforts to get the Kremlin to explain what it was doing and, later in 1974, to persuade the Soviets that they were undercutting "the position of the oil producers at a time when they were in conflict with the US over oil prices"[21] no doubt provided additional reminders that the USSR, like any other international actor, was above all concerned with advancing its own interests.

In a similar vein, Baghdad continued to enlist Soviet and East European help in expanding its petroleum production and oil-related infrastructure. In March 1974, Iraq and the USSR signed a contract for the construction of a 585-kilometer pipeline between Baghdad and Basrah. This was followed in May by an accord to expand production at the North Rumailah field. "In return, the Soviet Union would obtain crude oil at preferential rates."[22] In November the two states signed a major agreement on developing Iraqi industry, agriculture, energy, petroleum, mineral resources and on training the Iraqi personnel.[23]

In addition, between 1972 and 1975 the USSR and Iraq entered into numerous other economic, financial, and technical agreements. Cutting across the whole spectrum of economic activity, these agreements provided for Soviet assistance in developing Iraq's industry,[24] agriculture (including irrigation projects),[25] transportation,[26] energy,[27] fishing,[28] manpower training,[29] long-term planning,[30] and, last but not least, "use of nuclear energy in industry, medicine, science and agriculture."[31] Among the major projects were the construction of a power station at Zigar (in southern Iraq) at a cost of 88 million Iraqi dinars (ID), more than $300 million, and of an iron and steel complex at Basrah.[32] As in the past, most of these projects were financed by oil. Thus, of the 325.4 million rubles of Iraqi exports to the Soviet Union in 1975, 320.4 million were in petroleum.[33] As a result of the growing cooperation, the trade between the two countries expanded dramatically, rising from 49.4 million rubles in 1968 to 322.1 million rubles in 1973, 453.1 million rubles in 1974,[34] and 596.2 million rubles in 1975.[35] In addition to the USSR, the energy-poor countries of Eastern Europe were also able to secure some Iraqi petroleum in exchange for contributions to Iraq's economic development. As a result, in July 1975, Iraq was admitted to Comecon, Eastern Europe's regional economic cooperation community, with the status of observer.[36]

Even more notable, in terms of the long-range economic and political repercussions, were the successes scored by the Iraqi government in its efforts to secure Western markets for its oil after the nationalization of the Iraq Petroleum Company. During the visit of Saddam Hussein, the civilian leader of the Ba'th and vice-chairman of the Revolutionary Command Council, to France in 1972, a ten-year agreement was reached enabling Compagnie Française des Pétroles, which had a 23.75 percent share in the Iraq Petroleum Company, to purchase an equivalent amount of the nationalized oil.[37] In another important development, Italy undertook to increase its imports above the total of 20 million tons over a ten-year period agreed to in March 1972.[38] The

French and Italian accords were followed by large-scale purchase contracts with Brazil and Spain.[39] As a result of these measures and of the deals struck with its Soviet and East European customers, Iraq successfully averted the threat of a potential boycott by the major Western petroleum companies.[40]

In any event, the rapid increase in petroleum production after the nationalization of the Iraq Petroleum Company, coupled with the rise in the price of oil, enabled Baghdad to initiate an accelerated economic development program. One of its striking features was the assignment of the bulk of the petroleum-related projects to the Western countries and not, as was initially assumed, to the USSR and its allies. For example, in 1973 the Iraq National Oil Company and the U.S. firm of Brown and Root negotiated a contract for the installation of two deep-water terminals off Iraq's southern coast and for laying underwater pipelines connecting the terminals with the city of Faw. A West German consortium was contracted to build the land portion of the system.[41] In 1974, as part of an elaborate pipeline system connecting Iraq's northern, southern, and western terminals and pumping stations, a West German concern undertook to build the Iraqi section of a 980-kilometer pipeline from Kirkuk to the Turkish Mediterranean port of Dörtyol.[42] Japan provided the pipes for this project as well as for the Baghdad-Basrah pipeline.[43]

Other major oil-related deals included a $500 million loan from Japan for petroleum exploration, negotiated in 1973;[44] another $1 billion loan from Japan to finance several industrial projects, including a refinery and a petrochemical complex, agreed to in 1974;[45] and a $500 million contract for the building of a chemical fertilizer plant at Khor al-Zubair, awarded to a Japanese consortium in 1975.[46] Another important oil-for-aid agreement was signed with Italy in 1974. The aid, worth ID 900 million (L1.3 billion), was given in exchange for 10 million tons of crude a year in addition to Italy's regular purchases. It was to be used in financing a number of agricultural and industrial projects, including petrochemical installations.[47]

In addition to petroleum-related projects, the West also benefited from the Iraqi bonanza in a number of other ways. The trend for a steady (and, beginning in 1974, dramatic) expansion of trade was set in 1972. During that year Iraq's imports fell to ID 234.68 million, a drop of 5.3 percent from 1971, due to cuts in the import program.[48] However, while imports from the communist countries declined by 7.8 percent, imports from Western Europe increased by 15.3 percent with "Great Britain regain[ing] its place as Iraq's leading supplier."[49] In 1973 the USSR

Table 1   Iraq's Trade with the Industrial West and the USSR/Eastern Europe*

	1971	1972	1973	1974	1975
Imports:					
West	383	363	468	1,429	3,176
USSR/EE	165	167	190	297	298
Exports:					
West	1,257	15	16	16	5,068
USSR/EE	18	10	11	4	788
Total Trade:					
West	1,640	378	482	1,445	8,244
USSR/EE	183	177	201	301	1,086

*All figures in millions of U.S. dollars.
Sources: United Nations, Yearbook of International Trade Statistics, 1972–1973, p. 396; 1977, 1:513.

temporarily emerged as Iraq's leading importer only to lose this distinction to Japan in 1974 and 1975.

Among the Western powers, France played a particularly important role in the development of Iraq. In 1974 alone, during Prime Minister Jacques Chirac's visit to Baghdad, the two countries signed contracts worth more than $2 billion.[50] Among the major projects were steel, aluminum, and cement plants.[51] In March 1975, France contracted to undertake nine agricultural projects, worth approximately $1.4 billion, and, in September, agreed to provide scientific and technical assistance in developing an Iraqi nuclear energy program.[52] It was at this time that Baghdad also expressed an interest in purchasing "sophisticated French weapons," an initiative which eventually resulted in the emergence of France as Iraq's number two supplier of modern armaments, second only to the USSR.[53] The Baghdad-Paris rapprochement led to the description of the Iraqi-French relationship as "privileged" and "extremely cordial," a noteworthy definition when compared to the phrase "strategic alliance," coined later in the decade to describe the relations between Baghdad and Moscow.

Thus, Iraq's vastly increased revenues from the sale of oil, coupled with the capital borrowed from the industrial nations, resulted in an economic boom of major proportions. In 1974 alone, Baghdad received more than $6 billion from the petroleum exports. Of this amount, $4.5 billion were spent on imports.[54] It is highly noteworthy, however, that the heavy plunge into international commerce for the purpose of acquiring capital, goods, and services needed to implement Iraq's "development explosion" effected a marked shift in the country's trade policy. Whereas before 1974 Iraq relied to a considerable extent on barter deals with the USSR and the countries of Eastern Europe, the main beneficiaries in 1974 and later were the developed industrial nations of the West (table 1). As noted, the main reasons for the switch were the vast amounts of hard currency earned from the sale of petroleum and the natural preference for the superior quality of most Western products.

Relations from 1975–1980

In his perceptive study of Soviet-Iraqi relations, Francis Fukuyama noted, correctly, that "early 1975 was the high tide of Soviet influence in Iraq." Russian military supplies were reaching Baghdad in unprecedented numbers and contributed to the "solution" of the Kurdish question.[55] Relations between the Ba'th and the Iraqi Communist party were outwardly cordial—the Communists held three seats in the Iraqi cabinet and the two organizations were cooperating in the National Front. The Ba'th was also maintaining close organizational contacts with the CPSU. Finally, having nationalized the Iraq Petroleum Company, Baghdad continued to rely on the USSR for economic and technical assistance. In exchange for Soviet goods and services, Iraq paid cash or bartered oil—from Moscow's viewpoint, a highly desirable arrangement.

This, to the Kremlin, fortuitous state of affairs proved to be rather short-lived, however. In the latter 1970s, slowly but surely, Iraq began to assert itself against its Soviet patron. In retrospect, this turn of events was made possible by two previously mentioned, unrelated events: the dramatic rise in the price of petroleum effected after the 1973 war, and the defeat of the Kurds in the spring of 1975.

The former provided Iraq with huge amounts of cash, enabling Baghdad to meet its military and economic needs not only in the USSR and Eastern Europe but also in the West. The collapse of the Kurdish resistance released Iraq from heavy dependence on Soviet arms and on Russian political support, designed to offset the backing extended to the Kurds by Iran, Israel, and, indirectly, the United States. In short, it was the combination of full economic independence and of the military victory over the Kurds that enabled Baghdad to pursue its interests in relative disregard of Moscow's wishes. Under these circumstances, areas of disagreement which the Ba'th intentionally suppressed earlier in the decade resurfaced, shedding light on the incompatibility of some of the basic Soviet and Iraqi interests. Consequently, Moscow-Baghdad relations deteriorated sharply, reaching a near breaking point in the period between 1978 and 1980. The most publicized domestic issue over which the USSR and Iraq confronted each other was the fate of the Iraqi Communist party.

In 1975, as a result of the normalization of relations between Baghdad and Tehran, of the successful completion of the war against the Kurds, and of the growing economic independence from the Soviet Union, the National Front between the Ba'th and the Communist party lost much of its previous importance to the Iraqi government. As will be shown in chapter 4, relations between the two organizations deteriorated in 1976 and 1977, when the Communists, backed by Moscow, continued to exert pressure on the Ba'th for a larger role in governing Iraq. The ruling party struck back in May 1978 when twenty-one Communists were executed on charges of plotting to overthrow the government. Further repressive actions followed and, by the end of the decade, the Marxist organization ceased to exist as one of Iraq's important political forces. The Kremlin interceded with the Ba'th on behalf of the Iraqi Communist party. As the authorities were in no mood to compromise, however, the Soviet efforts were in vain, contributing to the sharp deterioration of Moscow-Baghdad relations.

In addition to the differences which arose from the Ba'th's treatment of the Communists, Iraq and the USSR were also divided over several important foreign policy issues. For one thing, they supported the opposing sides in the Ogaden conflict (1977–1978), which pitted Somalia against Ethiopia, and in Addis Ababa's war against the secession-minded nationalists in the province of Eritrea. During his 1977 visit to Moscow, Saddam Hussein reportedly urged the USSR to discontinue aiding Ethiopia. Otherwise, he admonished his Kremlin hosts, they would "lose" both Somalia and Eritrea. According to al-Thawrah, official organ of the Iraqi Ba'th, the Soviets chose to disregard Saddam Hussein's advice and, as a result, "had harmed . . . [their] own interests." For its part, al-Thawrah promised Iraq's unequivocal support both for Somalia and for the "Eritrean revolution."[56] In May 1978 Baghdad warned Moscow that Soviet aircraft, carrying military supplies to Addis Ababa, would not be permitted to refuel on Iraqi territory if the USSR continued to support the Ethiopian campaign in Eritrea. The threat was reportedly carried into effect.[57]

In the spring of 1978 Iraq also chose to confront the USSR in the Arab-Israeli sector. The Ba'th's fortnightly review al-Rasid argued that "basic differences" continued to separate Moscow and Baghdad. The Soviet

Union remained committed to the concept of Israel's existence, while Iraq insisted on its liquidation leading to the "liberation" and independence of Arab Palestine. On a more mundane but no less annoying level, the authorities ordered that the Soviet embassy, situated near the offices of President Ahmad Hasan al-Bakr, be moved to a more remote location. The Russians balked and obliged only after their electricity and water had been cut off.[58] Finally, in 1978 and 1979 Moscow and Baghdad clashed over the events in North and South Yemen[59] and especially over the Soviet invasion of Afghanistan. They also differed significantly in their evaluation of and in their respective policies toward the emerging fundamentalist regime in Tehran (chapter 6). Nevertheless, even in the late 1970s Baghdad and Moscow shied away from a total breakdown in their relations. In June 1978, when the Syrian foreign minister stated that Iraq was about to abrogate the 1972 Treaty of Friendship and Cooperation with the USSR, a high Iraqi official countered that "our strategic alliance with the Soviet Union will not change."[60]

Iraq's reluctance to break with the Soviet Union can be explained by the following considerations: in the late 1970s Baghdad continued to harbor far-reaching regional and international ambitions. Having historically been a proponent of "radical," that is, anti-Western brand of Arab nationalism, Iraq regarded the United States as its major international adversary. Under these circumstances, association with the USSR "strengthened" its "progressive" credentials. Neither did the total alienation of the Soviet Union make any practical sense. Although, in the latter 1970s, Iraq continued its efforts to diversify the sources of military and economic supplies, the USSR remained an important provider of both war materiel and of other types of goods and services. For its part, Moscow, too, had no interest in breaking with Baghdad. Staunchly "anti-imperialist" in its orientation, Iraq opposed many of Washington's policies in the Middle East, ranging from outright condemnation of the Camp David process and of the resulting peace treaty between Israel and Egypt to resistance to American initiatives in the Persian Gulf.

In short, in the late 1970s relations between Iraq and the USSR were marked by a significant coincidence of interests with respect to American policies in the Arab-Israeli sector as well as in the Persian Gulf and by concurrent conflicts over Moscow's own political and military activities in the Horn of Africa, the Gulf, and Afghanistan. As noted, the Kremlin was also unhappy with Baghdad's handling of the Iraqi Communist party. Put differently, the conflicts accounted for occasionally bitter strains in Soviet-Iraqi relations, but their partially overlapping interests ensured that these relations would not be broken.

Specifically, in October 1976 the USSR and Iraq concluded another arms agreement, providing for the delivery of T-62 tanks and of additional Scud missiles. Valued at $300 million, these systems were to be delivered in 1979.[61] In 1977 the Soviets undertook to supply Iraq with IL-76 long-range military transport planes and generally to upgrade its air force by means of additional MIG-21s and MIG-23s.[62] Finally, in 1979, in the last major deal concluded before the outbreak of the Iran-Iraq war in September 1980, the USSR contracted to supply Baghdad with MI-8 helicopters, MIG-23 and MIG-27 fighters, and MIG-25 fighter-reconnaissance aircraft. The ground forces were to be strengthened by means of SP-73 and SP-74 self-propelled howitzers.[63] As a result, by 1979, Iraq had emerged as Moscow's main Third World recipient of modern weaponry. This point is best illustrated by the statistics in Table 2.

To recapitulate, in the period between 1964 and 1973, Iraq ranked fifth on the list of major Third World recipients of Soviet military aid behind Egypt, North Vietnam ($2,090 million), India ($1,273 million), and Syria.[64] Between 1974 and 1978, in contrast, Iraq moved into first place, followed by Libya and Syria. It is equally important, however, that, whereas in the earlier period the USSR, Czechoslovakia, and Poland (with deliveries worth $742 million, $77 million, and $3 million, respectively) provided military assistance valued at $822 million out of a total of $874 million spent by Baghdad,[65] in the ensuing years the noncommunist suppliers succeeded in significantly increasing their share of the Iraqi market. Thus, between 1974 and 1978, the Soviet bloc countries exported arms and related services valued at $3,720 million (the USSR, $3,600 million; Czechoslovakia, $90 million; and Poland, $30 million) out of Iraq's total military budget of $5,300 million. The rest—$1,580 million (minus $10 million for the People's Republic of China)—accrued to Western suppliers and Yugoslavia. Of this amount, $430 million went to France, $150 million to West Germany, $70 million to Italy, and $900 million to others,[66] among them Brazil, Switzerland, Yugoslavia, and Spain. Put differently, between 1964 and 1973, the USSR and its satellites supplied 90 percent of Iraq's arms imports. The corresponding figure for 1974 through 1978 was 70 percent, and the downward trend continued in 1979 and 1980.

In the late 1970s France became Iraq's second-largest provider of modern weapons. The initial arms accord of 1974 was followed by agreements of 1976 and 1977.[67] The latter, in particular, provided for the delivery to the Iraqi air force of forty Mirage F-1 fighter aircraft.[68]

Table 2   Soviet Arms Supplies to Its Chief Arab Clients, 1964–78[*]

	1964–73	1974–78	Total
Egypt	2,305	430	2,735
Syria	1,153	2,700	3,853
Iraq	742	3,600	4,342
Libya	—	3,400	3,400

[*]All figures in millions of U.S. dollars.
Sources: U.S. Arms Control and Disarmament Agency, *World Military Expenditures and Arms Transfers, 1963–1973* (Washington, D.C., 1975), p. 70; *1969–1978* (Washington, D.C., 1980), p. 160.

Additional accords were negotiated in 1978 and 1979.[69] The agreements of 1979, valued at $1.5 billion, represented a "trebling [in Iraq's] purchases" of French military equipment. France was to be compensated by "increased and guaranteed oil supplies."[70] Finally, in early 1980, Baghdad ordered twenty-four additional Mirage F-1 fighters at a cost of $300 million.[71] Among Iraq's other major noncommunist arms suppliers were Brazil and Italy.

In examining the motives for Baghdad's interest in diversifying the sources of its arms supplies, some analysts have pointed to the reportedly unsuccessful attempts to acquire additional Soviet weapons at the height of the Kurdish campaign of spring 1975.[72] This line of reasoning overlooks the fact that Iraq's first major arms deal with France was entered into in 1974, well in advance of the final push in Kurdistan. Moreover, the implication that Iraq's decision to embark upon a major weapons procurement and diversification program was prompted mainly by the exigencies of the Kurdish campaign neglects not only Baghdad's ambition to play a leading role in Persian Gulf and Middle Eastern politics but also the fact that the major perceived threat to Iraq's security was thought to emanate not from the Kurds or even Israel but from Iran. It will be recalled that in the early 1970s the shah had initiated a massive military buildup program intended to establish Iran as the dominant power in the Gulf.[73] For this reason, Iraq's drive to upgrade its armed forces did not stop after April 1975 when Tehran and Baghdad had temporarily reconciled their differences and the Kurdish uprising had been subdued.

In short, it stands to reason that Iraq's decision to build up its armed forces was prompted by considerations which transcended the needs of the Kurdish campaign. The decision to diversify, on the other hand, was no doubt dictated by the desire not to depend exclusively on one source.

No matter how friendly at any given time, one supplier could seriously inhibit Iraq's freedom of action by denying weapons when they were needed most. The Ba'th was well aware of the incompatibility of some of the respective Iraqi and Soviet interests and hence of a possible temptation on Moscow's part to influence Baghdad's policies by withholding the supply of arms.[74]

Be that as it may, by the mid-1970s Iraq had made a determined effort to diversify the sources of its military supplies. However, because it takes years to translate orders for sophisticated weapons systems (such as aircraft) into actual deliveries, by 1980 Baghdad remained dependent on the USSR for the continued supply of much of its modern equipment as well as for maintenance and training. (Some two thousand Soviet military and civilian advisers were reportedly present in Iraq in early 1980.)[75] The following breakdown of some of the major weapons systems available to Iraq in mid-1980 (i.e., shortly before the outbreak of the war with Iran) will illustrate this point. The air force included five interceptor squadrons, consisting of 115 MIG-21 aircraft, and twelve fighter-bomber squadrons. In this group were four squadrons of MIG-23BS (eighty planes), three squadrons of SU-7BS (forty planes), and four squadrons of SU-20S (sixty planes). This category included also one squadron of British-made Hunter FB59/FR10S (fifteen planes). In addition, the air force had one squadron of TU-22 medium-range bombers (twelve planes) and one squadron of light IL-28 bombers (ten planes). Thus, of the total of 332 combat aircraft available to Iraq in 1980, 317 had been supplied by the USSR. The air force also had at its disposal eleven helicopter squadrons, consisting of 276 craft. Of these, 169 were Soviet-made (thrity-five MI-4s, fifteen MI-6s, seventy-eight MI-8s, and twenty-four MI-24s), a hundred were manufactured in France (forty-seven Alouette IIIs, ten Super Frelons, forty Gazelles, and three Pumas) and seven in Great Britain (Wessex Mk 52s). With the exception of two French-made Heron planes, Iraq's two transport squadrons consisted of fifty-four Soviet-made aircraft (nine AN-2s, eight AN-12s, eight AN-24s, two AN-26s, twelve IL-76s, two TU-124s, and thirteen IL-14s). The anti-aircraft missiles (SAM-2s, SAM-3s, and twenty-five SAM-6 batteries) had all been provided by the USSR. On order, but not yet delivered, were 150 MIG-23s, MIG-25s, and MIG-27s from the Soviet Union, sixty Mirage F IC/IBS and C-160 transports from France, as well as a number of Soviet and French helicopters.[76]

The composition of the Iraqi navy provided another illustration of Baghdad's continued dependence on the USSR. Although, in 1979 and 1980, major orders for frigates and corvettes had been placed in Italy, the navy, on the eve of the Gulf war, consisted of the following vessels, all of them Soviet-made: twelve guided missile patrol boats, twelve torpedo boats, five large patrol craft, ten coastal patrol craft, five minesweepers, and four landing craft. Finally, of the Iraqi army's tank force of 2,850 machines, all but two hundred had been supplied by the Soviet Union.[77]

Attempts at diversification were even more pronounced in the general sphere of Iraq's foreign economic relations. The USSR and the states of Eastern Europe were by no means precluded from taking part in the country's economic boom, but the ratio of their participation, unlike that of the industrial West, was steadily declining. Thus, Iraq's imports from the communist world fell from a high of 24.6 percent in 1973 to a low of 6.9 percent in 1979. The corresponding figures for the Western industrial countries, in contrast, rose from 50.7 percent to a high of 77.2 percent.[78]

Another important indicator of the decline of Soviet participation in Iraq's economic activity was provided by the amount of money borrowed by Baghdad to finance some of its development projects. In 1975, "Soviet loans . . . totaled 150 million rubles" (approximately $200 million). They decreased to some 75 million rubles in 1976 and to about 25 million rubles in 1977.[79]

During this period, Soviet economic assistance to Iraq centered mainly on large-scale irrigation projects. Following the completion of the first stage of the Lake Tharthar dam project in 1976, the USSR undertook to construct the Hindiyyah dam on the Euphrates in southern Iraq.[80] Shortly afterward, in December 1976, Moscow won another major contract for four irrigation projects valued at ID 300 million (more than $1 billion): the Hadithah and Habbaniyyah dams in western Iraq, a canal from Lake Tharthar to the Tigris, and the Kirkuk irrigation canal in the north.[81] In addition, the Soviet Union participated in the development of Iraq's fisheries and grain storage facilities.[82] It also contracted to build a $337 million assembly plant south of Baghdad, as well as a power station.[83] The plans for the construction of the Kirkuk Canal, a cement plant, a dam on the Tigris, and an electric power station were finalized in an agreement signed in Moscow in December 1978.[84]

But the center of gravity in Iraq's international economic relations in the period between 1976 and 1979 clearly and overwhelmingly shifted to the industrial West (table 3).

Because statistics on Soviet imports from Iraq for the period between 1976 and 1979 are not yet available, the evaluation of Moscow's position must remain somewhat tentative. Nevertheless, the added information is not likely to change the conclusion that, in relative terms, in

Table 3   Iraq's International Economic Relations, 1976–79[*]

Iraqi Exports to Noncommunist Countries:

1. France	8,099	6. Spain	2,193
2. Italy	6,829	7. United States	1,345
3. Brazil	5,112	8. India	1,292
4. Japan	3,549	9. The Netherlands	1,147
5. Great Britain	2,604		

Iraqi Imports from Noncommunist Countries:

1. Japan	4,120	6. United States	1,271
2. West Germany	3,790	7. Belgium	696
3. France	1,995	8. The Netherlands	652
4. Italy	1,518	9. Sweden	645
5. Great Britain	1,508		

Iraq's Leading Commercial Partners:

1. France	10,094	6. Great Britain	4,112
2. Italy	8,347	7. United States	2,616
3. Japan	7,663	8. Spain	2,483
4. Brazil	5,547	9. The Netherlands	1,799
5. West Germany	4,540		

[*]All figures in millions of U.S. dollars.

Source: IMF, *Direction of Trade Yearbook, 1980* (Washington, D.C.: International Monetary Fund, 1980), pp. 207–8.

the bilateral trade between Iraq and its major commercial partners, the USSR and Eastern Europe (with the exception of Yugoslavia) had steadily lost ground. This is clearly evident from an examination of the value of Iraqi imports between 1976 and 1979. During this period Soviet exports amounted to $763 million, placing the USSR in the seventh position, substantially behind the United States ($1,271 million). And the combined value of Soviet and East European exports to Iraq—$1,731 million—placed the group in the fourth place behind Japan, West Germany, and France.[85]

Evaluation

As the data on Iraq's military procurement program and foreign trade demonstrate, the ruling party was engaged in a broad effort to increase the size and to improve the quality of the armed forces and to expand the country's industrial and agricultural infrastructure. In these major undertakings, made possible by enormous profits resulting from the sale of oil, the "socialist" proclivities of Ba'thism as well as its general "anti-imperialist" (i.e., anti-Western) slant were not permitted to stand in the path of progress. Pragmatism was the order of the day, and better-quality Western technology, goods, and services were clearly preferable to those offered by the USSR and its allies. In addition, Western (above all French) arms were purchased to offset the near-monopoly position which Moscow held since the 1960s.

Economics affected—but did not determine—politics. In the latter 1970s prosperity and the resulting ability to satisfy the country's economic needs from the preferred Western sources enabled Iraq to assert itself politically with regard to the USSR. As a result, some of the important differences which, before 1975, were papered over (as, for example, the rivalry between the Ba'th and the Iraqi Communist party) resurfaced, producing visible strains in the "strategic alliance" between Moscow and Baghdad. In time, old issues were reinforced by new problems, such as the Horn of Africa, Afghanistan, and Iran. As a result, by September 1980 relations between the Soviet patron and the Iraqi client reached their lowest point of the post-1968 period. Under these circumstances, Moscow's highly negative reaction to the Iraqi attack on the Islamic Republic should have come as no surprise (chapter 7).

■ Part One *Domestic Problems*

At the time of the overthrow of the pro-Western monarchy in 1958, the oil royalties received from the Western-owned Iraq Petroleum Company (IPC) and its two subsidiaries, the Mosul Petroleum Company (MPC) and the Basrah Petroleum Company (BPC), constituted Iraq's main source of income.[1] After the revolution, the regime of Colonel Abd al-Kerim Kassem used the petroleum revenues to initiate a program of social and economic reforms and to modernize Iraq's armed forces by purchasing huge quantities of foreign (mainly Soviet) military equipment promptly used in an attempt to subdue the Kurdish nationalists. The large-scale diversion of funds into the defense sector as well as into the war effort in the northern region made it impossible for the Iraqi government to fulfill the promises of extensive socioeconomic change made shortly after the 1958 revolution.

To secure additional revenues, the authorities attempted to prevail upon the IPC to increase its production and, consequently, the amount of money receivable by the Iraqi government in the form of royalties. Because relations between the anti-Western regime and the IPC had deteriorated sharply after the revolution of July 1958, negotiations were marked by hostility and confrontation until they were abruptly suspended by Baghdad in October 1961. Kassem's next move was the proclamation in December 1961 of Law 80 which severely limited the concessionary territory handed over to the IPC and its subsidiaries in the 1920s and 1930s. Specifically, in expropriating all areas not in use in 1961, Law 80 left less than 1 percent of the original concessionary area under the control of the IPC.[2]

If the purpose of Law 80 was to pressure the IPC into increasing its production, the measure could only be classified as a failure: in the ensuing two years Iraqi output remained constant while that of the

other producers rose sharply.[3] In the long run, however, Law 80 proved
to be of immense importance because the territory regained from the
IPC and its affiliates contained vast reserves of petroleum which could
be exploited by Iraq's own budding oil industry without regard to the
Western companies.[4]

In 1967 the Iraqi government implemented two new laws—97 and
123—which provided clear indications of the general direction in
which Baghdad was moving. The first, promulgated in August, provided
for the transfer to the Iraq National Oil Company (INOC) of the concessionary area expropriated under Law 80. The second, put into effect in
September, conferred upon INOC the exclusive "right to prospect and
exploit in all areas not exploited by IPC and its associates."[5] The importance of these measures lay in the fact that they provided other foreign
companies with an opportunity to compete with the IPC. Baghdad did
not have to wait long—it soon became obvious that other outsiders
were interested in helping Iraq exploit its petroleum resources.

The initial understanding between INOC and a foreign company was
reached in November 1967, when the French state oil company, Enterprise de Recherches et d'Activités Petrolières (ERAP), secured exploration and exploitation rights in sections of the former IPC concessionary
area "where oil had not been found."[6] As noted by Majid Khadduri, this
agreement, signed in February 1968, established "a new pattern of relationship with foreign companies. No longer was oil to be produced in
the expropriated areas directly by any foreign company. The owner of
the oil industry must be I.N.O.C., and the foreign companies, in accordance with contracts signed between them and I.N.O.C., must act as
contractors on behalf of I.N.O.C."[7] Significantly, Abd al-Rahman Aref,
then president of Iraq, described the ERAP agreement as "the beginning
of steps to break the monopoly of our national resources, particularly
the oil resources."[8]

The next important step was taken in December 1967. In a letter of
intent signed by Iraq and the USSR, the latter "pledged the necessary aid
and equipment to INOC for the development of oil drilling in the south
and transport and marketing of oil products." The Soviets also undertook "to conduct a geological survey in northern Iraq."[9] In a related
move, pointing to the eventual Soviet involvement in the rich North
Rumailah oilfield in southern Iraq, Baghdad Radio announced in April
1968 that "all offers by foreign companies to exploit untapped areas" of
the North Rumailah region had been rejected by the Iraqi government.
Instead, "all exploitation rights had been granted to . . . [INOC]."[10] As
Khadduri notes, the ERAP and INOC projects were hailed in Baghdad's

nationalist circles "as bold steps enabling Iraq to establish a public oil sector in addition to the private sector (i.e., I.P.C.)."[11]

The Soviet attitude toward Iraq's efforts to nationalize the IPC becomes more intelligible in the context of Moscow's general view of the history of the petroleum industry in the Middle East. Writing in 1968, Ruben Andreasian, one of the USSR's leading authorities on the subject, distinguished among three separate stages of development. The first, dating back to the discovery of oil in Persia in the 1900s and lasting until the late 1940s, was described as "the golden age of oil monopoly domination in the Middle East." Its main feature was a "ruthless plundering [by oil imperialism of] the main natural wealth of the Arab countries and Iran."[12] Specifically, "the provisions of the concession treaties were emphatically unequal." The Western companies had gained unlimited access to the region's petroleum resources and were free to determine how to dispose of them. The governments of the producing countries, in contrast, were "confined to passive bargaining with the concessionaires for higher fixed royalties on each ton of oil extracted."[13]

The second or "Sturm und Drang period in the oil history of the Middle East" was inaugurated after 1945, when "the flames of the national-liberation struggle spread to the oil-producing countries of the Persian Gulf." This period was marked by an effort "to secure a radical solution of the oil problem," highlighted, in 1951, by Iran's nationalization of its petroleum industry. The attempt failed, but "the struggle was not in vain." Fearful of losing their positions in the other producing countries, the Western companies decided to make some concessions: the governments' royalties were increased to approximately "one-half of the concessionaire's earnings on oil exports (the so-called fifty-fifty principle)"; the governments were offered representation on the companies' boards; and the companies undertook to train and employ native specialists in "some engineering and technical posts."[14] (However, to compensate for the losses suffered in the process, the cartel "increased production in the Middle East and started production in Africa, thus reaping additional profits running into tens of thousands of millions of dollars.")[15]

Although the Iranian experience had demonstrated that "the more radical means of fighting oil imperialism had to be abandoned for the time being," it also made the producing countries aware of the fact that sustained pressure on the companies could gradually change the situation in their favor. New efforts in this direction were undertaken after 1956, leading to the third stage in the history of the Middle Eastern oil industry. This period was marked by "the disintegration of the colonial system and the growth of the world Socialist forces," as evidenced by the nationalization of the Suez Canal Company and the defeat of the tripartite attack on Egypt. According to Andreasian, these trends provided "favourable conditions for a [renewed] drive against the positions of oil imperialism in the Middle East." The opportunity was recognized and seized upon by the governments of the petroleum-producing states, which formulated and pursued the following objectives:

> (1) to ensure access for national capital to national sources of oil, directly or in cooperation with foreign capital, so as to create a national oil industry and start exporting liquid fuel independently; (2) to secure a revision of the oil concession agreements in order to increase the share of the profits, to establish effective control over the activity of the concession companies, and to 'Arabise' the personnel; and (3) to unite the efforts of the oil exporting countries to protect their rights on the world markets against the Consortium's arbitrary acts and to exert joint pressure on the monopolies to achieve the first two aims.[16]

Even though the new policy was not followed uniformly or consistently by Middle Eastern producers, it represented "a big step forward as compared with the state of affairs prior to 1951." Particularly noteworthy, according to Andreasian, were the efforts "gradually and indirectly [to] set up a national sector in the oil industry alongside the foreign one" and to place foreign oil monopolies under government control.[17]

Arrangements to strengthen the national sector by means of agreements with foreign companies which did not belong to the cartel[18] took two different forms: partnerships and commercial contracts. The idea of a "partnership between national and foreign capital" in the guise of a "mixed company" was initially proposed to Iran by the Italian ENI organization after the Suez war. Tehran accepted because, for the first time, an agreement between the producer government and a Western company was based on the principle of a complete equality of sides: it provided for "equal ownership of stock of oil extracted, and equal representation on the board." Equally significantly, Iran retained the right "to control the activity of the mixed company, to receive 75 per cent of the profits on oil exports, and solid royalties for the foreign partner's right to operate on Iranian territory." The initial accord was soon followed by similar agreements between Tehran and French, Canadian, West German, and independent U.S. companies; and Iran's example was emulated by other producers, among them Saudi Arabia and Egypt. Under another type of a concessionary agreement, concluded by Saudi Arabia and Kuwait with a Japanese firm in 1957 and 1958, respectively, the two states were guaranteed "more than one-half of the profits over the whole range of oil operations, the right to buy on easy terms a part of the stock and a definite share of the oil extracted." The Japanese company also undertook to build oil refineries in the two countries.[19]

In the latter 1960s the producers scored yet another major victory over the cartel by concluding commercial contract-type agreements with a number of foreign companies. Here, too, Iran led the way signing an accord with ERAP, and Iraq followed suit a short while later. The novelty and importance of this arrangement lay in the fact that ERAP agreed "to act as contractor for the local state company in prospecting and working oilfields at its own expense . . . and with the right to purchase some of the oil on favourable terms." This meant, in part, that the producing state retained "full legal title to all the oil extracted" and that the contracting company's expenses were "reimbursed only if commercial oil deposits . . . [had been] discovered."[20]

According to Andreasian, the new types of cooperation between the producers and the independent foreign petroleum companies were important not only because they set precedents for future dealings with the cartel but also because they effectively broke the latter's exclusive control over the Persian Gulf oil. This qualitatively new situation reflected "the continued weakening of positions of Anglo-American imperialism in the Middle East" and was an outgrowth of "the shrinking share of the U.S.A. and Britain in the world economy, on the one hand, and the relatively faster economic development of the Common Market countries, on the other." Last, it was also due to "the successes scored by the developing countries in their struggle for economic independence."[21]

An important step in protecting the rights of the producers was taken in 1960 with the formation of the Organization of Petroleum Exporting Countries (OPEC). Initially, it was rather ineffective, due to the members' inability to adopt "a concerted policy" toward the cartel, the oil importers, and each other. The main stumbling block in the last category proved to be the problem of "quotas for oil extraction in member countries," most of whom endeavored to sell as much petroleum as possible without any regard for the interests of the other producers. Nevertheless, even in the 1960s OPEC more than proved its worth—it "prevented another price cut and . . . secured some increase in the Gulf countries' share of the profit made by concession companies."[22]

But the biggest gain scored by the producers in the late 1950s and especially in the 1960s, according to Andreasian, was the establishment of national oil companies and the ensuing "gradual development of the whole range of the liquid fuel operations." The initial step was the ousting of foreign capital from the domestic oil market, a goal achieved (a) by securing petroleum "either from . . . [the producer-owned] small oilfields (Iran, Iraq, the U.A.R., . . .) or from . . . [the government's] share of the profits in mixed companies (Iran and the U.A.R.)" or by buying it from the concessionaires; (b) by setting up "a network of state-owned refineries" (Iran, Iraq, Kuwait, and Syria); (c) by constructing the petro-chemical industry (Iran, the UAR, Syria, Kuwait, Iraq, and Saudi Arabia); and (d) by "training of national personnel," usually in special schools established for that purpose by the foreign oil companies in response to the host governments' pressure.[23]

As a result of all of these developments, in the latter 1960s some Middle Eastern producers (such as Iran, Saudi Arabia, and the UAR) began exporting petroleum independent of the major Western oil companies, known as the "Seven Sisters." Among the early partners of these national petroleum companies were not only the states of Western Europe, Latin America, and Asia but also "the Socialist countries" which bartered "machinery, equipment and manufactured goods" for the Iranian and Saudi crude oil. In short, in the 1960s, the petroleum-exporting countries of the Middle East took their "first steps in the independent marketing of oil." The road ahead, Andreasian predicted, would be "long and hard . . . , but it is the only one in the struggle for a truly independent oil policy and against the dictates of the oil imperialists."[24]

Against this general background, it is now possible to proceed with an analysis of the Soviet attitude toward the petroleum policy of the Iraqi government. As might have been expected, the USSR came out openly in support of Baghdad's measures aimed at the weakening of the IPC's hold over Iraq's economy and, eventually, at the company's nationalization. Thus, in spite of the growing disenchantment with Abd al-Kerim Kassem, Moscow wholeheartedly backed his efforts at developing Iraq's own state-controlled petroleum industry. Specifically, the Kremlin criticized Kassem for abandoning a "progressive course" in domestic politics. As noted in chapter 1, this meant that the relative freedom of action which the Iraqi Communist party had enjoyed in the first year of the postrevolutionary period was rescinded in 1959 and 1960. Moreover, Kassem was judged guilty of unleashing a "fratricidal war" against the Kurdish "national-liberation movement." These measures detracted from one of the major tasks facing the revolutionary regime—the ongoing negotiations with the "imperialist oil monopolies." Given Baghdad's misguided preoccupation with the suppression of "democratic elements," the Soviet argument ran, there was no need for the IPC to make any far-reaching concessions.[25] Only after the talks were broken off in the fall of 1961 and Kassem was facing the choice between capitulating or taking a strong stand did his regime, "engaged in a balancing act between the reactionary and progressive elements," adopt Law 80. The decision was also influenced by "prestige considerations"—"repression of democratic elements" had caused a drop in Kassem's popularity. To help restore it, he struck at the "oil monopolies."[26] In spite of the negative connotations which this analysis of Kassem's policies evoked, Moscow clearly regarded Law 80 as a historical landmark worthy of full Soviet backing. As Gerasimov notes, its passage was seen by the "patriotic forces of the national bourgeoisie and the Iraqi Communists as the most important achievement of the Iraqi revolution."[27]

In the ensuing years "many factors" prevented Baghdad from developing its own oil industry after the passage of Law 80: "a shortage of specialists and funds, the . . . [IPC's] . . . efforts to capitalize on its monopoly position, [and] the political storms which were shaking the country." In addition, many influential Iraqis were advocating caution and resisted a complete break with the IPC, the main source of the government's income. A dramatic change in Baghdad's outlook occurred only after the 1967 war which drove home the danger of reliance on "unequal economic relations with the West, as typified by the agreement with Iraq Petroleum." It also "pointed up the need to search for new markets, demonstrated the community of interests of all the Arab countries, showed the Arab peoples who their true friends were."[28]

Not surprisingly, Law 97 of August 1967, which transferred to INOC the concessionary area withdrawn from the IPC under Law 80, also met with Soviet approval. As Gerasimov states, its adoption "in conditions of struggle against the Israeli aggression was greeted with great enthusiasm by Iraq's public opinion," ranging from the right-wing nationalists to the Communists.[29] The same was true of Law 123 of September 1967 which entrusted INOC with exploring and exploiting petroleum deposits in areas removed from the IPC's original concession by Law 80. A "logical extension of Law 97," Law 123, according to Gerasimov, had to be passed because decisive steps against the IPC were being blocked by those in the INOC leadership who favored "cooperation with foreign oil monopolies."[30] The measure was judged important not only because it excluded the IPC from participation in the development of North Rumailah's rich oil fields, but also because it empowered INOC to contract other petroleum companies to perform this task. Put differently,

Laws 97 and 123 resulted in a "general weakening of positions of the international oil cartel" and, more specifically, of the "political positions of the USA, Britain, and their allies in Iraq." Combined with the events of June 1967, they also created "real possibilities for the 'outsiders' of the oil business to participate in the exploitation of Iraq's oil resources." Thus, in September and October 1967 Baghdad approached "business circles in France, Italy, Spain, Japan, and other capitalist nations as well as the Soviet Union and the socialist countries with an official request to study the possibilities of aiding INOC in the exploitation of [Iraq's] oil resources."[31]

The first agreement between the Iraqi government and a foreign—in this instance, French—petroleum company was reached in November 1967, when ERAP was "granted the right to explore oil for a term of six years." If successful, ERAP could continue its operations for another twenty years. Of the amount produced, 30 percent could be purchased by ERAP "at privileged prices." The remaining 70 percent became the property of the Iraqi government. In return for this concession, the French concern undertook to pay Baghdad $15 million. Echoing the sentiments expressed by President Abd al-Rahman Aref,[32] the Soviet press hailed the INOC-ERAP agreement as a "fundamentally new type of deal for Iraq, it does not give the foreign entrepreneurs ownership of oil or a concession; it is merely a commercial contract." The official protests lodged by the United States and Great Britain with the French government merely reinforced Moscow's approval of the Iraqi initiative.[33]

Even more heartening, from the Kremlin's viewpoint, was the December 1967 Soviet-Iraqi agreement "on cooperation in the extraction of oil" which the Times of London described as "a deal that directly challenges the positions of Western-owned oil companies."[34] Not only was Iraq, "for the first time in her history," given an opportunity to exploit its petroleum resources, but it also called on the USSR to help break the "Iraq Petroleum's monopoly hold" on the country's economy. It was freely admitted that the time when "Iraq can be completely rid of exploitation of its wealth by imperialist monopolies" was some distance away. Nevertheless, a new situation had arisen, as Baghdad was now in the position to revise fundamentally its relations with the Western oil companies: the Iraqis had acquired an "ability . . . to produce and sell their own oil thanks to the increasing cooperation between their country and the Soviet Union."[35]

In the ensuing months, Moscow continued to lend its moral support to Baghdad's efforts to assert itself against the Western oil companies.

When Iraq and Algeria, in early 1968, agreed to continue the oil boycott against those Western states which had "aided Israel" in the June 1967 war, *Pravda* praised the decision "to continue the struggle against the expansion of the imperialist monopolies and to guard the national interests of the Arab peoples."[36] In April 1968 Prime Minister Taher Yahya announced that Great Britain had threatened to land paratroopers if Iraq began exploiting oil resources in areas taken over under the terms of Law 80 of December 1961. Moscow was incredulous: "one had to lose one's head completely to threaten aggression against a sovereign state which is taking steps to exploit its own natural resources." *Pravda* went on to say that the "imperialist monopolies" objected to Iraq's decision not only because it deprived the IPC of petroleum-rich areas, among them the North Rumailah fields, but also because it was bound to "intensify the struggle of the other developing countries for the return of their natural resources usurped by foreign capital."[37]

Oil Policy of the Ba'th

The trend toward the nationalization of the IPC continued after the Ba'th party returned to power in July 1968. In its proclamation Number 1, issued on July 17, the new regime announced "the adoption of a national oil policy, independent of world monopolies . . . , and the strengthening of the National Oil Company to enable it to set up an independent oil sector and start production as soon as possible."[38] Going one step further, the "Chapter for National Unity," made public on October 24, not only called for "a hard line against oil companies operating in Iraq," but also suggested that "the contract with . . . ERAP should be renegotiated 'in order to secure better terms.' "[39] This attitude was maintained over the next four years, leaving no doubt about the Ba'th's ultimate intentions. Baghdad's stand, marked by steadily increasing pressure, produced frequent confrontations as well as occasional concessions by the oil companies but did not lead to any lasting compromises.

Iraq's increasing public resentment stemmed from the IPC's unwillingness—conditioned by years of confrontation—to comply with two major demands: a significant increase in production and an adjustment in accounting procedures to allow for a more beneficial expensing of royalties. Specifically, while oil production and, consequently, the revenues in Saudi Arabia and Iran were rising at a rate of more than 10 percent annually in the late 1960s (11 and 14 percent, respectively),

Iraq's increase was only 4.7 percent. According to Baghdad's calculations the loss "to its income during the ten years following the enactment of Law 80" was more than half a billion Iraqi dinars (ID).[40] Under the pressure of public threats, such as those delivered by Bakr and Ammash,[41] the IPC gave some ground—it announced in October 1970 that, beginning in 1971, the annual production of crude oil would be increased by 16.5 million tons to 86.5 million tons.[42]

On the question of royalties, Iraq insisted that larger payments to the government should be made retroactive to 1964, when OPEC adopted the principle of expensing.[43] Acceptance of this demand by the IPC would have netted the Ba'thi authorities another ID 82 million. Instead, the company agreed to begin applying new expensing procedures in 1971, "when the subject was brought up for negotiations," and deferred the discussion of retroactive payments until such time as the IPC's own demands on the Iraqi government resulting from the implementation of Law 80 had been settled.[44] Nevertheless, in a move designed to appease the government, the IPC, in June 1971, agreed to raise the price of the Iraqi crude oil exported through the Mediterranean from $2.41 to $3.21 per barrel. (According to Baghdad Radio, Iraq's oil revenues would thereby be raised from L181 million in 1970 to L330 million in 1971.) At the same time, the IPC refused to comply with Baghdad's request for a "'quality premium' of 20 cents per barrel similar to that granted in April [1971] for Libyan low-sulphur oil"[45] on the ground that Iraqi northern crude had a sulphur content of more than 0.5 percent (the criterion used in the Libyan negotiations).[46]

In addition to these two major problem areas, Baghdad, in July 1970, demanded participation "to the extent of 20 percent in the capital of foreign oil companies operating" in Iraq. It also insisted that its "representative on the IPC board be made 'executive director' in order to enable the government to participate in the formulation and execution of the company's policy."[47]

Having initially rejected the government's demands as "unsuitable as a basis for discussion," the IPC group, in March 1972, nonetheless "agreed in principle to the Iraqi Government having a 20 percent holding in their concessions."[48] At the same time, however, INOC's preparations to ship North Rumailah oil to Iraq's Soviet-bloc and Western customers prompted the IPC, in March and April 1972, to threaten legal action against organizations violating the group's concessionary rights in Iraq.[49] These warnings were disregarded, leading the oil companies to slow down production and thus to lower the government's royalties. When its protests produced no results,[50] Baghdad on May 17 presented the IPC with an ultimatum—it had two weeks to meet Iraq's demands for "increased output, participation in the companies' assets and a readjustment of royalties from 1964 to 1970 amounting to some L95 million" or face the possibility of "drastic action."[51] The IPC's final offer to the government was found unacceptable and, on June 1, 1972, President Bakr announced the nationalization of the Iraq Petroleum Company.[52]

To keep this action in its historical perspective, it is worth repeating that, although there had been no Iraqi timetable for the nationalization of the country's oil industry, the principle itself had been openly espoused by all of Baghdad's leaders since Kassem. The Ba'th party, after 1968, was no exception. A noteworthy example was provided by RCC Vice-Chairman Saddam Hussein in an interview with Beirut's *L'Orient*, published on May 18, 1971. Asked if Iraq proposed to nationalize the foreign oil companies, he said, in part: "No regime in this part of the world that does not work for the liberation of its oil can claim to be nationalist or progressive. . . . We are not trying to attain all our objectives at once, but if we fail to do so in the future, we shall not be able to call ourselves progressive."[53]

Baghdad's reluctance to press for an early nationalization was explained by awareness that additional foreign financial and technical assistance as well as markets had to be secured to protect Iraq against the expected boycott by the powerful Western oil companies. To do otherwise, as was amply illustrated by the experience of Iran's Prime Minister Mohammed Mossadeq in the early 1950s, was to court an economic and political disaster. It was for all of these reasons that Baghdad attempted, prior to the nationalization of the IPC, to barter its oil to both Communist and some Western customers for capital, goods, and services. (This approach to foreign economic relations remained in effect until 1974 when, after the successful nationalization of the IPC and the quadrupling of the price of petroleum, preference was given to cash transactions.)

As it turned out, France and the USSR were the first great powers willing and anxious to meet Iraq's requirements. Sensing a unique opportunity to weaken some of the major Western economic interests in the Middle East and to strengthen its ties with an important Arab producer country, Moscow stepped in. Following up on the letter of intent of December 1967, an agreement between the two countries was signed in June 1969. Under its terms, Iraq received Soviet economic and technical assistance valued at $72 million for oil exploration and exploitation in the Halfayyah region of southeastern Iraq. The initial undertaking was followed, in July 1969, by a similar accord providing an additional $70 million for the development of reserves in the petroleum-rich North Rumailah area of southern Iraq, operated by INOC. Both loans were to be repaid in crude oil, an arrangement which netted Moscow considerable economic benefits following the sharp rise in the price of petroleum in 1973.[54]

Between 1969 and 1972 the USSR took additional steps to strengthen Iraq's capability to extract, process, and market its oil. The framework for stimulating bilateral economic relations was created by an agreement signed in March 1970. It provided for the establishment of a permanent joint committee "to study the expansion . . . of economic, technical and trade relations" between the two countries. Valid for five years, the agreement was to be "automatically renewed unless cancelled by either side."[55]

Among the important initiatives negotiated during this period were supplementary agreements to develop the North Rumailah field and to construct a 143-kilometer pipeline between it and the Persian Gulf deep-water terminal at Faw;[56] an undertaking to build a refinery in Mosul and a pipeline linking Baghdad with Basrah;[57] and an arrangement to lease to INOC a number of Soviet tankers to ship the North Rumailah oil to the USSR and Eastern Europe after production started in April 1972.[58] In addition, Moscow extended other forms of technical assistance to INOC, ranging from supplies of seismological and drilling equipment to the establishment of a training center for INOC personnel.[59]

Emulating the Kremlin's example and closely following in its footsteps were the USSR's oil-hungry satellites of Eastern Europe. As early as November 1969 Czechoslovakia, Hungary, and Poland (as well as Yugoslavia) had agreed to cooperate in the construction of a 560-mile Central European pipeline which would carry 19 million tons of Iraqi crude a year to these countries.[60] Subsequently, underscoring Baghdad's determination to secure markets for its oil in exchange for loans as well as for a variety of services designed to stimulate its petroleum production, Iraq entered into a number of other deals. Among the major projects were undertakings by Czechoslovakia to construct an oil refinery in Basrah[61] and by Hungary to help drill wells in the North Rumailah area and in the Kirkuk province.[62] In addition, Hungary, Bulgaria, Rumania, East Germany, and Yugoslavia provided INOC with credits for the purchase of equipment, services, and technical assistance. All these loans, as well as those extended by the USSR, were to be repaid mainly in oil and petroleum products.[63] The insistence on acceptance of Iraqi crude as repayment for loans and other forms of assistance was the most important feature of Baghdad's foreign economic policy before the successful nationalization of the IPC and the 1973 rise in the price of oil. Adopted in 1969, the policy was officially formulated in February 1970, when the Iraqi government announced that it was giving "preference in international tenders . . . to bidders who were prepared to accept at least partial payment in Iraqi crude oil or products."[64] Moscow's willingness to accommodate Baghdad explains, in part, the economic (and political) successes scored by the USSR and its satellites in Iraq in the late 1960s and early 1970s. The highwater mark of Soviet prestige was reached in April 1972, when Chairman of the USSR Council of Ministers Aleksei Kosygin visited Iraq for the signing of the Treaty of Friendship and Cooperation. In one of his speeches, the prime minister promised full Soviet support for Baghdad's drive to achieve "complete sovereignty" over the country's natural resources. This served as a clear indication of Moscow's stand on the nationalization of the IPC. In another symbolic gesture, Kosygin attended the ribbon-cutting ceremony to begin the flow of petroleum from North Rumailah. A few days later, the first Soviet tanker, carrying 21,000 tons of North Rumailah crude, sailed from Faw. According to a TASS report of April 14, 1 million tons of Iraqi oil would be shipped to the USSR in 1972, to be followed by additional 2 million tons between 1973 and 1975.[65]

However, as noted in chapter 1, even at this time of dramatic expansion of economic ties between Iraq and the countries of the "socialist commonwealth"—a course of action judged necessary to ensure the success of the nationalization of Iraq's oil industry—Baghdad also launched a major effort to expand economic relations with several Western states. In this pursuit, as in the case of the Communist bloc, preference was given to the countries willing to deal with INOC. The obvious purpose, indicative of the general approach which was to mark Baghdad's dealings with the outside world in the years to come, was not only to diversify Iraq's markets but also to secure the cooperation and, hopefully, goodwill of some members of the Western camp. Put differently, one of the cardinal features of the Ba'th's political and economic policies in the 1970s was the determination to avoid too deep an entanglement with any one state or a group of states (in this instance, the USSR and its allies) by diversifying its markets as well as its sources of assistance and support. Later in the decade, this approach was also followed with respect to the acquisition of modern weapons. In any event, in the early 1970s economic and technical cooperation in exchange for petroleum was also sought (and received) from France, Spain, Italy, and Brazil.

In May 1970 a French company was awarded the contract for the construction of a pipeline from North Rumailah to Faw, and in July another French firm was placed in charge of operating a gas bottling plant near Baghdad.[66] Although not without problems, such as the impasse reached in the negotiations between INOC and ERAP concerning the size of the latter's original concession area,[67] cooperation between Iraq and France continued and took a dramatic upturn after the nationalization of the IPC and Saddam Hussein's subsequent and highly successful visit to Paris in June 1972. Spain was another of Iraq's major Western trading partners. Its primary early contribution to INOC was a May 1970 agreement to deliver seven 35,000 ton oil tankers in exchange for North Rumailah crude.[68] In addition, in November 1970 INOC took possession of a lube oil plant, built near Baghdad by a subsidiary of the Italian state-owned ENI petroleum company, and in March 1972 the latter contracted to buy 20 million tons of Iraqi crude over a ten-year period. Payments were to be made in industrial equipment, machinery, services, and consumer goods provided by ENI and other Italian state-controlled enterprises.[69] Finally, in December 1971 an INOC delegation signed an agreement with the Brazilian state-owned and state-operated oil company Petrobras to supply it with an unspecified amount of Iraqi crude.[70]

On balance, it is clear that, in the period between 1969 and 1972, the magnitude of Soviet and satellite effort in support of INOC—and hence of the determination to nationalize the IPC—far surpassed that of France, Spain, Italy, and Brazil. Nevertheless, of importance in the context of this discussion is the fact that Iraq had no intention of relying exclusively on one international power bloc. Instead, moral and material support was sought from both the East and the West, establishing the pattern which Baghdad was to follow in the years to come.

In addition, Iraq also set out to secure moral backing of the Organization of Petroleum Exporting Countries and of the Organization of Arab Petroleum Exporting Countries (OAPEC), of which Baghdad was a member.[71] After intricate diplomatic maneuvering, both organizations came out openly in support of the Iraqi position. In the wake of the nationalization of the IPC, OPEC (with Iran dissenting) and OAPEC officially endorsed Baghdad's action as "a lawful act of sovereignty designed to safeguard . . . [Iraq's] legitimate interests."[72]

Thus, the June 1, 1972, nationalization of the IPC was the final act in an extensive and involved process whose success, the Ba'th understood well, depended on the completion of several separate but related tasks. Domestically, INOC had to be transformed from a paper enterprise into a vigorous and well-functioning organization whose efficiency rested on qualified specialists, reasonably developed infrastructure, and the availability of transporting capacity as well as of foreign markets.[73] This goal was reached in April 1972 when the North Rumailah fields, developed primarily with Soviet assistance, went into production with an intact market of both Eastern and Western customers. Internationally, in addition to markets, Iraq also had to assure itself of extended support from the communist as well as some of the major Western countries and from the oil-producers' organizations. With these pieces in place, all that remained was to demonstrate the "unreasonableness" of the IPC. This was accomplished by means of the May 17, 1972, ultimatum which, as Baghdad correctly suspected, the IPC had no choice but to reject. Upon the expiration of the two-week period, Iraq was free to announce the nationalization of the IPC.

It is significant that in moving against the IPC, the authorities not only decided to compensate it for the assets which had been nationalized—an accepted international legal practice—but also limited themselves to taking over of the company's northern fields only. This meant that the assets and the operations of the Basrah Petroleum Company, located in the southern part of Iraq, were not affected by the nationalization decree. In another display of moderation, Baghdad also negotiated an agreement with Paris "allowing the French partner in IPC to receive its share from the nationalized oil under the same conditions prevailing before nationalization for a period of 10 years."[74] While Iraq's attitude toward France could be explained, in part, by the fact that the latter had by then emerged as Baghdad's main Western trading partner, the circumspection shown by the authorities was also due to their reluctance to take over the country's oil operations all at once. As noted by Majid Khadduri, Iraq actually "needed the income from the BPC before it could run its own oil industry."[75]

On February 28, 1973, the IPC formally accepted the nationalization decree and resolved all of its outstanding differences with the Iraqi government. Specifically, the company agreed to recognize the legality of the nationalization laws of 1961 and 1972 (this meant, in part, the liquidation of the Mosul Petroleum Company and the transfer to Iraq of all of its local assets) and to pay Baghdad the sum of L141 million in settlement of the government's claim for outstanding royalties. In exchange, the authorities undertook to compensate the IPC for the nationalization of its northern fields with 15 million tons of Kirkuk crude, worth L128 million. Finally, the Basrah Petroleum Company agreed to increase significantly the production of oil in its concessionary area.[76]

The next step in the nationalization process was taken in the wake of the October 1973 war, when Iraq, "in retaliation for the hostile attitude of the American and Dutch Governments in their support of Israel against the Arabs," announced the nationalization of the U.S. and Dutch holdings in the Basrah Petroleum Company.[77] The process was completed in December 1975 with the nationalization of the remaining foreign interests in the Basrah Petroleum Company.[78] In retrospect, Iraq succeeded in its task because of the steadily growing economic and technical cooperation, as well as trade, with a large number of communist and Western partners, including the Soviet Union.

The initial step in the exploitation of the North Rumailah deposits was taken in July 1969, when Iraq and the USSR signed an agreement providing for Soviet assistance in developing the North Rumailah fields and in establishing Iraq's own national petroleum industry.[79] The Kremlin made no secret of its satisfaction with this turn of events: in expanding their national economies, the Arabs were "relying more and more confidently on the friendly assistance of the world socialist system." As a result, "mutually advantageous cooperation between Arab and socialist countries is being extended to an ever-widening range of economic problems, including the problem of creating a national oil industry for the Arabs." The June and July 1969 agreements between Iraq and the USSR were a case in point.[80] In addition, these two accords also represented a "most telling blow at the interests of the foreign oil monopolies."[81] The extent of the West's discomfort was evidenced by the fact that the Associated Press referred to the 1969 agreements as the "first fruit of a policy designed to strengthen the Soviet Union's influence in the Persian Gulf." *Izvestiia* found "the Yankees' irritation . . . understandable: they are disturbed not by the imaginary 'influence' of the USSR but by the fact that their own plans to control the Arabs' oil are breaking down."[82]

As time passed, Soviet publications offered variations on the theme of "Western monopolies'" scheming and plotting against the Iraqi government. For example, in November 1971 Pavel Demchenko, *Pravda*'s leading authority on the Middle East, attributed the growing unrest in the Kurdish region not only to the "lack of unity" among the Ba'th, the Iraqi Community party, and the Kurdistan Democratic party, but also to the "machinations of the imperialist powers, the oil companies, and their agents." Political discord and conflict between the Arabs and the

Kurds, Demchenko concluded, provided these forces with an opportunity "to retain their positions in the Iraqi economy and their profits from the Iraqi oil."[83]

In addition to warnings about "imperialist intentions," the Soviet media continued to express Moscow's satisfaction with both Baghdad's economic policies designed to strengthen the state sector and the continued expansion of Soviet-Iraqi economic relations. Commenting on the government's 1970 through 1974 five-year plan for economic development, *Pravda* wrote approvingly about the "intensification of the industrialization program [and] the development of the national oil industry." Plans to create petrochemical, shipbuilding, and other energy-related branches of the Iraqi industry were singled out for special praise, as were also plans to expand significantly the state sector of the economy.[84]

Moscow was equally pleased with the official position taken by Iraq on the matter of cooperation with the USSR. As early as August 1970, during Saddam Hussein's visit to Moscow, the Ba'thi leader spoke of Iraq's "deep gratitude to the Soviet Union for its great assistance" to his country's economic development.[85] He was even more profuse in his expressions of appreciation for Soviet support during the February 1972 visit to the USSR. Preceding as it did the signing of the Treaty of Friendship and Cooperation in April 1972 and the subsequent nationalization of the Iraq Petroleum Company, the trip was particularly important in that Baghdad may be assumed to have secured Soviet backing for the nationalization of the IPC not later than that date. Thus, in the speech at a Kremlin dinner, Saddam Hussein referred to "significant development in technical and economic cooperation" between the two countries and singled out Soviet assistance in the "utilization of the oil riches of Iraq." He went on to emphasize the "utmost importance of this problem in the life of our people who have decided to reclaim their lawful rights in the struggle with the monopolist companies and to guarantee their sovereign right to the national wealth." Saddam Hussein concluded by saying that in the pursuit of this goal Iraq relied on its "own strength, [and] on the assistance of . . . [its] friends, above all the USSR." This support, he said, "we value exceptionally highly."[86]

Although Prime Minister Kosygin, in his speech, made no references to Iraq's economic policies—an omission that would appear to support the contention that the USSR, "though tacitly agree[ing] on nationalization in principle, seems to have given Iraq no encouragement in the drive to nationalize Western oil operations"[87]—the language of the joint communiqué came very close to refuting that argument. In it, the two sides not only indicated their determination to broaden cooperation, "especially . . . [with the view to] further development of Soviet-Iraqi political, economic, and military cooperation and [to] the creation of the national oil industry in Iraq," but the Soviet Union also "expressed support of the petroleum policy implemented by the Iraqi government." Moreover, and significantly, the USSR specifically endorsed the "determined stand taken by the . . . [Ba'th] party and the Iraqi government with regard to the monopolist oil companies."[88] Kosygin's omission of the problem so vitally important to Baghdad from his Kremlin speech and the outright endorsement of Iraq's position in the joint communiqué could be interpreted as meaning that the Soviet side had been won over by Saddam Hussein in the negotiations which followed the opening ceremonies.

Be that as it may, in the ensuing months the USSR continued to voice its support of Baghdad's determination to gain control of the country's petroleum resources. As noted earlier, Kosygin's April 1972 visit to Iraq might have been viewed, among other things, as an official endorsement of the nationalization of the IPC, planned for later in the year. It will be recalled that his presence was utilized not only to sign the Treaty of Friendship and Cooperation but also to inaugurate the production of the North Rumailah field, which had been developed with Soviet assistance. Not surprisingly, Soviet publications described the event as "a truly revolutionary development for Iraq, whose oil has hitherto been monopolized by Western interests."[89] It was, moreover, "a practical embodiment of the slogan 'Arab oil for the Arabs,'" because "with the opening of the [North Rumailah] field the monopoly of Iraq Petroleum in extraction and export of Iraqi oil has come to an end."[90] Reciprocating, Saddam Hussein spoke of the opening of the North Rumailah field as a "striking symbol of Soviet-Iraqi friendship."[91] Finally, the joint communiqué, issued at the conclusion of Kosygin's visit, referred to North Rumailah as the "beginning of an important stage in the struggle of the Iraqi people against the penetration of the imperialist oil monopolies [and] for the achievement of complete economic independence of the Iraqi Republic."[92] The stage was now set for the nationalization of the Iraqi Petroleum Company.

Nationalization of the IPC

The USSR has consistently endorsed the principle of nationalization of major Western companies operating in the countries of the Third World. It is equally noteworthy, however, that the initiative for such actions invariably came from the developing nations themselves and that the Kremlin simply endeavored to reinforce their resolution by offering moral and, where applicable, material support. For example, in commenting on the proceedings of the conference of the OAPEC countries held in Kuwait in March 1970, *Pravda* praised the participants for urging their respective governments to use "one of the Arabs' greatest riches" for the benefit of the Arab peoples. The best way to achieve this goal was to nationalize the foreign oil companies.[93] Similar conclusions were reached at the Algiers colloquium of the Arab oil producers held in October 1970. Here, too, it was argued that the Arabs must coordinate their activities and "formulate a joint policy toward the monopolies." *Pravda* concurred, concluding that the "end goal of all these measures . . . [was] full liberation of the natural resources of the Arab countries from the power of foreign capital."[94]

Soviet commentators had no doubt about the ultimate outcome of the conflict between the major Western oil companies and the petroleum-producing countries: the "continued strengthening of . . . [the latter's] solidarity . . . will undoubtedly lead to the development of conditions in which the imperialist oil cartel . . . will be powerless to prevent the transfer of control over Arab oil into the hands of its real owners."[95]

In any event, matters came to a head in May 1972, when Baghdad accused the foreign oil companies operating in Iraq of "subversive activity." Specifically, it was argued that the curtailment of production in northern Iraq had deprived the state treasury of L33 million in revenues during March, April, and the first week in May. The authorities responded by presenting the IPC with an ultimatum demanding that it "increase oil extraction to the full capacity of the oil pipelines, draw up together with the Ministry of Oil and Natural Resources a long-term plan for oil extraction in Iraq, and take steps to insure its fulfilment." The IPC, according to the *New Times*, was given two weeks to respond, with the Iraqi government reserving "the right to take whatever steps it considers necessary to protect the legitimate national interests."[96] Soviet publications noted that the ultimatum as well as the "initiation of oil extraction through the nation's own efforts were a source of acute irritation to the monopolies." There was clearly, it was implied, a connection between the two events—the recent opening of the North Rumailah fields "created new opportunities for the Iraqi people in their struggle against the domination by foreign monopolies."[97]

In line with its previous stand, the Soviet government came out openly and unequivocally in support of the June 1, 1972, nationalization decree. In a joint communiqué published at the conclusion of Foreign Minister Murtada Said Abd al-Baki's June visit to Moscow, "the Soviet side declared its support for the Iraqi government's measures and for the just struggle of the Iraqi people, which is aimed at restoring their sovereign rights over the country's natural resources and at using its oil resources in the interests of developing an independent national economy. . . ."[98]

The Soviet media staged a major campaign in support of the nationalization decree. The *New Times*, quoting the *Baghdad Observer*, spoke of a "historic landmark," while *Pravda* described it as a "proof of the firm determination of the government and people . . . to strengthen [Iraq's] political and economic independence, to march along the path of social transformations."[99] Combined with Syria's decision to nationalize the assets of the IPC, the two measures were welcomed as a "new page in the struggle of the Arab peoples for full control over their natural resources [and] for the strengthening of [their] national sovereignty."[100] Finally, the nationalization of the IPC was highly important because it was "not simply an economic sanction employed against insolent monopolists but [was also] . . . a direct [political] challenge to the imperialist powers."[101]

Placing the events of June 1972 in historical perspective, a Soviet commentator noted that they followed Algeria's partial nationalization of the foreign oil companies and Libya's takeover of the property of the British Petroleum Company. Nevertheless, Baghdad's action came as something of a surprise because until then the members of OPEC had "consistently advocated a policy of gradual pressure on the international monopolies so as to push back, step by step, their positions as regards the terms and the size of the allotments from profit, the supply of oil . . . to the home market, the activity of national oil companies and a number of other issues." Iraq's action was understandable, however, because the country had been singled out by the international oil cartel as "the arena where the monopolies decided to give battle to OPEC, to try and split its ranks and once again demonstrate their strength." The monopolies miscalculated, and the Soviet analysts attributed the cartel's failure to several factors.[102] First, Iraq's success resulted from "the advance of the national liberation movement in the 'Third World' countries." Second, it was due to "the consolidation of forces by oil-producing countries" and to their determined support of Baghdad's and Damascus's nationalization decrees. OAPEC's decision to offer financial assistance to Iraq and Syria as well as OPEC's June 9 resolution not to replace Iraqi petroleum on the world market were a case in point. The latter action, in particular, "deprived the monopolies of a . . . powerful weapon, with the help of which they practically reduced to naught in 1951–54 the results of the nationalization of the Anglo-Iranian Oil Company . . . by replacing Iranian oil on West European markets by oil from other countries, including Iraq."[103] Third, there was the support extended by the USSR "and other socialist countries." *Pravda* pointed out that successful nationalization of the IPC depended, in part, on Baghdad's ability to launch its own oil industry. Soviet aid was described as having been crucial for two reasons. On the one hand, the July 1969 agreement on economic and technical assistance enabled Iraq to begin operating the North Rumailah fields. On the other, Moscow launched a major effort to revive INOC whose effectiveness, according to Ali Ghannam, member of the Ba'th party National Command, had been paralyzed by "reactionary forces" acting on the orders from the outside. Only because of Soviet assistance, said Ali Ghannam, was it possible to breathe new life into INOC.[104] In addition to helping to set up and run the national oil industry, the USSR and the countries of Eastern Europe also undertook to purchase Iraqi petroleum and provided tankers necessary for its shipment.[105] Fourth, there was the decision of a number of major Western consumers such as France, Italy, Spain, West Germany, Holland, Greece, Japan, and India to disregard the cartel's call for boycott and to continue buying Iraqi oil.[106]

In short, Iraq had scored an important victory. It not only gained general recognition of the legitimacy of the nationalization decree on the part of the international community—an effort spearheaded by "the socialist countries and all the anti-imperialist forces"—but also succeeded in securing "*de facto* recognition of nationalization by IPC," extended when the latter agreed to reopen negotiations with INOC. It is noteworthy, however, that even at this time of triumph Moscow sounded a note of caution: "The Iraqi Government understands that the nationalization decision by itself does not signify complete and final victory, that it is merely the beginning of a real battle against oil imperialism. Indeed, the monopolies have no intention of losing a source of such huge profits without resistance."[107]

Among the various avenues open to the cartel were control of the petroleum markets as well as of the tanker fleets; possible recourse to legal action against customers willing to purchase Iraqi oil; subversion and "encouragement of right-wing elements" with the view of destabilizing the Iraqi government;[108] and, last but not least, the threat or actual use of force. In this connection, the *New Times* informed its readers that, in the wake of the nationalization decree, the British, U.S.,

French, and Dutch governments had considered "taking joint action against Iraq" and that London was "trying to bring pressure to bear upon Iraq through the CENTO military bloc." Nevertheless, the Soviets found reassurance in the argument that "the days of gunboat diplomacy . . . are gone never to return" and in the statement by the Iraqi defense minister that the country's armed forces were "ready to defend the revolutionary gains of the people against all encroachments."[109] *Pravda* pointed out also that in its "just struggle" Iraq was not alone—it was supported by the "other Arab peoples [and] its strength . . . [was] doubled by the backing and aid of the Soviet Union and other socialist countries."[110] Subsequently, after it had become obvious that no major sanctions were going to be invoked against Iraq after all, Moscow went back to routine expressions of support for the nationalization of the IPC.[111]

In October 1972 the Arab petroleum-producing states of the Persian Gulf were said to have gained a "major concession" from the Western oil companies. By that was meant a 25 percent participation in such companies (to be raised to a 51 percent after a ten-year period). According to *Pravda*, all past efforts on the part of the producers to secure a share in the Western-owned companies had been unsuccessful because of the cartel's awareness that, once set into motion, the process would ultimately lead to complete nationalization. However, when Iraq and Syria succeeded in nationalizing the assets of the IPC, the monopolies were forced to adopt a more flexible and conciliatory attitude. They sounded tactical retreat in the hope that partial concessions would protect them against "more serious losses." This approach, *Pravda* concluded, was not likely to work—the situation "on the oil front has not of late favored the monopolies."[112]

Soviet publications were also elated at the February 1973 agreement between Iraq and the IPC. When President Bakr, in a radio and television speech of March 1, described the accord as "ensuring Iraq's sovereignty over her oil wealth" and thanked the world's "progressive forces," including the "socialist countries [and] especially . . . the Soviet Union," for their "support . . . [and] disinterested assistance," *Pravda* hailed Baghdad's "complete victory" over the IPC. The February 1973 agreement was judged to be important for the following reasons. It brought to an end the "bitter struggle . . . between Iraq and the Western monopolies unwilling to reconcile themselves with the loss of their positions" in that oil-rich country.[113] *Pravda* also noted that Baghdad remained determined to continue its "advance against the positions of foreign oil capital." Thus, the assets of the Mosul Petroleum Company were to pass into the hands of the Iraqi government, without compensation, on

March 31, 1973, while the Basrah Petroleum Company undertook not only to increase payments to Iraq but also to raise the production of oil to 80 million tons in 1976. In short, the cartel had proved unable to prevent Baghdad from "striking a blow against imperialist intentions to deprive the progressive Arab regimes of their important weapon in the struggle against imperialism [and] reaction. . . ."[114]

In the ensuing months, the Kremlin continued to voice its satisfaction with Iraq's handling of the "oil monopolies" and to emphasize the role which the USSR had played in enabling Baghdad to nationalize the assets of the IPC. In a Kremlin speech honoring Saddam Hussein during his March 1973 visit to Moscow, Prime Minister Kosygin expressed "happiness" with Iraq's recent successes and lauded the Ba'th's "determination and perseverance" in defending the country's "national riches." The premier went on to state: "In addressing the peoples who have gained their national independence, we say: build your life according to your own interests . . . , own your national riches, use them to raise [your country's] economy and culture [and] to improve the living standards of the people."[115] In his speech, Saddam Hussein thanked the USSR for the "important, positive role" it played in backing the Ba'th's efforts to "gain a victory for our people" but went on to ascribe Baghdad's success mainly to the "perseverance, struggle, and sacrifices" of the ordinary Iraqis.[116] On another occasion, Saddam Hussein listed the factors which contributed to the "successful nationalization of the IPC" in the following order: "steadfastness of the Iraqi people, [and] support of the Arab and other friendly nations, especially the Soviet Union."[117] Although Moscow and Baghdad differed on some nuances (i.e., how much weight should, by implication, be assigned to different factors), they were in general agreement that both the perseverance of the Iraqis and the Arab and Soviet support were of crucial importance in guaranteeing the success of the nationalization decree of June 1, 1972.

Subsequently, Moscow endorsed the October 1973 nationalization of the U.S. and Dutch holdings in the Basrah Petroleum Company. These "direct blows" were struck in response to the two states' "anti-Arab positions" held during the 1973 war.[118] Likewise, during his December 1973 visit to Baghdad, Boris Ponomarev, candidate member of the CPSU Politburo and Central Committee secretary in charge of relations with the developing countries, expressed the Kremlin's "approval and strong support" of the "decisive steps [taken] by the Iraqi government with respect to the nationalization of its petroleum riches."[119] Finally, in December 1975 President Bakr announced that the RCC had ordered the nationalization of the assets of the last two foreign companies operating in Iraq: the British Petroleum Company and Compagnie Française des Pétroles. According to *Pravda*, the decision was "warmly supported by the Iraqi people," including the Iraqi Communist party, because it completed "Iraq's lengthy struggle against the foreign monopolies for the right . . . to be the master of its own natural resources."[120] Moscow concurred. On the one hand, the takeover of the Basrah Petroleum Company "put an end to the foreign oil operators' grip on . . . [Iraq's] economy." On the other hand, as noted by Oil Minister Tayeh Abd al-Kerim, the decision was of great political importance as well. It strengthened "the entire Arab nation, which is confronted with imperialist conspiracies, reactionary machinations and Zionist aggression."[121]

Evaluation

As is evident from the above discussion, the problem of the nationalization of Iraq's oil industry was one of the few major issues facing the ruling Ba'th party in the early 1970s on which Baghdad and Moscow had found themselves in full agreement. Even before 1968, the USSR came out openly in favor of the measures adopted by the various republican governments to limit the scope of activities of the IPC and its subsidiaries, such as Laws 80, 97, and 123. The Soviets also endorsed the programs aimed at accelerating Iraq's economic development on the ground that more efficient agricultural production (to be achieved by means of a sweeping agrarian reform) as well as more intensive industrial growth would enable Baghdad to lessen its economic, and hence political, dependence on the West and would thus significantly contribute to the general weakening of the Western positions in the Middle East. With this in mind, the USSR was prepared not only to offer Iraq its vocal moral and political support but also to come to Baghdad's assistance in more tangible ways. As shown in chapter 1, the economic and military aid programs of the late 1950s and the 1960s were increased in the 1970s with the result that, during that decade, Iraq emerged as one of Moscow's major recipients of military assistance and, to a lesser extent, economic, financial, and technical aid in the developing world.

Baghdad was glad to avail itself of this Soviet support, regarded as indispensable for the attainment of two major goals which the various postrevolutionary regimes, and especially the Ba'th, felt had to be reached in order to secure Iraq's complete political and economic independence and to consolidate the authority of the central government. One of them was the problem of the Kurdish quest for autonomy. The other issue was the gaining of full control over the country's oil industry. This objective was regarded as being of utmost importance not only for its own sake—that is, because it eliminated Western control over a significant portion of Iraq's petroleum resources—but also because the IPC had become synonymous with foreign control over the country's economy and, to a lesser degree, of its political life.

In short, on this particular issue, the interests of Baghdad and Moscow coincided to a remarkable degree and thus contributed significantly to the impression that, in the 1970s, Iraq and the USSR had become very close friends, if not outright allies. This view was reinforced by active Soviet participation in the efforts to develop Iraq's petroleum industry in the fields nationalized under Law 80 (above all in the North Rumailah sector) and to help establish other branches of industry as well as to strengthen the country's armed forces.

Still, while there could be no doubt about the general, "strategic" confluence of Moscow's and Baghdad's interests with regard to the problem of nationalization of Iraq's oil industry, there was some uncertainty as to whether the USSR, for tactical reasons, actually favored a decisive action by the Ba'th in the first half of 1972. The Kremlin's hesitation, if indeed there was one, might have been caused by apprehension that the petroleum cartel had sufficient economic and political influence to persuade the Western consumers to boycott the nationalized Iraqi oil. Such a turn of events, as well as the possible threat or actual application of force, would have placed the Soviets in an unenviable position. They might have been asked to absorb much of Iraq's petroleum production—not an appealing prospect in 1972—or even to come to Baghdad's defense in case of Western military intervention. Whatever reservations the Kremlin may have had, however, appear to have been removed during Saddam Hussein's February 1972 visit to Moscow. The Treaty of Friendship and Cooperation was signed soon afterward, clearing the path for the nationalization degree of June 1.

Thus, the USSR and Iraq were in full agreement on the desirability of the nationalization of the Western oil interests. If the two states diverged at all, it was on the timing of the action. If so, and if the Soviet Union did in fact urge caution, it was Iraq's view which prevailed in the end. Faced with Baghdad's determination to proceed, Moscow was confronted with the choice of supporting the Ba'th or of opposing it and thus risking a deterioration of what, in 1972, must have appeared to the USSR as a very promising relationship with an important, oil-rich, and strategically located Arab state. The Kremlin decided to accommodate Iraq—but another instance of a client-state influencing the behavior of the patron. In the overall scheme of Soviet-Iraqi relations, this was not the most prominent example of Baghdad's ability to influence Moscow, but it was important, both in its own right and as a manifestation of the underlying reality of that relationship.

Last, since in the past the USSR had been highly vocal in its encouragement of the developing countries to nationalize the assets of major Western companies operating in their territory, the blame for the measures by the petroleum-producing nations to curtail the activities of the Western "oil cartel" has occasionally been laid at the doors of the Kremlin. Nothing could have been further from the truth. The gradual self-assertion on the part of the producers, a process in which the 1972 nationalization of the IPC was an important landmark, had been prompted by their own determination to control their countries' natural resources. To be sure, the producers not only found encouragement in Moscow's strong policy but also, as in the case of Iraq, sometimes approached the USSR in search of moral and material support. The latter was usually forthcoming, but the initiative for gradual or outright nationalization of the foreign petroleum companies came invariably from the producer countries themselves and not from the Kremlin.

The Kurdish drive for national assertion has been an integral and important factor in Middle Eastern politics for a long time. Before World War I
the Kurds staged periodic rebellions against Ottoman rule. After the
dissolution of the Empire in 1918, Kurdish aspirations received a significant boost when the Western powers, under the terms of the Treaty of
Sèvres (1920), recognized Kurdistan as an independent state. Its provisions were nullified in 1923, however, when the Turkish Republic negotiated a new agreement with the Allied powers. The Treaty of Lausanne
reestablished Ankara's control over the predominantly Kurdish parts of
southeastern Turkey.[1] The Kurds fared no better in post-World War I
Persia (Iran), Iraq, or Syria.[2] Of the four Muslim states where the Kurds
have resided after the dissolution of the Ottoman Empire, only Iraq
recognized them as an officially constituted minority with specific
constitutional rights, granted in 1925 by the League of Nations as a
condition for the inclusion of the oil-rich Mosul area in the Iraqi state.
This recognition has formed the basis for the Kurdish demands for
autonomy since 1961.[3]

Under the monarchy, the last major Kurdish uprising took place in
1945. It was staged by the newly formed Kurdish Democratic party,
which embraced leftist intellectuals, among them Ibrahim Ahmad and
Jalal al-Din Talabani, as well as conservative tribal elements headed by
Mulla Mustafa al-Barzani. In 1953, the organization was renamed Kurdistan Democratic party (KDP). The 1945 uprising was suppressed by the
government forces, but a group of Kurdish warriors, led by Mulla Mustafa, escaped to neighboring Iran and helped their compatriots in establishing the Kurdish Republic of Mahabad. After the latter was overrun
by the Iranian army, Mulla Mustafa and some of his followers found

refuge in the USSR, where they remained until the overthrow of the Iraqi monarchy in July 1958.[4]

The republican regime, headed by Colonel Abd al-Kerim Kassem, expressed itself in favor of Arab-Kurdish "partnership" and permitted the exiled Kurds to return to Iraq. The move was favored by the Iraqi left, including the Iraqi Communist party (ICP), and may have been influenced by Kassem's desire to strengthen the nationalist (as contrasted with pan-Arab) groups in order to counterbalance the influence of the Ba'th and other pro-Nasser factions in Iraq which favored a union between Baghdad and Cairo. (The Kurds, who constitute approximately one-quarter of Iraq's population and who would have been reduced to an insignificant minority in any larger Arab state, have been among the staunchest supporters of Iraq's independence.) When Mulla Mustafa, who soon emerged as his people's leading spokesman, began pressing demands for Kurdish autonomy, Kassem turned against him. Hostilities began in September 1961 and continued intermittently until spring 1963, when the Iraqi strongman was overthrown by a group of Ba'thist officers.[5]

On March 10, 1963, the new regime promised to guarantee "the rights of the Kurds on the basis of decentralization." The authorities preferred the term *decentralization* to *autonomy*. Recognition of the latter, it was feared in Baghdad, might be but a prelude to demands for Kurdish independence which no Iraqi government, regardless of its political leanings, was prepared to grant.[6] However, as in the case of Kassem's "Arab-Kurdish partnership," these "rights" were not defined. After a brief interlude, marked by unsuccessful negotiations and growing mutual suspicion, hostilities were resumed in June 1963. The regime of Abd al-Salam Aref, which came to power in November 1963, initially persevered in efforts to subdue the Kurds but proved no more successful than its predecessors. A truce was signed in February 1964, only to be broken in April 1965 when the Iraqi army resumed the offensive. It, too, ended in a failure.[7]

Relative calm was restored in the summer of 1966, after Prime Minister Abd al-Rahman Bazzaz announced a twelve-point peace program which recognized Kurdish autonomy in northern Iraq. Before his plan could be implemented, however, Bazzaz was forced to resign and his successors, who openly disapproved of his moderation, did nothing to carry it into effect.[8] Their inaction was prompted by reluctance to grant autonomy to the Kurds, by preoccupation with other pressing domestic problems, and, finally, by Iraq's participation in the Arab-Israeli war of 1967.

Moscow and the Kurdish Problem Before 1968

Since the overthrow of the Iraqi monarchy in 1958 the USSR has consistently backed what it described as legitimate Kurdish demands for national autonomy within the confines of the Iraqi republic. In the early stages this Soviet attitude was reflected, among other things, in the position adopted by the ICP. A report on the subject, published by the organization's Central Committee in March 1962, argued that "democracy will be meaningless, mere nonsense for the Kurdish people, unless they are guaranteed the real possibility of enjoying their national rights and managing their own affairs. This can be achieved only through autonomy." The term was explained to include "an administrative territory whose affairs should be in the hands of an elective legislative body which, in turn, would elect an executive body responsible to the people."[9]

The USSR and the ICP denied Baghdad's allegations that past Kurdish revolts against the central government of Iraq were a result of "foreign intrigues." They were, rather, the outcome of "national oppression being intensified to the extreme." For this reason, Kurdish aspirations were deemed worthy of Soviet and Iraqi Communist support. Moreover, "national autonomy for Iraqi Kurdistan would reinforce militant Arab-Kurdish fraternity against imperialism and . . . [domestic] reactionaries, would further democracy, safeguard national independence and contribute to social progress." Conversely, any attempts to subdue the Kurds by means of brute force would merely "facilitate the intrigues of imperialism and reaction aimed at disrupting the unity of the two peoples."[10]

The Bazzaz plan of June 1966, which recognized the Kurds' "right . . . to share in the administration of the areas they inhabit" and provided for development aid and for instruction in the Kurdish language in the region's schools, was regarded by Moscow as a step in the right direction. It soon became obvious, however, that the regime of Abd al-Rahman Aref was in no hurry to implement the promised reforms. Thus, "large-scale economic development," designed to upgrade the standard of living in the northern region, was found by a Soviet journalist who visited Iraq in January 1968 to be "a thing of the rather remote future." Instead, "the authorities and the Kurdish leaders are at present concerned primarily with the solution of political problems, which are extremely acute." In this respect, too, the government was not delivering on its promises. Taking the composition of local administrative bodies as an example, the *New Times* correspondent noted that "while in the lower municipal organs the Kurds often constitute the majority, in the higher organs the proportion is much smaller." Moreover, the selection process was described as "somewhat discriminatory." The followers of Mulla Mustafa found most of the administrative jobs allocated to the Kurds going to the members of "the breakaway Democratic Party led by Jelal Talabani." Finally, the widely heralded education reform was not being fully implemented, either. In most northern towns Kurdish was taught in the first four grades only; anyone wishing to continue education beyond the fourth level had to do so in Arabic.[11]

The fact that there had been no large-scale fighting in Iraqi Kurdistan since mid-1966 was thought to be "noteworthy in itself." However, the ceasefire, combined with a widespread desire to avert another war, was "evidently not enough to ensure the establishment of a real, lasting peace." On the Kurdish side, as noted, the *New Times* correspondent had recorded widespread and justified complaints with Baghdad's "inconsistency in observing the 1966 programme." On the government's side, he discovered that many Iraqi generals were longing for another opportunity to subdue the Kurds by means of armed force.[12] This attitude was particularly reprehensible, *Pravda* noted, because past wars in Kurdistan had significantly detracted from Iraq's contribution to Arab efforts to confront Israel.[13] Baghdad's stance was all the more unfortunate in that, in June 1967, Mulla Mustafa issued "a special statement expressing complete solidarity with the just cause of the Arabs."[14]

The Ba'thi Coup, July 1968

In its Proclamation No. 1, issued on July 17, 1968—the day on which the Ba'th overthrew the ineffective regime of Abd al-Rahman Aref—the regime of President Ahmad Hasan al-Bakr announced its determination "to achieve national unity . . . [and to] end the problems in the North."[15] As the Revolutionary Command Council (RCC) explained in a statement of August 3, the Kurdish problem would be resolved on the basis of the 1966 Bazzaz plan. The announcement signified official approbation on the part of the Ba'thi regime of the principle of Kurdish autonomy within the framework of the Iraqi union. Concurrently, the government took a number of other steps designed to persuade the Kurds of the sincerity of its intentions. It invited four Kurds to join the new cabinet, issued an amnesty to all Kurds who had taken part in the 1966 insurrection, and ordered Kurdish to be taught in the schools of the northern region.[16]

As in the past, however, little came of this auspicious beginning. In the period between the fall of 1968 and the spring of 1970, when another reconciliation attempt temporarily halted armed clashes between the followers of Mulla Mustafa and the government forces, relations between the two antagonists continued to deteriorate. They did so in spite of the Ba'th's continuing assurances of its dedication to the principle of Kurdish autonomy and in spite of the government's occasional efforts to deal with the actual grievances. For example, in July 1969 the Office for Kurdish Affairs, attached to the RCC and headed by Murtada al-Hadithi, was established in Baghdad. In early October, following the reorganization of the administrative structure of the country, two new governorates (or provinces) were created. One of them was the Kurdish governorate of Dahuk.[17] In December, in response to the deteriorating situation in Kurdistan, a special high-level committee was set up in Baghdad to implement government reforms in the northern region. An accompanying statement reiterated the authorities' determination to safeguard the Kurdish nationality, to recognize Kurdish as the official language "in areas which are predominantly Kurdish," and to make provision for "fair Kurdish representation in the government, public administration, the Armed Forces and elective offices." In addition, some development aid was extended to the northern region.[18]

Nevertheless, the majority of the Kurds remained skeptical about Baghdad's ultimate intentions. They mistrusted the Bakr regime for a number of reasons. Many believed that the major government offensive undertaken in the summer of 1963—when the Ba'th ruled Iraq for the first time and when Bakr was the prime minister—was a result of his personal initiative. The Kurds also could not help noticing that the government's pronouncements were not matched by its actions: the actual reforms were slow in coming and were not as far-reaching as had been promised originally.[19] Moreover, Mulla Mustafa and his followers were dismayed at what they perceived as the authorities' desire to effect a split in the Kurdish community by supporting rival groups, such as the KDP faction, headed by Jalal Talabani and Ibrahim Ahmad. Thus, of the four Kurds who joined the revolutionary government in July 1968, two were members of Mulla Mustafa's Kurdistan Democratic party while the others were followers of Talabani. The friction between them contributed, in mid-August 1968, to the resignation of the pro-Barzani ministers.[20] Another indication of the government's bias, as perceived by Mulla Mustafa, was provided by the authorities' treatment of *al-Ta'khi*, official organ of the pro-Barzani KDP, published in Baghdad. The newspaper, which had been repeatedly shut down in the past, was suspended again in October 1968. Instead, *al-Nur*, a new Kurdish newspaper reflecting the views of Jalal Talabani and Ibrahim Ahmad, was licensed and vowed to protect the interests of the "vigilant vanguard of the toiling masses of Kurdistan" in cooperation with the Ba'thi authorities. As hostilities in northern Iraq intensified in the fall of 1968, *al-Nur* came out squarely on the side of the central government. Among other things, it accused Mulla Mustafa's followers of "violent crimes against the Kurdish people" and described the Kurdish problem as "a conflict between Kurdish revolution and Kurdish reaction supported by imperialism."[21]

In 1969 the fighting intensified and was accompanied by increasingly bitter verbal exchanges. Bakr, in his address of July 18, warned the Kurds that he would not tolerate secession. Mulla Mustafa, in turn, accused the Ba'thi authorities of waging a "war of genocide" and appealed to UN Secretary-General U Thant to send a fact-finding committee to Kurdistan and to use his influence to end the hostilities.[22]

Nevertheless, in late 1969 signs began to appear suggesting the possibility of yet another attempt at a peaceful resolution of the Kurdish problem. In an interview with *Le Monde*, Mulla Mustafa defined the aims of the Kurdish revolution as "unity of our people and our proper autonomy within a democratic Iraqi state." At the same time, it was reported in Baghdad that contacts between the government and Mulla Mustafa had been initiated earlier in December. The reports proved correct when Saddam Hussein announced on January 24, 1970, that the authorities were negotiating with Mulla Mustafa "to lay down a final peace formula reestablishing fraternity between Arabs and Kurds and ending all forms of conflict between them."[23]

As might have been expected, the Kremlin applauded the Ba'th's initial commitment to the principles of a peaceful resolution of the Kurdish problem and of Kurdish autonomy within the Iraqi state. Subsequently, such measures as the proclamation of an amnesty affecting all Kurds who participated in the insurrection, the projected establishment of a Kurdish university and of an academy of the Kurdish language, and the setting aside of scholarships for Kurdish students, were also lauded in the Soviet publications.[24]

Soviet analysts initially shared the skepticism of Mulla Mustafa and his followers concerning the Ba'thi intentions. Commenting on the Provisional Constitution, adopted in September 1968, a Soviet author noted its "lack of precision" on the question of the Kurdish right to national autonomy, a fact "which . . . could not but alarm the leaders of the Kurdish liberation movement." Further cause for concern was provided in October 1968 by the government's reported backing of the pro-

Talabani military units in the ongoing clashes with Mulla Mustafa's forces, known as *Pesh Merga*.[25]

As the Ba'thi authorities stepped up their "repressive measures" against the Kurds,[26] Moscow came out openly in favor of Mulla Mustafa. In an important series of articles, which clearly reflected the attitude of the Soviet government, Evgenii Primakov, then a *Pravda* correspondent, reiterated the Kremlin's traditional sympathy for the Kurdish quest for autonomy. He admitted to presenting mainly the Kurdish point of view but justified his bias on the ground that he found "most of . . . [the Kurdish arguments] convincing." "In the name of objectivity," Primakov conceded that several valid arguments had been presented by the opposite side as well. For instance, an unnamed Arab leader held that a national minority should not attempt to weaken from within the Arab world while it was engaged in the "struggle against imperialism, [and] for the liquidation of the consequences of the [1967] Israeli aggression." But to Primakov, such views were but an "additional and extremely weighty . . . argument" in favor of a "final peaceful resolution of the problem of northern Iraq in the interests of the Arabs as well as the Kurds."[27]

Throughout 1969 the Soviet attitude on the Kurdish problem remained essentially unchanged. The media praised the Iraqi government for "progressive" steps taken in stimulating the country's economy, in strengthening the state sector, and in weakening the "positions of imperialism," particularly in the production of oil. On the Kurdish question, the USSR approved such measures as the opening of a Kurdish university in Sulaimaniyyah, the setting up of a new Kurdish province of Dahuk, and the channeling of financial aid to stimulate the economic development of the northern region. But the basic problem—that of granting the Kurds national autonomy—remained unresolved. This Primakov found all the more regrettable because "time spent without vigorous attempts to find acceptable forms of satisfying the national aspirations of the Kurdish population within the framework of the Iraqi state works to the benefit of extremist elements on both sides."[28]

Since the fall of 1969, Mulla Mustafa and the Ba'thi authorities had been engaged in intensive secret negotiations to reach a compromise settlement of the Kurdish question. Awareness of these efforts, combined with a desire to impress on both Baghdad and the Kurds the importance which Moscow attached to an early solution, was reflected in another major article in *Pravda*. Commenting on the abortive coup staged in Baghdad on January 21, 1970, Primakov wrote that the rebellion was the work of "extreme reactionary elements [who] had been 'nurtured' by the American intelligence service and other outside forces," meaning Iran. One of the coup's main objectives, Primakov argued, was to torpedo the Iraqi-Kurdish dialogue which, of late, had been "developing successfully." Desire to prevent the resolution of the Kurdish problem was dictated by the outsiders' determination to keep Iraq weak "at a time when the Arab peoples are waging a difficult anti-imperialist struggle." Noting the "extraordinary importance [which] a peaceful settlement in the north has for the Iraqi state" and for the Arab cause generally, Primakov concluded that the USSR "has always stood for the peaceful, democratic resolution of this highly important question. . . ."[29]

The Accord of 1970

Peace returned to war-torn Kurdistan in the spring of 1970. Announcing the termination of hostilities, President Bakr said that the authorities had recognized "the right of the Kurdish citizens to enjoy their national rights." Responding, Mulla Mustafa praised the Ba'th's "important and positive initiative" and promised Kurdish cooperation in the quest "to ensure a durable peace. . . ."[30] The agreement between the two parties, known as the March Manifesto, consisted of a fifteen-point program. Among other things, it recognized the Kurds' right to national autonomy within the framework of a united Iraq and provided for proportional Kurdish representation in the central government and the National Assembly. (The implementation of this provision depended on a new census to be taken at an unspecified future date.) It also called for the appointment of a Kurdish vice president and five Kurdish ministers; for an amendment to the provisional constitution whereby two nationalities (Iraqi and Kurdish) would be designated officially; and for the recognition of Kurdish as an official language in those areas where the Kurds constituted a majority of the population.[31] As became evident later, the agreement promised full implementation of all provisions not later than four years after its proclamation.[32]

The Kurdish leaders expressed their satisfaction with the March Manifesto. Mulla Mustafa said that it "fulfilled the ambitions of the Kurdish people and the objectives of its struggle for national independence" and Mahmud Uthman, member of the KDP Politburo, promised active Kurdish participation in the Arab struggle against Israel.[33] The General Congress of the KDP, held in July 1970, amended its statutes to emphasize the close links between Kurdish and Arab nationalism and

Mulla Mustafa, commenting on the March Manifesto on the occasion of its first anniversary, declared that the "settlement has been an important factor in . . . strengthening domestic unity, promoting peace and stability and putting an end to the chaos, corruption, killing and conflict which harmed the country."[34]

Initially, the Ba'thi regime was anxious to demonstrate its willingness to implement the provisions of the March 1970 accord. Later that month five Kurdish ministers were brought into the reshuffled cabinet. Of these, the most important post went to Mohammed Mahmud, a follower of Mulla Mustafa. He was appointed to the Ministry of Development of Northern Iraq and was responsible for the implementation of the economic program envisaged in the March Manifesto. The authorities also set up a nine-man committee "to supervise the implementation" of the accord.[35]

Other signs, too, pointed to the normalization of Iraqi-Kurdish relations. In March 1970 the government released all Kurdish prisoners held for political reasons and disbanded the irregular Kurdish units used in the fight against the forces of Mulla Mustafa.[36] In addition, al-Nur ceased publication in late March "at the request of the Ministry of Information," and al-Ta'khi reappeared in early May after a suspension of a year and a half.[37] The Kurds reciprocated by closing down the Voice of Kurdistan radio station and, in early 1971, by handing over to the Iraqi authorities "large numbers" of heavy weapons.[38]

In mid-July 1970 President Bakr announced the adoption of a new provisional constitution, Iraq's fourth in twelve years. Among other things, it endorsed the Kurdish rights granted in the March agreement. At a press conference of July 20 Bakr listed the reforms introduced by the central government and expressed confidence that peace in Kurdistan had come to stay.[39] In addition, the authorities appeared to have made a concerted effort to contribute to the economic development of Kurdistan. It was announced in January 1971 that Iraq's Planning Council had allocated ID 4 million for "the urgent implementation of a plan to develop industry, agriculture and communications" in the northern provinces. This was followed by another appropriation of ID 2.25 million in February, bringing the total allocation for the Kurdish areas since March 1970 to approximately ID 16 million.[40] It is important to note, however, that these and other figures advanced by the central government should not be accepted uncritically. As Keith McLachlan pointed out in his perceptive discussion of Baghdad's financial allocations in the Kurdish region in 1974 and 1975: "It is altogether unclear how much of the allocation was actually disbursed, and even less clear how much was spent on creating improved conditions for the inhabitants of the northern region against expenditures on military and quasi-military structures, strategic roads and the implementation of land reform."[41]

In any event, taken at their face value, actions and pronouncements by Iraq's Arabs and Kurds might have led to the conclusion that durable peace had finally been restored in the northern region and that relations between the two protagonists were at long last proceeding toward normalization. As is often the case with Middle Eastern politics, however, appearances were misleading. Even in the initial euphoria of March 1970, it did not take long for important differences to surface. Some of them, such as the issue of pensions to be paid to the families of Kurdish military personnel killed in action during the wars fought between 1961 and 1970, were resolved to Mulla Mustafa's satisfaction.[42] Others, however, were not and contributed to the poisoning of relations and, ultimately, to the resumption of large-scale hostilities in 1974 and 1975.

One such problem revolved around the appointment of a Kurdish vice president. Initially, it was rumored that Mulla Mustafa had withheld a nomination because of his irritation with Baghdad's failure to appoint Kurdish governors for the provinces of Kirkuk, Sulaimaniyyah, Arbil, and Mosul.[43] A short while later, however, Beirut's weekly al-Sayyad reported that the KDP had nominated Party Secretary Mohammed Habib Kerim, but that he was turned down by the government because his close association with Iran had made him "an undesirable person."[44]

The most significant differences separating the Iraqi government and the KDP, however, were the issues of demarcation of the area of Kurdish autonomy and of definition of the status of the city of Kirkuk. A basic prerequisite for the resolution of these problems was the holding of a national census—the first since 1957—to determine the distribution of the population in the disputed areas, above all in Kirkuk. (A city of approximately a hundred thousand inhabitants, Kirkuk has a mixed population of Arabs, Kurds, Turkomans, and Assyrians.) But, as noted by Le Monde, it became obvious as early as mid-1970 that the government was doing its best to postpone the holding of the census until the Arabs constituted a majority in Kirkuk as well as in other disputed areas. With this goal in mind, a concerted effort encouraging Arabs to settle in and around the city got underway soon after the March 1970 accord.[45] The Ba'th was not the only party attempting to strengthen its hand in the northern region, a fact evident in 1971, when the Iraqi Kurds, soon after the March agreement, began "importing" their Iranian compatriots and resettling them in Iraqi Kurdistan. According to the Ba'thi sources, some 100,000 Iranian Kurds had settled in Iraq after

March 1970. This came out into the open when *al-Ta'khi* demanded that the immigrant Kurds be granted Iraqi citizenship. The request was denied, and the ensuing bitter debate between the KDP organ and the government's *al-Jumhuriyyah* ended only after a personal intervention by Saddam Hussein.[46]

Additional strains in the tenuous KDP-Ba'th relationship surfaced in the spring and summer of 1971. Baghdad Radio announced on May 25 that Murtada al-Hadithi had met Mulla Mustafa in Kirkuk to discuss "the situation in the northern area." "Reliable sources" in Baghdad reported that the meeting had been prompted by a note sent by the Kurdish leader to President Bakr accusing the government of deliberately delaying the census while sending Arab settlers to Kirkuk "to dilute the Kurdish presence there." Bakr pointedly replied that the Iraqi army was "fully capable of maintaining law and order."[47]

Even before the March 1970 agreement was reached, the Kremlin had been of the opinion that traditional antagonism between Iraq's two major nationalities required not yet another transitory and ineffectual arrangement but a radical solution which would go to the roots of the Kurdish problem. For this reason, *Pravda* quoted approvingly the views expressed by Saddam Hussein in a January 1970 interview with Evgenii Primakov:

> The starting point of the settlement must be the recognition of the existence in Iraq of the Kurdish nation as well as the Arab nation. These two nations are territorially united, and they have a common destiny. We must not obstruct the finding of a . . . constitutional formula that would confirm the national rights of the Kurds. We do not want temporary, spur of the moment solutions. We must achieve a settlement of the Kurdish problem in Iraq for all time, so that the future generations will never suffer because it is unresolved.[48]

Writing a short time later, Igor' Beliaev and Evgenii Primakov agreed: "The proclamation of Kurdish national autonomy was an objective necessity, without which there could be no firm union of the two peoples, and was the sole means of resolving the national question in Iraq."[49]

In line with these views, the Kremlin enthusiastically supported the March Manifesto: "The Soviet people, who have always advocated a peaceful and democratic solution to a question of such major importance to Iraq's fate, sincerely welcome the agreement. . . ."[50] In an official telegram of March 17, 1970, Chairman of the Presidium of the

USSR Supreme Soviet Nikolai Podgorny and Prime Minister Aleksei Kosygin congratulated Bakr on the peaceful resolution of the Kurdish problem and expressed the Kremlin's conviction that "this important agreement will contribute to the strengthening of national unity and friendship between the two fraternal peoples of the Iraqi republic."[51] Moscow also expected that the March agreement would "facilitate the uniting in a single national front all of the country's progressive forces."[52]

The March Manifesto, it was generally agreed, represented a "triumph of good sense" for which both the Ba'th and the Kurdistan Democratic party deserved the highest Soviet praise. As Aleksei Vasil'ev explained in a lengthy commentary on the first anniversary of the agreement, the latter "required a serious political choice by the Iraqi government." The authorities "understood that without the resolution of the Kurdish problem, without the strengthening of national unity, it was impossible to implement social reforms and to pursue an [effective] anti-imperialist policy." Likewise, a "realistic position was also adopted by the leadership of the Kurdish movement. It proved capable of bypassing the obstacle of mistrust toward the Iraqi government, created during the years of open warfare."[53]

In examining other factors which contributed to the peaceful resolution of the Kurdish problem, the Soviet media noted also the "constructive role" played by the Iraqi Communist party as well as by the USSR. Beliaev and Primakov insisted that success in reaching the Iraqi-Kurdish accommodation was "to a large extent a consequence of the resolute struggle waged by the Iraqi Communists for the speedy peaceful [and] democratic settlement in the north."[54] In eliciting praise for the "favorable influence that the Soviet policy in the Near East had exerted on the search of [the Kurdish-Iraqi] agreement," *Pravda* quoted Mahmud Uthman to the effect that the "friendly Soviet Union had supported a peaceful settlement of the Kurdish question." Specifically, it "had helped . . . stimulate the dialogue and had facilitated the attainment of results that are necessary to guarantee Arab and Kurdish national interests."[55]

In addition, the Iraqi-Kurdish settlement was held to be of cardinal importance for the future development of Iraq because it deprived the imperialist powers of a major opportunity to intervene in the internal affairs of the country, "to weaken it militarily and economically . . . [and] to undermine the . . . all-Arab struggle [aimed at] liquidat[ing] the consequences of the Israeli aggression." The accord also struck a blow at the "internal pro-imperialist reactionary forces" which, by means of inciting the Arab-Kurdish conflict, had endeavored "to regain their lost positions" in Iraq.[56] Finally, the agreement "opened unprecedented opportunities for broadening cooperation between the Kurds and the Arabs."[57]

Alongside the delight at the conclusion of the agreement, a note of caution crept into early Soviet comments on the March Manifesto. The problems, as Moscow saw them, were twofold. On the one hand, the Arabs and the Kurds were warned that "forces hostile to . . . [them] have not ceased their subversive activities aimed at sabotaging the accord." Among such "forces" were the "domestic reaction" and the "agents of Israel and of the imperialist powers." Their purpose was "to aggravate the situation [and] to provoke conflicts between the Arabs and the Kurds . . . in the expectation of pushing Iraq into the abyss of a new civil war." On the other hand, both the Arabs and the Kurds were admonished that the implementation of a "successful national policy," as the experience of many countries had shown, was a "difficult task demanding painstaking daily work."[58] It required "discarding the burden of the past, overcoming the remnants of hostility and mutual distrust, and showing a maximum of patience, support, and mutual understanding."[59]

In reviewing the early implementation of the March agreement, the Soviet press lauded the Ba'th for attempting to achieve national reconciliation. *Pravda* praised the inclusion in the cabinet of five members of the KDP, the proclamation of a new Provisional Constitution which endorsed the rights of the Kurdish minority, and the lifting of the state of emergency, introduced in 1965.[60] Among other measures which the Kremlin regarded as important Ba'thist contributions to the normalization of the situation in Iraq were the legalization of the Kurdistan Democratic party; the appointment of Kurds to administrative and judicial positions in the northern region (including the governorship of the Sulaimaniyyah province); the reinstatement of Kurdish officers in their jobs in the Iraqi army; and the RCC's decision to allocate resources for an accelerated economic development of the Kurdish areas.[61]

Moscow was similarly impressed with the attitude adopted by the Kurdistan Democratic party. As an expression of the Kremlin's benevolence, extensive coverage was given in the Soviet press to the proceedings of the Eighth Congress of the KDP, held in July 1970.[62] In a subsequent article devoted to the twenty-fifth anniversary of the founding of the party and entitled "Tempered in Battle," Pavel Demchenko also commented on the congress. Its documents, as well as the speeches by the KDP leaders, made it clear that the "party considers the Kurdish democratic movement an inseparable part of the country's democratic forces and gives top priority to total implementation of the March agreement." Equally praiseworthy was the KDP's insistence on the "creation of a national-democratic front which would include all of the country's anti-imperialist forces: the ruling Ba'th party, the Kurdistan Democratic party, and the Iraqi Communist party."[63] In view of these considerations, the Central Committee of the CSPU, in its message to the Central Committee of the KDP, wished the latter "new successes on the path of strengthening the unity of actions of all the progressive, anti-imperialist forces of Iraq . . . in the struggle against imperialism and reaction, for the full implementation of the agreement on peaceful resolution of the Kurdish problem."[64]

Thus, the USSR expressed extreme gratification at the signing of the 1970 accord and supported its implementation with all the means at its disposal. At the same time, the Kremlin could not remain oblivious to the fact that important problems remained and serious differences continued to separate the leaders of the Ba'th and of the KDP. As early as March 1971, therefore, in commenting on the first anniversary of the agreement, Pravda once again called on both the Iraqi government and the Kurds to show "political sagacity, vigilance, and tolerance." It noted that during the past year there was achieved a "certain degree of trust and cooperation between the leadership of the KDP and the Iraqi Ba'th party. However, it sill remains a fact that the Arab-Kurdish conflict has left behind . . . mutual complaints and bitterness." In view of these considerations, Pravda warned that "extremist mood among the Kurds as well as the Arabs, which is shared by some politicians who do not possess sufficient restraint [and] maturity, could seriously harm Iraq."[65]

Deterioration of Iraqi-Kurdish Relations

In the summer and fall of 1971, relations between the Kurds and the central government deteriorated sharply. The process was accelerated, in late September, by an abortive attempt to assassinate Mulla Mustafa. Even though the Ba'th party on September 30 sent him "an urgent message" which condemned "the wicked attempt" as an effort to disturb peace in northern Iraq, many Kurds suspected that the assassination had been ordered by the Revolutionary Command Council.[66] Their attitude was shared by Mulla Mustafa. In an interview with Beirut's L'Orient-Le Jour, published on November 18, the Kurdish leader attacked his Ba'thi counterparts publicly for the first time since early 1970: "We cannot have confidence in the people in Baghdad—they have no notion of ethics. We cannot approve of . . . [their] arbitrary use of power." Mulla Mustafa noted also that some of the "essential elements" of the March Manifesto had not been implemented. Among them were withdrawal of Iraqi forces from the Kurdish areas, clear demarcation of the land area of Kurdish autonomy, definition of the status of Kirkuk, appointment of Kurds to government jobs proportionate to their percentage of the total population, and special allocations from the state budget for development projects in Kurdistan.[67] For these reasons, the KDP refused to subscribe to the National Charter, promulgated earlier in the month.[68]

The growing tension in Kurdistan displeased the Soviets and prompted another of Demchenko's periodic visits to Iraq. His extensive commentary shed some light on the evolution of Moscow's policy and, for this reason, deserves to be considered in detail. The article, entitled "Alarm in the Kurdish Mountains,"[69] reflected a decision to engage in a balancing act between the two forces which, once again, appeared to be on a collision course. It also indicated the continuation of attempts to persuade the antagonists to resume the dialogue in order to resolve their differences by political rather that military means. Specifically, Demchenko subscribed to several of Mulla Mustafa's basic arguments, among them his view that the assassination attempt had "exacerbated the situation throughout Iraq and [had] created the worst tension since March 1970." Moving to larger issues, Demchenko also supported Mulla Mustafa's contention that, even before September 1971, the implementation of the March Accord had encountered serious problems: "Some articles have been carried out slowly, while others have not been acted upon at all." *Pravda* used this opportunity to raise its own objections to the Ba'th's domestic policy. Demchenko pointed to "two additional circumstances [which] have been aggravating the situation" in Iraq. First, he blamed the government for the "lack of unity among the . . . political forces supporting a progressive platform—the ruling Ba'th party, the KDP, and the [Iraqi] Communist party." The absence of such unity was all the more regrettable in that "right-wing, reactionary circles have persevered in their efforts to replace the . . . [Ba'thi] regime and to assume power." Second, the Ba'th's intransigence appeared incomprehensible in view of the determination displayed by the "imperialist powers and their agents . . . to prevent the consolidation of authority and of stability" in Iraq and to interfere in Iraq's domestic affairs.[70]

Well aware of Iraq's importance to the USSR's overall position in the Middle East, the Kremlin still was unwilling to back the Kurds and thus totally alienate the Ba'th. For this reason, Demchenko not only stopped short of repeating some of Mulla Mustafa's stronger charges against the central government, but also actually subscribed to Baghdad's official view of the assassination attempt. According to *al-Thawrah,* "major provocations" in Kurdistan occurred whenever the country's political groupings were moving toward reconciliation and whenever the central government was attempting to wrest concessions from the "imperialist interests" in Iraq. Since the assassination attempt was made "on the eve of negotiations" with the Western oil companies, negotiations designed to limit their concession rights in Iraq, the conflict with the Kurds would significantly weaken the position of the central government. Hence the conclusion that the Ba'thi authorities were not in any way implicated in the attempt to kill Mulla Mustafa and that, therefore, it had to be the work of the "imperialist powers and their agents, [including] the domestic reaction."[71]

Moreover, while admitting to the difficulties in implementing the March Decree, Demchenko agreed with the Ba'th that the overall situation in Kurdistan had improved significantly over the past year and a half. He noted that Kurdish autonomy had been officially recognized by the Baghdad authorities, that the Kurds had been drawn into the national government and had been given important administrative assignments in the northern region, and that money had been made available to raise the economic and cultural standards of the Kurdish population. In addition, the activities of the Kurdistan Democratic party had been legalized, the publication of *al-Ta'khi* had resumed, and units of *Pesh Merga* had been entrusted with maintaining internal security in the north. The message *Pravda* delivered was clear: enough progress had been achieved to forestall the necessity of a renewed recourse to arms. This view, Demchenko noted pointedly, was also shared by Mulla Mustafa, who personally assured him that the Kurds would do their best to ensure that the hostilities did not resume. This important article concluded on an up-beat note: "the leaders of the republic and of the KDP have displayed enough wisdom and composure to prevent events from taking a dangerous turn."[72]

In 1972 and 1973 the ancient rivals continued to edge closer to another confrontation. There were still the familiar expressions of dedication to the principles of the "historic declaration" of March 1970.[73] More and more often, however, these sentiments were mixed with warnings, such as the one issued by Bakr at the 1972 May Day rally, of "difficulties and obstacles" created by "the enemies of the peaceful and democratic solution of the Kurdish problem."[74] Responding, the KDP, in an official statement of July 31, 1972, publicly threatened to resume civil war if the peace accord granting the Kurds regional autonomy was not implemented in full.[75] In the fall of 1972 the Ba'th and the KDP issued lengthy memoranda justifying their respective positions and blaming each other for the deterioration of the situation in northern Iraq.[76]

Finally, in a major article on November 2, *al-Thawrah* accused "certain prominent members" of the KDP of passing military secrets to Iran for transmission to the Israeli intelligence. Contacts between the KDP and Tehran's "reactionary rulers," the Ba'thi paper continued, were causing "great concern" in Baghdad. Moreover, Iranian arms were flowing into the northern region, the Iraqi Kurds were receiving military training in Iran, and members of the Kurdish "armed movement" were supporting Iranian forces in border clashes with the Iraqi units.[77] Allegations of Mulla Mustafa's cooperation with Iran as well as with the United States and Israel have since been well documented. The shah's involvement—a function of traditional Tehran-Baghdad hostility—began in 1958 and accelerated in the 1960s, and especially in the early 1970s. Jerusalem supported the Kurds to deflect Iraq's attention from the Arab-Israeli conflict, while Washington resented rapprochement between Baghdad and Moscow and as well as the 1972 nationalization of the Iraq Petroleum Company.[78]

By the summer of 1973, acts of sabotage against the Iraqi military installations and occasional clashes between army units and *Pesh Merga* had become a commonplace occurrence. The hopelessness of the situation was graphically illustrated by an interview which Mulla Mustafa gave to a correspondent of the *Washington Post* in June 1973. The Kurdish leader accused the Iraqi government of duplicity and doubledealing ("These Arabs seem to favor a no war, no peace policy everywhere. We have it here, too, where they make war under the cover of a peace agreement") and intimated that further clashes between the Kurds and the government forces were imminent. With this as a background, Mulla Mustafa appealed for "political, humanitarian or military help, open or secret," from the United States for his "small nation of poor and oppressed people." In exchange, "we are ready to do what goes with American policy in this area if America will protect us from the wolves. If support were strong enough, we could control the Kirkuk [oil] field and give it to an American company to operate." Referring to Baghdad's nationalization of the Iraq Petroleum Company's assets, Mulla Mustafa said that, if consulted, he would have opposed it and described the nationalization decree as "an act against the Kurds." He also admitted receiving military aid from Iran and implied that some assistance was reaching the Kurds from Israel as well.[79]

The seriousness of the situation was clearly recognized in Baghdad. In a speech commemorating the fifth anniversary of the Ba'thist revolution, Bakr, on July 17, 1973, admitted to "past mistakes" by both sides and assured the Kurds that his regime remained committed to the principles enunciated in the March Manifesto. He then called on the KDP to work with the authorities to restore order in the northern region. Echoing these sentiments, Saddam Hussein, in a press conference held the next day, promised that the Kurds would be granted self-government by March 1974.[80] These appeals and promises were of no avail, however. It appears in retrospect that, by mid-1972 at the latest, both Mulla Mustafa and the Ba'th no longer believed that a peaceful solution of the Kurdish problem was possible and proceeded with their plans for the next confrontation.

In 1972 there also occurred a perceptible shift in Moscow's stand on the Kurdish question. In retrospect, this change can be traced back to a number of what the Kremlin must have regarded as compelling reasons. The most significant one was no doubt the Iraqi government's desire to upgrade its relations with the USSR by signing a treaty of friendship and cooperation. It is true that Baghdad's wish for rapprochement was dictated by the perceived necessity of securing Moscow's support in the impending clash with the Western oil companies, and it stands to reason that the Kremlin was well aware of Iraq's motives. As noted in chapter 1, the Soviets unquestionably recognized in the Ba'thi overture an opportunity to weaken Western influence and to improve their own position in Baghdad. Hence, Moscow proceeded to back Iraq in its confrontation with the petroleum companies and agreed to enter into a formal treaty of friendship and cooperation. Because Mulla Mustafa had been opposed to the strengthening of the central government, achieved by the 1972 treaty with the USSR, and of the successful nationalization of the Iraq Petroleum Company, he sought (and received) renewed Iranian, Israeli, and U.S. assistance. The Kremlin, through Baghdad or its own intelligence sources, must have been appraised of and perturbed by Mulla Mustafa's activities. For all these reasons, the cooling of Soviet feelings toward the KDP should not have come as a surprise.

The shift in Moscow's position manifested itself in the following ways. First, in a marked departure from a decade-long practice, the Soviet press relegated the Kurdish issue to a state of near obscurity. Second, when it was raised, the Soviet statements exhibited an unmistakable tendency to accept and adopt the position held by the Iraqi government.

Thus, as high-level contacts between Moscow and Baghdad continued to grow in 1972, an interesting pattern emerged in their respective pronouncements on the Kurdish problem. In the course of that year, Saddam Hussein and Bakr visited the USSR, in February and September respectively, while Kosygin traveled to Iraq in April. The speeches by Saddam Hussein (in Moscow and, on occasion of the Soviet premier's visit to Iraq, in Baghdad) contained no references to the Kurds. The same was true of Bakr's public address in the Soviet capital. Kosygin and Podgorny, in contrast, invariably praised the "progressive policies" of the Iraqi government, including "successful implementation" of the 1970 agreement.[81] The joint communiqués, issued at the end of Saddam Hussein's and Kosygin's trips, noted merely that the Iraqi side had informed the Soviet government about measures to achieve a "peaceful [and] democratic solution of the Kurdish problem in accordance with the Declaration of March 11, 1970." The joint communiqué of September 1972, however, went one step further. In it, the Kremlin actually gave its full approbation to the Ba'th's handling of the problem: "The Soviet side valued highly . . . the progressive, anti-imperialist course [and] the successes achieved by the Iraqi people in the economic, political, and social spheres. It also expressed satisfaction with the measures undertaken in the implementation of the [March] Declaration . . . ."[82] Considering the true state of affairs in the northern region, acceptance of Baghdad's position provided a clear illustration of Moscow's decision to side with the Ba'th.

Additional light on the change in the Kremlin's attitude was shed by the decreasing volume of and a shift in emphasis in the commentaries on Iraqi-Kurdish relations which appeared in the Soviet press. To be sure, the USSR remained committed to the principle of a "peaceful democratic solution of the Kurdish problem" as provided for by the March Accord.[83] Along with the ICP, the Kremlin also continued to uphold the view that "the best solution of the national question [in Iraq] is to grant the Kurds autonomy within the Iraqi Republic."[84] At the same time, Moscow expressed renewed concern that major differences between the Arabs and the Kurds remained unresolved and continued to exert a negative influence on the political situation in Iraq. The Soviet press warned that "deviation" from Arab-Kurdish cooperation was bound to provide "imperialism and reaction" with new opportunities "to restore their positions" in Iraq.[85] Even more ominous were calls to combat "bourgeois nationalism" and "chauvinism," described as major roadblocks on the path to success "in the national and social revolutions."[86] In addition to the more pronounced urgency of these appeals, their importance lay in the fact that, in 1972 and 1973, they appeared to be directed not at Baghdad but at the Kurds.

For the time being, these Soviet references to the mounting problems in the northern region were, to some extent, offset by public insistence that important segments in the KDP, including Mulla Mustafa, remained committed to the principle of a peaceful resolution of the Kurdish problem. For example, at the meeting between high-level functionaries of the CPSU and the KDP, held on August 25, 1972, the latter assured the Kremlin of its determination to seek a peaceful solution of the Kurdish question and of its efforts in assisting the implementation of the March agreement.[87] However, no public pronouncements could conceal the fact that, by 1973, relations between the Baghdad authorities and the KDP were rapidly approaching a breaking point. In view of the delicacy of the situation and of its own commitment to support the Iraqi government, the Soviet press passed in relative silence the deteriorating situation in Kurdistan. (There was, for instance, no reference at all to Mulla Mustafa's explosive interview with the Washington Post.) The closest Pravda came to acknowledging the true state of affairs was an article by Evgenii Primakov. Having noted that the "culmination of the socioeconomic transformations in Iraq . . . [as well as its] future internal and external successes" depended on the "full settlement of the Kurdish problem," Primakov observed that the "enemies of the progressive regime in Iraq" had recently "doubled and trebled their energy" in an attempt to "foster Arab-Kurdish differences."[88]

In contrast with Soviet publications which, in spite of Moscow's obvious preferences, were publicly maintaining an attitude of detachment from Iraq's internal squabbles, the country's Communist party made no secret of its strong disapproval of the Kurdish position. Differences between the two groups surfaced in the summer of 1973, after the Ba'th and the ICP had agreed, in May, to form the National Front.[89] On several occasions (before and during 1973), the KDP expressed itself in favor of the Front[90] but, as subsequently became apparent, the Kurds refused to join it until the three parties had reached an agreement on "general principles and joint action." The ICP weekly al-Fikr al-Jadid, on August 28, found this Kurdish attitude "astonishing."[91]

Additional signs of the rapidly deteriorating situation appeared in early fall of 1973. On September 2 the National Front announced its decision to "draw up a comprehensive plan for self-government in Kurdish areas." It would then be submitted to the Iraqi people for "debate and approval." "Kurdish sources" responded three days later by accusing the government of obtaining "poison gas from the Soviet Union in preparation for an attempt to exterminate the Kurds."[92] Verbal exchanges soon gave rise to violence. On October 5, the ICP newspaper *Tariq al-Sha'b* accused *Pesh Merga* of attacking and killing Kurdish communists and of driving several thousand families from their homes.[93] Other incidents followed, prompting the Iraqi Communist party, on November 17, to issue a formal statement protesting what it described as "organized military action aimed at exterminating the Kurdish Communists. . . ." The hatchet was temporarily buried four days later, when the ICP and the KDP issued a joint statement calling for normalization of relations. It also supported Kurdish autonomy in northern Iraq and expressed hope that the KDP would soon join the National Front. However, this declaration produced no practical results.[94]

Although the Soviet press refused to take sides in the dispute between the Ba'th and the ICP on the one hand and the KDP on the other, the Kremlin's preferences were clearly on the side of the central government. At the same time, the USSR remained convinced that a major confrontation in the northern region was bound to weaken Iraq and to detract from its ability to resist Western pressures. Hence Moscow endeavored—genuinely, it would appear—to exert its influence with both parties to stop the dispute from developing into a civil war. One early effort was undertaken by Premier Kosygin during his April 1972 visit to Baghdad.[95] The Kurdish threat to resume the civil war, contained in the statement of July 31, 1972,[96] resulted in an invitation to the KDP to send a mission to Moscow to meet with Soviet representatives on August 25, 1972. The importance the Kremlin attached to the meeting was evidenced by the fact that the Soviet delegation was headed by Politburo member and chief party ideologue Mikhail Suslov. The statement issued at the end of the meeting noted that the KDP remained committed to the twin principles of "peaceful, democratic solution of the Kurdish problem in Iraq" and of the implementation of the March 1970 accord.[97] Yet another attempt to smooth over the differences between the KDP and the members of the National Front was undertaken by the Iraqi Communist party. In mid-June 1973 a high-level party delegation, led by First Secretary Aziz Mohammed, traveled to Kurdistan and conferred with Mulla Mustafa. According to *Pravda*, its stated purpose was to reaffirm the parties' continued adherence to the March Declaration as a basis for the peaceful settlement of the Kurdish problem.[98]

In November 1973, at the height of the armed clashes between the ICP militia and Mulla Mustafa's *Pesh Merga*, the CPSU Central Committee once again invited a KDP delegation to visit Moscow. Simultaneously, more talks were held in Baghdad between representatives of the Kurdistan Democratic party and of the Iraqi Communist party. The statement issued at the conclusion of the Moscow meeting expressed the parties' "conviction" that the resolution of the Kurdish problem had to be sought by peaceful means and that the March Accord had to be implemented "in the interests of strengthening the national unity of the Iraqi people [engaged in a] struggle against imperialism and reaction." The joint KDP-ICP communiqué of November 21 added that "the supreme interests of the republic and the struggle against imperialism, Zionism, and reaction constitute the common aims uniting the two parties with the other national forces" (i.e., the Ba'th).[99] Finally, in late November 1973, a CPSU delegation, headed by Central Committee Secretary Boris Ponomarev paid a visit to Baghdad. In addition to Bakr and Saddam Hussein, he also met with the leaders of the Iraqi Communist party and with the representatives of the KDP. The problems of Kurdistan were not mentioned in the official account of the visit, but it is probable that they were high on the meetings' agenda. The same applies to Saddam Hussein's February 1974 sojourn in Moscow.[100]

Soviet publications did not report the October–November 1973 clashes between *Pesh Merga* and the communists until February 1974. When they did so, blame for the incidents and for the Kurds' refusal to join the National Front was assigned to "the reactionary forces, as well as the extremist elements within the KDP."[101] By implication, the Ba'th and the ICP were absolved of any wrongdoing. The framework for Soviet analysis of the next round of hostilities between the Kurds and the Arabs had thus been set.

The most notable feature of the Soviet attitude toward the Kurdish question in the period between 1970 and 1974 was thus a major change in Moscow's position. Whereas during the first two years the Kremlin's sympathies were clearly on the side of the KDP, in 1973 and 1974 the USSR switched its support to the Ba'th and attempted to persuade Mulla Mustafa and his followers to compromise with the Baghdad authorities. Kurds viewed this Soviet shift as a hostile act and eventually, as evidenced by Mulla Mustafa's interview with the *Washington Post*, it brought them into an open conflict with the Kremlin. No subsequent attempts by Moscow were able to bridge this gap. As the Kurds intensified their search for outside support, the Ba'thi and Soviet attitudes hardened, moving all sides to the dispute closer to the ultimate showdown. It came in March 1974.

The 1974–1975 War

Hostilities in Kurdistan were precipitated by the government's promulgation, on March 11, 1974, of a new Autonomy Law for the northern region coupled with a fifteen-day ultimatum demanding its acceptance. Because the degree of autonomy was more limited than that promised in 1970 and the area of the autonomous region was smaller than provided by the March Manifesto (as no census was held—in violation of the document—only the predominantly Kurdish provinces of Sulaimaniyyah, Arbil, and Dahuk were included in the autonomous region, thus excluding all the oil-producing areas of Kurdistan, including Kirkuk), the KDP had no choice but to turn down the Autonomy Law.[102] As this reaction was entirely predictable, it is probable that Baghdad decided to force the issue by provoking a confrontation in order to "settle" the Kurdish question by military means.[103]

It appears in retrospect that a number of factors encouraged the Ba'th to adopt a tougher line with respect to the Kurds: a marked upgrading of Iraq's armed forces, strengthened by new weapons and training provided by the USSR as part of the process of the tightening of relations between Baghdad and Moscow; growing Soviet disillusionment with Mulla Mustafa; Ba'thist ability to secure the support of the Iraqi Communist party by drawing it into the National Front; successful Arabization of some key northern areas, most notably the Kirkuk province; and growing splits among Kurdish nationalists, many of whom had chosen to cooperate with the central government. (When hostilities resumed, the five Kurdish ministers in the Iraqi cabinet resigned and were replaced by their compatriots who were opposed to Mulla Mustafa's policies.)[104]

It is noteworthy that although Baghdad dispatched heavy reinforcements to Kurdistan in late spring and summer of 1974, major military operations did not begin until August. The government used the intervening period not only to strengthen its hand in the northern region but also to wage a political offensive against the KDP. In addition to the shifts in the Iraqi government, the RCC appointed Taha Muhiy al-Din Ma'ruf, one of Mulla Mustafa's rivals who had previously cooperated with Bakr, as the country's first Kurdish vice president. *Al-Ta'khi*, suspended in March, reappeared a short time later as a pro-government organ edited by Aziz Aqrawi, another opponent of Mulla Mustafa. Aqrawi also founded another Kurdistan Democratic party—using the same name as Mulla Mustafa's organization but strongly opposed to its policies.[105] On July 30, 1974, the RCC issued a decree establishing a Constitutional Council for the Kurdish region; all council members were outspoken opponents of Mulla Mustafa.[106] In the fall, the government allocated new funds to complete development projects initiated before March 1974.[107] In January 1975 the authorities announced a "system of administrative appointments for self-rule . . . in Kurdistan in implementation of the 11 March Manifesto and in completion of the stages of the peaceful and democratic solution of the Kurdish issue."[108] More important, Baghdad in the summer of 1974 initiated secret diplomatic contacts with Iran. Meetings were held in Istanbul then and in early 1975. Although unsuccessful at first, they laid the groundwork for the Algiers agreement of March 1975.

Heavy fighting in Kurdistan took place in late 1974 and early 1975. Although large concentrations of Iraqi troops equipped with tanks, artillery, and helicopters and enjoying fighter and fighter-bomber support succeeded in pushing the Kurds out of most of the northern region, the resistance of *Pesh Merga* could not be broken as long as it enjoyed the military backing of Iran. Put differently, the Ba'thi authorities realized that the rebellion could be crushed only if Tehran discontinued its support of Mulla Mustafa's forces. As it turned out, the shah proved willing to abandon the Kurds, but only at a price.[109]

From the outset the USSR extended its full support to the promulgation of the 1974 Autonomy Law, describing it as an event of "great historical significance." Placing the Ba'thi initiative into its "proper historical perspective," *Pravda* held that hostilities between Baghdad and the "liberation forces led by the Kurdistan Democratic party," which continued intermittently since 1961, constituted a "fratricidal war, spurred on by reactionary, chauvinistic circles and by the oil monopolies interested in dividing the nation." Chances for a peaceful resolution of the Kurdish question were said to have improved perceptibly after the Ba'th's accession to power in July 1968. The March 1970 Accord ended the fighting by guaranteeing the Kurds "basic national rights." It also stipulated that autonomy would be granted within a four-year period, a promise that had now been fulfilled. As encouraging as these developments had been, however, *Pravda* warned anew of the remaining obstacles which blocked the resolution of the Kurdish problem. Among them were the perennial intrigues of "foreign agents" and, above all, the "activity of rightist elements which penetrated the KDP as a result of its class heterogeneity and which are trying to arouse separatist sentiments."[110]

Pravda's apprehensions were soon borne out by events. After the KDP refused to abide by the autonomy law, military operations in Kurdistan were resumed. The Soviet press blamed Mulla Mustafa and his adherents for the outbreak of hostilities and charged that the Kurdish leaders had been influenced by "imperialist and other external reactionary forces, who are trying to sow discord between the Kurdish and Arab populations of Iraq" in order to "weaken the present progressive regime in that country." According to *Pravda*, the "democratic public" expressed "concern over the dangerous turn of events" in Iraq and regarded the "escalation of the conflict" as "intolerable."[111]

As Mulla Mustafa appealed for Western military and economic aid, Saddam Hussein announced that "the rebel Kurdish leaders" were receiving "massive military assistance . . . from the United States and Iran."[112] The KDP also requested a Soviet intervention on its behalf; on May 6, 1974, a Voice of Kurdistan broadcast said in part: "We demand that the Soviet Union should stop the bloodshed in northern Iraq. The autonomy we are fighting for is less than that enjoyed by each of the socialist republics in the USSR." The broadcast concluded with a hollow warning: "If the Soviet Union . . . [does] not take a stand, the Kurds would have to reassess their attitude toward Moscow and all Communist powers."[113]

The Soviet press responded by launching violent attacks on the Kurdistan Democratic party. Notable among them were two articles which appeared in *Pravda* and the *New Times*. Both reflected the attitude adopted by the Ba'th and examined the reasons which, in Moscow's opinion, had led to the breakdown of the Iraqi-Kurdish talks. The *New Times* argued that differences of opinion between the two parties had surfaced long before the promulgation of the Autonomy Law in March 1974. One of the important problems revolved around the future status of Kirkuk. The KDP motivated its demand for the city's inclusion in the autonomous region "by historical considerations and the fact that the majority of its population, in their opinion, was Kurdish." Because "no census has been taken there for a long time," the Ba'th argued that "the exact [numbers] and the distribution of the population among the various national groups" could not be determined with any degree of precision. For these reasons, Baghdad proposed that "a joint Arab-Kurdish administration" should be set up in Kirkuk "under the jurisdiction of the central government." The KDP objected, the negotiations stalled, and the authorities decided to promulgate the Autonomy Law unilaterally.[114]

According to *Pravda*, the Autonomy Law was an important and far-reaching step designed to satisfy the Kurdish quest for autonomy. It was noted that the administrative organs of the region would consist of two major bodies: a locally elected legislative council and an executive council, whose chairman would be appointed by the president of the republic from among the members of the legislative council. The region would have its own budget (to be set up as a part of the state budget), and Kurdish would be elevated to the status of an official language of the region on an equal footing with Arabic. These and other constructive measures, *Pravda* held, had met with the overwhelming approval of the majority of Iraq's Arab and Kurdish population and had given rise to expectations that the remaining differences would be worked out through negotiations between the interested parties. Such, however, was not to be the case. Following instructions from the KDP headquarters, most Kurdish cabinet ministers and many other high government officials left Baghdad for the mountains of northern Iraq; *al-Ta'khi* ceased publication; and *Pesh Merga* units took up positions in areas controlled by Mulla Mustafa's followers. Hostilities began shortly afterward.[115]

The rejection of Baghdad's offer of autonomy called into question the real motives of the KDP, Soviet publications insisted. Quoting an anti-Barzani Kurdish member of the Iraqi cabinet, the *New Times* stated that the real reason for KDP behavior was the establishment "in recent years . . . [of] an alliance with the local reaction and the imperialist forces." Among its manifestations had been the KDP's open opposition to the National Front; the opening of the frontier with Iran; public declaration of willingness "to accept aid from anyone, including the United States and Israel"; and offers "to grant Americans a concession in the rich Kirkuk oilfield." In retrospect, the *New Times* did not find such attitudes surprising: "The point is that most of the Kurdish leaders belong to the feudal element of the bourgeoisie, and their common class and purely personal interests impel them to resist the reforms effected by Baghdad."[116]

Replying to these denunciations, Voice of Kurdistan, on behalf of "the Kurdish people and the command of their liberation revolution," described Moscow's attitude as injurious to "the fraternal. . . relations between the Kurdish and Soviet peoples." The broadcast held "the Baghdad rulers and their supporters responsible for harming relations between the Arab and Kurdish people" and reminded the Kremlin that, in the past, the Ba'th had been particularly vicious in its treatment of the Iraqi Communist party. "How can the Baath Party with its criminal past be transformed into . . . a builder of socialism in Iraq?," Voice of Kurdistan inquired. "Anyone who expects such a transformation will be making a gross historical error which the people will not pardon."[117] Moscow Radio retorted that by rejecting the Autonomy Law, "the right wing of the KDP has chosen the path of outright deception of the Kurdish people and is fomenting fratricidal war." In so doing, the KDP chose to ignore the fact that "the implementation of the law . . . is closely linked with the fundamental interests of . . . [Iraq] and its future destiny as an independent sovereign state."[118]

With the lines clearly drawn, the USSR stepped up its military aid program to Iraq. The decision to do so may well have been communicated to the Ba'thi leaders during the surprise March 23–26 visit to the Iraqi capital of Soviet Minister of Defense Marshal Andrei Grechko. At the time, Western opinion ascribed Grechko's hurried trip to Moscow's desire "to mediate in the dispute with the Kurds with whom the Soviet Union still has good relations."[119] In retrospect, this evaluation appears to have been wrong on both counts. For one thing, by March 1974 the USSR could no longer have harbored any illusions about Mulla Mustafa's association with Iran as well as with the United States. For this reason, Moscow's relations with the Kurdistan Democratic party could not possibly have been "good." Moreover, given Western support of Mulla Mustafa with the view to weakening (if not entirely eliminating) the Ba'thi regime, and given that the final showdown between the two antagonists, therefore, appeared imminent, it may be assumed that Grechko arrived in Baghdad not "to mediate the dispute" but to assure the Iraqi government of full Soviet support.

This proposition is supported by three additional considerations. First, *Pravda*'s account of Grechko's visit contained a reference to his interest in "measures [taken by the Iraqi government] to strengthen the country's national unity, territorial integrity, and . . . sovereignty."[120] Stripped of its diplomatic vagueness, the statement clearly denoted concern about the state of Iraq's military preparedness. Second, it soon became evident that "new types of late model [Soviet] equipment" began arriving in Iraq in the latter half of 1974 and in early 1975. As noted in chapter 1, more prominent among them were Scud surface-to-surface missiles and MIG-23s.[121] The third, and perhaps most dramatic, manifestation of Moscow's apprehension was the permission to use Soviet pilots in flying bombing missions over northern Iraq in the fall and winter of 1974 and 1975. Such raids were undertaken by the medium-range, supersonic Tupolev-22 bombers, delivered to Iraq prior to the Arab-Israeli war of October 1973, and by the newly arrived MIG-23s. Because, at that time, no Iraqi pilots were qualified to fly either model, the combat deployment of the Soviet planes and pilots served as a tangible commitment to Baghdad's war effort against the Kurds.[122]

Not unexpectedly, Soviet assistance to Iraq evoked an extremely hostile reaction from the Kurdish leadership. In an interview with *The Times*, Mulla Mustafa accused the USSR of "pursuing a selfish policy, regardless of cost and of the human misery which it is creating" and urged the Western powers "to check Russian influence in Iraq" by helping the Kurds "morally, politically, militarily, [and] economically."[123]

As hostilities continued, the Soviet press centered its attention on two parallel themes: the growing isolation of the "reactionary elements in the Kurdish movement" and on the "normalization of the situation in the liberated areas." It was noted that the resumption of hostilities in northern Iraq had forced a "large number of Kurds, including some members of the KDP leadership, to break with [the party's reactionary] leaders." The new party came out squarely in favor of "strengthening ties with the country's progressive forces" and supported the March 1974 law on Kurdish autonomy.[124] The same source reported also that life in most Kurdish areas was now returning to normal. Industrial and commercial enterprises had resumed their work, as had also organs of local and regional self-government. Of particular importance was the convocation in October 1974 of Kurdistan's first regional Legislative Council. All this led *Pravda* to conclude that the government's policy aimed at "peaceful resolution of the Kurdish question corresponds with the aspirations of the entire Iraqi people" and will, therefore, "sooner or later gain the upper hand."[125]

The Defeat

As a result of the Iraqi-Iranian agreement signed on March 6, 1975, Tehran discontinued its assistance to Mulla Mustafa's forces. Although the Kurdish problem was not specifically mentioned in the Algiers communiqué, references to "strict and effective" border controls and to an "end to all subversive infiltration" clearly denoted an Iranian obligation to stop aiding *Pesh Merga*. A massive offensive against the Kurds was launched on March 7. Their resistance collapsed and tens of thousands Kurds fled to Iran. In short, the Ba'th succeeded where its predecessors had failed.[126]

Although the 1975 agreement between Iraq and Iran was potentially of major significance to the Soviet position in Baghdad,[127] the Kremlin limited itself publicly to "expressions of satisfaction . . . on the settlement of the problems" between the two states.[128] Otherwise, the USSR used the end of the Kurdish war and Saddam Hussein's sojourn in Moscow to reiterate Soviet support of the Ba'th's policy in the northern region. In his dinner speech honoring the Iraqi delegation, Kosygin expressed "great interest [in] the way in which the Kurdish problem is being solved in friendly Iraq." Saddam Hussein was assured that, because of the CPSU's own "rich experience in national construction," the Iraqi government could expect to find in the USSR "deep understanding of a policy which is aimed at a democratic resolution of the nationalities question and at ensuring not only the *de jure* but also the *de facto* equality of nations." Kosygin went on to say that the March 1974 Autonomy Law was "of particularly great importance for a peaceful, democratic solution of the Kurdish problem" and that "its successful implementation will be facilitated by . . . the enlistment of the broad masses in carrying out a constructive program for a peaceful settlement."[129]

Once in charge the authorities initiated a far-flung campaign designed to bring Kurdistan under Baghdad's firm control. Initially, emphasis was placed on massive punitive actions ranging from arrests and imprisonment to executions of those found guilty of antigovernment activities.[130] Moreover, large numbers of Kurds were uprooted from the fertile lands in the north and deported to the "less sensitive" arid flatlands of central and southern Iraq. To take their place, Arabs (mostly Iraqis but also some Egyptians) were encouraged to settle down in Kurdistan.[131] To prevent the flow of arms and "saboteurs" from Turkey to Iraq, the government also decreed "internal resettlement" of the Kurds living in the proximity of the Turkish border.[132] On the positive side, the authorities issued three separate amnesties, designed to induce Kurdish refugees to return home from the Iranian camps.[133] Judging by its public pronouncements—which were often misleading—the government also devoted considerable attention to developing the region's agricultural and industrial infrastructure and to improving its educational, cultural, and medical services.[134]

Although the Kurds had lost the war, their resistance was not broken. By the summer of 1975, some had found another patron—Syria—which, because of Baghdad-Damascus tensions, was willing to contribute to the discomfort of the Iraqi government. In July the Syrian Arab News Agency reported the formation of Patriotic Union of Kurdistan (PUK), headed by Jalal Talabani. Marxist in its orientation and politically militant, PUK disassociated itself from Mulla Mustafa's "rightist tribalist command" and announced its intention "to join all the progressive, Leftist nationalist forces in Iraq" in order to "liberate . . . [the country] from the economic and political chains of neo-imperialism." It was also determined to replace the "bloody dictatorial regime" with a "national democratic coalition authority . . . capable of giving democracy to all the Iraqi people."[135]

In addition, by the late 1970s the original KDP, now renamed Kurdistan Democratic Party's Provisional Command (KDPPC) and led by Mulla Mustafa's sons Idris and Masud, succeeded in shaking off the 1975 defeat and reemerged as the largest and probably most effective Kurdish political grouping in Iraq.[136] After the Iranian revolution, Tehran resumed its support of the Barzani KDPPC.

Initial reports of "serious incidents" involving the Kurdish guerrillas and the Iraqi security forces appeared in the spring of 1976.[137] New clashes were reported in the summer of 1976[138] and their occurrence may have been responsible for Baghdad's decision to discontinue the policy of dispersal of the Kurdish population. Fighting broke out again in the spring of 1977, prompting the authorities to allow 40,000 Kurds, relocated to central and southern Iraq in 1975, to return to their homes.[139] The Ba'th also attempted to settle its differences with Jalal Talabani. He refused, and sporadic hostilities between the Kurds and the government forces continued into the late 1970s.[140]

After the defeat of Mulla Mustafa's forces, the Soviet media continued to laud the Iraqi government for putting into effect what Kosygin described as a "constructive program for the peaceful settlement of the Kurdish problem." Among the measures singled out for Soviet praise were the amnesty decrees, steps to foster the economic and cultural development of Kurdistan, and efforts to rebuild the pro-Ba'th Kurdish Democratic party.[141] It was to Baghdad's credit, the Soviet press asserted, that it had recognized the enormity of the problem and had given high priority to the task of liquidating the lag between the northern region and other parts of Iraq as soon as the hostilities had come to an end. Thus, in 1975 alone, the government assigned ID 100 million for the economic development of Kurdistan. By the end of 1977, the total amount invested in the north since the March 1970 Accord was estimated at more than ID 700 million.[142] This massive allocation of resources resulted in the expansion of existing and the construction of new industrial enterprises engaged in the manufacture of sugar, cigarettes, canned goods, milk products, textiles, carpets, and building material. It also led to a sharp increase in housing construction and road-building.[143] Considerable progress had also been achieved in the agricultural sector. In addition to extensive irrigation work, an agrarian reform law was implemented in Kurdistan in 1975 to expropriate land from large feudal landlords and to distribute it among the peasants, who were then encouraged to join cooperatives and state farms.[144]

According to Soviet publications, Baghdad had exhibited similar concern about the cultural development of the Kurdish Autonomous Region. In late 1976, *Pravda* reported the opening of more than 150 new schools since the termination of hostilities in the spring of 1975. This brought the total of schools operating in the north to 938. During the same period the number of teachers, too, had been increased by 1,800. The number of students in the Kurdish schools was estimated at 198,000.[145]

The Soviet Union appeared equally gratified with the post-1975 reorganization of the Kurdistan Democratic party. In early May 1976, the "progressive wing" of the organization, which had earlier disassociated itself from the "reactionary leadership" of Mulla Mustafa, held the Ninth Congress of the KDP. The program approved by the Congress, *Pravda* reported, stated that the reconstituted party embraced the principles of Iraq's national unity and of Kurdish autonomy within the Iraqi state. The program also noted the "principled character" of the KDP's alliance with the Ba'th and expressed itself in favor of broadening cooperation, within the framework of the National Front, with "all the patriotic forces" of the country.[146] For the remainder of the decade, the Kremlin's basic position on the Kurdish question remained virtually unchanged. The USSR continued to extend its unqualified support to the March 1974 Autonomy Law; to condemn the anti-Ba'th KDPPC's attempts to block its implementation by means of armed struggle and sabotage; and to praise the Iraqi government for the reforms implemented in the northern region.[147]

It is noteworthy that even during the early years of glasnost Soviet publications did not challenge the main points of contemporary analysis summarized in this chapter. For example, in a scholarly collection dealing with modern history of the Arab states, it was noted that the ICP (and, by implication, the Kremlin) were aware of the shortcomings of the 1974 autonomy decree. Nevertheless, the argument ran, the Communists decided to support the measure because it incorporated the "main principles of a peaceful and democratic solution of the Kurdish question." In addition, the ICP held that "calls for separation" played into the hands of all those who did not favor the "positive changes [which] had taken place in Iraq."[148] After the end of the 1974–75 Kurdish campaign, the situation in northern Iraq continued to stabilize and, by 1980, normal conditions had been restored in war-battered Kurdistan.[149] After the outbreak of the Iran-Iraq conflict, the authorities went out of their way to appease the restive Kurds, and negotiations between them continued well into 1984.[150]

It was all the more surprising, therefore, that an article appeared in the popular weekly *Argumenty i fakty* in 1990 which was highly critical of the Ba'th; of many of its policies, including those in Kurdistan; and, explicitly, of the Soviet government. According to the article, entitled "Iraq without Stereotypes," the Kremlin decided not to oppose Baghdad's decision to fight the Kurds. It did so in spite of the fact that the autonomy conferred upon the Kurds in 1974 had been limited and that the area which had been offered to them excluded "indigenous and oil-rich Kurdish territories." Under these circumstances, the Kurds resorted to arms and the authors clearly implied that Mulla Mustafa did not have much of a choice. In the ensuing years, the "protracted guerrilla war" continued, and in the end, the Iraqi Kurds found themselves on the "edge of a national catastrophe."[151]

Evaluation

As noted by Majid Khadduri, the Ba'th was the first political party to understand that a strong and unified Iraq could be established only on the basis of cooperation between the central government and the country's Kurdish minority. This realization did not come easily, however. During the party's initial attempt at ruling Iraq in 1963, the Ba'th repeated many of the mistakes of the regimes which preceded it (monarchy, Kassem): it viewed the occasionally violent expressions of Kurdish nationalism as tribal insurrections to be suppressed by brute force. When removed from power in 1963, however, Khadduri argues, the Ba'thi leaders came to appreciate that unity of Iraq depended not on conflict but on harmony in the relations between the country's Arabs and Kurds. Hence, after 1968 the Ba'th endeavored to gain the good will of the Kurds by making important concessions to their national aspirations. They were embodied in the Manifesto of March 1970.[152]

Unfortunately, this promising initiative did not yield the desired results. The reasons for its failure lay not so much in the clash of personalities involved (although the old mistrust between Mulla Mustafa and Bakr was no doubt an important consideration) as in objective factors, such as the ultimate goals of the parties involved. Thus, although the Kurds subscribed to the principle of unity of the Iraqi state, they demanded full autonomy for the region in which they constituted a majority of the population. Since autonomy, as understood by the Kurds, implied unrestricted self-rule, this meant that the central government would have no authority over how the region would be administered. To guarantee self-rule, the Kurds also demanded the withdrawal of Iraqi forces from the Autonomous Region. These requests, too, proved unacceptable to the Ba'th for fear that they represented initial steps to Kurdish independence and, hence, secession from the Iraqi state. Another major bone of contention was the issue of the territory to be occupied by the autonomous Kurdish region. Mulla Mustafa insisted that it include the major oil-producing area of northern Iraq, including the city of Kirkuk. Again, no Iraqi government, regardless of its political persuasion, could seriously entertain the idea of a possible loss of a major source of revenue. For this reason, Baghdad refused to hold a new census and, in 1974, specifically excluded Kirkuk and the rest of the petroleum-rich area in the north from the autonomous Kurdish region.[153]

It appears in retrospect that, from the very beginning in 1970, the Ba'th and the Kurds found themselves attempting to reconcile the irreconcilable and were therefore on a collision course which ultimately led to the final showdown of 1974 and 1975. As in the past, Mulla Mustafa was openly supported by Iran and enjoyed the backing of the United States and Israel. Their attitude encouraged the KDP to abandon its previous strategy of waging a guerrilla war in favor of a frontal confrontation with the Iraqi army. As long as Tehran was willing to keep the supply lines open, *Pesh Merga* succeeded in staving off the Iraqi assault. When this support was withdrawn in March 1975, the Kurdish resistance collapsed. With Mulla Mustafa's leadership discredited, other leaders emerged and reverted to time-tested guerrilla activities. While successful in pressuring Baghdad into some concessions, such as repatriation of many of the resettled Kurds, however, these tactics could not significantly alter the basic fact of firm Iraqi control over much of the Kurdish territory.

When, in the wake of the July 1958 revolution, the Soviet government decided to involve itself heavily in the affairs of Iraq, the presence there of a relatively large and well-organized Kurdish minority, bent on achieving autonomy and capable of resisting the central government's pressure, was recognized by Moscow as a major factor facilitating the establishment and promotion of its interests in that country. Because of their previous experiences with the monarchy, the Kurds were opposed to the return of a pro-Western government and could therefore be counted on to help defend the revolutionary regime. At the same time, they also objected to the concept of Arab unity, which became so popular in the wake of the February 1958 union between Egypt and Syria, because Iraq's submergence in a regional political entity would have reduced the Kurds to a status of a small and hence inconsequential minority. Since the Kremlin, too, had endorsed the 1958 revolution while sharing, for reasons of its own, the Kurds' misgivings about Arab unity, their respective interests converged even at this early date. An outward manifestation of the resulting unity of tactical interests was Moscow's support of Kurdish autonomy "within the framework of the Iraqi republic," preceded by the dispatch to Iraq of Mulla Mustafa and his followers who had resided in the USSR since the collapse of the Iranian Kurdish Republic of Mahabad in 1946.

Throughout the 1960s, the Soviet Union was well aware that the continuing Arab-Kurdish rivalry made it imperative for the Baghdad authorities to secure outside political and military support. In the early 1970s the shah accelerated the shipment of arms to Mulla Mustafa's forces, leaving the Ba'th no choice but to seek large-scale military assistance from the USSR. This turn of events, coupled with the Ba'th's determination to nationalize the country's oil industry, precluded rapprochement between Baghdad and the Western powers and facilitated the pursuit by Moscow of its own objectives in Iraq. The Kremlin, however, must have been aware of the serious dangers inherent in the "Kurdish problem." Western support was likely to encourage Mulla Mustafa to press the Iraqi government for concessions which the latter would be reluctant to grant. The resulting tension could once again give rise to another major confrontation, threatening the country's stability and internal cohesion. Whatever its outcome, a Kurdish-Arab war was certain to have important negative repercussions for the Soviet policy in Iraq. A KDP victory would result in the removal from power of the Ba'th, a party with which the Kremlin, since 1968, had succeeded in establishing a close working relationship and whose cooperation had been solicited even more eagerly after the Russians' 1972 ouster from Egypt. A victory by the central government, on the other hand, could not but destroy the political influence of the Kurds who, along with the ICP, were regarded by Moscow as important domestic checks on the ruling Ba'th party. In addition, Baghdad's victory was likely to reduce Iraq's reliance on the USSR. For these reasons the Kremlin appears to have genuinely preferred a political settlement of the Arab-Kurdish dispute which would have reduced (but not entirely eliminated) the tension while leaving the internal balance between the two communities intact. Only in these circumstances could the Soviets expect to have optimum opportunities to advance their own interests in Iraq and, through it, in the neighboring Gulf area as well.

With these considerations in mind, the USSR in the early 1970s exerted pressure on both the Ba'th and the KDP urging them to reconcile their differences by political means. For a while, these Soviet efforts appeared to be paying off. In retrospect, however, there can be no doubt that peace in Kurdistan was maintained not because of Moscow's persuasion but because of Baghdad's preoccupation with the planned nationalization of the Western oil interests in Iraq. Success in this important venture, the Ba'thi leaders recognized, was predicated on their ability to secure Kurdish cooperation. Once the nationalization had been effected in 1972, however, Baghdad's attitude toward the Kurds stiffened appreciably. For a while the Kremlin persevered in its attempts to reconcile the Ba'th-KDP differences, but Soviet influence proved insufficient to prompt them to moderate their respective positions.

By 1972–1973 there could no longer be any doubt that Mulla Mustafa had openly adopted a pro-Western stance and was pressing for a degree of autonomy which would have severely limited the political and economic power of the central government. Specifically, the detachment of the Kirkuk oil fields and the resulting loss of income would have dealt a heavy blow to the Iraqi economy. In the process, the political power and credibility of the Ba'th, too, would have been shattered. As seen from Moscow, the net result would have been a major gain for the Western powers and a corresponding loss for the USSR. Therefore, once Mulla Mustafa's intentions had become known, the Soviets had no choice but to throw their support behind the Iraqi government. It may be assumed that the decision to do so had not been arrived at easily or painlessly; it did, after all, signify an abandonment of an old and time-tested policy. And even when it was resolved to support Baghdad against the Kurds, the Soviet approval of an allout endeavor to crush the rebellion was withheld for a long time after Mulla Mustafa publicly announced his pro-Western stand. Moscow's attitude was probably a reflection of apprehension that, given large-scale Western and Iranian support of the Kurds, a major military conflict in the northern region might lead to the collapse of the friendly Ba'thist regime in Iraq. In such an eventuality, the new leadership in Baghdad might move the country away from its pro-Soviet orientation and toward closer association with the moderate Arab states (such as Egypt) or even with the Western powers.

When it finally became obvious that a showdown was inevitable, the USSR not only openly abandoned the Kurds and sided with the Ba'th but also extended Iraq large-scale military and political support. After Baghdad won the war, due to a significant degree to the agreement with Iran, the Soviet Union remained steadily supportive of the central government's activities in the northern region and rejected all Kurdish nationalist claims of the severity and injustice of Iraqi policies.

The Kremlin's decision to support the Ba'th in its confrontation with the KDP resulted mainly from the initiatives taken by Mulla Mustafa—his policy created a common ground in the respective Soviet and Iraqi positions on the Kurdish issue. Put differently, Moscow's own efforts at exerting influence with Mulla Mustafa and with the central government proved futile. Even when the two protagonists did exhibit moderation in the period between 1970 and 1973, they did so not because of Soviet pressure but because of their independent decisions temporarily not to seek a military showdown in northern Iraq.

Likewise, Moscow's espousal of Baghdad's cause in 1974–75, too, could not be attributed to the Kremlin's own initiatives. Rather, it was a reaction to Mulla Mustafa's resolution to confront the Ba'thi authorities with the support of Iran, the United States, and Israel. It does, of course, stand to reason that Iraq had strongly urged the USSR to abandon the Kurds. However, the Soviet decision to do so—in seeming compliance with Baghdad's wishes—was taken primarily in response to Mulla Mustafa's initiatives which threatened Moscow's interests in Iraq rather than to the pressure exerted by the Ba'th.

In short, the Kremlin's handling of the Kurdish question demonstrated some of the limits of both Moscow's and Baghdad's ability to influence each other's policies. It also provided a good illustration of the proposition that, in the Middle East, the Soviets are usually at the mercy of initiatives taken by the local actors. As a result, the Kremlin's policies are often designed to minimize losses in situations which affect Soviet interests but over which the USSR has little or no control. The Kurdish problem in Iraq and Moscow's handling of it offer good illustrations of this contention.

The Iraqi Communist party (ICP), historically one of the more effective Marxist organizations in the Middle East, was formally established in 1934. Its first National Congress was held in Baghdad in 1945 and adopted the Party Program and Rules.[1] For the next thirteen years, the ICP belonged to a loose alliance of anti-royalist political parties and led the existence of a persecuted, clandestine organization committed to the overthrow of the Iraqi monarchy.[2]

In the wake of the 1958 revolution, the ICP, for the first time in its existence, emerged from the underground and, in a surprisingly short time, became one of republican Iraq's important political forces. However, independence from the government, relative freedom of action, and the resulting violence perpetrated by some party zealots against political opponents (the "Red Terror") soon brought the ICP into conflict with Abd al-Kerim Kassem, the country's new strongman. As a result, between mid-1959 and the "glorious leader's" demise in February 1963, the ICP lost some of its former effectiveness.[3] Nevertheless, its relative decline did not save the party from the wrath of the militantly anticommunist Ba'th which controlled Iraq between February and November 1963. A major bloodbath instituted by the Ba'th not only crippled the ICP's infrastructure, but also deprived it of its leader, Secretary General Hussein al-Radi, otherwise known as Salam Adil. Its ranks depleted and the surviving members driven underground, the ICP required several years to overcome the defeat inflicted by what was subsequently labeled as the "pro-imperialist and reactionary wing of the Ba'th party."[4]

The next five years (1963–68)—marked by the rule of the Aref brothers—were used by the ICP to rebuild the organization with the view to becoming, once again, one of the principal political forces in Iraq. A major step toward solving the leadership crisis was taken before the July

1968 revolution. After extensive behind-the-scenes maneuvers, Aziz Mohammed (a Kurd and a Communist moderate who found refuge in Moscow in 1963) was elected the party's first secretary. Another challenge facing the ICP in the late 1960s was the threat to party unity emanating from the radical faction, led by Aziz al-Hajj Ali Haydar. Following abortive attempts to impose his radical brand of ideology on the ICP, Aziz al-Hajj and his followers were expelled from the party and, in the summer of 1968, used the widespread dissatisfaction with the central government among the poor Shi'i peasants of southern Iraq to initiate a guerrilla war against the regimes of Abd al-Rahman Aref and, after his overthrow by the Ba'th in July 1968, of Ahmad Hasan al-Bakr. The uprising was squashed by government forces a few months later.[5]

Purged of "deviationist elements" and united under the leadership of Aziz Mohammed, the Communist party reemerged as an important factor in Iraq's political life. Its "arrival" was made possible by the relative circumspection with which the ICP as well as the victorious Ba'th initially treated each other. Specifically, having drawn appropriate conclusions from the experience of the 1958 through 1963 period, the ICP was careful not to provoke the Ba'th. What the Communist party needed above all was a period of relative tranquility to help it recover from the losses suffered in 1963. The ICP leadership understood that this goal could be attained only by means of an accommodation with the Ba'th. Moreover, in 1968 the Communists (as well as the USSR) found themselves in agreement with some of the Ba'th's basic policy objectives, among them the anti-Western orientation of its foreign policy and, on the domestic scene, the proposed nationalization of land as well as of Iraq's oil industry.

The Ba'th, too, showed an interest in coexisting with the ICP. Domestically, its leaders recognized the need of acquiring widespread political support, causing the Bakr regime to seek political accommodation with the Communists as well as the Kurds. The Ba'th was equally aware that the planned socioeconomic reforms (particularly the nationalization of the country's oil industry) and the resulting alienation of the Western powers made it imperative for Baghdad to secure Soviet cooperation and support. In view of the USSR's strong reaction to the 1963 persecution of the ICP,[6] Moscow was not likely to back the Ba'th if the latter reverted to the policy of open suppression of the Communist party.[7]

In short, the groundwork for limited cooperation between the Ba'th and the ICP was laid in the early years of the Bakr regime. It rested on mutual recognition that their respective interests could be best advanced by limited political accommodation and not open confrontation. However, even under the best of circumstances, it was a strictly tactical alliance: mistrust and mutual dislike, if not outright hatred, remained an integral part of the Ba'th-ICP relationship.

The Ba'th and the ICP: The Early Years

As might have been expected, the ICP came out in favor of the July 17, 1968, revolution. An official statement, published later that month, hailed the overthrow of "the Aref . . . dictatorial clique . . . [as] the inevitable fate of all tyrants and reactionary rulers hostile to the people."[8] However, careful reading of the document made it clear that approval of the revolution signified neither sympathy for nor unqualified support of the new regime. The statement did not mention the Ba'th by name but made several poignant references to the party's failure to recognize the people's desire for moderation and reform. Specifically, "the people" demanded "an immediate . . . release of all prisoners [and] the reinstatement of all dismissed civilians and servicemen. . . ." "The people" were also in favor of putting "an end to the lawlessness perpetrated by the terroristic punitive apparatus, to tortures, disfranchisement, dismissals and arrests." On the positive side, the ICP called for recognition of "democratic freedoms: the freedom of political activity of parties and patriotic groups, the freedom of trade union and public activity of mass organizations, [and] the freedom of press, convictions and manifestations. . . ." Finally, the Communists expressed themselves in favor of "a democratic coalition government which would solve the burning problems of the country and satisfy the demands of the people."[9]

Given these Communist preferences, the initial organizational activities of the Ba'th, designed to secure for the party a preponderant position in Iraqi politics, found little sympathy with the ICP. The statement noted that the establishment of the Revolutionary Command Council (manned exclusively by the members of the Ba'th), of an " 'enlarged national council' made up of ministers and servicemen, [and] the concentration of power in their hands can only sow . . . doubts . . . [about the Ba'th's willingness] to put an end to . . . despotism and to establish democratic constitutional institutions."[10] This public exposition of the ICP position could not but alert the Ba'thi authorities to the continuing incompatibility of their and Communist long-range goals. As a result, barely concealed hostility between them surfaced early on and remained a basic feature of their relations well into the 1970s.

In any event, heading the list of the ICP demands were the twin requests for the release of the imprisoned "patriots" and for an end of persecution of "progressive elements." The RCC complied by freeing some political prisoners and, in a symbolic gesture, by closing the notorious Nurqat al-Salman prison. These measures were greeted by the ICP as "steps in the right direction," but mistrust toward the Ba'th remained, reinforced by rumors that many Communists detained at Nurqat al-Salman had been transferred to other prisons.[11]

Tension between the two parties increased in late 1968-early 1969, when the ICP accused the Ba'th of "stepping up violence against the opponents of its policy": the latest campaign resulted in the arrest of "more than 200 patriots." The statement of March 1969 protested against what was termed "a disgusting manifestation of dictatorship" and demanded "an end to the terror and tortures and the release of the arrested patriots."[12] Such allegations were heatedly denied by the Ba'thist officials. President Bakr, during a press conference held in July 1970, said: "I can affirm that we have not arrested any citizen because of his political beliefs. . . . The mighty revolution has closed forever all prisons and detention camps in which political prisoners were being held under previous regimes."[13] In addition to those imprisoned, "some 35 leading Communists" were reportedly assassinated between 1968 and 1970. Among those killed were two members of the ICP Central Committee.[14] It is not known whether the authorities had been implicated in these murders, but the Iraqi Communist party thought they were and said so publicly.[15]

The program, adopted by the Second Congress of the ICP in September 1970, described the Ba'th as "generally speaking . . . anti-imperialist" but, at the same time, "in essence antidemocratic." It went on to add that "in spite of a certain relaxation of persecutions and the release of several Communists and democrats from prison, provocations continue and attempts are still being made on the lives of Communists."[16] These charges were borne out by events. At least one more prominent Communist, Thabit Habib al-Ani, was reportedly kidnapped by "armed security men" in May 1971 and "taken to an unknown . . . [location]." Lebanese Communist daily *al-Nid'a* described his abduction as "part of the Iraqi Baath Party's campaign of terror against local Communists who refuse to join the Baath-dominated government . . . ."[17]

Tied to the issue of "democratic freedoms" was another important domestic political problem: the establishment of what was then called a "united front of democratic forces." In an effort to strengthen its political base, the Ba'th, in early August 1968, invited representatives of various political groups, including the ICP, to discuss the possibility of creating a "united front." Concretely, in return for recognition of the ruling position of the Ba'th, the left-wing parties were offered government seats and a voice in running the affairs of the state. According to a Soviet source, this proposal was turned down because the government refused to restore respect for civil rights, to permit freedom of activity to the left-wing parties, and to hold elections for a new "General Assembly." There was also considerable resentment against the Ba'th's determination to control all the key positions in the government and the armed forces.[18] Uriel Dann offers a somewhat different explanation. In the course of 1968 negotiations the ICP demanded to be treated as an equal of the Ba'th. In the government, the Communists coveted the Ministry of Defense. They also insisted on the immediate licensing of a party daily newspaper. Confronted with these requests, the authorities broke off the talks.[19]

Be that as it may, in November 1968 the ICP issued its own "Charter of Cooperation of National Forces in a United Front" calling for unity of the "workers, peasants, revolutionary intelligentsia, petty bourgeoisie, and progressive . . . national bourgeoisie." Among the tasks of the "national-democratic nature" which were awaiting the front's attention, the ICP singled out the "mobilization of all forces for the struggle against imperialism, neocolonialism, and Zionism; for the liquidation of the remnants of feudalism, . . . of large landownership, and . . . of the Kurdish problem." The ICP also repeated its earlier insistence on the creation of a "representative coalition government" which would not be "subordinated to the wishes of one party."[20] Because the charter challenged the political preeminence of the Ba'th, the authorities did not avail themselves of the Communist proposal. Instead, they intensified their pressure on the ICP.

In July 1969 President Bakr announced his decision to resume contacts with the left-wing parties and, in early August, the authorities issued another call for the creation of a "united front."[21] Nothing came of this initiative, either. Describing the stalled negotiations as a "stalemate," Saddam Hussein explained that the talks between the Ba'th and the leftist parties (including the ICP) "had broken down on three major points: the question of the existence of Israel, Kurdish nationalism, and joint efforts to begin political indoctrination 'immediately and at the lowest level.' "[22]

Saddam Hussein's analysis was essentially correct. The Ba'th and the ICP did in fact differ profoundly over the question of Israel's existence. While the ruling party insisted on the annihilation of the Jewish state, the Iraqi Communists, who had accepted Moscow's leadership in the international Marxist movement, were simply following the Soviet line. As is well known, the USSR had recognized Israel's right to exist and was demanding only that the territories occupied in 1967 be returned to the Arabs. Put differently, in contrast to the Iraqi Ba'th, both the Soviet Union and the ICP were urging a political, and not a military, solution to the Arab-Israeli conflict.

On the Kurdish question, too, Moscow and the Iraqi Communists held complementary positions. Both regarded Kurdish nationalism as a manifestation of legitimate national aspirations and supported it as a bona fide revolutionary movement worthy of Communist backing.[23] The Ba'th, in contrast, recognized the Kurdish right to autonomy but refused to sanction any concessions which might lead to an end of Baghdad's control over the northern region.

Finally, the question of indoctrination of the masses was used by Saddam Hussein to conceal differences on the fundamental issue of political parity between the Ba'th and the other political parties of Iraq. Since the authorities were committed to a de facto one-party rule, no compromise on this issue was possible in 1968 or later. However, although in the early 1970s the Ba'th would bend considerably on this and other issues, there was no overriding need to do so in the 1960s. Instead, irked by Communist insistence on equality of Iraq's left-wing political parties and by ICP protests against continued "discrimination," the government occasionally struck back. For instance, when such sentiments were expressed by an ICP representative at the July 1970 Congress of the Kurdistan Democratic party, al-Thawrah inquired "whether, if the Communists, and not the Baathists, had seized power in July 1968, they would have given equality to all progressive parties." The paper concluded by saying that "in a national front the Communists will have to accept the leadership [i.e., dominance] of the Baath Party."[24]

In any event, in the late 1960s and early 1970s the Ba'th and the ICP appeared occasionally to be moving toward a compromise. No real progress was achieved, however, because the basic issues separating them remained unresolved. A good illustration of this proposition was provided by the deliberations of the new party program, adopted by the Second Congress of the ICP in September 1970. While the delegates appealed to the Ba'th "to take steps to strengthen national unity" and repeated earlier calls for "a national conference of all patriotic parties and national groups to discuss the formation of a national front,"[25] the party program was explicit in expressing the ICP's disapproval of the government and its policies. The document emphasized the "dual nature" of the Ba'thi regime. As for the July 1968 coup, it "served only to put the middle and small bourgeoisie in power while the military dictatorship was transferred into a 'Baathist' party dictatorship." As a result, "many of the revolution's goals have not been achieved."[26]

The 1970 party program was also noteworthy for the relative frankness in presenting the organization's long and short-term aims. "A national-democratic revolution and transition to a socialist revolution" were said to fall into the latter category. "The ultimate goals of the ICP," in contrast, were "to achieve socialism and communism in Iraq." The document went on to state that "the leading role in the revolutionary struggle to fulfill the goals of the national-democratic revolution" belonged not to the Ba'th but to "the working class of Iraq led by the ICP." However, since it was obvious that, in the foreseeable future, the "working class" would not be strong enough to implement the "national-democratic revolution," the party program advocated the establishment of "a national front of progressive parties and forces which are to act jointly, by common agreement." To make certain that, by joining the front, the ICP would not lose its separate identity, the program called for recognition of "each party's . . . [right] to political and organizational independence" and rejected "attempts to impose domination by one or another party upon other groups. . . ."[27] Such candor was not likely to please the Ba'th, and in late 1970 and early 1971 relations between the two parties deteriorated once again.[28] This state of affairs seems to have alarmed the USSR. It may well have been that the May 1971 visit to Moscow by an ICP delegation, headed by Aziz Mohammed, was an outward manifestation of growing Soviet concern and an indication that the Kremlin was taking measures to improve relations between the Iraqi Communist party and the Ba'th. It certainly appears significant that between May and November 1971, public recriminations between the authorities and the ICP had ceased. In this atmosphere of unaccustomed calm, President Bakr, in a major speech delivered on November 15, submitted the Ba'thi version of the "Charter of National Action" for nationwide discussion.

Turning to the USSR, it is noteworthy that the 1968 revolution received a relatively good treatment at the hands of the Soviet press. For those who remembered Moscow's (as well as the ICP's) 1963 experiences with the Ba'th, this positive response may have come as something of a surprise. The Kremlin's attitude becomes more understandable, however, if it is borne in mind that, by the time they staged the coup, Bakr and most of his associates had openly disassociated themselves from the Ba'th's earlier excesses. As noted by Evgenii Primakov, the resolutions adopted by the party conference, held in Beirut in early 1968, underscored the Ba'th's determination to avoid the "mistakes of the past" and to work for the establishment of a "united front" with "all Arab progressive and nationalist organizations," including the Arab Communist parties.[29]

The Soviets traditionally favored the creation of "united fronts" of "progressive, national forces" in the developing countries whose indigenous Communist parties were not strong enough to seize and hold power. (In the late 1960s and early 1970s this applied to Iraq as well as to Syria, ruled by the local branches of the Ba'th.) The Kremlin preferred such an arrangement because it legalized the existence of the Communist parties, offered them relative freedom of organizational activity, and provided a degree of protection from excesses by the ruling party. It is true that "united fronts" implicitly guaranteed the Ba'th a position of superiority over the Communist "junior partners." Given the political realities in Syria and Iraq, however, such a state of affairs, although deplorable, was no doubt seen in Moscow as inevitable and, in any event, preferable to massive persecution of the Communist parties.

Moreover, in the case of Iraq, the Soviet government found in the Ba'th's initial position on international and domestic problems much that was considered encouraging and praiseworthy. For example, an unidentified party leader, interviewed by Primakov in early August 1968, admitted that the Ba'th's "anti-Communism . . . had caused its defeat in November 1963." The party learned from past mistakes and was now determined to seek the support and cooperation of the other political groups in Iraq. Likewise, the RCC communiqué of August 2, 1968, ordering the release of all political prisoners was seen as a step toward restoration of a healthier political climate in Iraq.[30]

At the same time, while praising Baghdad's pronouncements, the Soviets also followed its actions and, in late August, found that its deeds did not quite match its words. On the issue of political prisoners in particular, *Pravda* noted that the list of detainees released after the coup contained only three hundred names. This reportedly left several hundred Communists in government prisons. According to *Pravda*, "all these facts cannot but diminish the importance of the statements made by the new Iraqi leadership. They do not contribute to the stabilization of the situation in the country which, according to the Iraqi leaders, is a goal they are trying to attain."[31]

Although the initial Soviet (as well as parallel ICP) pressure did not produce immediate results, the tenor of the remarks directed at Baghdad at the end of 1968 was rather calm. This was probably due to the fact that many of the measures introduced by the Ba'th after its advent to power did meet with Moscow's approval. Specifically, the authorities had released many imprisoned Communists, had promised unconditional amnesty to the Kurds, had initiated a far-reaching agrarian reform, and had contacted the ICP and other "progressive organizations" with a view to establishing a "popular front."[32] The Kremlin's commendation of these measures contrasted sharply with the ICP's initial hostility toward the victorious Ba'th.

An interesting example of the relative restraint with which the USSR treated the Ba'thi regime in the early post-revolutionary period was provided in the spring of 1969. In March, the Iraqi Communist party issued a strong statement protesting against continued detention of political prisoners. It appeared much later in the year in the *Information Bulletin* but was ignored by the mainline Soviet press. In contrast, the joint ICP-Arab Socialist Movement declaration of April 1969 was promptly reported by *Pravda* on April 5. A comparison of the texts of these two documents provides a clue to their differing treatment by Moscow. Whereas the first protested against the persecution of the Iraqi Communists, the second called for the establishment of a "united front of national, patriotic forces." The publication of one document and the de facto official disregard of the other left no doubt about Soviet priorities: the creation of a national front had been elevated to an important policy objective which took precedence over other considerations, including the fate of the imprisoned members of the ICP.[33] It is equally noteworthy that reports on the "united front" appearing in the Russian press consisted of quotes from materials published in the Iraqi and other Arab Communist sources but contained no *Soviet* comments. This meant that, although Moscow favored the establishment of a national front in Iraq, it had no intention of exerting direct public pressure on the Ba'thi government which, or so it seemed at the time, was adopting an "anti-imperialist" foreign and "socialist-oriented" domestic policies.

A clearer indication of the trend toward accommodation with Iraq was given in the fall of 1969 in one of Primakov's articles from Baghdad. It was based on an interview with Abd al-Khaliq al-Samarrai, then assistant secretary general of the Ba'th. First, Samarrai listed the reasons which had prompted his party to revise its initial anti-Communist stance: the fiasco of November 1963; the experience of Syria, where the Ba'th and the Communist party began to cooperate in February 1966; and the necessity of uniting "progressive" Arab forces after the defeat of June 1967. At the same time, as he freely admitted, "it is hardly to be imagined that the earlier attitudes prevalent in the Ba'th . . . had suddenly and completely vanished." On the contrary, staunch anti-Communists continued to occupy high party and government positions. All in all, however, forces opposed to "exclusiveness" were now dominant in the party councils.[34]

Commenting on the Ba'th's current attitude toward the ICP, Samarrai noted that "one of the most influential figures of the new Iraqi regime" expressed a desire to appoint some Communists to ministerial positions. "We could not do so [earlier] because . . . we had no links with the leadership of the Communist party which was operating . . . underground." A dialogue became possible, the source told Samarrai, after the authorities had freed all the political prisoners arrested by the Aref regime and "not one Communist was left in prison."[35] The fact that such assertions were hotly disputed by the ICP did not impress *Pravda*. What seemed to matter to Moscow was the implied promise, contained in the statements by high Ba'thi functionaries, that former excesses against the local Marxists were a thing of the past and that the ruling party was now moving in the direction of the "united front." If true, Baghdad's changing attitude could lead to a recognition of the legitimacy of the ICP and, presumably, to the discontinuation of government persecution. Moreover, the Kremlin no doubt understood that exerting influence on behalf of the Iraqi Communists would not improve their position; it would, however, increase the level of tension in Moscow-Baghdad relations.

For a while, *Pravda*'s guarded optimism appeared to have been justified. As quoted by Primakov, *al-Thawrah* expressed the Ba'th's appreciation of the "need for an alliance with progressives, first and foremost the Iraqi Communist party." The ICP was now seen in a particularly favorable light: it proceeded from the "ideas of scientific socialism, which represents the interests of the proletariat"; it had "important links with the broad popular masses"; and it had "international links with the socialist countries . . . which have come out on the side of the Arab revolution." An open expression of such views, Primakov continued, "demonstrates that the Ba'th party is undergoing a definite ideological evolution." He was under no illusion that "important historical obstacles" remained and had to be "overcome and eliminated." However, the dialogue between Iraq's two major parties had begun and was continuing "in a milieu of auspicious changes that are opening new horizons for Iraq." Primakov's article was important because it ran counter to views expressed by the ICP and, as such, served as another indication of Moscow's changing attitude toward the Ba'th.[36]

Upbeat reporting of developments in Iraq marked most Soviet comments appearing in 1970 and 1971. Occasional acts of terror committed against prominent members of the ICP were either passed over in silence or were mentioned only in passing. (Such was the case in the March 1970 murder of Mohammed Ahmad al-Khudayri; of the central Soviet press, only *Sovetskaia Rossiia* reported his death as well as that of two other ICP functionaries.)[37] Moscow's circumspection, coupled with continuing calls for the creation of a "unified national democratic front of all progressive parties in Iraq,"[38] stood in sharp contrast to the reaction of the ICP which, in a public statement, held the authorities responsible for Khudayri's death.[39] Likewise, Soviet publications managed to "overlook" the important Second Congress of the Iraqi Communist party held in September 1970, while devoting considerable attention to Saddam Hussein's August visit to the USSR. Along with the text of the ICP Program, adopted at the Second Congress, the documents issued at the meeting of the Jordanian, Syrian, Iraqi, and Lebanese Communist parties, held in January 1971, were once again made public only in the *Information Bulletin*.[40] In short, in 1970 and 1971 the Soviet press gave no inkling of the seriousness of the situation facing the ICP—a clear indication that the Kremlin had no intention of jeopardizing its rapidly improving relations with the ruling Ba'th for the sake of Iraq's Marxist organization.

Nevertheless, the sharp deterioration of relations between the Ba'th and the ICP, which took place in the early 1970s, made it impossible for the USSR to ignore the subject entirely. Significantly, however, the venue chosen to protest the repressive policies of the Iraqi government was not a major Soviet publication but the *World Marxist Review*. Entitled "Who Profits From Persecution of Communists in Iraq?," the 1971 article by Ara Kachadoor (a pseudonym) accused the ruling Ba'th party of arresting, imprisoning, torturing, and executing members of the ICP. Alluding to the venerable Leninist concept of the "dual nature of the national bourgeoisie," Kachadoor acknowledged that "the best part of the Baathists are friendly towards the Communists and do not shy away from contacts with them." Nevertheless, especially "among influential Baathists," there were many who could not "shed their ingrained anti-communism" and were anxious "to . . . oust the Communists from public and political life." The ICP had no doubt that these elements controlled the actions of the Iraqi authorities: "It would be naive to believe that the security service initiated this campaign against Communists . . . without the knowledge of the Baath Party and the government." The ICP, Kachadoor concluded, remained committed to the principle of "unity of the democratic movement" but warned that it could be implemented only after government repressions stopped. If they did not, Iraq would not be able to "win genuine independence and progressive development."[41]

It was in this general atmosphere of the tightening of Ba'thist controls over the political life of Iraq, of growing ICP resentment and clamor for Soviet protection, and of the USSR's apparent unwillingness to involve itself publicly in the domestic affairs of a client-state that a high-level Communist party delegation, headed by First Secretary Aziz Mohammed, traveled to Moscow. The visit took place in May 1971 and encompassed meetings with Mikhail Suslov. According to the Soviet account, Aziz Mohammed informed his hosts "about the situation in Iraq, the activity of the Iraqi Communist party, and the difficulties that it is encountering in its work." In the course of the discussions, the USSR "expressed its solidarity with the Iraqi Communist party . . . and with its efforts to unite the country's patriotic and national-democratic forces within the framework of an anti-imperialist front." Both parties agreed that "imperialist and reactionary intrigues . . . as well as the persecution of the Communist party impede the achievement of unity of progressive patriotic forces and facilitate the subversive activity of hostile elements which strive to prevent Iraq from . . . strengthening its national independence and [achieving] social progress."[42]

The formula left little doubt that, in the accelerating conflict between the Ba'th and the ICP, the Kremlin's public sympathies were on the side of its fellow Marxists. At the same time, it was equally obvious that the difficulties encountered by the Iraqi Communists would not be permitted to jeopardize the growing friendship between Moscow and Baghdad. This point was well illustrated not only by Soviet unwillingness to criticize the Ba'th's repressive behavior with respect to the ICP openly, but also by the continuing public praise of "new" and "progressive" aspects of Baghdad's domestic policy.[43] Nevertheless, the overall situation did place the USSR into an uncomfortable position. For this reason, the Soviets may be safely assumed to have applied behind-the-scenes pressure in an effort to persuade the Iraqi authorities to discontinue, or, at the very least, to moderate their anti-Communist practices. Indeed, during his mid-1971 visit to Moscow, Saddam Hussein was reportedly told that continued Soviet support of Iraq depended on Baghdad's willingness to end "the repression of the Communists."[44] Pressure to show more flexibility must also have been exerted on the ICP since it, too, had its share of hard-liners, unwilling to compromise with a party at whose hands the Marxists had suffered a great deal. Moscow's desire to settle the Ba'th-ICP feud was also prompted by the realization that the advancement of the USSR's own interests in Iraq was greatly hampered by public quarrels between the two parties, by the repression of the Communists, and by their appeals for Soviet support.

"Charter of National Action" and Ba'th-ICP Cooperation

On November 15, 1971, President Bakr announced that the work of drafting the National Action Charter had been completed. The draft proclaimed the Ba'th's desire to strengthen the political and economic independence of Iraq through cooperation with the USSR and other members of the "socialist bloc." It reiterated Baghdad's determination to support the Arab struggle against "imperialism" and "Israeli aggression." Domestically, the draft envisaged the creation of a National Front, embracing all of the country's "progressive forces." It also provided for the adoption of a permanent constitution guaranteeing "democratic freedoms" for Iraq's "progressive" political parties.[45]

At a press conference, held two days later, Bakr said that the "cornerstone" of unity to which his party aspired was an alliance between the Ba'th, the Iraqi Communist party, and the Kurdistan Democratic party. He went on to add, however, that joining the alliance was predicated on acceptance of the principle that "the responsibility for leading the Army and directing it politically falls on the RCC alone. . . . No party other than the Baath . . . will be allowed to carry out any forms of political or organizational activity within the armed forces."[46]

In a statement issued on November 27 the ICP Politburo expressed "great interest" in the draft Charter. It appealed to the Communists because it was "anti-imperialist in character" and emphasized "the importance of . . . strengthen[ing] . . . cooperation with the socialist countries"; because it "rejected . . . the capitalist path" and envisaged a program of "progressive socio-economic change"; because it reasserted "the importance of a peaceful democratic solution of the Kurdish problem"; and, above all, because it contained an implicit promise to avoid "the mistakes and failures suffered by the revolutionary movement in Iraq. . . ."[47] The ICP also approved of the provisions guaranteeing "all democratic freedoms for the popular masses . . . , including freedom of political parties, . . . the press, [and] freedom of opinion. . . ." At the same time, the ICP insisted that "the requirements of the victorious struggle against imperialism, Zionism and reactionary forces call for the confirmation of certain [other] principles. . . ." Leading among them was "the liquidation of all manifestations of suppressions of the masses and their political institutions (especially their patriotic parties)." Finally, in order to "achieve . . . more comprehensive and precise formulation[s]," the ICP suggested holding "direct meetings and constructive discussions" by the Ba'th, the ICP, and the KDP.[48]

As noted by Majid Khadduri, a number of high-level consultations between the Ba'th and the ICP was in fact held in Baghdad in the spring of 1972. The former was represented by Saddam Hussein and RCC member Tariq Aziz and the latter by Aziz Mohammed and Central Committee member Amir Abdallah. In the course of the discussions, "the differences between the two parties were narrowed down and agreement on fundamental principles was reached." Specifically, the ICP agreed to cooperate with the Ba'th on the basis of the draft Charter, provided that the latter was regarded "as a set of proposals for discussion and possible changes." The Ba'th consented and, in the ensuing meetings, the document "was subjected to a close scrutiny, but the substance remained essentially the same as [originally] proposed."[49]

According to a Communist account, during these talks the ICP informed the Ba'th leadership that, in order "to heighten the effectiveness and usefulness" of Marxist participation in the political life of Iraq, party members should be allowed to serve on the newly formed Council of Ministers. In addition, the ICP requested permission to publish a daily newspaper [*Tariq al-Sha'b*]. Both proposals were accepted by the Ba'th.[50] The addition of ICP Central Committee members Amir Abdallah and Mukarram al-Talabani to the Iraqi cabinet as ministers of state and irrigation, respectively, was announced on May 14, 1972.[51] While the Ba'thi press spoke glowingly of "new perspectives" for the strengthening of national unity, the ICP praised the step as "still another form of cooperation" implemented by the party "for the purpose of finding positive solutions to the political, economic and social problems confronting our country."[52]

The ICP's decision to cooperate with the Ba'th was dictated by a number of considerations. First, it rested on a shared desire to proceed with the nationalization of Iraq's oil industry.[53] Moreover, the draft Charter was received favorably in the USSR, and it may be safely assumed that the Kremlin had strongly counseled moderation. In addition, the Iraqi Communists must have understood that open opposition to the Charter would lead to renewed oppression by the authorities. Conversely, cooperation with the Ba'th could be expected to result in several short-term gains. The ICP could hope to step up its propaganda and organizational activities with less fear of government retaliation. Likewise, its prestige and influence in and outside Iraq were likely to grow as the party acquired "respectability" by working with the ruling Ba'th. Nevertheless, accommodation was agreed to reluctantly and certainly did not mean submission to the will of the Ba'th. Above all, the ICP was determined not the give in on the question of political supremacy in Iraq, an issue of cardinal importance to the Communists as well as to the Ba'thists. And since this basic matter had not been resolved then (or later), major differences between the two parties could be expected to resurface at some future date.

As subsequently explained by the ICP, the difficulties which the party encountered in its drive to play a legitimate role in the affairs of Iraq fell into two major categories. First, the Communists endeavored to push the country "along the path of progressive development . . . to more advanced revolutionary positions." These efforts were met with "mounting conspiratorial activities on the part of imperialism and its lackeys . . . , [such as] feudals, big bourgeoisie and certain groups of middle bourgeoisie." Together, they attempted to inhibit "the . . . alliance of the patriotic parties within a national front; nurturing alarm against cooperation with the Communist Party and sowing mutual suspicions and misgivings among the patriotic parties."[54] Second, the Communists also ran into problems in their dealings with the Ba'th. Specifically, some of the ICP's basic demands for "concrete measures necessary for reinforcing and broadening democratic freedoms" had not been met. Among them were the requests for:

1. Legality of action for all the patriotic parties, including our Iraqi Communist Party. . . .
2. Preparing the climate for the election of a national assembly through direct free secret suffrage. As a preliminary step, . . . a national assembly should be formed based on the coalition of the progressive parties and forces and entrusted with full constitutional prerogatives to act as an interim legislative body. . . .
3. Reconsidering the . . . [form] and tasks of the existing popular councils and reformulating them as local councils directly elected by the masses . . . on the basis of the coalition of the patriotic political parties. . . .
4. Achieving comprehensive cooperation among the political parties within social organizations, such . . . as trade unions, peasant associations . . . and student, youth and women's organizations. . . .
5. On the basis . . . [of the] above, . . . [it was concluded] that the participation and cooperation of the patriotic parties within the state power should assume the nature of the coalition government entrusted with the task of realizing the patriotic, national

and democratic tasks embodied in the program of the national progressive front.[55]

In spite of these clearly defined differences, the Ba'th and the Iraqi Communist party announced on July 17, 1973, the formation of the Progressive National and Patriotic Front (PNPF).[56] The document legalized the ICP for the first time since its establishment in 1934. However, it was evident from the very beginning that the Ba'thist-Communist "alliance" rested on a shaky foundation. At the signing ceremony, Aziz Mohammed stated that "our ambitions . . . do not stop at the limits of this militant document." Al-Thawrah responded, warning the Communists to "take extreme care to act as allies and friends who love their Baathist . . . comrades."[57]

As might have been expected, Moscow applauded President Bakr's November 1971 decision to submit the National Charter draft for nationwide discussion. In an early reaction, Pavel Demchenko agreed with al-Thawrah's assessment that this step would open a "new page in the relations between patriotic and progressive elements in the country, Arabs as well as Kurds." One of the Charter's more important aspects, he noted, was the proposed creation of a "national coalition in which all . . . progressive forces will participate." Equally significant were promises of the legalization of political activity, made to "progressive" parties and groups; of freedom of the press and of "other basic rights of the people"; and of the establishment of a representative National Assembly.[58] The Soviet press praised the draft Charter also because it reflected the Ba'th's determination "to build a socialist society." Among the projected initial measures were the termination of "the country's dependence on foreign capital" and the nationalization of "its oil resources, which are now being exploited by the foreign monopolies." With respect to foreign policy, the draft Charter expressed Iraq's "resolute support [of] the struggle against imperialism and Israeli aggression" while emphasizing "the need further to consolidate . . . relations with socialist countries." It also urged "the unity of all progressive and patriotic forces in the Arab world."[59]

In short, the draft Charter was hailed by the Soviet press as "a major positive step . . . along the path of national independence and social progress."[60] The euphoria engendered by Soviet discussion of the draft Charter stood in sharp contrast to the serious reservations expressed by the Iraqi Communist party.[61] It is true that excerpts from the ICP's initial statement on the Charter were reproduced in Pravda on December 4, 1971. However, none of the Iraqi Communists' objections were reflected in the discussions of the document to appear in the Soviet press. This observation reinforces the earlier conclusion that, in its dealings with Iraq, the USSR was above all interested in maintaining and broadening its relations with the Ba'thi regime.

Thus, the groundwork for improved relations between the Ba'th and the Iraqi Communist party was laid in the spring of 1972. In retrospect, there can be no doubt that there was a definite connection between their willingness to reach a modicum of cooperation and the April 1972 visit to Baghdad of Prime Minister Aleksei Kosygin. During his stay the Soviet dignitary held talks with the representatives of the Ba'th, the ICP, and the KDP. In urging moderation and in advocating a coalition of "progressive forces," Kosygin exerted direct pressure on all of Iraq's major political parties, and his efforts were partially successful: the Ba'thist-ICP consultations resulted in an agreement to cooperate on the basis of the draft "Charter of National Action."[62]

In line with its preferences expressed earlier in the year the Soviet press welcomed the inclusion of two Communists in the Iraqi cabinet, announced in May 1972. *Pravda* described this "consolidation of the nation's progressive forces" as an important feature of the present stage of Iraq's struggle for national assertion. "All the parties upholding the interests of the broad strata of the nation—the ruling Ba'th party, the Communist party, and the Kurdistan Democratic party—are acting as a united front for liberation from the pillaging of foreign predators."[63]

Public enthusiasm aside, however, Moscow remained aware that serious problems continued to hamper Soviet efforts to manipulate the actors on Iraq's political scene. Some of these difficulties were spelled out with uncharacteristic candor by Viktor Kudriavtsev, *Izvestiia*'s prominent political commentator. He praised the Ba'th for its "movement toward socialism," but also cautioned Baghdad that the "tasks confronting Iraq . . . [in its quest for] social and economic transformation are so great that the Ba'th . . . alone cannot cope with them. It would be an illusion to believe that this program can be fulfilled without cooperation between the Ba'th on the one hand and the Iraqi Communist party and the Kurdistan Democratic party on the other." Significantly, this admonition was not addressed to the ruling party alone. Praise of the three parties for showing awareness of the need to cooperate with each other was tempered by regret that the "initial talks on the draft Charter have shown that it is not such a simple matter to agree on the Charter's final text." The main obstacle to an early agreement, Kudriavtsev stated, was the "persistent *mutual* distrust and wariness toward one another that had become ingrained during the long years of mutual hostility." He admitted that "reality . . . cannot be ignored," but called on all concerned "to rise above narrow party interests and to think on the scale of the entire country, of all strata of the population that are ready to advance along a progressive path of development."[64]

A similar point was made later in the year by Rostislav Ul'ianovskii, deputy head of the CPSU Central Committee's International Department. In an article devoted to the subject of "national fronts," Ul'ianovskii addressed the major participants in Iraq's political life in the following fashion: "What is needed for the front's success is mutual trust, sincere cooperation and militant unity of all its participants, notably of the forces forming the nucleus: the national democrats, who wield the power, and the Communists, who are being drawn into active common work to carry out the progressive programme of fundamental social reforms advocated by the ruling party."[65] The same message was delivered personally by Suslov, Ponomarev, Ul'ianovskii, and other CPSU officials to an ICP delegation, led by Aziz Mohammed, which visited the USSR in October 1972.[66]

Whatever the CPSU might have preferred, however, it soon became apparent that Moscow and Baghdad differed widely on the importance which they attached to the establishment of the National Front. For example, in his dinner speech honoring Saddam Hussein during the latter's March 1973 visit to the USSR, Kosygin praised the Ba'th's resistance to the "pressure from imperialist monopolies attempting to prevent the development of Iraq along the path chosen by its people." One of the prerequisites for success, he continued, was the "consolidation of the National Front of progressive forces in Iraq." Significantly, neither Saddam Hussein in his speech nor the joint statement on his visit alluded to this subject.[67]

Saddam Hussein's refusal to mention the National Front, while speaking at length about a number of domestic and international issues, made it clear that, on the Ba'th's list of priorities, the Front was clearly a secondary issue. Of much greater importance were the Kurdish problem and the necessity of developing the oil industry after the nationalization of the Iraq Petroleum Company. Because the pursuit of these twin goals required the assistance and support of the USSR, the Ba'th was not likely to challenge the Soviet leaders publicly. At the same time, by ignoring the National Front on such important occasions as Saddam Hussein's visits to Moscow, Baghdad was delivering a clear message—the Front was destined to remain a politically insignificant organization which would not be permitted to challenge the Ba'th's dominant position in Iraq. The attitude of the ruling party should not have been surprising: its determination to remain at the helm of the state was coupled with deep-seated suspicion that behind all the ICP rhetoric and appeals for cooperation lay the eventual ambition to seize power in Iraq.

The National Front

The text of the "Charter for National Action" was broadcast by Baghdad Radio on August 26, 1973. The document dealt with both ideological and organizational matters; it examined various facets of the Ba'th's domestic and foreign policies and promised "a peaceful and democratic solution of the Kurdish issue within the framework of the national front." It also called for the establishment of a "Supreme Committee" to preside over the activities of the Front. Headed by a member of the Ba'th, it was to consist of eight members of that party, three Communists, three Kurdish Democrats, and one each of two minor political groupings. Disagreements among member parties would be resolved by "democratic discussion," and "mistakes" would be "corrected through . . . self-criticism and fraternal and constructive criticism on the basis of safeguarding the alliance." The Front members were expected to "abide fully by the national action charter. . . ."[68] On September 25, it was announced that the National Front had appointed Naim Haddad as its secretary general. In this capacity, he would preside over a secretariat consisting of four Ba'thi and two Communist representatives.[69]

One of the significant benefits gained by the ICP was the legalization of its information and propaganda activities; on September 16, 1973, *Tariq al-Sha'b*, the party daily, made its first appearance since the early 1960s.[70] On the debit side, the Iraqi Communist party had no choice but to subscribe to the Ba'th's position on the Kurdish question. As noted in chapter 3, the resulting tension between the Communists and the Kurds led to violence in northern Iraq that cost many Marxists their lives.[71]

Initially, the ICP expressed satisfaction with the establishment of the Front. The resolutions passed by the party's Central Committee on January 25, 1974, noted that the adoption of the National Charter and of the Front Statute was "of programmatic importance for the development of the revolutionary movement in Iraq." The ICP was particularly pleased that a "spirit of cooperation has developed between the rank-and-file and supporters of both parties and the masses of the people" after the National Front had been established six months ago.[72] Nevertheless, even then, the ICP Central Committee warned that serious problems had prevented the Front from developing into an effective mass organization. Although expressed in a circumspect manner ("it must be said that the work of the Front has not yet reached a level which fully meets the aspirations of the broad masses . . ."), the criticism of the Ba'th served as a clear indication that the ICP was unhappy with the ruling party's unwillingness to implement changes which the Communists regarded as a prerequisite to turning the Front into an effective instrument for political and socioeconomic change.[73] Among the concrete measures recommended by the ICP were the following: transformation of the Front into an "effective vehicle for leading" the Iraqi people; adherence to the Charter; resolution of the Kurdish problem in a manner designed to foster "patriotic unity"; and "implementation of economic, cultural and political agreements . . . between Iraq and the socialist countries." Such cooperation, it was concluded, would "assist the revolutionary development of Iraq . . . [and] pave the way for . . . the construction of a socialist Iraq."[74]

The January 1974 resolutions of the ICP Central Committee attested to Communist determination to use the Front to spread the party's influence among the Iraqi masses. Confronted with what many Ba'thists perceived to be an open Communist challenge, the ruling party had a choice of playing the ICP game or clamping down hard. As it turned out, the Ba'th proved the epitome of tact and, on the surface, did nothing to antagonize its newly won political ally. In reality, however, the Front remained what the Ba'th intended it to be—part window-dressing and part an instrument through which the authorities were hoping to achieve several important goals. Specifically, along with the 1972 Soviet-Iraqi friendship treaty, the Front helped move both the Kremlin and the ICP into the Ba'thist camp. In 1974 this was particularly important because of Baghdad's determination to develop the country's economy in the wake of the nationalization of Iraq's oil industry and to attempt a "final solution" of the Kurdish problem. The Ba'th regarded Soviet and domestic Communist support as highly important for the success of both of these ventures. With this in mind, the RCC in March 1974 appointed three members of the ICP Central Committee (Nazihah Dulaymi, Rahim Adjina, and Mahdi Hafez) to the National Front Secretariat.[75]

The ICP reciprocated by continuing to voice its support for the National Front and to back the Ba'th's efforts to deal with the rebellious Kurds. Adel Haba, alternate member of the ICP Central Committee, praised both parties for overcoming past differences and for resisting divisive "political and ideological pressures to which they were subjected during the talks." One of the Front's "distinctive feature[s]," Adel Haba continued, was the linkage of "national objectives with social change." This was possible because the Front's "social base comprises . . . classes and social strata interested in development on non-capitalist lines." Moreover, the Front was organized "on a democratic basis, guaranteeing the political, ideological and organizational independence of each Party."[76] The ICP also endorsed the government's efforts to "settle" the Kurdish question: Rahim Adjina described the March 1974 autonomy decree as "a good foundation for the peaceful and democratic solution of the Kurdish problem." When the KDP rejected the decree and, with it, an invitation to join the Front, Amir Abdallah blamed the "actions of the reactionary elements" in the party's leadership for the resumption of hostilities in northern Iraq.[77]

In 1975, as a result of the normalization of Iraq's relations with Iran and a number of Arab states, of the successful completion of the war against the Kurds, and of growing economic independence from the Soviet bloc, the Front lost much of its previous importance to the Bakr-Saddam Hussein regime. It continued to exist, but was of no practical political significance. In spite of that, for the next three years the ICP continued to voice support of the National Front and promised to cooperate with the Ba'thi authorities in implementing "progressive" reforms.[78]

Theoretical justification for continued cooperation between the Communists and "progressive" nationalist elites in the developing countries was provided by a conference of representatives of several Third World Communist parties, organized by the *World Marxist Review* and devoted to the theme "Revolutionary Democrats and Socialist Orientation." The participants, including Adel Haba and member of the Politburo of the Syrian Communist party M. Salibi, endorsed the proposition that "as a force of social progress and vehicle of advanced social and political trends in Afro-Asian countries, the revolutionary democrats are, objectively, allies of the Communists."[79] Nevertheless, enough was said to indicate that serious strains existed in the relations between the Communists and "revolutionary democrats" in countries such as Iraq and Syria. For example, Haba bowed to Moscow's line by referring to "present-day revolutionary democracy as a qualitatively new socio-political category" but warned that "the revolutionary democrats . . . have retained what Lenin once described as the vacillations and inconsistencies of the petty bourgeoisie."[80] In adhering to its "alliance strategy," Haba continued, the ICP would "support the positive tendencies in the program and practical activities" of the Ba'th and would attempt to resolve "any differences of opinion . . . on the basis of the PNPF Charter." The reason for this position, succinctly put by Haba, was very informative: "We have no alternative alliances."[81]

Salibi agreed with Abel Haba on the need for cooperation between the Communists and the "revolutionary democrats" and avowed that the former had "no illusions about . . . [the national] fronts as organs of power." Still, the alliance policy was worth adhering to not only because there were no alternatives but also because such fronts had the potential of developing into "genuine alliance[s] of the working people and . . . platform[s] for jointly mobilizing the masses against imperialism and for social progress."[82] Yet, Salibi also was quite explicit in calling attention to "factors complicating closer association between revolutionary democrats and Communists." He listed "the disparities in political outlook . . . , certain ideological differences, and . . . past inter-party misunderstandings, the burden of which it is difficult to eliminate overnight." Moreover, he argued that "anti-Communist elements . . . existed in all the revolutionary-democratic parties."[83]

The statements by Haba and Salibi illustrate the degree of disenchantment felt by the Iraqi and Syrian Communist parties due to their inability to persuade the ruling Ba'th party to share power with the Communists and to implement comprehensive socioeconomic reforms. It is only in the light of the frustrations, building in the period between 1975 and 1978, that the subsequent break between the ICP and the Ba'th can be seen in its proper perspective.

In their public pronouncements, as noted earlier, the leaders of these two parties continued to reiterate their desire to "strengthen the union of all [of Iraq's] patriotic forces. . . ." However, it soon became apparent that the gulf separating them had grown progressively wider. Thus, the Communists emphasized the need for cooperation "with the view to *completing* the national-democratic stage of the revolution" and expressed their preference for a national front capable of "actively participating in the major plans of development [and] in the movement toward social progress, national unity, . . . freedom, and democracy."[84] The Ba'th, in contrast, was primarily interested in "intensifying the joint struggle of the Iraqi patriots against the intrigues of imperialism, Zionism, and reaction, carrying into effect plans of economic and social development of the Iraqi republic."[85]

The report adopted by the Third Congress of the Iraqi Communist party, held in Baghdad in May 1976, summarized the organization's position on a number of problems, above all its relationship with the ruling Ba'th.[86] Generally speaking, as contrasted with the Second Congress (1970), the ICP now elected not to publicize its "ultimate goals," such as achievement of "socialism and communism" in Iraq, or its conviction that leadership in the "national-democratic revolution" belonged to it rather than the Ba'th. Instead, the 1976 report insisted that the Second Congress had "favorably assessed the achievements of the Baath Party" and had concluded that " 'the policy of patriotic cooperation and the United Front are not a passing tactic' . . . but a firm principled course of action." To be sure, the Second Congress had recognized that the task of establishing cooperation with the Ba'th was "fraught with many difficulties. . . ." In spite of that, the ICP had decided in 1970 to overcome the existing problems "as a prelude to an alliance with the Baath." Communist efforts were crowned with some success, as evidenced by the signing of "the National Action Charter and [of the] Agreement [to establish] . . . the Progressive National Patriotic Front."[87]

In the ensuing years, the 1976 report continued, the Front achieved some successes. "Foremost among . . . [them] is the Law on Autonomy for Kurdistan and suppression of the reactionary, rightist rebellion in that area." Nevertheless, the report demanded "stronger action by the Front and a firmer patriotic alliance." Specifically, the ICP requested:

(a) continued mass and Party education on the basis of the National Action Charter, which must be a common program of all patriotic forces united in the Front; the formation of specialized committees of the Front under the auspices of the Higher Committee . . . to draw up such programs, carry out the decisions adopted and implement the provisions of the National Action Charter;

(b) a greater role of the Front in the political life of the country and in its institutions so that the Front could carry out . . . public control over the government bodies, effective participation in the drawing up and realization of the programs for economic, social and cultural development, and the creation of a climate of trust and comradely solidarity among the parties affiliated . . . [with] the Front;

(c) turning the Front into a broad and active mass body comprising all the progressive forces of our people, and spreading its various branches all over the country to ensure the broad mobilization of the people;

(d) adoption of a formula of alliance of the Front by all mass organizations, primarily the Trade Union Federation, peasant cooperatives, women's, student and other youth organizations . . .

which play the main part in translating the Front's Charter into life and in implementing its decisions;

(e) the principle of equal opportunities for all citizens and the employment of . . . personnel from all the parties of the Front . . . in the bodies, offices and institutions of the state without discrimination; . . .

(f) a common policy of the Front in the field of information for popularizing the aims of the National Action Charter . . . for strengthening the militant brotherhood and patriotic unity of the parties united in the Front, and for combating hostile reactionary propaganda, which strives to split the national ranks, sow discord and play on the sensitive relationships of the Front's forces;

(g) an end to the wrong practices toward members of our Party and other patriots, practices contradicting the laws, rights and freedoms of the citizens, for they may have negative consequences for the entire activity of the Front and for relationships within the Patriotic Alliance.[88]

(Reference was probably made to reported arrests of some hundred Iraqi Communists in January 1976.)[89] Finally, the ICP also challenged the Ba'thist policy in Kurdistan. The report noted that, after the elimination of "the reactionary armed rebellion" in 1975, "better objective possibilities for a peaceful and democratic solution of the Kurdish problem" had been created but were not being used by the Ba'th.[90]

The 1976 report has been quoted at length because it presented both a frontal attack on the Ba'th as well as an open challenge to its undisputed authority. As such, the document reflected the true state of ICP-Ba'th relations and served as an indication that, in the Iraqi Communist opinion, the authorities were using the Marxist organization to advance their own goals. The only course of action available to the ICP was to bring matters to a head and hopefully to force the Ba'th into making concessions. This is not to say that in openly voicing its position the ICP had declared "war" against the Ba'th. On the contrary, the hoped-for concessions to the Communist party were envisaged within a collaborative framework. Thus, in a declaration issued at the conclusion of a plenary session of the ICP Central Committee in February 1977, the party reiterated its insistence on "rallying the forces belonging to the . . . Front . . . , deepening national unity, transforming the Front into an active political force, [and] overcoming the erroneous practice in the relations between the Communists and the Ba'thists." All of these steps were described as an "urgent necessity," contributing to "Iraq's march toward socialism, [and] a guarantee of frustrating hostile attacks against the republic."[91] Whatever the Communist intentions might have been, however, the Ba'th was not about to turn the other cheek. Instead, in 1977 the authorities initiated a policy of measured repression against the ICP.

In line with their stated position, the Soviets were very much in favor of the Ba'th-ICP agreement of July 1973 to promulgate the Charter of National Action and to establish cooperation within the framework of the Progressive National and Patriotic Front. The event was described by *Pravda* as a "major step on the road to the creation of the National Front" and a "great success in the cause of the [country's] progressive and democratic development." The accord was judged to be particularly important in the light of the unstable domestic situation, as reflected in the abortive coup attempted in late June and early July by Chief of Security Police Nazim Kazzar. *Pravda* argued that "internal stability based on the consolidation of all democratic forces is a vitally important condition for the implementation . . . of socioeconomic changes."[92]

In 1974 and 1975, with the Kurdish war in full swing, the Ba'th did nothing to annoy the USSR, its foreign patron, or the ICP, its principal domestic ally. On the contrary, in March 1974, three members of the ICP Central Committee were appointed to the Secretariat of the National Front, and both Communists kept their jobs in the cabinet reshuffle announced on November 11.[93] The Soviets were pleased. In a March 1974 telegram to the ICP, the CPSU Central Committee acknowledged that the Iraqi Communist party had "emerged . . . as an important national force" and had become an "integral part of [Iraq's] national-democratic movement." Together with the Ba'th, the message said, the ICP was now engaged in an "active struggle against imperialism and reaction, for the strengthening of national independence and social progress of the Iraqi Republic."[94]

In retrospect, there can be no doubt about the importance which the USSR attached to the continuous strengthening of the National Front. On November 13, 1974, at a Kremlin ceremony, Aziz Mohammed was awarded the Order of Friendship Among Nations. Judging by President Nikolai Podgorny's statement, one of the subjects discussed by the Soviet leaders and the visiting ICP delegation was the future of the National Front. Podgorny praised the Iraqi Communist efforts on its behalf and said that the creation of the Front "marks the birth of a new sociopolitical force which can become one of the main guarantees of the strength of Iraq's national independence [and] of the success . . . of national-democratic transformations."[95]

One of the themes which emerged prior to the end of the Kurdish war and which was widely used by the Ba'thi, ICP, and Soviet sources was summarized in a statement by Amir Abdallah, then a Communist cabinet member. Commenting on the "growing viability" of the Front, he reiterated the ICP's determination to strengthen the cooperation between Iraq's main political parties and went on to say: "Our colleagues from the Ba'th party say that the creation of the National Front is not a tactical but a strategic step. Agreeing with them, we emphasize that by cooperating within the framework of the Front we must set an example for others," above all the Kurds. *Pravda* concurred.[96]

The next three years—the period between the end of the Kurdish war in 1975 and the crackdown on the Marxist organization in 1978—were marked by growing tension between the Ba'th and the ICP. Initially, the Soviets attempted to minimize these differences. Indicative of Moscow's efforts was selective coverage of the relevant events and pronouncements by the Iraqi political leaders. For example, *Pravda* was pleased to report that, at a National Front meeting of June 1975, Saddam Hussein spoke of the Ba'th's determination to "strengthen the alliance of all of . . . [Iraq's] progressive forces."[97] For its part, Moscow praised the Ba'th and the ICP for their willingness to cooperate and, in line with its earlier stand, described the creation of the National Front as the "greatest achievement of the Iraqi revolution."[98] Likewise, Soviet coverage of the ICP's Third Congress omitted criticism of the Ba'th, contained in the Congress report. Instead, *Pravda* published excerpts from the speech by Aziz Mohammed who hailed the Front as the "most important event in the life of Iraq. . . ." The ICP, he went on to say, would "do everything in its power to deepen cooperation with the Ba'th party . . . with the view to preparing the necessary conditions for the victorious march toward socialism."[99]

Nevertheless, Moscow could not indefinitely ignore the growing rift between the Ba'th and the ICP. In early 1976, the Soviet press published the statements by the Iraqi Communist and Ba'thi representatives attending the Twenty-fifth Congress of the CPSU, held in February and March 1976. While both Aziz Mohammed and RCC member Zayd Haydar agreed that Iraq should become a "socialist country," their speeches attested to far-reaching differences dividing their respective organizations. Thus, Zayd Haydar spoke of the need to establish an "up-to-date industry and developed economy" and to "construct . . . a democratic, socialist society." He also said that major steps in that general direction had already been taken—"unity of the people has been achieved along with the unity of its progressive forces within the framework of the . . . National Front and the [National] Charter. . . ." Speaking for the ICP, Aziz Mohammed confirmed that "alliance with the Ba'th . . . and other progressive national forces" remained the "basis of . . . [the party's] policy." He went on to say that the Communists were determined "to strengthen this alliance" in order to complete the "national-democratic stage of the revolution" and move on to "socialism." He added, however, that, to achieve these goals, it was necessary for the National Front "to become a mass movement, so that the participation of the masses in the political, economic, and public life in the conditions of democratic liberties should be strengthened, as was invisaged in the National Charter."[100] The clear implication was that these conditions had not been met.

Indications of strained relations appeared also in subsequent statements by the two parties. In May 1976, in separate interviews with a *Pravda* correspondent, both Tariq Aziz (then minister of information and member of the RCC) and Aziz Mohammed spoke of the "long-range nature" of cooperation between the Ba'th and the Iraqi Communist party but warned of "certain complications" in their relationships.[101] In February 1977 the ICP used the antigovernment disturbances in the predominantly Shi'i Najaf province[102] to express its support of the Ba'th. However, the Central Committee meeting of February 18 also restated its conviction that "to rally the forces belonging to the National . . . Front, to deepen national unity, to transform the Front into an active political force, to overcome the erroneous practices in the relations between the Communists and the Ba'thists is an urgent necessity and an important condition of Iraq's march toward socialism."[103] In reporting these disquieting developments, *Pravda* offered no editorial comment.

The situation that the Soviets faced in Iraq in the mid-1970s was, in many ways, a familiar one: they could not entirely ignore the complaints of fellow Marxists but were equally determined not to antagonize the ruling Ba'th whose continued anti-Americanism and cooperation with the USSR were important in the context of the Kremlin's Middle Eastern and Third World policies. Caught on the horns of this dilemma, Moscow once again responded by engaging in a balancing act. On the one hand, the Soviets publicly praised both parties, above all their efforts at cooperation in the National Front, as well as the Front itself.[104] On the other hand, the USSR exerted pressure on both the ICP and the Ba'th to reach a practical compromise. Since, in the Iraqi context, it was the Communist party that was openly urging the authorities to modify their rigid stand and to grant the ICP a role in governing the country, the Kremlin had no choice but to address itself to these demands. It did so by means of strong public endorsements of Iraq's Marxist organization[105] and of unusually frequent high-level contacts between the CPSU and the ICP.

Two Iraqi Communist delegations visited Moscow in 1975, and one in 1976 and 1977. The first, headed by Politburo member Zaki Khayri, stayed between June 7 and 21, 1975; the other three were led by First Secretary Aziz Mohammed. On two of these occasions (December 1975 and December 1977) the Iraqis were received by Mikhail Suslov—an indication of the importance which the Kremlin attached to the negotiations—while in October 1976, the Soviet side was represented by Boris Ponomarev.[106] It is likely that relations between the ICP and the Ba'th or, more precisely, the nature of the problems impairing their cooperation in the National Front, was one of the top items on the agenda. It appears equally certain that the Kremlin tried hard to persuade Iraq's Communist leaders to be more flexible in their dealings with the ruling party. If these assumptions are correct, the Soviet side was not entirely successful for, as shown, in 1976 and 1977, the ICP intensified its public pressure for a more meaningful participation in the political life of Iraq.

In a parallel effort the Kremlin attempted to persuade the Ba'th to be more forthcoming in its relations with the Communist party. In his June 1, 1976, speech on Iraqi television, Kosygin clearly implied that the country's future depended on the viability of the National Front and that, for it to become effective, the role which the ICP was permitted to play in Iraqi politics had to be upgraded:

> Concern for the well-being of the country and for its future has united the democratic forces of Iraq in the Progressive National-Patriotic Front. The [Ba'th] party . . . , the ICP, and other patriotic forces which have joined the . . . Front direct their efforts at advancing . . . the cause of social progress, raising the economy and culture of the country, struggling against the intrigues of imperialism, Zionism, and reaction, and [assuring] broader . . . participation of the masses in public activity.[107]

Similar sentiments were again expressed by Kosygin in a speech delivered during Saddam Hussein's 1977 visit to Moscow. It is noteworthy, however, that on that occasion the not too subtle Soviet pressure was publicly rebuked by the Iraqi leader. During his previous trips to the

USSR, Saddam Hussein had refrained from mentioning the National Front. This time he did so and left no doubt about the Ba'th's stand on this matter. Specifically, he alluded to efforts to strengthen Iraq's independence, "socialist experience, . . . [and] our *internal* National Front." He also reiterated Baghdad's commitment to "securing democracy for the broad popular masses. . . ." Saddam Hussein then went on to say, however, that these goals would be achieved *"under the leadership of the Ba'th party, and with the support of all progressive forces of the country."*[108] The unmistakable implication was that "forces" opposed to the Ba'th's preeminence in Iraqi politics would not be regarded as "progressive." What that meant should have been clear to all concerned. The timing of the message as well as the place where Saddam Hussein chose to deliver it left no doubt that it was intended to place the Kremlin leaders on notice that Baghdad would tolerate neither Soviet nor ICP pressure to modify its position on a matter of the utmost importance to the Ba'th, namely its *exclusive* control over Iraq. Moscow had no choice but to accept the facts.

Deterioration in ICP-Ba'th Relations

As *Tariq al-Sha'b* disclosed subsequently, "persecution of the Communists in Iraq [as well as] repression of the ICP affiliates and the press" were instituted by the Ba'thi authorities in the fall of 1977.[109] The party's initial reaction was mixed. On the one hand, the ICP stepped up its criticism of the Ba'th: economic relations with the outside world were devoid of ideological underpinnings (as demonstrated by fifteen-fold increase in trade with the United States in the period between 1965 and 1975); political and economic cooperation with imperial Iran and the conservative Arab monarchies was on the rise; and relations with the USSR, the "strategic ally," were on the decline.[110] On the other hand, with respect to the government's mounting anti-Communist campaign, the ICP reaction was rather mild—the party may have hoped that relative restraint would persuade the Ba'th of the genuineness of the Communist offers of collaboration. For instance, the report on the party's March 1978 Central Committee meeting complained that the ICP had been "subjected to various forms of discrimination and persecution during 1977 and that this has negatively affected the activity of the Front and the popular masses." The report went on to say that "these negative phenomena" served only to "encourage the reactionary forces" and called upon the Ba'th to adopt "vigorous measures . . . to strengthen the unity of . . . [the] people." As for the ICP, it remained committed to "the consolidation of relations between . . . [itself], the Baath Party and other national forces, [and to] elimination of disagreements between them. . . ."[111]

ICP moderation proved of no avail. In the spring of 1978 the government accused the Communists of "subservience to Moscow"—a clear indication that Soviet-Iraqi relations were on the decline—as well as of "royalist attitudes." The meaning of the latter term was explained in the following manner: the ICP was "raising questions and . . . [presenting] demands which could not be met under the prevailing circumstances, with the object of embarrassing the revolution."[112] This was a different way of saying that the Communists were challenging the leadership of the ruling party. On May 28, 1978, al-Thawrah pointedly reminded the non-Ba'thist members of the National Front that they had been strictly forbidden to infiltrate Iraq's armed forces and that any violation of this rule would result in the execution of the offenders.[113]

As rumors of the execution of a number of Communists began to spread,[114] Tariq al-Sha'b, on June 6, published a long lead article, "For Stronger Confidence and Closer Relations of Alliance Between the Parties of the Progressive Patriotic and National Front." It lavishly praised the Front ("an outstanding revolutionary gain of our people . . .") and reiterated the ICP's "commitment to safeguarding and developing this progressive alliance."[115] Tariq al-Sha'b flatly denied the charge that the Communist party had "use[d] the Front . . . as a means to take over power through treachery and by stabbing its allies in the back." On the contrary, the ICP participated "in disclosing and foiling a series of . . . conspiracies aimed at the power of the Baath Party even before the establishment of the Front" and had helped "counter the reactionary rebellion in Kurdistan."[116] In closing, Tariq al-Sha'b called on the authorities to abide by the National Charter which stipulated that differences between the Front members were "to be dealt with by the method of democratic discussions in order to rectify mistakes through constructive criticism . . . in the interests of maintaining and consolidating the alliance."[117]

The Ba'thi rebuke was delivered on June 7 (one day after the publication of the article in Tariq al-Sha'b) by Naim Haddad. The secretary general of the PNPF announced the execution, in May, of twenty-one members of the Iraqi Communist party. He said that all of them were military men who, in the period between 1975 and 1978, had been found guilty of "forming secret groups inside the Iraqi armed forces." In justifying the harshness of the measure, Haddad repeated the arguments advanced by *al-Thawrah* on May 28: the National Charter stipulated that political activity inside the armed forces was reserved exclusively for the Ba'th party. He added that executions were designed to "deter others from trying to organize political activity in the armed forces" and not to destroy the ICP.[118]

As the purges and arrests continued, *Tariq al-Sha'b* mounted another attack against the Ba'th. The editorial of November 21, 1978, reiterated the need of cooperation between Iraq's "progressive parties and organizations" at a time when a "major effort was underway to undermine the National Front by driving a wedge between its two major partners. . . ." However, while the ICP, aware of the implications of such a rift, was said to have gone out of its way to prevent further deterioration of relations with the Ba'th, the latter persevered in repressing the "progressive elements." As a result, *Tariq al-Sha'b* concluded, the "gains [made by] the revolutionary movement in Iraq" had suffered "great damage."

Undeterred by ICP protests, the authorities ordered a new wave of arrests and executions. Among those detained was Majid Abd al-Rida, member of the ICP's Central Committee. On January 15, 1979, Voice of Lebanon, quoting Iraqi Communist sources, reported that thirty more Communists had been executed two days earlier.[119] The beleagured Marxist organization, according to Kuwait's *al-Watan*, boycotted the January 29 meeting of the National Front. The move was reportedly ordered when executions of party members in Iraq's armed forces were followed by arrests of civilian Communists and by "general harassment" of ICP activities. Summarizing the results of the government crackdown, *Le Monde* quoted "sources close to the ICP" as saying, on February 23, that "over 1,900 militant members and sympathizers of the . . . Party have 'disappeared' since 1 January."[120]

Indicative of Communist desperation was a public appeal by Nazihah Dulaymi, published in the *World Marxist Review* in March 1979. It stated that, in spite of "unwarranted charges . . . , the scale of persecutions, and the bitterness and anguish caused by the executions," the Iraqi Communist party "publicly declared its firm adherence to the course it had chartered at its Third Congress. . . ." Nevertheless, "the savage repressions and persecution against the ICP . . . continue." Specifically, Dulaymi charged that, since May 1978, "more than 10,000 persons have been arrested and subjected to physical and mental torture" in violation "even . . . [of] the undemocratic laws passed during the last three years." Concluding, she called on "the fraternal Communist and workers' parties . . . [to] upgrade the solidarity campaign, demanding an immediate end to the repressions against Communists and their friends in Iraq."[121] In the meantime, the ICP leaders left the country, and the party "froze" its membership in the National Front.[122]

Speaking for the authorities, Naim Haddad announced the arrest of twenty-seven more militiamen belonging to the ICP. The action was made necessary by the Communists' "duplicity": they maintained the appearance of collaborating with the Ba'th but continued to work "behind . . . [its] back." In early April 1979 the government suspended *Tariq al-Sha'b* for publishing a reply to a National Front statement criticizing the ICP, and on April 10 *al-Thawrah* attacked the Communists for "attempting to create ideological diversions in Iraq. . . ."[123] Later in the month Haddad called upon the Communists "to make up . . . [their] minds whether to pull out formally from the . . . Front or return to it on the Baath Party's terms." According to Haddad's April 22 statement, representatives of the two organizations held a meeting during which the Ba'th reportedly urged the ICP to reconsider its position. Moreover, Mukarram al-Talabani, the sole remaining Communist member of the cabinet, was dispatched to Moscow to appraise the self-exiled ICP leaders of the Ba'th's desire to resume cooperation and to urge them to return to Baghdad.[124] His mission ended in failure: on May 5, Talabani was ousted from his post as minister of transportation. As a result, the cabinet was left without Communist representation.[125]

On May 28, 1979, the ICP Central Committee, meeting in Beirut, issued a statement urging the creation of a new "democratic front" and of a coalition government in which "all the national parties and forces, including Arabs, Kurds and other minorities" would participate on an equal footing.[126] As might have been expected, the Ba'th had no intention of complying with these demands. The break between the two organizations was finalized on July 11, when the National Front, in an official statement, accused the "leaders of the Iraqi Communist Party . . . of acting as agents of Israel and the United States."[127]

ICP reaction to the events of the preceding two years was contained in a report of the party's Central Committee, adopted in late July 1979. Because it represented a thorough analysis of the differences dividing the Communist party and the Ba'th, the document deserves to be considered in detail.[128] First, the Central Committee noted that, since its last plenary meeting of March 1978, there had taken place "a serious reversal in the policy of the Iraqi regime." Before that date, the Ba'th's internal policy had exhibited occasional "negative streaks within a generally progressive line." Since then, the situation had grown progressively worse: in an attempt to impose "one-party rule" on Iraq, the Ba'th "crippled and then totally wrecked" the National Front. Occasional meetings of its Higher Committee were held "not for discussing and tackling essential problems . . . , but in order to listen to some measures taken by the top level of power." The Secretariat occasionally occupied itself "with the complaints . . . [of] the victims of persecution," but its limited efforts produced no results.[129]

The emasculation of the National Front was but one manifestation of the Ba'thist determination to monopolize "all legislative, executive and judicial powers [held] by the Revolutionary Command Council." Other measures included the intensification of the anti-Communist and anti-"national democrat" campaigns, highlighted by "the execution of 31 military and civilian Communists . . . in May 1978"; the continued "Baathization of the state organs, the social organizations, the education system and culture . . ."; and the adoption of a "chauvinist stand" on the problem of national minorities, evident particularly in Kurdistan.[130]

In analyzing Iraq's foreign policy, the ICP accused the government of softness on "Israeli aggression," the Camp David accords, and the Egyptian-Israeli peace treaty. In offering only "minimum resistance" to these initiatives, the Ba'th had bowed to the will of the "imperialist" powers and of the "reactionary [Arab] regimes," led by Saudi Arabia. At the same time, the authorities thought nothing of "provok[ing] a deliberate quarrel with the Iranian revolution" or displaying hostility toward "progressive" Afghanistan, Ethiopia, and the PDRY. In the world arena the Iraqi Ba'th equated "U.S. imperialism—enemy of the peoples, . . . [with] the Soviet Union—the faithful friend and staunch ally of the Arabs." The ICP also criticized Iraqi purchases of military equipment from the Western countries.[131]

After rejecting the main planks of the Ba'th's domestic and foreign policies, the ICP advanced its own "democratic alternatives." High on its list of priorities remained the creation of a "democratic national front." Embracing "the people and all the opposition parties and forces," it was to be "democratic in form and content." This signified, in part, that it would "consist of ideologically, politically and organizationally independent parties, organizations and forces." It also meant that the Front's decisions would be "taken unanimously." Members would enjoy "the right of criticism" and "any disagreements between them [would be solved] by democratic means." In conclusion, the ICP called for a "revolutionary struggle . . . by the broadest masses of the people . . . to end the [Ba'thist] dictatorship."[132] Among the purposes of the struggle, the ICP listed the following: "democratization" of Iraq's political life;

"an end to the state of emergency . . . ; transforming the army into a democratic institution" (meaning freedom of Communist activity in the armed forces); "a peaceful, democratic solution to the Kurdish question . . . ; the adoption of scientific planning" in the Iraqi economy; "safeguarding and developing the gains of the working class and the peasantry . . . ; effective contribution to the Arab nation's fight against imperialism, Zionism and reaction . . . ; closer militant solidarity between the Arab peoples . . . ; [and] an independent foreign policy based on . . . cooperation with the Soviet Union."[133]

Thus, by mid-1979, the Iraqi Communist party was driven underground and ceased to be an important factor in Iraqi politics. Hundreds of its members had been executed and thousands more had been jailed. Most party leaders escaped and found refuge in the USSR. Occasionally, they held meetings, participated in conferences, and issued proclamations, thus maintaining some visibility in the international Communist circles. In those troubled times the ICP enjoyed Soviet moral and no doubt material support. Nevertheless, it lost much of its native base and has remained a party in exile.

An early sign of Moscow's displeasure with the Ba'th appeared in February 1977, when the ICP appeal to the ruling party "to overcome the erroneous practices in [their] relations" was published not in the World Marxist Review (let alone its Information Bulletin) but in Pravda.[134] It is important to reiterate, however, that, in 1977, when the authorities unfolded their anti-Communist campaign or later, the USSR showed no inclination of breaking with Iraq. On the contrary, for more than a year Soviet publications paid little attention to the plight of the ICP. Instead, the Soviet press addressed the topics of Iraqi Communist calls for improvement in Moscow-Baghdad relations (the "strategic alliance" theme);[135] ICP insistence on playing a major role in Iraqi politics;[136] and ICP praise of the USSR and its manifold achievements.[137]

On March 14, 1978, the ICP Central Committee, for the first time since the early 1970s, publicly complained against government discrimination and "other violations" against the party members. In commenting on the Central Committee session, Pravda declared that the Communists continued to adhere to the principle of "solidarity of all [of Iraq's] progressive and democratic forces" and remained convinced that "serious efforts must be made to strengthen the unity of the Iraqi people."[138] It was not easy to gather from Pravda's account that relations between the ICP and the Ba'th were rapidly approaching a breaking point. Subsequently, the Soviet media passed in silence the ICP report of March 1978 and the early May campaign in the Iraqi press accusing the

Communists of "subservience to Moscow" and of "royalist" attitudes.[139]

If the Kremlin's reserve was prompted by expectation that the differences between the two parties would somehow be smoothed over, Soviet hopes were dashed in late May 1978, when it was announced that a
number of Iraqi Communists had been executed. The USSR reacted
with unaccustomed caution: only on June 18, that is after a delay of two
weeks, did *Pravda* reproduce, without commentary, lengthy excerpts
from the editorial which appeared in *Tariq al-Sha'b* on June 6.[140] Public
acknowledgment of the executions was delayed until the Soviets had an
opportunity to consult with the Ba'thist leaders. This was accomplished by means of a hurried visit to Baghdad by roving ambassador
Leonid Mendelevich. He arrived on June 3, reportedly at Iraq's invitation, and, accompanied by Ambassador Anatolii Barkovskii, held several meetings with high officials, including Saddam Hussein.[141] It may
be safely assumed that the Ba'thi-ICP conflict as well as its impact on
Iraqi-Soviet relations were among the subjects discussed and that Moscow strongly urged Baghdad to cease the persecution of the Communist
party members. If these suppositions are correct, the Kremlin's pressure
not only failed to produce the desired results but actually precipitated a
public warning to stay out of Iraqi affairs. This point was illustrated by
the exchange between the Syrian and Iraqi branches of the Ba'th party.
In an obvious attempt to embarrass Baghdad, Syrian Foreign Minister
Abd al-Halim Khaddam observed on June 6 that Soviet-Iraqi relations
had never been worse and that Iraq was about to expel its Russian
advisers and to abrogate the 1972 treaty with the USSR. His statement
prompted a public rebuke by Naim Haddad. On June 7 the secretary-
general of the PNPF dismissed Damascus' "vulgar insinuation" and said
that Iraq continued to regard Moscow as a "strategic ally" and a "friend
with whom we can cooperate, *provided there is no intervention in our
internal affairs.*"[142] Judging by subsequent Iraqi comments, this warning was not heeded by the Soviet government. Information Minister
Saad Kassem Hammudi's statement that, in Iraq, the Communists had
"much greater opportunity for freedom of action" than Marxists "in
their own countries" and that no "crocodile tears" should be shed for
them, allows no other conclusion.[143]

Diplomacy aside, the Soviet media said nothing about the persecution of the Iraqi Communist party in May or June of 1978. In the long
run, however, given the magnitude of Baghdad's "provocations," Moscow could not remain totally silent, and criticism of the Ba'thi authorities was finally voiced in July 1978. One example of the toughening

Soviet stance was provided by Pavel Demchenko's commentary on the twentieth anniversary of the Iraqi revolution. In reviewing the history of the republic, Demchenko observed that Iraq "developed most successfully in periods when its national-patriotic forces were acting together." In contrast, "when the Patriotic Front disintegrated [and] the struggle among . . . [its] participants intensified, . . . failure was inevitable." Hence, the main task facing Iraq's "progressive forces" was to make the Front work. Demchenko admitted that "it would be wrong to ignore the difficulties emerging in the activity of the Front," but agreed with *Tariq al-Sha'b* that conflicts among allies must be resolved "by means of a discussion on a democratic basis, of correction of errors through friendly criticism and self-criticism."[144] Demchenko's article appeared during the visit to the USSR of an ICP delegation, headed by the first secretary of the party's Baghdad Regional Committee,[145] and was thus probably intended both to offer the beleaguered Communists some public support and, after some two months, finally to voice the Kremlin's concern about the turn of events in Iraq. Nevertheless, Demchenko's reference to "fruitfulness" of Soviet-Iraqi cooperation served as an indication that despite the persecution of the ICP and a general deterioration of Moscow-Baghdad relations, the Kremlin remained determined to avoid an open break with Iraq.

Another lengthy article, appearing in the July 1978 issue of *Aziia i Afrika segodnia*, came close to an open condemnation of the Ba'th. Like Demchenko, its author P. Pak spoke approvingly of the ICP's insistence that "controversial" positions of the Front members be discussed, and problems be resolved, in a "business-like, constructive" fashion. He also noted that the Iraqi Communists regarded their association with the Ba'th as a "strategic alliance" which was not limited to the "resolution of the tasks of the national-democratic stage of the revolution" but was also intended to serve as a basis of cooperation in "constructing socialism."[146]

Pak blamed "imperialist and local reactionary circles" for aggravating relations between the ICP and the Ba'th. He also found these "circles" guilty of attempts to "undermine and destroy" the National Front by "sowing doubts about . . . [the members'] readiness to carry out obligations undertaken under the terms of the National Charter." These anti-Front intrigues made it imperative for its members "thoroughly to weigh . . . their steps, to widen the sphere and to raise the level of interaction and cooperation." Pak warned the Ba'th that the "effectiveness of the Front can be guaranteed only if its positive essence is preserved, if a decisive rebuke is handed to the efforts by international and internal reaction to drive a wedge between the national progressive parties. . . ."[147]

Another glimpse at the Kremlin's displeasure was provided by the text of the obligatory telegram, congratulating President Bakr on the anniversary of the Iraqi revolution. In previous years the signatories included the Presidium of the Supreme Soviet, the Council of Ministers, and the CPSU Central Committee. In July 1978 the list was shortened by omitting the party. The contents of the message, however, were rather similar to those preceding it and included a reference to the "important role" played by the National Front "in the struggle against imperialist intrigues." The cooling of relations between Moscow and Baghdad was also reflected in Bakr's reply—although couched in familiar terms, it made no reference to the Front.[148] But the Ba'th's real attitude was revealed with unusual candor by Saddam Hussein. In an interview with *Newsweek*'s Arnaud de Borchgrave, the Iraqi leader insisted that those executed in May were put to death "not because they were Communists but because they tried to subvert the state." Turning to the USSR, Saddam Hussein made a statement that would have been unthinkable at any other time after the 1968 revolution: "The Soviets won't be satisfied until the whole world becomes Communist. They believe their most effective means for changing the world to their advantage is with arms."[149] A few days later, Saddam Hussein issued an explicit warning: "No country, whether friend or enemy, can decide Iraqi policy."[150]

Whatever the merits of Saddam Hussein's arguments, Moscow must have been shocked by the bluntness of his statements—they were designed to place everybody on notice that Soviet-Iraqi relations had in fact reached a new low. It is revealing, however, that the Kremlin chose neither to reply to Saddam Hussein nor, for the time being, to react publicly to the continuing plight of the ICP or to the sharp deterioration of Soviet-Iraqi relations. Even the November 21 *Tariq al-Sha'b* editorial, which protested against the government's "atrocities" and complained that "nothing had been done to end them,"[151] was not reproduced in the Soviet press until January 10, 1979. By then, a suitable period of time had elapsed since the conclusion of the visits to the USSR of high Iraqi military and civilian delegations in late 1978.

As Moscow kept its silence, however, Baghdad abruptly changed its tune. On October 17 Saddam Hussein declared that the USSR was Iraq's "best friend." The Ba'thist leader admitted that differences between them remained and cited "Eritrea's conflict with [pro-Soviet] Ethiopia" as an example of his contention. He went on to say, however, that the

Kremlin "always sides with the Arabs" and that the latter should there-fore "act accordingly."[152]

In the wake of Baghdad's conciliatory gesture, Defense Minister Ad-nan Khayrallah and Saddam Hussein visited Moscow in November and December 1978, respectively.[153] Saddam Hussein was received by Sec-retary-General Leonid Brezhnev—an indication of the importance which the Kremlin attached to his visit—and signed two agreements on continued economic and technical cooperation between Iraq and the USSR. In the joint communiqué the parties condemned Washington's peace initiatives in the Middle East and appealed for "unity of all forces in the Arab world opposed to the policy of capitulation." They also announced that the Kremlin agreed "to strengthen Iraq's defensive ca-pabilities." It is equally noteworthy that in his speech honoring Saddam Hussein, Kosygin stated that Soviet-Iraqi cooperation transcended "mo-mentary ups and downs" and, for the first time on such occasions, made no reference to the National Front.[154] Moreover, on January 10, 1979, the very day *Pravda* reproduced *Tariq al-Sha'b*'s lament of November 21, 1978, Moscow's Radio Peace and Progress program in Arabic warned that continued persecution of Iraqi Communists could create "suitable circumstances for the domination by reaction" but did not directly criticize the Ba'th.[155]

Similar circumspection marked also an important article by Iurii Zhukov, one of *Pravda*'s leading political commentators. During his February 1979 visit to Iraq, Zhukov interviewed several Ba'thist and ICP functionaries. According to his account, both parties continued to advo-cate cooperation, despite the fact that "there appeared regrettable dan-ger signs . . . [pointing to] the weakening of the united front." Zhukov did not dwell on the reasons for this state of affairs but urged the Ba'th and the ICP to settle their differences: "The guarantee of success of the progressive forces lies in their unity. . . . Any weakening of this unity is fraught with dangerous consequences, playing into the hands of the imperialists [who] strive to separate the progressive forces in order to strike at them one at a time."[156]

In March 1979 the CPSU Central Committee congratulated the Iraqi Communist party on its forty-fifth anniversary. The telegram spoke glowingly of the ICP's accomplishments: "Your party . . . has made an important contribution to [Iraq's] independence and progress. The . . . long struggle of the Communist party for the freedom of the mother-land and the happiness of the people has guaranteed it . . . respect of the . . . [toiling] masses." Otherwise, given the continuing efforts by the "imperialist and reactionary" elements, the CPSU continued to advocate "unity of action" among the various "progressive" parties of the Middle East.[157]

In short, in 1978 and 1979 Soviet sympathies were clearly on the side of the hard-pressed Marxists.[158] However, in no instance did the Kremlin actually condemn the Iraqi Ba'th for persecuting the Communists. Moscow's unwillingness to attack Baghdad directly, even after a public ICP appeal for Soviet support,[159] can be attributed to several important considerations. First, attempts undertaken in 1978 to intervene on behalf of the ICP not only did not produce the desired results but led also to an open denunciation of the Soviet Union by high Ba'thist functionaries, including Saddam Hussein. Second, and as a partial consequence of the first, relations between the USSR and Iraq had reached a new low, reducing the Kremlin's leverage in Baghdad to an inconsequential level. Third, and most important, Moscow's uncharacteristic reticence in the face of Iraqi "provocations" as well as Saddam Hussein's about-face of October 1978 can be attributed to the dramatic events unfolding in the Middle East, that is, to Egyptian President Anwar Sadat's November 1977 journey to Jerusalem and to the subsequent attempts by the Carter administration to resolve the Arab-Israeli impasse by means of the so-called Camp David process. Because Iraq was playing an important part in the Arab efforts to prevent the signing of a peace treaty between Egypt and Israel, the USSR—a leading opponent of Washington's diplomatic initiative—chose not to antagonize Baghdad at this crucial juncture. Not only that, the Kremlin was actively seeking Iraq's cooperation, as evidenced by a flurry of high-level consultations and by the signing of economic and military aid agreements. For its part, Iraq, too, recognized the importance of Soviet backing of the Arab position and, brushing aside its earlier reservations, chose to normalize relations with the USSR. The relative calm did not last: after the Russian move into Afghanistan in December 1979, Baghdad reemerged as one of Moscow's most outspoken critics in the Arab world.

A scathing indictment of the Ba'th as well as of the Soviet government's passivity in the face of the wholesale destruction of the ICP did not appear in the Soviet press until 1990. An article in *Argumenty i fakty* explained the Ba'th's decision to secure Communist cooperation in terms of the necessity to subdue the Kurds.[160] Having solved that problem, however, the authorities subjected the ICP to "most cruel repressions." By the late 1970s "thousands of Communists, who were declared traitors, were destroyed." The bloodletting in Iraq could be compared only with analogous events which had taken place in Indonesia in 1965 and in Chile in 1973.

Evaluation

The main political objective of the Iraqi branch of the Ba'th after the seizure of power in July 1968 has been to maintain itself in the position of undisputed authority. With this in mind, the Ba'thi leaders have worked hard to keep Iraq's other political parties in a subordinate position. Among other parties were the Kurdistan Democratic party, the Iraqi Communist party, and, after the Iranian revolution, *al-Dawah al-Islamiyyah* (Islamic Call), a militant underground organization of Iraq's large Shi'i community. All three were eventually suppressed by the authorities. A civil war was fought against the Kurds, while the ICP as well as *al-Dawah* were subjected to severe government persecution. As a result, by the early 1980s the effectiveness of all three groups was significantly reduced.

In the particular case of the Iraqi Communist party, it will be recalled that the Ba'th traditionally mistrusted and disliked the pro-Soviet Marxists, an attitude that resulted in a major crackdown on the ICP during the Ba'thist rule of 1963. In contrast, after the 1968 coup, initial hesitancy was followed by concerted government efforts to secure Communist cooperation and support. In retrospect, it is obvious that the Ba'thi position was dictated not by a major change of heart but by realization that achievement of two major internal objectives—nationalization of the oil industry and the "resolution" of the Kurdish problem—depended on the good will and cooperation of the USSR as well as of the ICP. (Given the Ba'th's pronounced anti-Westernism, the Soviets were the logical source of military, economic, and political support.) Because the Kremlin had long expressed concern about the fortunes of Iraq's Marxist organization, the Ba'thi leaders understood that Moscow's willingness to extend support depended, in part, on their treatment of the Iraqi Communist party. In addition, the Ba'th had learned from the mistakes committed in 1963. A crackdown on the ICP had not only deprived the government of Marxist support but also antagonized other left-wing groupings (among them the National Democratic party). Efforts at post-1968 collaboration with the Communists reflected this lesson. Finally, the ruling party was aware that it would be easier to watch the ICP within the framework of a Ba'th-controlled coalition than to have it serve as a disgruntled opposition.

Although the Kremlin was not indifferent to the fate of the ICP, on the scale of Soviet priorities, the party's fortunes were, of necessity, of secondary importance.[161] Of primary significance were the growing anti-Westernism of the Ba'th accompanied by moves to improve relations with the USSR and the introduction of "progressive" socioeconomic reforms at home. To encourage these "positive" trends, Moscow became engaged in a complex effort of applying pressure on all the major actors on Iraq's political scene: the Ba'th, the ICP, and the KDP. The former was urged to show more leniency toward the Kurds and the Communists, while the latter two were encouraged to support the "progressive tendencies" displayed by the ruling party. Initially, these Soviet efforts appeared to be paying off. As noted in chapter 3, Baghdad accommodated some of the Kurdish demands by means of the March 1970 autonomy decree. The authorities also moderated their attitude toward the Iraqi Communist party by releasing many imprisoned Communists, by promulgating the National Charter, by legitimizing the ICP, and by incorporating some of its members into the Iraqi cabinet.

However, outward cooperation did not conceal a major divergence of views between the ruling Ba'th and the ICP. The former never wavered in its insistence on monopolizing power, while the Communists were equally determined to share it. Nevertheless, in the early 1970s, when Soviet influence in Baghdad had reached its peak, the two parties temporarily buried the hatchet and it may be assumed that their relative affability owed much to Moscow's pressure.

In the end, in contrast, the Kremlin failed in its efforts to reconcile the Ba'th with its Kurdish and Communist counterparts (chapter 3). As tension between the government and the ICP continued to grow after 1975, the USSR, outwardly, remained aloof. However, there were indications of Soviet pressure on both Iraqi parties to reach a compromise, although the Kremlin's efforts at influencing their respective attitudes fell short of the mark. In the latter 1970s, due to vastly increased oil revenues, Baghdad was no longer dependent on exclusive Soviet support.

In the spring of 1978, when the ruling Ba'th announced the execution of twenty-one Communists, Moscow dispatched a high foreign ministry official to Baghdad. It may be safely assumed that one of the purposes of his visit was to persuade the Ba'thi authorities to stop the anti-Communist campaign. The effort failed. Baghdad continued to accuse the Iraqi Communist party of "subservience to the Soviet Union" and, in so doing, challenged not only the ICP but the USSR itself: the Kremlin was warned to stay out of Iraqi politics. In short, the Soviets attempted and failed to exert influence on behalf of the ICP. As a result, Soviet-Iraqi relations hit the lowest point of the post-1968 period, but, significantly, there was no break between Moscow and Baghdad. The circumspection with which the USSR treated Iraq was due, in part, to the prominent role the latter was playing in the Arab campaign to isolate Egypt in the wake of the Camp David accords—another indication that, to the Kremlin, state-to-state relations were more important than the fate of a Third World communist party.

■ Part Two   *Regional Problems*

5 The Persian Gulf, 1968–1975: Problems of Security and Stability

During his November 1967 visit to the Gulf, Minister of State at the Foreign Office Goronwy Roberts had assured Mohammed Reza Shah that Great Britain would not eliminate its military presence in the Persian Gulf before 1975.[1] It therefore came as a considerable surprise when Prime Minister Harold Wilson announced, on January 16, 1968, that "all British forces in the Far East (except Hong Kong) and the Persian Gulf were to be withdrawn by the end of 1971."[2] The mission to explain London's decision to the rulers of the Gulf states and principalities was once again entrusted to Goronwy Roberts. He was also instructed to urge the rulers to take steps to help maintain regional security and stability in the aftermath of Britain's far-reaching decision. Specifically, London suggested adoption of two separate but related measures: the creation of a regional defense pact and the establishment of a federation of smaller Arab principalities, to include Bahrain, Qatar, and the seven sheikhdoms of Trucial Oman (Abu Dhabi, Dubai, Sharjah, Ras al-Khaimah, Ajman, Umm al-Qaiwain, and Fujairah).

With respect to the first objective, Roberts advocated a regional alliance embracing Iran, Saudi Arabia, Kuwait, and the smaller Arab principalities.[3] While Tehran, even before the Wilson announcement, declared "its readiness to participate in 'any form of regional cooperation for the defense of the area,' "[4] the Arab states showed no interest in the British initiative. Before anything else happened, however, U.S. Undersecretary of State Eugene Rostow, in a Voice of America interview broadcast on January 19, expressed Washington's endorsement of a "joint [regional] defense system" built around a nucleus consisting of Turkey, Iran, Pakistan, Iraq, Saudi Arabia, and Kuwait. Its stated purpose was "to fill the vacuum left by Britain's withdrawal from the Gulf."[5]

The two proposals pursued the same objective, as London and Washington endeavored to establish a framework for regional security before the projected withdrawal of British forces from the Gulf. Given the strong anti-Western attitudes then prevalent in the United Arab Republic, Syria, and Iraq, these leading Arab states launched a major propaganda effort to discredit the British and U.S. plans. This left Saudi Arabia and Kuwait no choice but to deny "any intention of joining either a military or political pact or bloc."[6] Even Iran, which had initially offered to cooperate with the other Gulf states in ensuring the area's defense, reacted negatively to the Rostow proposal.[7] In the end, Western efforts to create a Gulf regional defense organization to compensate for the projected withdrawal of British forces accomplished nothing.

London's second objective, the creation of a federation of the Trucial Oman principalities with the view to fostering regional stability, was met on December 2, 1971, when seven sheikhdoms joined to form the United Arab Emirates (UAE). The new entity did not include either Bahrain or Qatar, which proclaimed their independence in August 1971. These events, signifying an abandonment of a three-year-long effort to establish a "maxi-federation," were something of a political setback for Great Britain, the project's main sponsor, as well as for Saudi Arabia and Kuwait, its main Arab backers. However, while not going as far as originally planned, the new entity was preferable to no union at all, as a fragmented and mutually hostile Arab lower Gulf was widely regarded as a fertile ground for subversion by radical elements, then active in neighboring Oman.[8]

Regional Security, 1968–1971

In the intricate patterns of Gulf politics of the late 1960s and early 1970s an unaccustomed harmony prevailed with respect to two major issues: the unanimous rejection of the British and American suggestions for the establishment of a pro-Western regional defense system and public insistence on the need for British military withdrawal from the area. In this regard, Iraq shared the position held by most of the other Gulf states, among them Iran, Kuwait, and Saudi Arabia. (Privately, some sheikhdoms had opposed the British departure.)

Baghdad's anti-British attitude manifested itself in the pronouncements of the Iraqi leaders and of the state-controlled media which periodically accused London of determination not to leave the Gulf. Thus, Baghdad Radio ascribed the difficulties encountered by the proposed Federation of Arab Emirates to British intrigues designed to enable London "to go back on its pledge of military evacuation by 1971."[9] In January 1971 Baghdad Radio insisted that the Conservative government had reversed the Labour's decision to withdraw from the Gulf, causing an Iraqi Foreign Ministry spokesman, on March 3, to demand a "complete liquidation of the imperialist presence" in the area.[10] Concurrently, Iraq discounted claims that a power vacuum would be created as a result of the British withdrawal. Baghdad Radio described the vacuum theory as "an absurd imperialist claim," since the Gulf region was not "a land without people and *the Arab people* are more capable than any foreign power of managing their own affairs."[11]

In January 1969 the shah insisted that "if the British are now leaving by the front door, they should not come back again by the back door." According to Foreign Minister Ardeshir Zahedi, Tehran's views were shared by Saudi Arabia and Kuwait.[12] No agreement prevailed with respect to the vacuum theory, however. Kuwait simply dismissed the idea,[13] but Tehran intimated that if a vacuum were to arise as a result of the British withdrawal, Iran was "able, preferably with the cooperation of other riparian states, to do the job."[14] Iraq, in contrast, implicitly excluded Iran from regional security considerations by insisting on the *Arabs'* ability to solve their own problems.

This discrepancy in their respective positions was but one of the manifestations of the deep-seated hostility which marked Baghdad-Tehran relations in the 1960s and early 1970s. While Iran, most of the Arab states, as well as the USSR appeared primarily concerned with the elimination of the British (and U.S.) presence from the Persian Gulf, Iraq also focused its attention on the regional ambitions of the shah. Part and parcel of the long-standing regional rivalry between the two states, Baghdad's anti-Iranian policy served a twofold purpose: to isolate Tehran in inter-Gulf relations and to project Iraq into the forefront of regional politics.

An early indication of this policy was provided in August 1968, when the victorious Ba'th announced its determination to "defend the Arab character of the Gulf area."[15] (Iran's regional territorial ambitions extended to the islands of Bahrain, Abu Musa, and the two Tunbs.) Variations on this theme appeared frequently and regularly in the late 1960s and early 1970s.[16]

Mohammed Reza Shah responded to Baghdad's campaign by reiterating Tehran's claim to Bahrain and by insisting that "the future of the Persian Gulf is a matter which concerns only the littoral countries."[17] In July 1970 Foreign Minister Zahedi went one step further claiming that "*all* the states of the Gulf maintain the view that Gulf affairs must be handled by the countries of the region without outside interference."[18] One week later, President Bakr rejected "any *foreign* claim to any part of the Gulf area" and proposed the establishment of an "*Arab* defence organisation comprising the Arab states *outside the Gulf* and the independent emirates" to guarantee the region's security.[19]

In pushing for the creation of a broad-based Arab military alliance to confront the shah's political and territorial ambitions in the Gulf, Bakr not only challenged Iran's claim to regional leadership but also reiterated Iraq's determination to champion the Arab cause in the Gulf. It should therefore have come as no surprise that swift rejections of Bakr's idea were registered not only in Tehran but also in Kuwait.[20] (The latter, for reasons to be discussed, was reluctant to isolate Iran and, in so doing, to help increase the political and military influence of Iraq.)

Undaunted, Baghdad continued to call on the Arabs to resist "British attempts at entrenchment" in the Gulf and "to close the door to U.S.-Iranian infiltration."[21] In December 1970 Baghdad Radio accused the shah of being "a British and US agent" and said that Western arms being supplied to Tehran would be used "not only against the Iran people but also against the Arabism of the Gulf."[22] The two antagonists clashed again in March 1971. In commenting on the British offer of a friendship treaty to the Arab emirates, Tehran argued that "The maintenance of peace and security in the Gulf . . . [is] solely the concern of the states bordering it and others . . . [have] no right to interfere in the affairs of the region."[23] Baghdad countered that "the Arabian Gulf and Arab emirates are Arab territory, and guaranteeing the sovereignty of that territory is an Arab responsibility."[24] The line separating Iran and Iraq was thus drawn early and clearly.

Moscow's reaction to the Western proposals for a regional alliance, too, was predictably negative. Initially, "Commentator" distinguished between the U.K. and U.S. initiatives, noting that Rostow's "clumsy" idea had provoked an "irritated reaction from London."[25] Yet the "TASS Statement" of March 1968, for obvious propaganda reasons, lumped the Western initiatives together and accused London and Washington of determination to set up a Gulf "military bloc" under their joint aegis. The reasons for the "frenzied imperialist activity," the Soviet news agency TASS explained, were twofold. First, Great Britain and the United States were doing their utmost "to maintain and strengthen the positions of the capitalist oil monopolies which for many years have extracted billions of dollars in profits through brazen plundering of the natural resources in the Persian Gulf zone." Second, and consequently,

the "imperialists" were hard at work "to prevent the successful development of a true national-liberation movement and to retard the process
of the strengthening of national independence . . . of the states of the . . .
Middle East." A Western-controlled Gulf defense pact was designed to
facilitate the attainment of these twin objectives.[26]

TASS went on to note that Turkey, Iran, Iraq, Kuwait, and Pakistan had
rejected the British and U.S. proposals and found their attitude both
understandable and praiseworthy. After all, "states located many thousands of kilometers from the Persian Gulf" had no right "to claim a role
of 'guardians' or 'spokesmen' for the interests of the states and peoples
of this region." For its part, the Kremlin argued that the "imperialist
plans . . . [were] also directed against the security of the USSR's southern
frontiers. . . ." For this reason, Moscow was "resolutely opposed to new
attempts by . . . the United States and Great Britain to interfere in the
affairs of countries in the Persian Gulf region and to impose their will
on them." TASS concluded by stating that "The peoples of these countries—and they alone—have the right to determine their destiny."[27]
This Soviet stance was clearly designed to bring the USSR into tune
with the views held by most of the Persian Gulf states, including Iraq
and Iran.

In a parallel action, the Kremlin also endeavored to ease the apprehension of the Gulf's conservative regimes that the withdrawal of British
forces would create a regional "power vacuum" which the USSR might
try to fill.[28] Attributing such "fabrications" to the Western powers'
reluctance to lose their political and economic "monopoly" in the
Persian Gulf, Soviet media argued that this line of reasoning implicitly
denied the peoples' ability "to exist independently" and to determine
their own fate. "Why, if the colonizer goes away, must . . . [another
outsider] replace him?," Pravda asked. "Why should a country, region,
continent, having liberated itself from colonial slavery, become a vacuum? Have not all these vacuums been invented by those who . . . want
to legalize colonialism in a new form . . . ?"[29]

Another early theme, on which a wide range of variations appeared in
the ensuing years, was reflected in the title of an article by Evgenii
Primakov—"They Leave in Order to Remain"—which appeared in
Pravda on January 20, 1968. It noted the Labour's decision to withdraw
British forces from the Persian Gulf and went on to say that, even if
Britain kept its word, it would spare no effort to protect Western interests by means of close collaboration with the region's "conservative"
regimes. Thus, Great Britain was in the process of constructing a "large
military base" in Sharjah and of expanding its facilities in Oman. More-

over, six thousand British soldiers and officers, as well as some RAF fighter squadrons, remained on station in Bahrain.[30]

In a similar vein, the 1970 electoral victory of the Conservative party was interpreted as signifying a "revision" of the Labour's 1968 decision to withdraw from areas "East of Suez." The "intention of maintaining . . . [British] military presence in the Persian Gulf" was described as "an act of political blindness" in that it "absolutely . . . [disregarded] the striving of the peoples for freedom and independence."[31] Even in mid-1971, when events had clearly overtaken some of the Soviet pronouncements on the subject, Moscow continued to insist that the withdrawal of British forces from the Persian Gulf meant but a "minor transfer" of military personnel. For example, after Bahrain proclaimed its independence in August 1971, forcing evacuation of RAF and army units, *Pravda* noted that they had merely been moved to Ras al-Khaimah and were "transformed" into the sheikh's armed forces. In addition, four hundred British officers and NCOs remained in Abu Dhabi as the "nucleus" of its "defense force."[32]

Finally, when it became obvious that the Conservative government would abandon all of the military bases in the Gulf itself, Moscow claimed that the overall Western position in the region would not be weakened appreciably because Great Britain remained "the real master" of Oman. The evacuation from Bahrain and Sharjah was offset by control of the Masirah Island and of such facilities as "the main operational base" at Salalah (Dhofar province), the naval base at Mukalah, and the air base at Ras al-Had, situated on the eastern coast of Oman.[33]

Although in the period between 1968 and 1971 Soviet attention in the Persian Gulf was focused on Great Britain, the policies of the United States were also scrutinized. According to "Commentator," the 1968 idea of a "joint security system" in the Gulf had been advanced "not only by Britain but also by the United States, which has an even greater interest in reinforcing its economic, political and military priorities in the Arab East." Following the Gulf states' refusal to heed "imperialist" advice, the two Western powers intensified their efforts to strengthen relations with the region's "conservative" forces, above all "the ruling group in Saudi Arabia and the feudal elements and Sheikhs of Arab tribes." In a complementary endeavor, Washington was said to be "preparing to increase the U.S. presence in the Persian Gulf area and to fill the vacuum which will allegedly result from the departure of the British forces."[34]

The joining of the United States and Great Britain in their presumed determination to undermine the resurgent Arab nationalist movement may have made good sense in the context of Moscow's propaganda campaign aimed at "exposing imperialist machinations" in the Arab world. Nevertheless, such a formulation also presented Soviet analysts with a touchy theoretical problem, for Marxism-Leninism rests on the assumption of the irreconcilability of "inter-capitalist" conflicts. What better place for the U.S. and British economic (and hence political) interests to clash than in the petroleum-rich Persian Gulf? As one Soviet specialist put it: "It would seem that the logic of the inter-imperialist struggle should prompt the U.S. ruling element to abolish the economic and political positions of the British so as to dictate the destinies of the Persian Gulf area [by] itself." This had not been the case, however, the argument ran, because of Washington's awareness "that the development of Anglo-American rivalry into an open struggle could in present-day conditions result only in weakening the position of the West in general. Hence the tendency towards a back-stage resolving of contradictions."[35]

In any event, the United States had encouraged Great Britain to reverse its decision to withdraw from areas "East of Suez." At the same time, Washington endeavored to improve its own positions by means of maintaining U.S. naval presence in the Gulf and by "utilising the services of the Jufeir base" in Bahrain. What the United States had really been after, Drambiants concluded, was to establish regional "military superiority" which would "serve as a basis for introducing U.S. neo-colonialism both in the Gulf and the Arabian Peninsula, and in the Middle East as a whole."[36]

The Federation

Iraq was one of the first Gulf states to endorse the concept of a federation embracing the region's smaller principalities. Even before the July 1968 revolution, *al-Jumhuriyyah* expressed Baghdad's "appreciation of the necessity for unifying the Persian Gulf amirates" to prevent what was described as "imperialist efforts to swallow" the area under the pretext of "filling a vacuum." The government newspaper promised that Iraq would render "any assistance" to the Persian Gulf emirates and would recognize their union "in order to assist it in playing its role in the cause of strengthening the national struggle in this region."[37] In addition to Iraq, the idea of a federation was also endorsed by Bahrain, Kuwait, Saudi Arabia, and the UAR.[38] As it soon turned out, however, outward enthusiasm on the Arab side of the Gulf was not shared by Iran. "In principle," the shah did not object to the proposed federation but, in

April 1968, Tehran expressed concern about the emergence of what was described as an "anti-Iranian grouping in the Gulf." This was not acceptable to the shah, who insisted that responsibility for the maintenance of peace and stability in the Persian Gulf rested exclusively with the littoral states and could be achieved only by cooperation among them.[39]

In short, the issue of the Gulf federation became another focal point in the gradually intensifying dispute between the Ba'thist Iraq and imperial Iran. As already noted, Baghdad not only challenged Tehran's claim to regional leadership but also attempted to rally the other Arab states under the banner of "protecting the Gulf's Arabism." Hence, Iraq expressed itself unequivocally in favor of a "federated Gulf," noting merely that the form and the substance of the union were to be settled by "the parties concerned."[40]

Simultaneously, Baghdad continued its efforts to gain a position of leadership among the Arab Gulf states. The task of persuading them to follow the Iraqi line was initially entrusted to Defense Minister Hardan al-Takriti. In November 1968, he traveled to Kuwait and, in April 1969, to Bahrain, Qatar, Abu Dhabi, and Dubai. According to al-Thawrah, the trip represented "a significant step" toward strengthening relations with the Gulf emirates.[41] In September 1969, Foreign Minister Abd al-Kerim al-Shaykhli visited Kuwait, Qatar, and Bahrain, and, in May 1970, Hardan and Shaykhli returned to Kuwait. In the meantime, in May 1969, Saudi Defense Minister Price Sultan bin Abd al-Aziz traveled to Iraq.[42] "Arabism of the Gulf" was one of the issues discussed during all of these visits.

As it turned out, Baghdad's anti-Iranian campaign proved unsuccessful. Although most of the region's conservative rulers rejected the shah's claim to the Gulf islands, they were instinctively uneasy about Iraq's revolutionary regime, its socialist slogans, and, above all, its regional ambitions. Leading among them was the Saudi monarchy, and its attitude manifested itself, in part, in Riyadh's conciliatory attitude toward Iran. As early as October 1968, the two countries signed an agreement for the demarcation of the continental shelf boundary line, followed by the shah's official visit to Saudi Arabia.[43]

The extent of Iraq's frustration with its inability to isolate Iran made itself evident in April 1970, when Baghdad elevated "the question of the Gulf's future" to a level "parallel with the struggle against Israel, and of even greater importance on its list of political priorities." A statement, issued by the Pan-Arab Command of the Iraqi Ba'th party, warned of "suspicious movements" in the Gulf and said that they were a part of "imperialist reactionary schemes." Specifically, the statement "accused

'Arab reaction' of collaborating with Iran, Britain and the U.S. in an effort to keep the region 'under the domination of imperialism and the international monopolies.' "[44] Under the circumstances, it should have come as no surprise that Bakr's July 1970 proposal for the establishment of an "Arab defense organization" to replace the British forces in the Gulf was rejected not only by Iran but also by Kuwait.[45]

Strained relations with its Gulf neighbors were also reflected in Iraq's treatment of the proposed federation. In May 1970, Vice-President Salih Mahdi Ammash argued that the union's primary responsibility was "to check Iranian designs in the area." In a marked contrast to Baghdad's earlier enthusiasm, however, Ammash noted merely that Iraq "did not object" to the federation—it was still hopeful that independence and membership in the Arab League and the United Nations would provide "a certain amount of protection . . . for the Arabism of the Gulf."[46]

Matters came to a head in late 1971, when Iranian forces occupied the islands of the Abu Musa and the Greater and Lesser Tunb over the objections of most Arab states. Iraq, whose attitude toward the federation had grown even more ambivalent, actually refused to recognize the United Arab Emirates unless the new state complied with three publicly stated conditions. According to *al-Thawrah*, the UAE should repudiate Sharjah's agreement with Iran sanctioning the takeover of Abu Musa, should issue a statement annulling that agreement, and should refrain from establishing diplomatic relations with Tehran until the islands were returned to their Arab owners.[47] None of these conditions were met, attesting to the loss of the battle for influence in the Gulf which Iraq had waged incessantly since 1968.

The initial Soviet reaction to the idea of a union of the smaller Gulf principalities was markedly reserved. First, in contrast to Baghdad, Moscow claimed that the initiative for the establishment of a federation had emanated not from the local rulers but from Great Britain. The latter had suffered major setbacks in the collapse of the South Arabian Federation and in the emergence of the "progressive" People's Republic of South Yemen. It was also confronted with the "heroic struggle of the Yemeni and Omani patriots." Under these circumstances, "it would be naive to suppose that London would not take countermeasures." The attempted creation of a pro-British federation of Arab sheikhdoms was a step designed to retain Western control over the "economically and strategically important [Gulf] area."[48]

In addition, Moscow was well aware that political survival of the various Gulf rulers had, in the past, depended on cooperation with Great Britain. Whether "objective considerations" (such as a desire to control their respective oil resources) would eventually prompt the sheikhs to initiate policies inimical to the interests of the Western powers remained to be seen. In early 1968, however, the Soviets saw little cause for optimism. Not only were the rulers described as Britain's "willing accomplices," but London and Washington, despite their "other contradictions," were also said to be working together to place the future federation under the protectorate of Saudi Arabia, one of the 'imperialists' " most trustworthy Arab allies. In short, what the Western powers were aiming to achieve in the Gulf was not an "independent federation of emirates," but "united British protectorates" designed to ensure the survival of the "old colonial order."[49]

In the ensuing months it became evident that no unanimity prevailed among the local rulers attempting to form a union of the Gulf emirates. This turn of events required of the Soviet analysts to refine the earlier proposition that Great Britain and the United States were cooperating closely in sponsoring the projected federation. In the summer of 1968 the two Western powers were therefore said to be in agreement on one issue only—the new political entity in the Gulf had to serve as a "bridgehead for the suppression of the national-liberation struggle in the Arabian peninsula." Otherwise, "acute contradictions between the British and American oil monopolies" made progress difficult, explaining the rulers' inability to reach an accord.[50] As for the local actors, *Pravda* noted, the "sheikhs and emirs" were preoccupied mainly with such problems as the "structure and the budget of the federation." The "peoples of the region," in contrast, had other concerns: "will the union become a new independent Arab state contributing its share to the general struggle of the Arab peoples against imperialism . . . or will it become a willing instrument in the hands of the neocolonialists?" Events to date, *Pravda* concluded, provided no answer to this "all-important" question.[51]

While *Pravda*'s comments may be assumed to have reflected the view widely shared in the Kremlin circles, it is noteworthy that it was not uniformly accepted by all Soviet analysts. A more sophisticated analysis of events of late 1967 and early 1968 appeared in the July 1968 issue of *Aziia i Afrika segodnia*. Its author, V. Bodianskii, echoed the accepted line, noting that the events in Aden had prompted London to transfer its attention to the Persian Gulf and that the decision to withdraw from areas "East of Suez" had resulted in British and U.S. efforts to establish a regional collective security system. As it turned out, however, these plans had to be abandoned after "storms of protest" had swept the entire Arab East, including the emirates. It was then that the *local rulers themselves* set out to form a federation. This formulation enabled Bodianskii to arrive at a conclusion which differed significantly from those reached by other Soviet commentators: the "very fact that the initiative had passed from the British and U.S. ruling circles to the local rulers is fraught with a serious danger for the West." In the long run, such local initiatives were likely to threaten the "interests of the [Western] oil monopolies." Bodianskii noted also that although the "imperialist powers," in cooperation with some local rulers, would strive to maintain control over the Gulf after the withdrawal of the British forces, the "broad toiling masses" of the region were likely to oppose such efforts.[52]

Some of Bodianskii's predictions seemed to have been borne out by events sooner than expected. The Soviet press reported with glee the formation, in September 1968, of the Liberation Front of the Persian Gulf Region (formerly the Dhofar Liberation Front), an organization which recognized "the ideology of scientific Socialism as the only instrument capable of . . . achieving genuine independence in the . . . Gulf principalities." The Front was said to be devoted to "unit[ing] in its ranks all the revolutionary forces fighting against imperialism, feudalism and reaction" in the Gulf area. One of its stated purposes was "to overthrow the existing regimes before the withdrawal of British troops from the Persian Gulf region in 1971 and to establish its power from the frontier of South Yemen to the Trucial Oman principalities, and later to Qatar and Bahrein, excluding only Kuwait."[53]

Another important assessment of the situation appeared in the fall of 1970, when Drambiants offered what might be described as a guarded endorsement of the federation idea. He freely admitted that "with the protectorate treaties [with Great Britain] still in force and the Gulf states in a position of dependence [on the Western powers], the proclaimed Federation bears the imprint of a Holy Alliance designed to unite the sheikhs and the sultans and to stabilise the existing regimes."[54] Nevertheless, the February 1968 initiative had been welcomed by "many Arab countries"—the first such admission to appear in the Soviet press. Their attitude was purportedly conditioned by the "desire to stimulate the growth of national consciousness among the population of the emirates, to enliven their political and economic life, and to strengthen Arab unity." Moreover, Drambiants asserted that "the political and economic drawing together of small Arab states which, by the will of the colonialists have been disunited and isolated from the outside world, is a positive development." The creation of a federal union of the Gulf principalities, he explained, "would promote social,

economic and cultural progress in an area which suffered colonial oppression for more than 150 years and whose population lives in conditions of extreme poverty and backwardness." If the federation also chose
to establish close "cooperation with independent states," it would per
force be drawn into the Arab "liberation movement."[55]

In his discussion of the "deep and protracted crisis" which marked the
efforts to form the federation, Drambiants struck another innovative
note—he conceded that the explanation offered by many Western commentators had in fact some validity, as in the assertion that the lack of
progress was due to deep-rooted "antagonism among some rulers of the
Gulf states." Citing the territorial disputes between Bahrain and Qatar,
Qatar and Abu Dhabi, Abu Dhabi and Dubai as examples of this contention, he agreed that "the sediments of tribal hostility, religious divergen-
cies, personal squabbles and conflicts, which were kept up and fo-
mented by the colonialists, have indeed produced an extremely tangled
skein of contradictions which laid their imprint on relations between
the states." Still, "the real reasons" for the difficulties encountered by
the federation were to be found "in the unceasing crude pressure exerted
on the . . . [rulers] by the imperialist forces."[56]

Specifically, "class interests" drove the Gulf rulers "into the camp of
the colonialists." At the same time, as evidenced by the oil embargo
imposed on the Western powers during the June 1967 war and by the
financial assistance extended to the Arab "front-line" states in the wake
of that conflict, "they are even more afraid to become puppets of the
imperialists. In this sense," Drambiants argued, "it is possible to speak
not so much about the crisis of the Federation as about the crisis of the
policy designed to keep its member states in colonial bondage." The
only way to resolve this problem was for the members of the federation
to "discard British guardianship." It was not an easily attainable goal,
since London and Washington were determined to maintain control
over the Gulf region. In the long run, however, the "imperialists" were
doomed to failure because it was impossible to "restrain the onslaught
of the liberation movement, whose victory will signify the end of the
era of colonialism in the Persian Gulf area."[57]

Similar conclusions applied to the July 1971 decision of six principalities to form a "mini-federation." The abandonment of the effort to
create a larger union—described as a major setback to British policy—
was explained in terms of "stubborn resistance on the part of some
sheikhdoms" to London's attempts "to turn the federation into a pliant
tool of its policy." For this reason, the refusal by Bahrain, Qatar, and Ras
al-Khaimah to join the new entity met with open Soviet approval. The

establishment of a truncated union, in contrast, signified a "tacit acceptance of British colonial domination by the [six] sheikhs . . . [and] the preservation of the old British protectorate under a new label." In short, London and Washington, having "taken advantage of the natural striving of the people in the Arab sheikhdoms for unity," were said to have scored a partial victory. More significantly, however, "the retreat from the 'big' to the 'mini' federation reflects the deep-going crisis of British colonialist policy and the futility of London's efforts to retain the Persian Gulf sheikhdoms under Britain's rule."[58]

In discussing the proclamation of independence by Bahrain, Qatar, and the UAE, Soviet publications again focused their attention on the policies of the Western powers. While conceding that London's "unlimited rule on the southern shores of the Persian Gulf" had indeed come to an end, Moscow restated earlier concerns that British military presence was being maintained not only in the neighboring Oman but also in Sharjah.[59] Similarly, the United States was described as "getting ready to use the former complex of British military bases in Bahrain." American military presence in the Gulf was established also to serve Washington's "imperialist ambitions" in the Indian Ocean basin.[60] In any event, official Soviet sanction was conferred upon the new Arab states by Prime Minister Kosygin. During his February 11, 1972 speech in honor of Saddam Hussein, he "applaud[ed] the gaining of independence by the people of Bahrain, Qatar, and the United Arab Emirates."[61]

The Islands

Another issue involving Iraq and Iran in the late 1960s and early 1970s was the future of the Gulf islands of Bahrain, Abu Musa, and the Tunbs. Mohammed Reza Shah addressed the problem of Bahrain in January 1969: he would respect the wishes of "the people of Bahrein" if they chose "not to join" Iran and would "never resort to the use of force to oblige them to do so." The shah went on to say, however, that Tehran could not "accept that this island, which was separated from our country by the British, can be just handed over by them to other people at our expense. This is a matter of principle on which Iran cannot compromise."[62] The shah's unwillingness to renounce Tehran's claim provoked strong criticism in Bahrain. In June 1969, its Department of Foreign Affairs expressed "concern and strong opposition . . . [to] Iran's untenable claims."[63]

Iraq's response to the renewal of Iran's claim was predictably swift and strong. In line with the position taken in August 1968,[64] the statement, issued by the Ba'th party in early February 1969, insisted that the "Arab character of the Gulf must be preserved." Later in the month, the crown prince of Bahrain visited Baghdad and reported that he had found "understanding among Iraqi officials on questions concerning Bahrein and the Gulf."[65] In February 1970 Assistant Secretary-General of the Regional (Iraqi) Ba'th Party National Command Shibli al-Aysami stated that Tehran's ambitions threatened to transform the Gulf "into another Palestine" and called upon "the Arab nation to act quickly." For its part, Baghdad was "fully prepared to give all material, military and economic assistance to the Arab Gulf states to repulse the invader . . . and preserve the Arabism of the Gulf."[66] Among other regional states, Saudi Arabia and Kuwait joined Iraq in rejecting the shah's claim to the Gulf islands.[67]

Nevertheless, neither Riyadh nor Kuwait shared the intensity of Baghdad's anxiety over Tehran's ambitions. Their attitude was influenced by the following considerations: while all four (Iran, Iraq, Kuwait, and Saudi Arabia) agreed on the necessity of Britain's military withdrawal from the Gulf, they diverged widely on other issues such as the questions of regional security and of the islands. This state of affairs forced Saudi Arabia and Kuwait, which found themselves in the middle of the Baghdad-Tehran dispute, to perform a balancing act between their feuding neighbors. On the one hand, they sided with Iraq on the future of the Gulf islands. On the other, along with Iran, they rejected the notion of an Arab regional security pact in which Baghdad would emerge as the dominant power. They also seem to have preferred to guarantee the area's security in cooperation with, and not in opposition to, the shah[68] who was much closer to the Gulf's Arab monarchs ideologically than the revolutionary, socialist Ba'th regime in Baghdad. Iraq, rather annoyed by the attitude adopted by Saudi Arabia and Kuwait responded by initiating an "anti-imperialist" as well as an "anti-reactionary" campaign.[69]

By mid-1970 the Bahrain problem was resolved. In March, Iran and Great Britain requested UN Secretary-General U Thant to determine whether the people of Bahrain preferred independence to unity with Iran. The report, submitted in early May, said that "the overwhelming majority" of the island's population wished "to gain recognition of their identity in a fully independent and sovereign state. . . ." A short while later, Mohammed Reza Shah dropped his claim to Bahrain.[70] As the Gulf governments applauded U Thant's handling of the Bahrain problem,[71] it was widely believed that a serious obstacle on the path of the projected union of the emirates had been removed. Appearances proved misleading, however. In October 1970 the shah informed the Gulf principalities that Tehran's acquiescence to the federation was predicated upon their recognition of Iran's ownership of Abu Musa and the Tunbs.[72] In November he threatened the use of force if Tehran's claims to the islands were not accepted by the Gulf principalities.[73]

Although the Anglo-Iranian dispute over the ownership of Abu Musa and the Tunbs had dated back to the 1920s,[74] the reasons for Tehran's interest displayed in the late 1960s and early 1970s were of a more contemporary nature. For example, it was assumed that sizable oil deposits were located in the Gulf nine miles from Abu Musa. Moreover, the islands were situated near the Strait of Hormuz at the mouth of the Persian Gulf. Military presence on Abu Musa and the Tunbs, it was argued in Tehran, would enable Iran to control the flow of petroleum from the Gulf to the Indian Ocean and beyond.[75] Finally, and most important, the acquisition of the islands was intended to demonstrate the shah's determination to establish Iran as the leading power of the Gulf. It was precisely this ambition that netted him the hostility of Iraq which, for its part, aspired to a leadership role among the region's Arab states.

While Egypt and Saudi Arabia chose not to become embroiled in this particular controversy, most of the other Arab states refused to recognize Iran's claim. In the Gulf, the rulers of Sharjah and Ras al-Khaimah proclaimed Abu Musa and the Tunbs a part of "Arab territory" and, in early November, called upon the Arab states to "adopt a unified stand on the issue."[76] A similar attitude was adopted by Kuwait: in November 1971 it broke off diplomatic relations with Iran.[77] The most vocal opposition to Tehran's ambitions, however, came once again from Iraq.

On June 29, 1971, Foreign Minister Shaykhli rejected Iran's claim on the grounds that the islands "were, are and always will be Arab" and that the past "colonialist Persian control" did not establish Iranian "ownership of them." He also called attention to the fact that Tehran's current drive represented a "grave threat to peace and international navigation in the whole area." For these reasons, Shaykhli called on the other Arab states to unite against Iran's "expansionist schemes."[78] The Iraqi efforts to isolate Iran and to prevent the shah from occupying the islands met with failure.

On November 29, 1971, the shah and the ruler of Sharjah reached an agreement permitting the deployment of Iranian troops on the island of Abu Musa. Ras al-Khaimah objected, but its attitude was of no consequence: on November 30, Iranian units landed on Abu Musa and the Tunb islands.[79] Of the Arab states, Egypt and Saudi Arabia, as noted, refrained from formally condemning Tehran (thus tacitly accepting the islands' occupation), while most of the others, with varying degrees of emphasis, expressed disapproval of the Iranian move. One of the strongest stands was taken by Libya which, on December 7, ordered the nationalization of the operations and assets of the British Petroleum Company.[80] Along with Libya, Iraq, and Algeria, the PDRY denounced Tehran's action as an "Anglo-Iranian plot." Baghdad broke diplomatic relations with London and Tehran and called for an urgent meeting of the UN Security Council "to condemn [Anglo-Iranian collusion] in the occupation of the islands."[81] In the ensuing weeks, Iraq confined itself to periodic appeals, calling on all Arabs to exert pressure on their respective governments "to bring an end to Iran's illegal infiltration of the Arabian Gulf emirates."[82] The failure of these efforts provided additional evidence for the conclusion that in its Gulf policy of the early post-1968 period, Iraq had encountered serious problems. Lip service to "preservation of the Gulf's Arabism" notwithstanding, the conservative Arab regimes were reluctant to accept Baghdad's leadership and, in so doing, to endanger their own security and their relations with Iran.

Between 1968 and 1971 the USSR exhibited a lively concern with such issues as the withdrawal of the British forces and the projected Gulf federation. The reasons for Moscow's interest were obvious—the evacuation of British troops was bound to weaken the Western positions in the vitally important Gulf area. Moreover, in a classic application of the zero-sum game theory, the Kremlin seemed to have assumed that any Western loss would automatically result in a Soviet gain. Similarly, since the USSR was also apprehensive that a union of Arab emirates might somehow provide Great Britain with an opportunity of "staying while leaving," the Soviet media did not hesitate to take a strong stand on that issue as well. The future of Bahrain (but not of Abu Musa and the Tunbs), too, fell into this category.

The island had been "assigned an important part in the unseemly game London . . . [was] playing in the Gulf": after the loss of Aden, "the hub of Britain's entire military and political system in this area" was transferred to Bahrain. Because of its importance to Great Britain, London had been hard at work "trying to turn Bahrein into a bone of contention between Iran and some Arab states"—tension enabled the British to hang on to their valuable outpost. Fortunately, the Soviets argued in the fall of 1970, this state of affairs was not likely to last long. In May the UN Security Council had "welcomed the findings . . . of a special mission which visited . . . [Bahrain and ascertained] that the overwhelming majority of . . . [its] people . . . want their country to be recognised as a fully independent and sovereign state."[83]

Subsequent events were not entirely to Moscow's satisfaction, however. Although the Kremlin applauded the proclamation of Bahrain's independence in August 1971 and welcomed the termination of British military presence on the island, the signing of a friendship treaty with Great Britain was interpreted to mean that the ruler was willing, "in a round-about way," to let London maintain its *political* influence in the Gulf region.[84]

The status of Abu Musa and the Tunbs, in contrast, was not regarded by Moscow as an issue of political importance equal to those of the union of the Lower Gulf emirates or of Bahrain. First, the problems of ownership and control of the islands appear to have been of no relevance to the Kremlin. Moreover, the Soviets lacked the means to influence the course of events even if they had wished to do so. Last, it simply made no sense to become embroiled in the vociferous contest for regional supremacy between Baghdad and Tehran when the USSR was attempting to improve relations with both.

For these reasons, Moscow reacted in a characteristic fashion: the Soviet media gave a brief factual account of events but judiciously refrained from taking sides. On December 2, 1971, *Pravda* quoted from Prime Minister Amir Abbas Hoveida's statement of November 30. It said, in part, that the landings of Iranian forces on Abu Musa and the Tunbs were carried out in accordance with an understanding previously reached with Sharjah and Ras al-Khaimah. The paper then went on to quote Baghdad Radio to the effect that the "occupation of the Arab islands represents a violation of the principles of the UN Charter" and of "international treaty obligations." (Reference was made here to the treaty of protectorate between Great Britain and the Trucial Oman principalities and to the fact that the Iranian troop landings occurred one day before the treaty's expiration.) *Pravda* concluded by informing its readers of Iraq's decision to break diplomatic relations with Iran and Great Britain.

On December 3 *Pravda* reported on the Arab reaction to the Iranian occupation of Abu Musa and the Tunbs. The general tenor of the comments emanating from a number of Arab capitals was predictably negative but not violent. Most protested the use of force by the shah, insisted that Great Britain was legally bound to protect the islands, and demanded the withdrawal of Iranian troops. *Pravda* noted also that Iraq had requested a special session of the UN Security Council to deal with the island issue and there the matter was allowed to rest.

Relations Between Iraq and Iran, 1968–1975

The rivalry between Iraq and Iran was one of the dominant features of Persian Gulf politics in the late 1960s and early 1970s. In addition to the problems of the federation and of the islands, Baghdad and Tehran also clashed on the issues of oil rights in the continental shelf, demarcation of boundaries, and navigation rights in the Shatt al-Arab. All three preceded the 1968 revolution and remained dormant during periods of cooperation between the two states, before the overthrow of the Iraqi monarchy in 1958. Conversely, these problems emerged as focal points of the ongoing dispute when relations between Tehran and Baghdad took a turn for the worse. This was particularly true after the advent to power of the Iraqi branch of the Ba'th party, which was viewed with suspicion by its conservative Gulf neighbors, including Iran.

Of the three issues, the delineation of the offshore continental shelf was the least conspicuous and surfaced only when some Gulf states concluded demarcation agreements on oil rights without consulting Iraq or invited international tenders for offshore exploration.[85] The two remaining problems enjoyed more limelight because it was around them that the Iraqi-Iranian dispute usually revolved. Both had their origin in the history of the Ottoman and Persian empires. Specifically, the Erzerum Treaty of 1847 and the Constantinople Protocol of 1913 addressed the question of what is now the Iraqi-Iranian frontier. While some border areas had not been delineated carefully, giving rise to future Iraqi claims to territory which Iran regarded as rightfully its, relative clarity prevailed with regard to the Shatt al-Arab estuary. (Formed by the confluence of the Tigris and Euphrates rivers, the waterway has been of vital importance to both neighbors: it connects Iraq's major port of Basrah and the Iranian ports of Khorramshahr and Abadan with the Persian Gulf.) The treaties provided for free access to and use of the Shatt by both the Arabs and the Persians. However, yet another undertaking, the Iraqi-Iranian treaty of 1937, was in force at the time of the 1968 revolution. This document fixed the Iranian frontier at the low-water line on the Shatt's eastern bank, thus giving Iraq sovereignty over most of the waterway.[86] Since Great Britain had insisted on this formulation at the time, Tehran had no choice but to comply. But after the 1958 revolution in Iraq, Mohammed Reza Shah denounced the 1937 treaty as "unprecedented" and "intolerable."[87]

A brief survey of Iraqi-Iranian relations in the period between 1968 and 1975 is necessary at this point. The shah recognized the new Ba'thi regime four days after the revolution of July 17 and, toward the end of the year, Defense Minister Hardan al-Takriti and Foreign Minister Shaykhli visited Tehran and initiated discussions on the delineation of the continental shelf, the boundaries, and the expansion of trade. Upon his return, Hardan stated that "past differences" between the two countries had been resolved.[88] The honeymoon did not last long, however. In April 1969 Iraq announced the decision to enforce its "territorial rights" in the Shatt al-Arab: Iranian ships using the waterway were to "strike their colours" and to "refrain from carrying Iranian Imperial Navy personnel." The shah retaliated by abrogating the 1937 treaty and warning Baghdad that "all necessary steps" would be taken "to safeguard . . . [Iran's] interests." Tehran then dispatched naval vessels into the Shatt to guard against a possible Iraqi attack on its commercial traffic.[89] None occurred.

In spite of the mediation efforts by Saudi Arabia, Kuwait, and Jordan,[90] relations between the two countries continued to deteriorate. As Baghdad instituted deportation proceedings against thousands of Iranians, Tehran arrested a number of Iraqi "spies and saboteurs." In June 1969 Iraq accused Iran of massing troops along the border and announced the creation of the Arabistan Popular Front.[91] (The area referred to as "Arabistan" is the oil-rich Khuzistan province of Iran. Situated on the eastern side of the Shatt al-Arab, it has a large Arab population.)

Tension reached a new high in January 1970 when the Iraqi authorities uncovered a plot to overthrow the government. Baghdad Radio announced on January 21 that the conspirators had acted "in collusion with foreign parties," including "the reactionary government in Iran." Iraq then expelled the Iranian ambassador and closed all Iranian consulates. Tehran retaliated in kind.[92] In spite of mediation attempts by Turkey and Kuwait, Iranian-Iraqi relations remained strained, fed by the bitter controversy over the issues of Gulf security, the islands, and the proposed federation. In December 1970 it was Tehran's turn to accuse Iraq of plotting to overthrow the shah.[93]

Relations reached a new low in late November and December 1971, following the Iranian occupation of Abu Musa and the Tunbs and Baghdad's decision to break diplomatic relations with Tehran. Forcible evacuation of Iranian citizens was resumed in the fall of 1971 and carried over into 1972.[94] Border clashes intensified and, in the spring, both countries sent letters to the UN Security Council accusing each other of provocation, subversion, and aggression.[95]

The situation quieted down in mid-1972, primarily because of Baghdad's preoccupation with the nationalization of the Iraq Petroleum

Company, and it appeared that both sides were interested in lowering the level of the conflict. Mohammed Reza Shah reportedly asked President Sadat to arrange talks in which the parties could "thrash out" their differences, while President Bakr in his July 17 speech expressed Baghdad's desire to "establish neighbourly links with Iran. . . ."[96] Nothing came of these initiatives, and in December 1972 and January 1973 tension along the Iraqi-Iranian border flared up again.[97]

Following the outbreak of the Arab-Israeli war of October 1973, diplomatic relations between the two countries were restored, on Baghdad's initiative. This turn of events did not lead to the resolution of the outstanding issues, however, and major border clashes took place in February and March 1974. After a cease-fire agreement was signed on March 7, the UN Security Council dispatched a special representative to study the Iraqi-Iranian conflict. On his recommendation, Baghdad and Tehran "agreed to enforce the ceasefire, to withdraw concentrations of armed forces along the entire border . . . and to begin talks . . . on a comprehensive settlement of all issues."[98]

In line with this understanding, the foreign ministers of Iran and Iraq met in Istanbul in August and in New York in October 1974 but were unable to reach an agreement.[99] In the meantime, border hostilities were resumed in August and continued intermittently into early 1975.[100] One of the potentially most serious incidents occurred in mid-December 1974, when two Iraqi air force planes were shot down over Kurdish territory in the vicinity of the Iranian border by U.S.-made Hawk surface-to-air missiles. Iraq accused Iran and the United States of intervention in its internal affairs; Tehran justified its action by saying that the Iraqi planes had operated over Iranian territory. Following renewed mediation attempts by Egypt and Jordan,[101] Foreign Ministers Sa'dun Hammadi and Abbas Ali Khalatbari met in Turkey in January 1975. According to Hammadi, the talks "had achieved nothing positive."[102]

The protracted crisis ended abruptly in March 1975, at the OPEC summit conference in Algiers, when the shah and Saddam Hussein signed an agreement resolving the differences between their states. Iraq made major concessions with respect to border demarcation—it agreed to the land boundary contained in the 1913 Constantinople Protocol and to the division of Shatt al-Arab "along the *Thalweg* line in the middle of the deepest shipping channel in the . . . estuary," both solutions favored by Iran. In return, Tehran promised "to maintain 'strict and effective control' over its border with Iraq and to put an end to 'all subversive infiltration.' "[103] The Ba'th was the main beneficiary of this provision—it represented the shah's promise to cut off all forms of aid to the Kurdish forces of Mulla Mustafa; the agreement spelled an end to the Kurdish uprising in Iraq. Baghdad reciprocated by abandoning support of the revolutionary movements in the Gulf area.[104] In June 1975 the Algiers accord was incorporated into a formal treaty, marking a dramatic improvement in relations between the two ancient rivals.[105]

In the late 1960s and early 1970s the USSR saw no advantage in becoming involved in the Tehran-Baghdad conflict. Not only did the Soviets lack the ability to influence it in any significant fashion, but they also thought it unwise to take sides in a regional quarrel between the very states the Kremlin was trying to woo. For these reasons, and because of superpower competition, Moscow preoccupied itself instead with the activities of the "imperialist" powers. Seen in this perspective, the Iraq-Iran feud was, to the USSR, an unwelcome development—it consumed an inordinate amount of the local actors' energy and detracted attention from the "machinations" of the Western allies.

In an effort to make the best of this difficult situation, the Kremlin developed the following strategy: it blamed "neocolonialism" for all of the region's problems, including the conflict between Baghdad and Tehran; called upon Iraq and Iran to resolve their disputes; and made a major effort to improve relations with both protagonists. Even before the Ba'thist revolution in Iraq, Moscow claimed that the Western powers' primary objective in the Persian Gulf had been to create conditions which would render their military and political withdrawal impossible. Specifically, the "neocolonialists" were accused of efforts "to poison . . . [the Gulf countries'] relations with each other, to harm the unity of the Arab states, . . . [and] to cause a conflict between Iran and the Arabs."[106] Drambiants leaves no doubt about Moscow's disapproval of the "conflicts between the Gulf states"—they "only play into the hands of the external imperialist forces." He argues that in such "an atmosphere of hostility and squabbles, it is easier to preserve the existing colonial order and the western oil concessions, and, what is most important, to divert the attention of the people of this area from the most burning and vital problems of the Arab East."[107]

Iraq and Iran, at whose leaders these Soviet arguments were primarily directed, appeared unconvinced. Although both capitals shared the Kremlin's insistence on the "necessity" of the British military pullout from the Gulf, they gave no indications of a desire to resolve their differences. Instead, they proceeded to seek Moscow's support for their respective positions. For its part, the USSR refused to take sides but showed a marked interest in improving bilateral relations with both protagonists. In this undertaking, the Soviets were relatively success-ful. Their developing ties with Iraq have been discussed in chapter 1; in the case of Tehran, it should be kept in mind that Mohammed Reza Shah had resolved to pursue an independent foreign policy and to ad-vance Iran's interests by means of cooperation, and not confrontation, with *both* power blocs.

Tehran's position was not identical with that adopted by the propo-nents of "positive neutralism" or "nonalignment," who refused to dif-ferentiate between the two major blocs but concentrated their attention on gaining maximum benefits from both by playing one side against the other. Because of Iran's geographical proximity to the USSR and the shah's acute awareness of the history of Russo-Persian relations, he could not have underestimated the "northern neighbor's" capacity for mischief-making. (Most of the nonaligned regimes, in contrast, had had no such experiences.) At the same time, convinced that, at the current historical stage, the Soviets were interested not so much in geograph-ical expansion as in their competition with the United States, the shah was eager to normalize relations with the USSR in the hope that a "balanced" position in international politics would enable him to pur-sue a more effective policy in the Persian Gulf. In this context, he was seeking Moscow's neutrality in the unfolding rivalry between Tehran and Baghdad. The shah's calculations proved essentially correct. In spite of their close cooperation with Iraq, the Soviets supplied Iran with some military and large-scale economic and technical assistance.[108] The Kremlin's attitude reflected its determination to remain an impor-tant regional actor. Rapprochement with revolutionary Iraq was to be tempered with outward cordiality in Soviet-Iranian relations. Moscow adhered to its policy in spite of the shah's refusal in October 1971 to "review the old friendship agreements [between the two countries] in the light of the evacuation of the Gulf by the British"[109] and of the ensuing rapprochement between Tehran and Washington.

In any event, in the period under discussion, the USSR became en-gaged in performing a balancing act between Iraq and Iran. Closer exam-ination of the official documents (that is, of public speeches and joint communiqués or statements) generated by high-level visits of the repre-sentatives of the Soviet Union and the two Gulf rivals reveals that Moscow's views were in closer harmony with Baghdad between 1968 and 1971, tilted toward Tehran between 1972 and 1974, and swung sharply toward Iraq in late 1974.

Specifically, in the period between 1968 and 1971, documents issued in conjunction with high-level Soviet-Iranian contacts contained no references to the problems of the Gulf, although it is likely that the subject was broached in the bilateral discussions. This observation applied to Prime Minister Kosygin's April 1968 visit to Tehran, the shah's September–October 1968 sojourn in Moscow, and President Podgorny's March 1970 trip to Iran.[110] In contrast, joint USSR-Iraqi pronouncements of this period alluded to their mutual concern about the Gulf. Thus, regional problems were touched upon in the joint communiqué issued at the conclusion of Foreign Minister Shaykhli's March 1969 visit to Moscow—the first high-level contact between the Soviet and Ba'thist officials. Both sides expressed their "resolute support of the people of Oman . . . and of [unspecified] other territories . . . fighting against imperialist oppression."[111] Because both countries were on record as supporting the Omani Liberation Front, an allusion to that country was not surprising. Of more significance was the fact that the joint communiqué failed to mention such important regional problems as the Iraqi-Iranian feud or the projected union of Arab emirates.

The first direct expression of concern over the Gulf itself was contained in the joint communiqué published during Saddam Hussein's initial visit to the USSR which took place in August 1970. The sides agreed that the "main task of the present stage of the national-liberation movement . . . [in] this area is complete liquidation of the imperialist presence." This meant, in part, the end of "colonialist domination and influence, the elimination of all foreign military bases, and the withdrawal of foreign forces from the Persian Gulf region. . . ." Attainment of these goals, it was concluded, would "enable the Arab peoples of the . . . [Gulf] to gain [their] independence and freedom."[112] The communiqué served as a clear indication that on the question of the British military presence in the Gulf the views of Moscow and Baghdad were complementary. It is important to reiterate, however, that the two were in disagreement on such regional issues as the proposed federation and, even more significantly, on Iraq's relations with Iran. While the Ba'th consistently accused the shah of determination, in collusion with "British imperialism," to "crush the Gulf's Arabism," the Kremlin carefully refrained from endorsing such claims. Instead, it was hard at work improving relations with Tehran.

This important divergence between the Soviet and Iraqi interests emerged even more clearly after the British withdrawal from the Gulf in late 1971. In February 1972, Saddam Hussein paid his second official visit to the USSR. It was an important trip, intended to finalize the details of the Soviet-Iraqi Treaty of Friendship and Cooperation, and it was marked by Saddam Hussein's unusual public attempt to secure

Moscow's support for Iraq's position on a number of Gulf issues, including relations between Baghdad and Tehran. The opportunity to do so was provided by the ceremonial Kremlin dinner and the speeches customarily delivered on such occasions by high officials of both states. While Kosygin, in addition to the standard "anti-imperialist" tirades, congratulated Bahrain, Qatar, and the UAE on achieving their independence, Saddam Hussein seized the opportunity to blame Iran for fomenting hostility between Tehran and Baghdad. In an unusual and poignant rebuttal, *Pravda* did not reproduce this section of his speech, saying merely that Saddam Hussein "touched on the question of Iraqi-Iranian relations and presented the position of his government." Moreover, in the joint communiqué of February 17, the two sides condemned "imperialist domination, foreign military bases, . . . intrigues and plots," and expressed their "full support for the struggle of the Arab states and peoples of the Persian Gulf region for the right to decide their fate by themselves,"[113] but said nothing about relations between Iraq and Iran.

The formulation demonstrated that the USSR was determined publicly to ignore Saddam Hussein's pleas. Specifically, it may be safely assumed that prior to and during his visit, the Iraqi leader had made a concerted effort to win Moscow's support for Baghdad's anti-Iranian position. To have given in, however, would have meant openly antagonizing the shah, a step which the Soviets were clearly unwilling to take. When Saddam Hussein proceeded to air the issue in public, he was rebuffed. The Iraqis must have found this Soviet attitude offensive, but since they were playing for higher stakes—securing the Kremlin's support in their confrontation with the IPC, nothing more was said about it at the time. Another novel element in the context of Soviet-Iraqi communiqués was the reference to "the right [of the Arab states and peoples of the Persian Gulf region] to decide their fate by themselves." Although the phrase could not be labelled as offensive to Baghdad, it came very close to Tehran's insistence that *all* the states of the area should "decide their own fate without outside interference." In any event, in February 1972 the Kremlin clearly demonstrated its intention not to support the Ba'th in its feud with the shah and not to become involved in the Iraqi-Iranian dispute.

This conclusion was reinforced by subsequent developments.[114] The Soviet account of Premier Kosygin's April 1972 visit to Baghdad for the ceremonial signing of the Treaty of Friendship and Cooperation contained no references to the Gulf.[115] The Kremlin's detachment was demonstrated again in September 1972, during President Bakr's first state visit to the USSR. In his dinner speech of September 14 the Iraqi leader claimed that the regional situation was threatened by "imperialist intrigues against progressive Arab regimes and forces" and, in a pointed reference to Iran, spoke of "actions against the historical rights of the Arab nation" in the Gulf region. He concluded by noting that "in our opinion, these conditions demand even greater solidarity and cooperation between our two nations. . . ." Podgorny, in contrast, said nothing about any of these matters, and the joint communiqué of September 19, issued at a time when the Kremlin was getting ready for another visit by the shah, went back to the original formulation: support was once again promised to "the Arab peoples of the Persian Gulf . . . [struggling] to repulse the aggressive imperialist plans which threaten their freedom and independence."[116]

Additional illustrations of Moscow's decision to steer clear of the Iraq-Iran entanglement were provided by the handling of the Gulf problems in the official documents issued in conjunction with the visits exchanged by Soviet and Iranian dignitaries. Thus, the key sentence, contained in the joint communiqué of October 21, 1972 (issued during the shah's visit to the USSR), and repeated in all such Soviet-Iranian documents prior to 1975, read: "The Soviet Union and Iran expressed firm conviction that questions concerning the Persian Gulf region must be resolved in accordance with the principles of the UN Charter, and *without outside interference*, by the states of the area themselves."[117] Since this formulation reflected Tehran's official position on the Gulf, its adoption by Moscow could have been interpreted as a Soviet concession to the shah. In reality, however, it mirrored the Kremlin's position as well—the USSR did not wish to become directly involved in the Iraqi-Iranian feud.

Nevertheless, the Soviet-Iranian communiqué also contained a sentence which Baghdad must have found highly offensive: Tehran and Moscow agreed to base their relations on principles of "equality, [of] respect for sovereignty, independence, [and] *territorial integrity*, and [of] noninterference in [each other's] internal affairs."[118] Since the October 1972 communiqué was the first public statement issued by the two countries in the wake of Tehran's occupation of Abu Musa and the Tunbs, the Soviet obligation to respect Iran's territorial integrity could have been interpreted as acquiescence in an action which Iraq had strongly opposed. In any event, the formulation supports the proposition that, beginning in 1972, on the matters of the Gulf, Moscow was more supportive of Tehran than of Baghdad.

As noted, this Soviet attitude was maintained for more than two years despite Moscow's growing uneasiness about Iran's massive military buildup program and the concurrent rapprochement between Tehran and Washington.[119] In March 1973 Kosygin paid another visit to Iran. Neither his nor Prime Minister Hoveida's speeches made any references to the Gulf, but the joint communiqué repeated verbatim the first of the formulas contained in the document of October 21, 1972.[120] The same was true of Hoveida's August 1973 trip to the USSR.[121] Significantly, the Gulf was not mentioned during the high-level Soviet-Iraqi contacts either. This applied to Saddam Hussein's third and fourth visits to Moscow, undertaken in March 1973 and February 1974, and of the November 1973 visit to Iraq by a CPSU delegation headed by Boris Ponomarev.[122] The conspicuous silence on a subject of considerable importance to Iraq could only have been interpreted as a reflection of a divergence of Moscow's and Baghdad's opinions and of their mutual disapproval of each other's positions.[123]

The situation changed dramatically in the late fall of 1974 as a result of another shift in the Kremlin's position, and, after considerable foot-dragging, the USSR came down on the side of the Iraqi government in its confrontation with the Kurds. Once that happened, the prolongation of the conflict, made possible by Tehran's support of the insurgency, was viewed by Moscow as highly undesirable. Breaking with previous restraint and caution, the Soviets used the opportunity provided by Mohammed Reza Shah's November 1974 visit to intervene directly in the Iraqi-Iranian dispute.

In his dinner speech, Podgorny noted that international peace was negatively affected by "all regional conflicts," including that of the Persian Gulf. He then proceeded to spell out the reasons for Soviet concern: "We want to say in all frankness [the diplomatic equivalent of a high degree of annoyance] that tension . . . in relations between Iran and Iraq does not correspond to the interests of . . . peace." For this reason, the USSR had long favored a resolution of their differences "at the negotiating table [and] on the basis of the principles of peaceful coexistence and good neighborliness." In line with this position, Podgorny concluded, "we shall welcome constructive steps which, we hope, the sides will take with the view to finding ways to resolve the controversial questions in a peaceful manner."[124] Podgorny's bluntness, uncharacteristic of the diplomatic exchanges of this kind, was clearly motivated by the seriousness of the situation in Iraqi Kurdistan and attested to Moscow's decision to throw its weight behind Baghdad's efforts to bring it to a swift and successful resolution.

The shah must have been taken aback by Podgorny's attack. Nevertheless, his answer, although couched in a more diplomatic language, was equally firm:

> I merely want to note that if in its relations with us Iraq would exhibit an attitude similar to that which you, our great neighbor, have adopted toward us, and would not, with such zeal, promote the legacy of British imperialism, no problems would exist between us on this score. In any case, Iran will . . . continue its efforts aimed at settling this question by means of negotiations.[125]

Although the statement on the shah's visit reaffirmed that, "as before, the sides are convinced that questions concerning the Persian Gulf region must be resolved by the countries of the region themselves in accordance with the principles of the UN Charter,"[126] the Soviets had clearly made their point.

On March 5, 1975, Iraq and Iran agreed to resolve their differences. Baghdad's position was explained to the Soviet leaders during Saddam Hussein's fifth, mid-April 1975, visit to the USSR. While Kosygin, in his speech, omitted the subject, the Iraqi leader spoke at some length about the recent developments in the Gulf. He mentioned that an "alarming hotbed of tension, endangering the peace" of the area had existed for some time and went on to say that, after the Algiers accord, "sincere efforts are being made to restore relations with our neighbor, Iran, in the interests of both our . . . countries." The Kremlin appeared highly pleased. In the joint communiqué, the "Soviet side expressed its satisfaction . . . with the recent agreement between the Republic of Iraq and Iran. . . ."[127]

As explained by the Soviet press, Moscow was gratified because "armed clashes . . . threatened to develop into a serious confrontation between the two neighboring countries" and because "Iran and Iraq were involved in a harassing frontier dispute that caused considerable tension and poisoned the atmosphere in the Middle East."[128] Moreover, the settlement of the Iraqi-Iranian dispute was "of great significance . . . [because] it has frustrated the plans of those who would like to see these two neighbouring countries pitted against each other in the role of political gladiators."[129]

Nevertheless, the signing of the Algiers agreement must have been unsettling to Moscow—reached without consultations with the USSR, the accord could not but lessen Soviet ability to influence Baghdad. It will be recalled that one of the main reasons for the normalization of relations between the two Gulf rivals was Iraq's determination to crush the Kurds, a goal that could be achieved only by securing Tehran's cooperation. In the early 1970s, the Soviets had resisted Baghdad's efforts to defeat Mulla Mustafa's forces. The Kremlin's main objective was to utilize Kurdish nationalism as a source of political leverage on the Iraqi government. Only in 1974, after it became clear that Mulla Mustafa had thrown in his lot with the United States and Iran, did Moscow come out openly in favor of Baghdad's decision to subdue his forces. Once that decision had been made, the Soviets had less reason to oppose the Iraqi-Iranian agreement. At the same time, the Kremlin had to know that the resulting consolidation of the Ba'th's domestic position, coupled with the growing accumulation of hard currency and the normalization of relations with Iran, were bound to lead to implementation of more independent domestic and foreign policies, thus decreasing Iraq's reliance on the USSR.

Iraq-Kuwait Crisis, 1973

In June 1961, Great Britain relinquished its 1899 protectorate over Kuwait. A few days later, Baghdad's strongman, Colonel Abd al-Kerim Kassem, announced that the sheikhdom was an "integral part" of Iraq. It had been "usurped" by means of an "illegal . . . document" and would now be joined with the mother country. The claim was opposed by Great Britain and the other Arab states which dispatched military units to guarantee Kuwait's independence.[130] After Kassem's ouster in 1963, relations between Iraq and Kuwait were normalized but did not become close as the sheikhdom continued to harbor suspicions about Baghdad's ultimate intentions.

A major incentive for closer political cooperation between the two states was provided by Britain's January 1968 resolution to pull out of the areas "East of Suez." Iraq and Kuwait were in agreement on two major issues arising out of that decision: they expressed themselves in favor of unconditional British military withdrawal from the Gulf and, at least initially, endorsed the establishment of a Federation of Arab Emirates.[131] However, this apparent harmony could not for long conceal a fundamental divergence of interests. As soon became evident, the two neighbors disagreed over the related problems of regional security and of Kuwait's relations with Iran. Specifically, apprehensive about Baghdad's intentions, Kuwait worked hard to maintain a regional balance in the Gulf in the hope that the area's other states, above all Iran, would check Iraq's attempts at territorial expansion. In line with this approach the sheikhdom resisted Baghdad's efforts to promulgate an Arab Gulf defense organization and endeavored to maintain close relations with Tehran.[132]

Lack of support for some of Iraq's political initiatives did not signify wholesale endorsement of the regional ambitions of the shah. Along with the other Gulf states, Kuwait strongly opposed Iran's claim to Bahrain and the other Gulf islands.[133] When Abu Musa and the Tunbs were occupied, Kuwait joined Baghdad in protesting that action and in breaking diplomatic relations with Tehran. But the sheikhdom "refused to lend its name to a call to the UN Security Council by five Arab States, led by Iraq, to condemn Iran for its seizure of the islands."[134] Relations were restored in November 1972, reportedly to "counter Israeli influence in Iran."[135]

In short, situated next to Iraq and Iran and mindful of its own security and independence, Kuwait endeavored to maintain a balance between the Gulf's two major rivals. However, Baghdad's previous territorial claims required that Iraq not be challenged openly except in situations where Kuwait's own vital interests were at stake. This was true of the continuing efforts to isolate Iran and of Iraqi attempts to annex parts of the sheikhdom's territory. Otherwise, Baghdad usually found Kuwait willing to accommodate and to cooperate.[136]

In addition to some of the wider political problems of the Gulf, Iraq and Kuwait differed also on a number of other issues that in the period between 1968 and 1973 ranged from the demarcation of the continental shelf to occasional deportation of Iraqi citizens.[137] The most intractable problem of all, however, proved to be the Iraq-Kuwait border; 130 miles long, it had been delineated in 1932, with Great Britain (the sheikhdom's protector since 1899) negotiating on behalf of Kuwait. Since then, Baghdad had repeatedly voiced reservations about the settlement and, in 1961, Kassem threatened to annex the sheikhdom. Two years later, his successor recognized Kuwait's independence but insisted that the border question had to be resolved through future negotiations.[138]

The matter was taken up again in January 1968 during Premier Taher Yahya's official visit to Kuwait. Although the joint communiqué referred to an agreement to continue discussions on this subject, many Kuwaitis remained apprehensive. The reason for their concern was Yahya's public insistence that "Iraq did not believe in artificial borders 'because we are advocates of unity.' "[139] From then on, the border problem remained one of the bones of contention between the two states. In April 1969, with Baghdad and Tehran edging closer to a military confrontation, Kuwait reluctantly agreed to the stationing of Iraqi units on its side of the frontier, reportedly to protect the port city of Umm Qasr against "an impending Iranian attack."[140] The 1969 crisis passed but the Iraqi troops remained; their presence on Kuwaiti territory ultimately resulted in the confrontation of March 1973.

In 1971 Saddam Hussein reopened the border issue by saying that an agreement between the two countries would be signed in the near future.[141] Nothing transpired until December 1972, however, when Iraq began massing troops along the Kuwaiti border.[142] A flurry of diplomatic activity, culminating in a February 1973 visit to Baghdad by Foreign Minister Sheikh Sabah al-Ahmad al-Jaber Al Sabah, produced no settlement and, on March 20, additional Iraqi units crossed the frontier and occupied the police post at al-Samitah.[143] At the outset, Iraq claimed to have been the victim of "Kuwaiti aggression." Seven days later, however, Foreign Minister Murtada al-Hadithi openly admitted Baghdad's responsibility for the attack. In an interview with Beirut's *al-Nahar*, he insisted that Samitah was situated within Iraqi territory and "commanded military positions in that area." This consideration, rather than any "wider strategic plan for expansion in the Gulf," was responsible for the "Iraqi action."[144]

Most of the Arab states, as well as the Arab League, strongly disapproved of Baghdad's resort to force. As they urged restraint and offered to mediate, Kuwait countered with demands of its own: no discussions could begin until Iraq evacuated Samitah and, in any event, future border delineation between the two states had to be based on the agreements of 1932 and 1963. It is noteworthy that this attitude led *al-Thawrah*, on March 27, to accuse Kuwait of artificially "magnifying the incident" and of "collusion" with the United States and the "reactionary Arab forces."[145] Nevertheless, on March 30—ten days after the incursion—the Iraqi troops withdrew from Samitah, due primarily to considerable Arab and Soviet pressure. The military stage of the conflict was over. Before proceeding with the discussion of the second, diplomatic phase, it might be appropriate to examine Baghdad's reasons for initiating the crisis.

Before the war with Iran, Iraq was heavily dependent on the Persian Gulf as the major avenue of the country's foreign trade. However, unlike that of the other regional states, Iraq's access to the Gulf was severely restricted. Its major port, Basrah, is situated some sixty-five miles from the Gulf on the western shore of the Shatt al-Arab, a short distance from the Iranian border. Given the state of relations between the two countries, the Iraqis regarded Basrah as strategically vulnerable. These considerations prompted a search for another outlet to the sea and, in the late 1960s, it was decided to turn Umm Qasr into Iraq's major Gulf port. This location, too, had its problems, however, as access to the Umm Qasr inlet from the Gulf is controlled by the Kuwaiti islands of Bubiyan and Warbah. Therefore, to guarantee the safety of Umm Qasr and to prevent the possibility of a blockade of its Gulf coast, Baghdad demanded from Kuwait a narrow strip of its coastline, including the frontier post at Samitah (situated near Umm Qasr) as well as the two islands.[146] In addition to strategic considerations, control of this territory would also have "bolster[ed] Iraq's claim to a large share of the Gulf's undemarcated continental shelf."[147]

Iraq's position was finally explained during the diplomatic phase of the conflict. In an interview with the Lebanese magazine *al-Sayyad*, published two days prior to the opening of the April 6–8 negotiations between Baghdad and Kuwait, Hadithi stated that the islands were of "extreme importance" because, without them, Iraq could not hope to become a "Gulf state." He went on to explain that if any foreign forces were to land on Bubiyan and Warbah, his country's access to the Gulf would be cut off. Reviving Kassem's 1961 claim, he insisted that "the whole of Kuwait is disputed" because "there is a document saying it is Iraqi and no document saying it is not." Nevertheless, Baghdad did not wish to annex the entire sheikhdom. Rather, it was prepared to abandon its claims "in return for the islands" and a narrow coastal strip. On April 7 a high Kuwaiti official countered that Bubiyan and Warbah were part of the territory of Kuwait. Its boundaries had been recognized by the Arab League as well as by the United Nations and were not, therefore, subject to negotiations.[148]

Given the inflexibility of their respective positions, the talks between the two countries were conducted in "a frank and fraternal manner."[149] The reason for their failure, according to Kuwait's foreign minister, was the attitude adopted by Baghdad. Sheikh Sabah quoted his Iraqi counterpart as announcing: "I am not authorised to negotiate; I have conditions which I wish to offer. . . . I am authorised by my government to claim the islands of Warba and Boubiyan and the coastal belt facing them on the grounds that this land belongs to Iraq." Sheikh Sabah retorted that "there will be no dialogue before the delineation of the border on the basis of [the 1932 and 1963] agreements." In spite of the impasse, the sides consented to continue discussions "at future meetings."[150] Following protracted negotiations, in July 1977 Iraq and Kuwait agreed to withdraw troops from the border areas.[151]

One of the more striking aspects of the 1973 border crisis was the relative speed with which the Iraqis had evacuated the occupied territory without securing any concessions from Kuwait. In retrospect, it would appear that, in addition to the pressures generated by the Arab states and Iran, the USSR, too, had played an important part in defusing a potentially explosive situation in the Gulf.

Publicly, Moscow had little to say about Baghdad's action. Soviet discretion was understandable, as the tension involved the two Arab Gulf states with which the Kremlin attempted to remain on friendly terms. (It will be recalled that, in addition to Iraq and Iran, Kuwait was the only other Gulf country to have established diplomatic relations with—in 1963—and to have purchased arms from the USSR. It was also an important member of the conservative Arab Gulf community and hence a possible valuable future asset.) Nevertheless, Soviet press coverage of the incident reveals some interesting insights. On March 21, one day after the Iraqi incursion, when a reference to it might ordinarily have appeared in its pages, *Pravda* treated its readers instead to a brief account of a speech Saddam Hussein delivered on March 20. The vice-chairman of the RCC praised the USSR for supporting Iraq in the "struggle against imperialism and Zionism." He then criticized those who, "in flirting with the West, attempt to call into question Soviet friendship" and warned that such an attitude "harbors a serious danger"—it diverts attention from the Arabs' main task which is the "struggle against imperialism."[152]

Saddam Hussein's remarks represented a skillful diplomatic maneuver, making it difficult for Moscow to be overly critical of Baghdad. To place the events of March 1973 into their proper perspective, it should be reiterated that, since late 1972, the USSR chose not to support Iraq's assertive policy in the Gulf openly.[153] Initially applicable to Iran, the attitude could have been expected to extend also to Kuwait, a state whose friendship the Kremlin was trying to cultivate.

In any event, the first and, for the rest of the month, only reference to the incursion appeared in *Pravda* on March 22. It was short, factual, and based exclusively on Baghdad's initial version of the event: on March 20, an Iraqi border patrol, training in Iraqi territory, was attacked by Kuwaiti troops. The Iraqis returned fire, acting in self-defense. *Pravda* then quoted from a statement by the Iraqi Ministry of Internal Affairs which expressed incomprehension at Kuwait's action. The account concluded by noting the apprehension expressed by the other Arab states and their appeals for a speedy resolution of the crisis.

Because only the Iraqi version of the incident was reported (and never refuted) in the Soviet press, and because so little was said about it at the time, Moscow's relative passivity could have been interpreted as lack of concern with the developments in the Gulf, or as indirect backing of Baghdad's initiative, or both. As soon became evident, however, these impressions were misleading. Although the USSR had no intention of openly humiliating Iraq, the Kremlin left no doubt about its concern as well as about its serious misgivings with Baghdad's action. An opportunity to do so publicly was provided by Saddam Hussein's arrival in Moscow, "at the invitation of the Soviet government," on March 21, 1973.[154] Because such high-level visits are customarily planned in advance and the Soviets usually announce them ahead of time, the trip may be assumed to have been arranged at a very short notice. Moreover, the dinner speeches delivered by Saddam Hussein and Kosygin on March 22 contained no references to any pressing problems that might have necessitated the visit.[155] The same was true of the account of Saddam Hussein's March 23 meeting with Brezhnev and of the joint statement of the next day.[156] It may therefore be concluded that the visit was arranged primarily to deal with the situation which had arisen as a result of the Iraqi incursion into Kuwait.

Moreover, careful reading of Kosygin's speech, made on the very day when the Soviet press published the Iraqi account of the Samitah incident, revealed Moscow's real attitude toward the events of the past two days. In an apparent bow to Baghdad, the premier allowed that the "dissolution of the world colonial system" had left a "painful legacy . . . [of] unequal and predatory agreements and treaties." He then went on to insist, however, that it was the "wish of the peoples that just norms of international relations prevail and dominate in the world." This meant, Kosygin elucidated, "equality, mutual respect, [and] noninterference in the sovereign life of peoples." The USSR and "our Communist party consistently adhere to these principles in our foreign policy."[157] The implicit question was, Should Iraq be expected to do less?

On the basis of these observations it may be concluded that Baghdad had not consulted Moscow on its planned move into Kuwait. Whether such a course of action was required under the provisions of the 1972 treaty is debatable.[158] The Ba'th certainly did not seem to have thought so, since it claimed that the territory in question belonged to Iraq. Kuwait, on the other hand, disagreed and, on this particular issue, the USSR chose to side with it and not with Baghdad. In any event, there is little doubt that the Soviets disapproved of Iraq's action and invited Saddam Hussein to Moscow to pressure him to withdraw the Iraqi troops from Kuwaiti territory, which was done by March 30.

On reflection, there appear to have been several reasons for this Soviet position. The Kremlin, since 1972, was interested less in supporting Iraq's political ambitions in the Gulf than it was in improving relations with Iran and, as it turned out, also with Kuwait. A glimpse at the state of Moscow-Kuwait relations at the time of the crisis was provided by the exchange of telegrams between Foreign Ministers Andrei Gromyko and Sheikh Sabah occasioned by the tenth anniversary of the establishment of diplomatic relations. The messages expressed both gratification at the expanding ties between the two countries and conviction that relations would continue to develop on the basis of "friendship and mutual understanding."[159] While not too much should be read into this formulation, it, as well as the very exchange of the telegrams, supports the proposition that Moscow valued its association with Kuwait and was not interested in jeopardizing it by support of Baghdad's bullying tactics.[160] Moreover, the Soviets must have been annoyed with the timing of the attack—it came shortly after Gromyko's friendly telegram to Sheikh Sabah and only four days after Premier Kosygin's return from an official visit to Iran.[161]

Outside the Gulf, in the spring of 1973, the USSR was devoting considerable attention to the Arab-Israeli problem. For instance, in the statement issued at the conclusion of Saddam Hussein's visit, the "sides noted the great importance of strengthening the solidarity and unity of actions of the Arab states and of the mobilization of all of their resources in the struggle against imperialism, Zionism, and reaction."[162] Seen in this light, the Iraqi intrusion into Kuwait was totally counterproductive—it split the Arab ranks and diverted their attention from what, to Moscow, were much more important issues. As subsequently noted by the *New Times*, the dispute had "caused anxiety in Arab capitals, . . . as Zionist and imperialist quarters have seized upon it to sow dissension in the Arab world and to weaken the Arab . . . struggle to eliminate the consequences of the Israeli aggression."[163]

Another intriguing aspect of the Kremlin's involvement in the border crisis was the visit to Iraq of the commander in chief of the Soviet navy, Admiral Sergei Gorshkov, and of a Russian naval detachment which remained in Umm Qasr between April 3 and 11, 1973.[164] The questions of whether their presence in Iraq had been related to the crisis and, if so, what role they had played in it have been thoroughly examined by Anne M. Kelly. While no exhaustive answers can be given even now, some tentative conclusions are possible. First, the timing of the visit indicated that it had nothing to do with the first phase of the conflict which concluded with the withdrawal of Iraqi troops from Kuwaiti territory. The evacuation was completed by April 1, or two days before the arrival of the Soviet naval detachment in Umm Qasr. Hence, although I believe that the USSR was in fact instrumental in effecting an early pullout of Iraqi units from Samitah, Moscow's views were initially and forcefully communicated to Baghdad not by Gorshkov but by the CPSU leadership, including Kosygin and, most likely, also Brezhnev.

As for the second or diplomatic phase of the crisis, highlighted, in early April, by the delivery of a virtual ultimatum to Kuwait to redraw the frontier according to Iraqi specifications, it could be argued that the presence of the Soviet naval detachment in Umm Qasr was meant to strengthen Baghdad's hand in the forthcoming negotiations. However, since Moscow was by then on record as opposing the use of force in the resolution of the border problem, the presence of Gorshkov and his flotilla did not seem to have made much practical difference. Given Kuwait's resolution to resist Iraq's diplomatic pressure, it is likely that the sheikhdom, too, arrived at this conclusion.

Another possible explanation revolves around the theory that the Soviet navy and its commander were dispatched in order to prevent Baghdad from once again resorting to military force in case of Kuwait's expected refusal to hand over a part of its territory. Such a hypothesis has little evidence to support it. Iraq had withdrawn its troops from Samitah in the face of the mounting Arab and Soviet opposition and would not likely have seriously entertained the thought of a new invasion just a few days after completing the pullback. In short, if the naval visit was in any way connected to the border dispute, its purpose was likely to stabilize a dangerous situation which affected regional stability and involved the two Arab Gulf states with which Moscow attempted to stay on good terms.

On the other hand, as Kelly demonstrates, the arrival of Gorshkov and his detachment was probably arranged well in advance of the Iraqi attack and was therefore totally unrelated to the crisis. It might, instead, have been intended to help secure for the Soviet navy access to Umm Qasr, a port built with Russian assistance. An attempt to acquire such a foothold in the strategically important Persian Gulf would have been in line with Moscow's similar efforts elsewhere in the Middle East and with the USSR's general forward naval deployment policy in the Mediterranean and the Indian Ocean. If this reasoning is correct, the two events—the border crisis and the Soviet naval visit—were purely coincidental. Either way, the presence of Gorshkov and his ships proved to be of little use to Baghdad and did not net Moscow free access to Iraqi naval facilities. On the contrary, the Kremlin's attitude during the 1973 crisis appears to have had the opposite effect—in view of Baghdad's failure to achieve its own objectives, the Soviet stand could not but reinforce the Ba'th's determination not to accommodate the USSR's desire to establish its naval presence in the Gulf through the use of the port of Umm Qasr.

Thus the Soviet position in the 1973 crisis can be summed up as follows: first, the Kremlin acknowledged that Iraq had a legitimate grievance against Kuwait. Echoing Kosygin's earlier pronouncement, the *New Times* argued that "the border line dat[ed] back to the times of British colonial rule . . . [and had] never been precisely defined."[165] At the same time, however, Moscow disapproved of the use of force while urging Baghdad to withdraw its troops from Kuwaiti territory and to negotiate a peaceful settlement of the border problem. Once the Iraqi units had been evacuated, the USSR expressed its satisfaction with this turn of events and proceeded to offer moral support to Baghdad's insistence on redrawing the frontier.[166] Under the circumstances, this could only have meant acquisition by Iraq of some of Kuwait's territory. With the use of force being ruled out, however, Moscow's verbal support was of little practical significance, leading to the conclusion that the USSR's real objective was to keep the lid on a potentially explosive situation while attempting to remain on good terms with both protagonists. This may have worked in the case of Kuwait but did not go over too well in Baghdad.

Moscow, Baghdad, and the Gulf, 1972–1975

The Kremlin remained keenly aware of London's continuing influence in the Persian Gulf even after the British withdrawal had been completed in December 1971. For example, *International Affairs* argued in late 1972 that "British imperialism" did not leave the Gulf region after all. Rather, "by making use of . . . various military-political machinations . . . ," London succeeded in shoring up its dwindling positions. On the political plane, the United Kingdom replaced the old "colonial treaties with the Persian Gulf principalities by 'friendship and cooperation' agreements . . . [which acknowledge] 'Britain's vital interest' in the affairs of the Persian Gulf, and [contain] an obligation for the principalities to consult London on every problem of their foreign policy." Great Britain continued also to exert considerable military influence in the Gulf. "Numerous army units" remained stationed in the area and the U.K. retained a "network of bases," ranging from Bahrain and Sharjah to the Omani facilities in Salalah and on the island of Masirah. Finally, the Gulf was frequently visited by units of the Royal Navy.[167] In view of these considerations, it was concluded that "despite some changes, Britain's policy in this part of the globe has clearly not undergone any essential revision." Instead of withdrawing, London simply regrouped its forces and continued to play an important role in the affairs of the Gulf. "Its strength is not what it once was, [as] the collapse of Pax Britannica is [an] . . . incontestable reality." Nevertheless, "it would be a dangerous mistake to underestimate Britain's role in the Persian Gulf area."[168]

Still, from 1972 on, Moscow's attention in this part of the world was clearly focused on the United States. The reasons for Washington's concern with the events in the Persian Gulf, the Soviet commentators argued, remained military, economic, and political. But the nature of U.S. involvement did change, as the course of events forced the United States to adapt itself to new realities. Specifically, in the 1950s, when Great Britain was the dominant Western power in the Gulf, the two capitalist giants competed with each other over the region's oil reserves. During the 1960s, due to the growth of the Arab nationalist movement, London and Washington reached an agreement on a "division of labor." The United States supported Great Britain's political and military preeminence in the Gulf in exchange for London's protection of American economic interests. Only in the late 1960s and the 1970s did London's "inability to maintain the necessary 'order' impel Washington to move toward establishment of US military and political domination in the area."[169]

According to Soviet analysts, one of the objectives pursued by the United States was to strengthen American military presence in the Gulf area. In this connection, an important role had been assigned to "the US [naval] squadron . . . which had been operating in the Persian Gulf for almost 25 years." To ensure the "legitimacy" of the U.S. naval presence in the Gulf, Washington in 1972 "hurriedly concluded an agreement on United States use of the Bahrain base for the 'modest charge' of a few hundred thousand dollars a year."[170] In addition, Bahrain was also said to occupy an important place in the "wider plans" of the American strategists. Thus, in the wake of the 1971 war between India and Pakistan, Washington decided to establish a permanent naval presence in the Indian Ocean. With this in mind, the United States began constructing a major base on the island of Diego Garcia. It was intended to supplement the naval facilities available to the U.S. navy in Australia and South Africa, forming what the Soviet press described as a "triangle of bases" to embrace the entire Indian Ocean basin. The "northern tier" of this system would rest on the "strong points" retained by Great Britain in Oman and on the bases situated in Bahrain.[171]

Otherwise, Moscow rejected Washington's argument that the withdrawal of British forces from the Persian Gulf would lead to regional instability. On the contrary, stability was being threatened by the "constant interference of the British and American imperialism in the affairs of this region. . . ."[172] According to Soviet analysts, the Western powers were determined "to retain the Gulf countries within the sphere of their influence and control." This goal was being pursued along two parallel tracks. On the one hand, a considerable effort was being made to keep "the Persian Gulf countries weak, divided . . . and thus incapable of withstanding the dictates of imperialism." On the other hand, Soviet commentators argued, Washington continued to push the discredited idea of setting up, "under US sponsorship, a broad regional military-political alliance in the Persian Gulf area." In pursuing its policies, the United States enjoyed the full backing not only of Great Britain—now Washington's "junior partner"—but also of the "local reactionary circles," whose interests coincided with those of the "imperialist powers." All of them were dedicated to "fight[ing] against the forces of national liberation and social emancipation."[173] The Soviet policy in the Gulf, in contrast, was depicted as the exact opposite of that conducted by the Western powers and their local supporters. Moscow backed the Arab national liberation movement and favored radical political and socio-economic reforms. The Kremlin also denied allegations about a Soviet threat to the security of the Persian Gulf.[174]

In addition to military-strategic and political considerations, Soviet publications continued to emphasize the economic importance of the Persian Gulf to the Western powers in general and to the United States in particular. In an article, "Oil and Politics," it was noted that, by 1972, the U.S. companies accounted for more than half of the petroleum extracted in the Gulf region. Not only did they secure "marvellous profits," but the United States also became more dependent on imported petroleum for its domestic consumption. For these reasons, Washington, like London before it, was striving to gain "guaranteed control" over Persian Gulf oil through exertion of "military pressure" on the producer countries.[175] This state of affairs was not acceptable to Moscow. Falling back upon the Iranian formulation, the Soviets argued that "questions related to the Persian Gulf area should be solved by the states of the area in conformity with the principles written into the UN charter, and without outside interference."[176]

According to the Soviet press, the Arab-Israeli war of October 1973 contributed to a general weakening of the Western positions in the Persian Gulf. Large financial assistance was extended to the "front-line" states by the Arab Gulf countries, accompanied by an oil boycott of some Western consumers, including the United States. A particularly telling blow against the "capitalist monopolies" was struck by Kuwait which, in 1974, assumed control of 60 percent of the shares of the Anglo-American Kuwait Petroleum Company. On the negative side, however, Soviet publications expressed concern about the continuing lack of progress in achieving regional security and stability. As in the past, the Western powers were held responsible—they persisted in maintaining military presence in the Gulf and in "inflaming regional conflicts." The United States did not withdraw its naval detachment from Bahrain, although the latter had abrogated the 1972 agreement after the outbreak of the 1973 war. Washington was also supplying vast amounts of military equipment to Saudi Arabia and Iran thus stimulating a regional arms race of "unheard of proportions." As a result, Tehran emerged as the dominant military power in the Gulf, arousing considerable apprehension about its ultimate intentions among its Arab neighbors. In 1974, Moscow found their concern well justified, as attested to by its condemnation of the shah's decision to dispatch Iranian forces to assist Sultan Qabus in his war against the rebels of the Popular Front for the Liberation of Oman.[177]

In early 1975 the USSR stepped up its propaganda efforts designed to depict the United States as the major destabilizing factor in the Persian Gulf and the entire Indian Ocean basin. *Pravda* reported that the Bahraini facilities, used by the U.S. navy, were being expanded.[178] Moreover, a major effort had been launched to secure for the U.S. air force the use of the British base on Masirah: a secret agreement was reportedly reached during Sultan Qabus's January 1975 visit to Washington.[179] In addition to the Persian Gulf, the access to Masirah was bound to strengthen the overall U.S. strategic posture in the Indian Ocean where, according to Admiral Elmo Zumwalt, the United States should not hesitate to use military power in the pursuit of its national interests.

The Soviet commentators remained unshaken in their belief that, in the long run, the "imperialist" efforts in the developing world were destined to fail.[180] Nevertheless, for the near term, Moscow remained visibly concerned about the growing U.S. presence in the Persian Gulf and in the Indian Ocean generally. It was therefore ironic that Soviet apprehensions were not shared by any of the Gulf states, including Iraq, whose attention from 1972 through 1975 was focused not so much on the activities of the outsiders as on the affairs of the region itself. Baghdad, in particular, remained too preoccupied with its internal problems and the steadily deteriorating relations with Tehran to pay much public attention to issues that were of central concern to Moscow. The Ba'thist attitude must also have been influenced by the perception of the Kremlin's pro-Iranian stand on problems separating Tehran and Baghdad.

In any event, the determination to protect the "Arab character of the Gulf," announced in the late 1960s and designed to isolate Iran, remained an integral part of most of Baghdad's regional diplomatic initiatives in the period between 1972 and 1975. In the sense that all of the Arab Gulf states, except Oman, continued to oppose the shah's proposal for a regional mutual assistance pact, Iraq may be said to have scored an important victory. However, Baghdad's efforts to drive a wedge between Tehran and its Arab neighbors proved only marginally successful. In 1974, only the PDRY announced itself in full agreement with Iraq's stated determination to defend the "Arab character of the Gulf."[181]

Initially, that is in 1972, Baghdad appeared to have secured the backing of such important members of the Gulf community as the United Arab Emirates and Kuwait. In March the UAE foreign minister denounced Iran's occupation of the Gulf islands and described them "an integral part of the Arab homeland which must be retrieved in due course." Kuwait concurred—the islands as well as the Shatt al-Arab were "indivisable parts of the Arab homeland, proved by the facts of history, population and law"—but said nothing about the islands' recovery.[182] In the fall of 1972 Kuwait appeared to be moving closer to the Iraqi position when some of its publications accused Iran of collusion with "British and US imperialism" as well as with Israel for the purpose of "occupying other parts of the Gulf." Nevertheless, in November, Kuwait restored diplomatic relations with Iran.[183]

Iraq's efforts to elicit support from Bahrain and Qatar, too, proved unsuccessful. When Foreign Minister Hadithi revisited both countries in the spring of 1972, no joint statements were issued—a clear indication of the sheikhdoms' determination to steer a neutral course in the Baghdad-Tehran dispute.[184] But the most serious blow to Iraq's efforts to isolate Iran was delivered by Saudi Arabia. In December 1972 Minister of State for Foreign Affairs Omar al-Saqqaf visited Tehran for the stated purpose of coordinating Saudi and Iranian policies in the Gulf. In an interview with *Kayhan International*, Saqqaf unequivocally distanced Riyadh from the anti-Iranian campaign waged by the "so-called radical Arabs" over the question of Abu Musa and the Tunbs. He went on to say that "the radicals' voices were not raised because the islands were Arab, or even because they valued them, but because they wanted 'to spoil the atmosphere of the region and create conflict.'" Saudi Arabia condemned such efforts and was determined to cement its friendship with Iran, a relationship which Saqqaf described as "the cornerstone of our foreign policy."[185] Two assumptions underlay this Saudi view: Communism and the Soviet influence represented the main threats to the stability and security of the Gulf region and the most efficient method of countering them was regional cooperation built around the Riyadh-Tehran axis. Equally implicit was the proposition that Iraq's anti-Iranian campaign, wittingly or otherwise, served to advance Soviet interests. In addition, the notion of a Tehran-Riyadh alliance was strongly encouraged by both the Nixon and Carter administrations as part of their "Twin Pillar" policy in the Persian Gulf. These considerations left Saudi Arabia no choice but to come out openly in opposition to Baghdad's policy in the Gulf, a turn of events which doomed the Ba'thist efforts to forge an anti-Iranian alliance.

No major events in the context of Gulf security occurred until the fall of 1974, when Bahrain revoked its decision to deny the U.S. navy the use of its facilities. According to the *International Herald Tribune*, Bahrain reversed its position due to "discreet pleas from the United States and Iran" which, along with some unspecified Arab states (presumably Saudi Arabia), had expressed growing concern over regional security due to "increasing Soviet sea and air activity in and around the Gulf."[186]

Partly in an attempt to counterbalance the negative reaction which its decision evoked among the "radical" Arab states, Bahrain also suggested the creation of a formal military alliance embracing all of the Arab Gulf states. On November 20, 1974, Kuwait's *al-Siyassah* quoted the island's foreign minister to the effect that, since the region's Arab countries had "established co-operation and co-ordination in all other fields, it is desirable that we establish co-operation in the military field as well." Otherwise, the "existing co-operation between the Arab states of the Gulf would not be 'fruitful.'"[187] Lest the Bahraini initiative be construed as a threat to the security of Iran, however, the minister, in an interview with *Kayhan International*, assured Tehran that his country had "always" advocated cooperation among the Gulf states, including "those beyond the immediate area" (a curious formulation presumably meaning Iran). Moreover, Bahrain was in favor of Mohammed Reza Shah's insistence that "the affairs of the Gulf should be the concern of the littoral states only, and that the Gulf should remain a 'zone of peace.'"[188]

Aimed at solidifying the Arab position and at establishing a degree of political harmony in the Gulf, the Bahraini overtures had no immediate impact on regional affairs. They may, however, have triggered renewed Iraqi efforts to seize the political initiative at a time when Baghdad-Tehran relations appeared to have reached another low.[189] In January 1975 Foreign Minister Sa'dun Hammadi visited Saudi Arabia, the UAE, Qatar, and Bahrain. The stated purpose of the trip was to "co-ordinate" Arab policy in the Gulf.[190] The intent of Iraq's policy was explained by Saddam Hussein. In an interview with Cairo's *al-Ahram*, the vice-chairman of the RCC reiterated that Iraq would make "every effort and support any policy aimed at preserving the Arab nature of the Gulf." He suggested, specifically, the signing of a bilateral defense agreement with Saudi Arabia which would include, among other things, "the formation of a joint navy."[191] Given the well-known Saudi mistrust of Iraq's intentions, which resurfaced during Hammadi's January visit to Riyadh (his conversations with King Faisal were described as having been conducted "in a frank and fraternal atmosphere"),[192] nothing, predictably, came of this initiative. As it happened, this did not matter because Iraq's diplomatic efforts aimed at isolating Iran were soon overtaken by events. As noted earlier, in March 1975 Baghdad and Tehran agreed to resolve their outstanding differences.

Evaluation

An examination of the respective Soviet and Iraqi positions on some of the major political problems facing the Persian Gulf after the announcement of Great Britain's intention to withdraw its forces from the areas "East of Suez" reveals a partial coincidence of views but also a significant divergence of interests. Specifically, Iraq, along with most other Gulf states, favored London's decision and explicitly rejected the argument that the pullout of the British forces would result in a "power vacuum" which would eventually be filled by the USSR. On the contrary, Baghdad and others pronounced the area's governments and peoples both willing and able to handle their own as well as regional affairs and insisted on the speedy evacuation of the British troops from the Gulf. Moreover, Iraq and the rest of the Arab Gulf states refused to join any Western-sponsored pacts and insisted that the region's defense should be entrusted to the governments of the littoral countries, all views wholeheartedly shared by Moscow.

The Kremlin adjusted easily to positions on which relative harmony prevailed in the Persian Gulf. It did encounter difficulties in attempting to deal with some of the area's more complex political issues, however.

One of them revolved around the substance and the form of regional cooperation to be achieved after the withdrawal of the British troops. For example, Iran's participation in any regional defense organization was strongly and consistently opposed by Iraq—an early manifestation of Baghdad-Tehran tensions that grew appreciably in the late 1960s and early 1970s. The shah, in contrast, favored a regional defense alliance in which Iran would play an important, if not a dominant, part. Competition between the two rivals presented the USSR with a major political problem which Moscow, for all of its efforts, proved unable to solve.

Another illustration of diverging Soviet and Iraqi interests was provided by the decision to proceed with the formation of the Lower Gulf Federation. Iraq had endorsed the plan early and unconditionally, but its attitude underwent a gradual change and resulted in nonrecognition of the UAE in December 1971. Moscow reacted differently. The project was initially greeted with reservation, was given guarded approval in 1970, and the new state was recognized by the USSR soon after its inception. It was hardly a coincidence that there were no references to Iraq's position in the Soviet pronouncements on the federation. Moreover, the USSR cared little about the future status of the disputed Gulf islands, whereas Baghdad was deeply involved in that dispute.

In short, the disharmony in Soviet and Iraqi approaches to various regional problems was caused by diverging interests which the two countries were pursuing in the Gulf. While Moscow was concerned primarily with undermining the Western position and strengthening its own, Baghdad was preoccupied with the contest for political leadership in the Persian Gulf which it had long waged with Iran. The rivalry between the region's two most powerful states, whose cooperation the Soviets had been actively seeking, confronted the USSR with a dilemma. It could offer its support to one of the sides and risk alienating the other, or it could adopt a neutral stance and attempt to maintain cordial relations with both. The latter course of action harbored the obvious danger of antagonizing both parties without securing any tangible returns from either.

It is evident that the Kremlin, opting for what it no doubt regarded as the lesser of the two evils, chose the second alternative. In so doing, the USSR, albeit indirectly, came out in opposition to Iraq's efforts to isolate Iran and to project itself into a leadership role in Gulf affairs. Put differently, as a result of their desire to remain on good terms with both Baghdad and Tehran, the Soviets wound up performing a balancing act, leaning toward Iraq in the period between 1968 and 1971, tilting toward Iran from 1972 to 1974, and coming out strongly in support of Iraq in late 1974. In conducting this type of policy, the Kremlin occasionally scored some points with one of the antagonists but invariably alienated the other.

More specifically, during the period from 1968 through 1971, Moscow and Baghdad shared common ground in their opposition to Western efforts to stabilize the Gulf region, with the USSR maintaining a discreet silence on Iraq's rivalry with Iran and working to improve relations with Tehran. From 1971 to 1974, a period which, in retrospect, deserves to be labeled the high water mark of Moscow-Baghdad relations, the Kremlin turned down Saddam Hussein's public request for Soviet backing of the Ba'th's Gulf policy and continued to voice respect for the shah's insistence on the legitimacy of Iran's role in regional affairs. The late 1974 shift in favor of Iraq was caused by the rapidly deteriorating situation in Kurdistan, a turn of events to which Mohammed Reza Shah had made an important contribution and which Moscow regarded as inimical to its interests. In 1975 Iran and Iraq reconciled their differences. Although the Soviets applauded the outcome, the rapprochement between Baghdad and Tehran provided another example of Iraq's determination to conduct an independent foreign policy in spite of its heavy reliance on the USSR.

In addition to the Baghdad-Tehran rivalry, the USSR also became actively involved in the Iraq-Kuwait crisis of March 1973. The Kremlin not only chose to oppose the Ba'th's efforts to acquire parts of Kuwait's territory by military means but also exerted its influence in Baghdad to effect the withdrawal of Iraqi forces.

In sum, an analysis of Soviet and Iraqi policies in the Persian Gulf in the period between 1968 and 1975 brings to light complementary positions (such as their joint, pronounced anti-Western as well as "anticonservative" attitudes) but also conflicting aspirations and interests (as in the case of the Iraqi-Iranian and Iraqi-Kuwaiti relations). In retrospect, Moscow appears to have initially disapproved of Baghdad's hostility to Tehran and to have occasionally (as was the case in February 1972) attempted to exert influence on the Ba'th to moderate its anti-Iranian stance. These efforts were unsuccessful despite Iraq's dependence on the USSR and the signing, in April 1972, of the Treaty of Friendship and Cooperation. Significantly, the same was true of Saddam Hussein's attempt, made also in February 1972, to prevail upon the Soviets to support Iraq's aspirations in the Persian Gulf. In late 1974, for reasons described in chapter 3, the Kremlin shifted its position and tried to persuade the shah to discontinue his policy of support of the Kurdish nationalists in Iraq. This initiative, as well as pressure to scale down arms purchases from the United States, proved counterproductive.

The only positive exercise of Soviet influence occurred in March 1973, when the USSR, along with the rest of the Arab states, prevailed upon Iraq to withdraw its forces from the Kuwaiti territory. This time Moscow's efforts were crowned with success but it is probable that its intervention was resented bitterly by Baghdad and served as an additional illustration of the basic incompatibility of the two countries' long-range interests. The Ba'th had no choice but to swallow this bitter pill, but it may be safely assumed that the lesson learned by the Iraqi leaders had been neither forgotten nor forgiven. It was merely shelved, being subordinated to bigger and more important issues. Leading among them was the unsettled situation in northern Iraq and the growing likelihood that the Kurdish problem would have to be resolved on the battlefield, a development requiring large-scale Soviet military and political support. Nevertheless, even the experiences of 1974 and 1975 drove home to the Kremlin the limits of its ability to influence the major policies of the Iraqi Ba'th. Having used the USSR for its own purposes, Baghdad proceeded to assert itself across the entire spectrum of governmental activities without consultation with Moscow and regardless of whether its actions were agreeable to the Russians.

Problems of Security and Stability

The Ba'th's determination to subdue the Kurds helped pave the way for the Algiers agreement of March 1975. In its wake, Iraq adopted a more moderate and pragmatic policy designed to improve relations with the conservative Gulf states, a policy that was reasonably successful, although its Iranian component disintegrated after the shah's downfall in 1979.

In any event, relations between Baghdad and Tehran improved rapidly after the signing of the Algiers accord. In late March, Prime Minister Hoveida traveled to Baghdad and conferred with President Bakr and Saddam Hussein. According to the joint communiqué of March 29, the sides undertook "to expand co-operation in all fields, including political issues, trade and economic relations."[1] One month later, an Iraqi delegation, consisting of Saddam Hussein, Foreign Minister Hammadi, and Minister of Interior Izzat Ibrahim al-Duri, arrived in Tehran. According to Saddam Hussein, the purpose of the visit was to "extend . . . [the] spirit [of the Algiers accord] to other areas," one of which was military cooperation among the Gulf states.[2] This flurry of diplomatic activity led, in June 1975, to the formal signing of the Iraqi-Iranian treaty, which was based on and incorporated the main provisions of the March agreement.[3]

The next step in the rapidly developing cooperation between the two states was taken in August 1975. During the visit to Baghdad of Iranian Minister of Interior Jamshid Amuzegar, Iraq and Iran agreed "to promote the further development and strengthening of bilateral relations."[4] High-level contacts continued later in the year and into 1976— in August, Hammadi traveled to Tehran, while Foreign Minister Khalatbari and Hoveida visited Baghdad in December 1975 and January 1976, respectively.[5]

Relations cooled temporarily in January 1976, after the information ministers of the Gulf's Arab states approved a Kuwaiti proposal for the establishment of the Arabian Gulf News Agency. The decision provoked a storm of protest in Tehran. On January 7, Khalatbari announced Iran's decision to "review" its policy toward the neighboring Arab states should they persist in using "a fictitious name" for the Persian Gulf. Four days later, Mohammed Reza Shah ordered Iranian ambassadors to the Arab Gulf states to return home "for consultations."[6] Iraq proved equally inflexible. In April, Foreign Minister Hammadi "refused to accept two messages from the Iranian Government" because they had contained references to "the Persian Gulf." Tehran described the incident as "totally unacceptable" and expressed concern over Baghdad's seeming unwillingness to improve relations between the two states.[7] Tension eased in June 1976, when Hammadi visited Tehran and exchanged the "final copies" of the 1975 treaty. A few weeks later, President Bakr spoke of Iran as a country with which Iraq enjoyed "relations of good-neighbourliness."[8]

For the next three years—until the shah's overthrow in 1979—relations between Iraq and Iran continued to improve. This was evidenced in an unusually high number of top-level visits, in the warm praise for their cooperation emanating from both capitals, and in a multitude of bilateral agreements. Thus, in January 1977 Hammadi returned to Tehran. In the joint communiqué, the sides expressed their "determination to expand [bilateral] relations" and "reaffirmed" their adherence to "the principles of full respect for national sovereignty, non-interference in internal affairs, and the peaceful settlement of disputes."[9] In March, Iran and Iraq signed an agreement delineating the frontier areas to be exchanged between them.[10] In July they agreed on the organizational framework to foster bilateral cooperation. The Joint Ministerial Committee, set up in 1975 and meeting for the first time, established subcommittees to deal with "energy, agriculture and fisheries; trade, transit, customs and communications; oil, gas and geology; education and tourism; and consular affairs." In addition, Iran and Iraq signed agreements expediting "trade, cultural co-operation, co-operation between the . . . ministries of Interior, tourism, agriculture and fisheries, and the establishment of a link between the Iraqi and Iranian railway networks." In November 1977 Iraq and Iran signed another trade agreement.[11] One of the few major policy differences to arise between them was the issue of a regional security pact, a subject to be discussed later in this chapter. The problem, although serious, was not allowed to disrupt the rapidly developing cooperation between Iran and Iraq.

Relations continued to expand in 1978. Among highlights was the second session of the Joint Ministerial Committee which met in Baghdad in late February and early March. It concerned itself with "promoting co-operation in such areas as fishing, commerce, power, communications and diplomatic representation." (According to rumors circulating at the time, Foreign Minister Khalatbari requested the Iraqi government to expel Ayatollah Rohollah Khomeini who was then living in the Shi'i religious center of Najaf. The reports proved correct. On October 6, after being refused asylum in Kuwait, the Ayatollah left Iraq for France.)[12] Finally, an important tourism agreement permitting 40,000 Iranian pilgrims to visit the Shi'i holy places in Iraq was signed in May.[13] Close relations between the two countries were terminated abruptly in the first half of 1979, when the shah's overthrow brought to power the fundamentalist religious regime headed by Ayatollah Khomeini.

The Algiers accord weakened Moscow's ability to influence Baghdad, but, nevertheless, the USSR adopted a benevolent attitude toward Iraq's efforts to normalize relations with Iran. This position was consistent with the general themes advanced by the Soviets throughout the 1970s: local and regional tensions in the Gulf area had been fostered by the "imperialist" powers; settlements of disputes served the cause of universal peace; and Iraq and Iran, in resolving their differences, had set a worthy example which others would be wise to emulate. Moreover, the Kremlin had long urged the Gulf states to base their mutual relations on what Foreign Minister Gromyko described as "trust and goodneighborly cooperation."[14] Public displays of friendship toward Tehran, reinforced by extensive high-level contacts and steadily growing trade relations between the USSR and Iran,[15] appeared frequently in the Soviet publications in the latter 1970s, despite occasionally bitter criticism of the shah's military buildup program and of his rapprochement with the United States.

Gulf "National Liberation" Movements

A more visible illustration of the diverging Soviet and Iraqi interests in the Gulf was provided by their respective attitudes toward the self-styled "national liberation" movements, above all the Popular Front for the Liberation of Oman (PFLO)[16] and the National Liberation Front of Bahrain (NLFB).

According to The Voice of the Oman Revolution radio, broadcasting from Aden in mid-1975, Iraq, along with Libya, the PDRY, and the Palestine Liberation Organization, were classified as staunch Arab sup-

porters of the PFLO. Opposed to them were the forces of the "reactionaries, slackers and defeatists," led by Iran, Saudi Arabia, and Jordan.[17]
Nevertheless, soon after the March 1975 reconciliation between Tehran
and Baghdad, rumors began to circulate that Iraq had decided to terminate its backing of the Popular Front. (Baghdad had in fact undertaken to
do so as part of the Algiers accord.)[18] An early indication of the reported
change in Iraq's position was contained in a PFLO communiqué, made
public in Aden in August 1975. Among other things, it attacked plans
for convening a Gulf security conference as "a damaging conspiracy . . .
which aims to subject the Arab people of the Gulf to Iranian-American
influence."[19] Because Iraq was on record as favoring the conference, the
PFLO statement represented a veiled attack on Baghdad—it is inconceiv-
able that language of this kind would have been used against a friendly
Arab government. Put differently, by August 1975, the Popular Front
must have come to the conclusion that, due to its rapprochement with
"reactionary" Iran, Iraq had decided to abandon the PFLO to its own
devices.

Another straw in the wind was a report that, on the shah's insistence,
Iraq was revising its hostile attitude toward Oman. Although *al-Thawrah*, on September 8, 1975, called for "increased action in the guerrilla
war" in Dhofar as well as for the overthrow of Sultan Qabus, Beirut's
usually well-informed *al-Nahar*, only two days later, predicted an impending change in Baghdad's attitude.[20] The rumors proved correct. In
January 1976, Iraq and Oman established diplomatic relations, a move
followed by a violent anti-Baghdad campaign from the PFLO.[21] These developments were correctly interpreted to mean the termination of Baghdad's policy of support of the PFLO and of opposition to Sultan Qabus.
This conclusion was subsequently reinforced by a Damascus Radio
broadcast which asserted that the Iraqi Ba'th had issued an "internal cir-
cular" announcing the end of the Dhofar rebellion. The Iraqis reportedly
argued that the uprising "had been a mechanical copy of non-Arab revolutions, . . . the circumstances had not been ripe, and . . . the Arab people
were not ready to engage in such an adventure." As a result, Damascus
Radio announced, the Baghdad offices of "the armed organizations and
fronts of the liberation movements in the Arabian Gulf area" had been
ordered closed.[22] In spite of the Iraqi denials,[23] Damascus Radio was
telling the truth. This conclusion was reinforced by Baghdad's concerted
efforts to improve relations not only with Iran, but also with the conservative Arab Gulf states, above all Saudi Arabia, well known as a staunch
supporter of Sultan Qabus and a resolute opponent of the PFLO.

The region's other "national liberation" movement which initially enjoyed some Iraqi support was the National Liberation Front of Bahrain. In October 1975 the Iraqi News Agency reported that a NLFB delegation had arrived in Baghdad "to explain the circumstances and dimensions of the national struggle in Bahrayn."[24] Although the arrival of the delegation and the publicity which it received indicated a measure of Iraqi backing, the organization's fortunes, like those of the PFLO, were soon subordinated to larger considerations of Baghdad's Gulf policy. It was no coincidence that Bahrain's prime minister visited Iraq soon afterward, in November 1975. According to official reports, his "talks centered on bilateral relations and the question of Gulf security." It is also important to note that the first economic agreement between the two states was signed during the premier's visit.[25] In short, in the overall context of Baghdad's attempted reconciliation with the Gulf's conservative rulers, there was clearly little room for the "national liberation" movements in Oman or Bahrain.

As already noted, in the late 1960s the USSR openly favored the Popular Front for the Liberation of Oman and the Arabian Gulf (PFLOAG).[26] In the early 1970s this stance was reinforced by Moscow's rapprochement with the PDRY, a staunch supporter of the Dhofari rebels, and, in more general terms, by the Soviet Union's intensifying regional competition with its major international rivals, the United States and the People's Republic of China.[27] In addition to moral backing, the Soviets also provided the Popular Front with light arms, ammunition, and military training administered by Cuban advisors stationed in the PDRY.

It is equally significant, however, that after 1975 the USSR did not strongly object to the Iranian involvement in the Dhofar war, an attitude prompted by unwillingness to antagonize the shah over an issue in which the Soviets were interested only peripherally but which could negatively affect their steadily improving relations with Tehran.[28] In any event, in 1975, as the PFLO's position continued to deteriorate, *Pravda* expressed apprehension about the shift of military operations into the vicinity of the PDRY border. Aleksei Vasil'ev wrote that the "renewed interventionist activity in Dhofar . . . [had] created a dangerous source of tension" and warned that in their struggle to prevent the "establishment in Arabia [of] colonialism of a new type . . . , the patriots of Arabia are not alone."[29] In retrospect, it would appear that the veiled warning of Oman and its chief backer Iran was not an expression of major concern over the fate of the PFLO. Rather, it was intended to preclude the possibility of military action spilling over into the PDRY, by then a major Soviet client in the Arab world.

The joint Soviet-Kuwaiti communiqué of December 5, 1975, provided additional insights into Moscow's changing position on the Gulf's
"national liberation" movements. It said that the sides favored the
"establishment of trust and goodneighborly cooperation between *all*
states of the Gulf zone on the basis of noninterference in their internal
affairs [and] of respect for their right to free and independent development."[30] While reference to "noninterference in . . . internal affairs"
might have been construed as condemnation of Iran's efforts to help
subdue the PFLO, the phrase could just as easily have been interpreted as
defending Sultan Qabus's right to take whatever action he wished to
insure "free and independent development" of Oman.

Be that as it may, examination of the material on the Gulf "national
liberation" movements which appeared in the Soviet press in the latter
1970s reinforces the conclusion that the Kremlin had lost most of its
interest in the PFLO. The Popular Front was not entirely forgotten, but
references to it became rare. For example, in the spring of 1976, *Pravda*
lent its pages to expressions of concern voiced by the Iraqi Communist
party. Addressing the Third Congress of the ICP, First Secretary Aziz
Mohammed spoke of "new attempts . . . to suppress the national-
liberation movement in Oman and in the Arabian peninsula." He then
proceeded to call for the "expulsion of the Iranian and British hirelings
participating in the operations against the Omani patriots."[31] While the
publication of this part of Aziz Mohammed's speech in the official
organ of the CPSU could have been interpreted as continuing Soviet
support of the PFLO, it was, in retrospect, clearly devoid of any specific
policy implications.

Another article on the "continuing struggle" in Oman appeared in
1978. In tracing the history of the various organizations committed to
the overthrow of the monarchy, the author admitted that the PFLO had
in fact been wiped out in Dhofar. By recognizing the impact of the
reforms instituted by Sultan Qabus as a factor in the defeat, however, he
introduced a novel element into standard Soviet explanations of the
failure suffered by the Popular Front. Nevertheless, in the Soviet accounts, the main cause for the PFLO's defeat remained, as before, the
presence in Oman of foreign troops from Jordan and, above all, Iran.[32]
Otherwise, Moscow's attention remained focused on the PDRY and
particularly on the anti-Aden activities of the Gulf's "reactionary regimes" (Oman, Iran, and Saudi Arabia) which reportedly enjoyed the
support of the "imperialist powers" as well as of the People's Republic of
China.[33] The latter's rapprochement with Oman, in particular, was
subjected to strong Soviet criticism.[34]

In addition to the PFLO, the Kremlin maintained contacts with the National Liberation Front of Bahrain: in the spring of 1976 a NLFB delegation visited the USSR.[35] However, its political value (or, rather, the lack of it) to Moscow was underscored by the benign neglect afforded the Bahraini Front by the major Soviet publications.

A comparison between the respective Iraqi and Soviet positions on PFLOAG-PFLO indicates a considerable convergence of views in the early 1970s, when both states, as well as the PDRY, emerged as the Popular Front's main outside backers. Baghdad's moral and material support of the Dhofari insurgents, extended as part of its "anti-conservative" campaign, was discontinued in the wake of the Algiers accord of March 1975 and its demise was sealed with the establishment of diplomatic relations with Oman. In 1975 and 1976, the USSR, too, lowered the volume and the pitch of its expressions of commitment to the PFLO, voicing public concern only when faced with the possibility of an Iranian-Omani intrusion into the PDRY. When it became obvious that none was forthcoming, Moscow toned down its public interest in the Popular Front.

There is no evidence of any Soviet pressure on Iraq in the general context of the Omani situation. Nor is there any reason to believe that the USSR would have attempted to exercise what influence it had in Baghdad over an issue of only marginal importance to both states. Not only would such an endeavor have detracted from Moscow's overall ability to influence the Ba'th, it would have also, without doubt, proved counterproductive. Relations between Baghdad and Tehran, which had a direct bearing on Iraq's Gulf policies, were much more important to the Ba'th than the fate of the region's "national liberation" movements.

Thus, relative harmony prevailed between Iraq and the USSR on this issue until the Baghdad-Tehran agreement of 1975. After that, Moscow continued to pay occasional lip-service to the PFLO, while the Ba'thist regime proceeded to improve relations with the Popular Front's chief antagonists—Oman and Iran. During the latter 1970s, the divergence of Soviet and Iraqi interests had thus become apparent. However, not too much significance should be attached to this; for both Moscow and Baghdad, the PFLO (let alone the NLFB) remained, at best, a sideshow, and not too significant a one at that.

Regional Security and Cooperation, 1975–1976

The conference of Islamic foreign ministers, meeting in Jiddah (Saudi Arabia) in July 1975, worked out a formula for regional security that was acceptable to all of the Gulf states. They expressed themselves in favor of excluding the outside powers and of keeping the region free from foreign military bases. They also reiterated their insistence that the area's security was the exclusive responsibility of the Gulf states.[36] However, this façade of harmony could not conceal the differences, which continued to divide some of the Gulf's major actors, on how best to promote regional security.

Iraq's position, after the signing of the Algiers accord, retained some of its former features but also contained new elements. Specifically, shortly before his spring 1975 visit to Tehran, Saddam Hussein spoke of Baghdad's determination to explore with the other Gulf states "the possibility of establishing 'security structures' to replace foreign military alliances." He then proceeded to make two important points. First, reiterating an earlier theme, Saddam Hussein said that the Gulf as well as the Indian Ocean should be declared "a peace zone, cleared of *all* foreign military bases." Second, in a new departure, he suggested that the Iraqi-Iranian rapprochement "could lead to a decrease in the arms race in the Gulf." Saddam Hussein went on to add, however, that although relations between Baghdad and Tehran were "proceeding in such a way as to reduce the search for procurement of arms," the continuing occupation of Arab territory by the "Zionist enemy" left Iraq no choice but to continue acquiring modern weapons.[37]

President Bakr shed additional light on Baghdad's position when, in his revolution day speech of July 17, 1975, he disclosed that Saddam Hussein's recent visit to Iran had resulted in an agreement between the two states "to impose controls to ensure freedom of navigation in the Gulf."[38] Because that particular issue (along with the problem of regional military alliances) had been a major bone of contention between Tehran and Baghdad, Bakr's statement created the impression that it had been resolved on Iran's terms. Specifically, Mohammed Reza Shah had favored "a restrictive legal regime governing the rights of outside powers to transit the Straits of Hormuz."[39] Iraq, in contrast, insisted on "maximum freedom of navigation" in the Gulf. In retrospect, Baghdad's stand was governed by political rather than legal considerations. Iraq's outlet to the Gulf was limited and its navy was no match for its Iranian counterpart. Under these circumstances, to give in to the shah would have been tantamount to recognizing Iran's role as the Gulf's leading power. In any event, as it turned out, Bakr's reference to "imposition of controls" did not mean Iraq's submission to Iranian pressure.

Bakr also went out of his way to emphasize that the Algiers accord did not signify adoption of "the 'formulae and concepts of regional alliances.' " On the contrary, their rejection remained "a central principle in our policy." The speech was noteworthy for yet another reason. In a major foreign policy departure, Bakr announced that, following the Algiers agreement and in line with "our clear pan-Arab outlook," Iraq was now determined to "deepen understanding with the Arab countries in the Gulf, particularly Saudi Arabia. . . ."[40]

The statements by Saddam Hussein and Bakr served as another indication that although Baghdad and Tehran agreed on the necessity of protecting the security of the Gulf by local or regional means, they continued to differ on how to achieve that goal. Additional evidence supporting this conclusion was provided shortly thereafter. In August 1975 Kuwait's *al-Siyassah* reported that the two states had circulated memoranda among the other Gulf states to describe their respective views on regional security. The Iraqi document favored "the setting up of a joint fleet of warships to protect the waterway of the Gulf," whereas the Iranian "note emphasized the need for a [regional] military pact for the protection of the territorial integrity of member states."[41]

Soon afterward, Saddam Hussein offered a clarification of the Iraqi position. In an interview with Beirut's pro-Iraqi *al-Dustur*, the vice-chairman explained that the question of Gulf security had not been raised during the Algiers negotiations with Iran but was brought up later (meaning, presumably, during his visit to Tehran), on Iraq's initiative. Baghdad had no intention of entering bilateral or multilateral accords on regional security but was prepared to discuss "initiatives based on analysis" (whatever this may have meant). "One of the 'most important requisites' of the Algiers agreement" was " 'to respect national sovereignty' of all the Arab countries." Should Iran attempt, under whatever pretext, "to occupy an Arab country in the Gulf," Baghdad would rush to the victim's assistance.[42]

In the ensuing months Iraq continued to insist that regional security should be achieved by assuring freedom of navigation and by eliminating "friction and unstable conditions" in the Gulf area. In his speech of July 16, 1976, President Bakr urged all of the region's governments to issue a "collective proclamation" guaranteeing "freedom of navigation in the Gulf for all littoral states and the international parties concerned." He again rejected Iran's insistence on the conclusion of a formal regional defense pact: "Any formula which deviated from . . . [the above] framework, tried to 'restrict the freedom of navigation . . . or which in any way resembles the formula of imperialist blocs and alliances, is absolutely unacceptable to us.' "[43]

In the wake of the Algiers agreement Iraq also moved to improve relations with the Gulf's conservative regimes, such as Bahrain, Qatar, the UAE, and Kuwait.[44] In January 1976 Iraq established diplomatic relations with Oman. However, a special place in Baghdad's diplomatic offensive was reserved for Saudi Arabia: Riyadh had long held a preeminent position among the Gulf's conservative Arab states; its stance had corresponded closely to that of Tehran; and it had been traditionally hostile to Iraq's aspirations to Gulf leadership. In short, along with Iran, Saudi Arabia occupied an important place in regional affairs, and Baghdad's ability to play a meaningful role in the Gulf depended, to a considerable degree, on Riyadh's relative good will and cooperation.

Iraq's attempts to normalize relations with Saudi Arabia were off to an auspicious start. In April and July 1975, respectively, the two countries reached agreements demarcating their 760-kilometer-long border and dividing their oil-rich desert neutral zone.[45] In April 1976, Saddam Hussein traveled to Riyadh and told a press conference that relations between the two states were "expanding and being consolidated in all spheres." But he also took this opportunity to emphasize "the need for strengthening pan-Arab relations in the Gulf 'to enable the Gulf states to establish sound and balanced relations with all parties, remote from any form of imperialist influence.'"[46]

As it soon turned out, however, outward politeness did not mean an abandonment of Saudi Arabia's traditional reserve toward Baghdad; nor did it result in any major changes in Riyadh's Gulf policy. Thus, in early July 1975, a high-level delegation, headed by Minister of Interior Prince Fahd, visited Iran. In the joint communiqué, the sides "expressed 'extreme satisfaction' at the development of Saudi-Iranian relations and affirmed their determination 'to maintain this growth in all fields.'"[47] While not outwardly directed against Iraq, the tone of the communiqué suggested a degree of intimacy clearly lacking in relations between Riyadh and Baghdad. Even more to the point was the Saudi decision, made in July 1975, to proceed with the construction of a major military base in the vicinity of the Kuwaiti and Iraqi border.[48]

In the summer of 1976, new strains appeared in Iraqi-Saudi relations caused primarily by events taking place outside the Gulf, such as the Syrian military intervention in Lebanon. Although Riyadh had little to say about these matters publicly, it continued to supply petroleum to Syria. Having cut off the flow of its own oil to Damascus in a protest against the Syrian entry into Lebanon, Baghdad found it difficult to conceal its irritation not only with Syria but also with Saudi Arabia. For its part, Riyadh remained distrustful of Iraq, suspecting the ruling Ba'th party of clandestine support for "radical and revolutionary movements throughout the Arab world."[49]

Otherwise, in terms of Gulf security, the conservative Arab states maintained a cautious middle of the road position. For example, in the Saudi-Iranian communiqué of July 1975 the parties agreed that the Gulf should remain "secure, stable, peaceful and free of any foreign intervention or bases."[50] Occasionally, some high officials were less diplomatic. In an interview with Kuwait's *Daily News*, the country's minister of interior endorsed the principle of holding a regional conference to discuss "security measures" in the Gulf. He went on to add, however, that Kuwait's willingness "to participate in any form of co-operation between Gulf states" should not be construed as an endorsement of "formal military alliances such as that proposed by Iran."[51]

Muscat Conference, 1976

Another concerted effort to establish a framework for regional security was made in late November 1976, when the foreign ministers of the Gulf states met in the Omani capital of Muscat. (The conference was preceded by three secret meetings of the Gulf foreign ministers, held in 1975 and early 1976, which Iraq, because of its opposition to a formal regional alliance, did not attend.)[52] The November 1976 conference, sponsored by Oman, was strongly supported by Iran: Sultan Qabus was one of the few Gulf rulers who favored the shah's preference for a formal regional defense alliance and a "restrictive legal regime" governing the freedom of navigation in the Gulf.

Before the opening of the Muscat conference, Iraqi Foreign Minister Hammadi visited the capitals of the other Gulf states and urged their governments to postpone the projected meeting on the ground that it was "premature." According to Baghdad's own account, Hammadi's trip was "fruitful": the other governments reportedly agreed to endorse Iraq's concept of guaranteed "freedom of navigation in the Gulf." They also stuck to their decision to participate in the Muscat conference, however. When it became obvious that the meeting would take place, the Iraqis, at the last moment, decided to attend.[53]

According to Iranian Foreign Minister Khalatbari, the conference was neither a "complete success" nor a "complete failure." He went on to explain that "the participants had agreed on the whole with the paper put forward by Oman outlining the principles that should govern relations between Gulf states" and that "only Iraq had called for changes in the paper."[54] Other observers offered a different assessment. Since no agreement on regional security and cooperation had been reached and no communiqué had been issued, the Muscat conference was a "success for Iraqi strategy" but otherwise a failure.[55]

In retrospect, it would appear that all of the governments represented at the Muscat meeting subscribed to the view advanced by the foreign minister of Bahrain who said that his country's position on regional security rested on two basic premises. First, "the Gulf region is the most important and strategic in the world and its control must be solely in the hands of the countries of the region." Second, "peace and security of the Gulf depended on ending the influence in the area of both the United States and the Soviet Union. That," he added, "is our only solution."[56]

The differences—which were aired but remained unresolved at Muscat—revolved around the old problem of how to achieve these goals; conference participants were unable to reach a compromise between the conflicting positions held by Iran and Oman on the one hand and Iraq and Kuwait on the other.[57] The former supported the establishment of a unified organizational structure (that is to say, a regional defense alliance), while the latter argued against a formal defense pact and favored bilateral arrangements among the various Gulf states. At Muscat, the situation was further complicated by the stance of Bahrain, which, to a degree, complemented the view advanced by Iraq. As subsequently explained by the Bahraini foreign minister, his government was of the opinion that "each country . . . had its own local needs and pressures to consider," but thought that these problems would eventually be overcome by means of "continuous direct discussion" among the Gulf states. Having said that, however, Bahrain parted company with Iraq: "Since the Gulf formed 'the eastern side of the Arab nation,' " the foreign minister concluded, "it had been agreed *with Egypt* that the security of the Gulf should be the joint responsibility of an 'Arab national plan.' "[58] No one else agreed. Instead, the participants in the Muscat conference appeared to have shared the view expressed by UAE President Sheikh Zayyid, who said that "the security of the Gulf region was a vital issue for all the countries *bordering the Gulf*,"[59] thus implicitly rejecting the involvement by the nonlittoral Arab states.

The failure of the Muscat conference to arrive at a regional consensus coincided with Baghdad's growing estrangement from its Arab neighbors which occurred in the latter half of 1976 and early 1977. To an extent, this state of affairs reflected a larger picture, as the Iraqi Ba'th, once again, found itself outside the mainstream of Arab politics. Among the contributing factors was the opposition to the Syrian presence in Lebanon, an involvement that had been sanctioned by the Arab League. This attitude brought Baghdad into conflict with Saudi Arabia and Kuwait, the Gulf's leading champions of the Syrian entry into Lebanon. Further complications arose when its two Gulf neighbors rejected Iraq's proposals for petroleum production quotas and for a 25 percent oil price increase, made in August and November 1976, respectively. (It was probably no coincidence that, in September, Iraqi forces were reported reentering Kuwaiti territory.)[60] The degree of Baghdad's isolation was reflected in its refusal to attend a conference of the foreign ministers of the "confrontation" and Arab oil-producing states, held in Riyadh in early January 1977.[61]

To rectify the situation, Iraq embarked upon another major effort to improve relations with its Gulf neighbors. This, in any event, was one of the stated purposes of the trip to Kuwait, Qatar, the UAE, and Iran that the Iraqi minister of planning undertook in January 1977.[62] In February, Baghdad made a point of attending the Riyadh conference of the Gulf foreign ministers.[63] Nevertheless, relations with Saudi Arabia remained strained. In March the Iraqi press finally turned its attention to the Muscat conference. Not surprisingly, Baghdad's resentment was directed not at Oman and Iran but at Saudi Arabia: Riyadh saw "the security of the Gulf as a matter of guaranteeing American interests and organizing a conspiracy against the Arab liberation movement."[64]

In April and May 1977, another high-level delegation, which was led by Minister of Interior Duri and included Foreign Minister Hammadi as well as the minister of trade, visited Kuwait, Bahrain, Qatar, the UAE, Saudi Arabia, and Oman. According to press reports, the delegation was empowered to discuss with the Arab Gulf governments a variety of political and economic problems, ranging from "Gulf security [and] Palestinian issues [to] oil prices [and] economic cooperation."[65] As became evident later in the year, Baghdad's efforts to broaden cooperation with the other Arab Gulf countries were crowned with some success. In October 1977 Iraq hosted the first conference of trade ministers, attended by officials from Saudi Arabia, Kuwait, Bahrain, Qatar, the UAE, and Oman. Reflecting Baghdad's position, the joint statement said, in part, that "the differing social and political systems in the countries of the area must not and should not prevent the establishment of economic co-operation among . . . [them]."[66]

Regional Security, 1977–1979

Iraq's attitude toward Gulf security, as explained during the Duri mission, was restated by Saddam Hussein before the delegation's departure from Baghdad. In an interview, published in Tehran on April 17, 1977, the vice-chairman of the RCC continued to insist that bilateral cooperation rather than any general formal arrangements was "the best way to attain security and stability" in the Gulf. He went on to explain that, "owing to the different character of the various regimes of the Gulf states, it would be impractical to expect the formation of 'some kind of group' in the Gulf in the near future." Saddam Hussein also, more forcefully than before, reiterated Iraq's determination "to put an end to the interference of foreign powers in the Gulf" and added that he personally did " 'not feel easy' about the visits of U.S. naval units to the region, *nor about the visits of Soviet units to Iraq.*"[67] Unnoticed at the time, the latter phrase represented a significant shift in Baghdad's public stance. Whereas prior to 1977, Iraq's reserve was expressed implicitly, at this time the authorities left no doubt about their desire not to receive Soviet naval vessels in their Gulf ports. Such an unambiguous position—another clear indication of the gradually deteriorating relations between the two countries—left Moscow no choice but to bow to Baghdad's wishes.

Given the fundamental disparity of views on ways and means to achieve regional security in the Persian Gulf, it was obvious that no early accord would be reached on what everyone agreed was an important problem. The views of the majority were once again expressed by Sheikh Zayyid, who argued that to be effective, regional security "would require an agreement on a joint system for the benefit of everyone." Should reaching a "unanimous agreement" prove impossible, he recommended "freez[ing] the subject for the time being." Giving it "more study and thought" might yet result in an acceptable solution to the problem.[68]

In November 1977 the Arab world was shocked by President Sadat's trip to Jerusalem, followed, in 1978, by the Camp David accords. In addition, in the late 1970s, the Gulf states were preoccupied with three sets of problems which were seen as threatening regional stability. The first was a U.S. decision, reportedly taken in September 1977, to safeguard Western interests in the Gulf by any available means. The second concerned the rapidly deteriorating relations between the Yemen Arab Republic and the PDRY which resulted, in June 1978, in the assassination of the YAR president. The third was the Islamic revolution in Iran. All of these events prompted Iraq to move farther away from Moscow and closer to the Gulf's conservative regimes.

Reflecting its previous opposition to outside interference in regional affairs, Iraq reacted sharply to Washington's resolve to use military power to guarantee Western access to the Gulf's petroleum resources. President Bakr protested publicly against what he described as "American threats to use force in the Arabian Gulf on the pretext of protecting the sources of oil." Such "repeated American declarations," he continued, "reveal continuing aggressive intentions against the peoples and security of the region."[69] Not surprisingly, Bakr also objected to the establishment of the Rapid Deployment Force, announced in February 1978,[70] while al-Jumhuriyyah warned the "imperialists" that they were "playing with fire" and reminded them that "oil is a readily combustible material."[71]

Concurrently, Iraq continued its efforts to improve relations with its Gulf neighbors. When Saudi Defense Minister Prince Sultan traveled to Tehran and Baghdad in the spring of 1978, Kuwait's usually well-informed al-Siyassah reported on April 19 that the visits were "aimed at establishing some sort of co-operation in security among the three Gulf countries."[72] Additional light on the trilateral contacts was shed by Iraqi Minister of Information Saad Kassem Hammudi on June 23, 1978. He noted that his government's policy of opposition to regional "military pacts and collective agreements" and of support for bilateral cooperation had remained unchanged, but he stated that Iraq, Iran, and Saudi Arabia were working together "to avert disturbances that might disrupt freedom of navigation" in and near the Gulf.[73]

Other incentives for regional cooperation were provided by the April 1978 Communist coup in Afghanistan and by the assassination, on June 24, 1978, of North Yemeni President Ahmad Hussein al-Ghashmi. Because he was killed by a bomb that was carried in a briefcase by a South Yemeni envoy,[74] Ghashmi's violent death was generally regarded as a retaliation for San'a's policy of rapprochement with Saudi Arabia to which the PDRY was strongly opposed. Nevertheless, two days later, South Yemeni President Salim Rubayyi Ali himself was executed "ostensibly for his part in the assassination of . . . Ghashmi. . . ."[75] He was replaced by the staunchly pro-Soviet Abd al-Fattah Ismail. Since Aden was an ally of the USSR, Ghashmi's assassination and Ismail's coup were seen as additional manifestations of Soviet aggressiveness in the Arabian peninsula. Sufficiently alarmed, the Gulf states intensified their efforts "to strengthen . . . joint security co-ordination to confront" what *al-Siyassah* described as "the Soviet role in the Gulf."[76]

In February 1979, following border skirmishes, PDRY units occupied parts of North Yemeni territory. As the fighting intensified, President Jimmy Carter ordered a carrier task force into the Arabian Sea, while Saudi Arabia placed its armed forces on full alert. In late March, after an intervention by the Arab League, South Yemeni troops were pulled out of North Yemen.[77] Iraq reportedly played an important part in effecting their withdrawal: Saddam Hussein told the PDRY ambassador that in case of noncompliance with the Arab League request, South Yemen would have to face the Iraqi army.[78]

In contrast to its objections to the possible use of U.S. military power in defense of Western interests in the Gulf, Baghdad did not directly accuse the USSR of involvement in the affairs of North Yemen. Iraq did, however, participate in efforts to coordinate regional security measures undertaken in the wake of Ghashmi's assassination and reacted strongly to the PDRY incursion into North Yemeni territory. Moreover, in a clear indication that Baghdad shared apprehensions of the conservative Gulf governments, Saddam Hussein publicly warned the USSR against harboring aggressive designs on Saudi Arabia and, by implication, on any of the Gulf states:

> We must draw our weapons against any foreigner . . . who violates our sovereignty; we must not differentiate in this between a progressive or non-progressive; a Zionist or a Frenchman or a Soviet citizen or an American. Regardless of the relationship of friendship that connects us on the official level, we cannot allow the Soviet Union, which is a friend of Iraq, to occupy the land of the Saudis, because Saudi Arabia does not lie outside the Arab map.[79]

Finally, in 1978 and 1979, the security and stability of the Gulf had been affected by the overthrow of the Iranian monarchy. To deal with these problems, in September 1978, Saddam Hussein announced his intention to visit the Gulf states to "speed up bilateral security arrangements" in order to keep the region out of superpower competition and possible conflicts.[80] Additional impetus for concern among the Arab Gulf states was provided by a remark made by U.S. Secretary of Defense Harold Brown. During his January 1979 visit to Saudi Arabia, the secretary warned that the Iranian events could lead to a Soviet-American confrontation in the Gulf. Speaking for all the Arab Gulf states, a high Kuwaiti official declared that the region's governments had "no intention of getting involved in superpower rivalry" and remained opposed to "any form of foreign interference in the Gulf, no matter where it . . . [came] from,"[81] a view that had been communicated directly to the visiting Soviet envoy Oleg Grinevskii by Kuwait's Foreign Minister Sheikh Sabah. The Russian reportedly replied that the USSR "could not possibly interfere in the internal affairs of any other state." As a result, the Soviet Union and Kuwait "agreed to the exclusion of the Gulf region from international conflicts."[82]

In the meantime, Brown was also reported to have raised in Riyadh the subject of a "Gulf military pact under U.S. supervision," an idea that, minus American participation, seemed to have attracted at least some governments. In an interview with Riyadh's al-Jazirah (published on February 8, 1979), the UAE minister of information argued that the region was "exposed to the ambitions of the major powers" and called for "unification of the security forces of the Gulf states." (While not tantamount to an endorsement of a regional military alliance, the statement could nevertheless be interpreted as a step in that general direction.) Other reports attributed to Oman's minister of state for foreign affairs amounted to outright support of the idea of a Gulf security pact. These allegations were subsequently denied by a spokesman for the Omani Ministry of Foreign Affairs: the minister had expressed "the need for mutual co-operation among the Gulf states in all fields but 'had not referred in any way to the idea of establishing a security pact.' "[83]

Notwithstanding these denials, in September 1979 Muscat advanced a "technical project for the maintenance of [regional] security." Designed to guarantee the safety of the oil traffic in the Gulf, the Omani plan envisaged a "cooperative arrangement" between some Western and Arab Gulf states.[84] (This wording was widely understood to mean the stationing in the Gulf of some Western, above all U.S., naval units.) The project was to cost approximately $100 million and was to be financed by the United States, Great Britain, West Germany, as well as by some conservative Arab countries.[85] Because direct Western involvement was an integral part of Sultan Qabus's plan, the initiative received no public support among any of Oman's neighbors and was rejected outright by Iraq, Kuwait, Bahrain, the PDRY, and revolutionary Iran.[86]

Baghdad was particularly upset at the Muscat initiative. In late September, Minister of Defense Adnan Khayrallah traveled to Kuwait and Bahrain carrying personal messages from Saddam Hussein—who had replaced Bakr as president on July 16, 1979—to the rulers of these states. Judging by the statement Khayrallah made upon his return to Baghdad, the mission was an unqualified success: Kuwait and Bahrain fully shared Iraq's assessment that the project had been inspired by the "imperialist powers" and that it represented an "inadmissible outside interference into the internal affairs of the Gulf states."[87]

Baghdad's attitude—consistent with its previously held views—was explained in the Iraqi press. *Al-Thawrah* blamed Washington for initiating the idea and argued that, by means of direct participation in the proposed "security pact," the United States was hoping to "strengthen its military presence" in the Gulf region.[88] Since it was "precisely these designs that present[ed] a real threat to peace in the . . . Gulf," *al-Thawrah* noted on another occasion, the Arab states had no choice but to reject them.[89] As in the past, Iraq and the other Gulf states would "resolutely oppose all attempts by the West to organize aggressive military pacts, to force the Arab peoples to conduct policies desired by Washington, [and] to draw them into the sphere of American imperialism."[90]

Iraq's position on regional security and stability, as enunciated by its leaders in the late 1970s, can be summed up as follows:

1. The Gulf (as well as the Indian Ocean) was to be declared a "zone of peace." This meant, in part, that the region was to remain outside superpower competition, let alone possible conflicts. To achieve this aim, no foreign bases were to be situated in the area and no foreign warships were to be allowed to enter it—a provision that Saddam Hussein stated in 1977 was meant to apply to the Soviet naval vessels as well.

2. The principle of freedom of navigation in the Gulf was to be upheld by all the littoral states by means of a "collective proclamation" and protected by a "joint fleet of warships."

3. Regional security was to be guaranteed not by means of a formal military alliance but through bilateral arrangements among the littoral states.

4. The principle of bilateral cooperation applied also to efforts to enhance the domestic security of the Gulf countries.

Moscow and Regional Security, 1975–1979

In the latter 1970s, Baghdad concentrated its attention on regional affairs and explicitly urged the superpowers to stay out of the Gulf. The USSR, in contrast, while echoing many sentiments expressed by Iraq, focused mainly on the activities of the United States. In general, Moscow continued to insist that the region occupied an important place in Washington's global strategy: the U.S. bases in the Gulf were intended to serve as a "strategic beachhead" and the "extreme Western link in the chain of bases which the Pentagon is creating in the basins of the Indian and Pacific oceans."[91] Stretching from "Japan, [Taiwan, and the Philippines] to Australia and across the Indian Ocean [i.e., Diego Garcia] to southern Africa and the Persian Gulf," these U.S. "strongholds" formed a "part of a gigantic strategic arc"[92] and were designed to serve a variety of purposes. In addition to military considerations, they were intended to "exert pressure on the internal and foreign policies of the developing Asian and African states." In the context of the Gulf, they were also to "protect the flow of oil" to the Western markets.[93]

According to Soviet publications, the United States was employing a variety of means to protect and enhance Western interests in the Gulf. Some were old and time-honored, such as the continuing search for military bases and attempts to establish a pro-Western regional military alliance. Other methods, although not necessarily new, were conditioned by situations that were peculiar to the late 1970s. Among them were massive arms sales to a few selected clients, above all imperial Iran and Saudi Arabia, as well as threats to use force against the oil-producing countries in an attempt to dissuade them from increasing the price of petroleum.

The Continuing Search for Military Bases. Developing the arguments presented in the late 1960s and early 1970s, the Soviet analysts continued to insist that the United States began to pay special attention to the Gulf after the British withdrawal in 1971. The most important U.S. position remained the island of Bahrain, where access to the Jufair naval base reportedly enabled the Pentagon "to control the Gulf region and to exert pressure on the oil-rich littoral states." For this reason, in the 1970s, Moscow consistently called for the eviction of the U.S. Middle East Naval Task Force from Bahrain.[94]

Otherwise, the United States was said to have scored a major success in Oman. In early 1977 *Pravda* argued that, despite public denials, Sultan Qabus had placed the facilities on the island of Masirah at the disposal of the U.S. navy and air force, an initial agreement was reportedly reached during the sultan's 1974 visit to Washington. The consequences of the U.S. involvement with the sultanate were "far-reaching." In addition to strengthening American military capabilities in the Indian Ocean basin, access to Masirah also enabled Washington to control the Strait of Hormuz—the "strategically important entry into the Persian Gulf." As a result, the United States improved its ability to "block . . . [the efforts] to transform the Indian Ocean into a zone of peace and cooperation, [and] to slow down the process of international détente."[95] In the Arabian peninsula, Masirah, as well as the British bases in Muscat and Salalah, were being used as staging grounds for attacks against the "Dhofar patriots" and for "aggressive raids" against the PDRY. Finally, the acquisition of the Omani bases also enhanced the Pentagon's ability "to defend the interests of the oil monopolies in the face of . . . the growing determination of the region's petroleum-producing states to bring under their control the extraction and sale of oil."[96]

Efforts to Establish a Military Bloc. Paralleling efforts to acquire naval and air bases in and near the Gulf were Washington's attempts to organize a pro-Western regional defense alliance. For example, *Pravda* charged that "imperialism and reaction" remained determined to set up a "military bloc, subservient to the West, under the false pretext of defending the Gulf's oil riches from an imaginary 'Communist threat,'"[97] endeavors "contrary to the interests of the region's Arab peoples."[98]

In line with this position, the USSR reacted negatively to the Omani-Iranian plan for a regional defense pact, advanced in Muscat in November 1976. The Soviet attitude, although hardly surprising, was noteworthy for two reasons. First, the Kremlin took a long time to pass its judgment—public stand on the Muscat conference was not taken until the spring of 1977. Second, when it did come, Moscow's ire was directed not so much at Oman and Iran as at Saudi Arabia. In both respects, the Soviet position paralleled closely that held by Baghdad.[99] Otherwise, *Pravda* agreed with Iraq's judgement that the task of "guaranteeing security [and] freedom of navigation" in the Gulf was indeed a legitimate issue for regional deliberation and action. However, since the Muscat conference was held under the "false slogan" of a "struggle against the Communist threat" and refused to recognize that the "real danger to the security and independence of the littoral countries stems from the imperialist circles," its failure came as no surprise.[100]

This setback notwithstanding, the Soviet press insisted in the months ahead, the United States was forging ahead with plans "to establish a military alliance in which the main role will be played by Saudi Arabia and Iran."[101] Moscow's prognostications proved only partially correct. The next step in the direction of a regional pact was taken after the overthrow of Mohammed Reza Shah; in September 1979 Oman circulated among the Gulf states another "technical project" for Gulf security, a proposal that was promptly denounced by several littoral states, above all Iraq and Kuwait.

Not surprisingly, the USSR found itself in full agreement with the opponents of the Muscat initiative. This was reflected, in part, in the voluminous comments devoted to the rejection of the Omani proposal by some of the leading Iraqi and Kuwaiti officials and in the meticulous reporting of the sentiments aired by the Iraqi and Kuwaiti press. Thus, *Pravda* featured prominently the Kuwait government statement to the effect that it "does not believe in the usefulness of alliances and blocs and does not under any circumstances approve of their establishment."[102] The Soviet press also quoted freely from unfavorable reactions of such newspapers as *al-Thawrah* and *al-Jumhuriyyah* (Baghdad) and *al-Siyassah* and *al-Rai al-Amm* (Kuwait). For example, the latter noted that the very countries which Oman wished to elevate to the status of regional "protectors" were those which "increase tension and conduct intrigues in the Persian Gulf." They also "spread discord and strain the atmosphere by means of concentrating . . . their navies and creating military bases" in the vicinity of the Gulf. For these reasons, *al-Rai al-Amm* concluded, the "adoption of the Omani plan would be tantamount to a [foreign] occupation of all of the Persian Gulf states."[103]

As for Moscow, it saw the Omani initiative as an "Arab packaging for American neocolonialist plans."[104] Placing the "Qabus plan" in a historical perspective, Nodari Simoniia, a noted authority on the developing world, saw it as the latest link in a chain of U.S. attempts to penetrate and dominate the Gulf. Describing "Oman's 1976 "technical project" as the initial step, Simoniia argued that, in mid-1978, the United States had come close to persuading Iran and Saudi Arabia to form the nucleus of a pro-Western regional military alliance. That plan had to be abandoned because of the overthrow of the shah. Washington's next project was the Middle East Treaty Organization, consisting of Saudi Arabia, Oman, Egypt, Somalia, and Israel. Simoniia insisted that one of the purposes of Defense Secretary Brown's February 1979 visit to a number of Arab capitals (including Riyadh and Muscat) was to persuade them to join this proposed military grouping. The attempt failed as did the push for an "Islamic pact," an idea concocted at the secret March 1979 meeting of U.S. diplomats in New Delhi.[105]

The *New Times* spoke sarcastically about American preoccupation with the safety of the oil routes in and near the Gulf: Washington reportedly "hinted" that "the security of the Persian Gulf area . . . [was] endangered by the 'hand of Moscow' and 'Palestinian terrorists.'" U.S. apprehension was triggered by the CIA which "released a pseudo-scientific paper alleging that the Soviet Union's oil resources would soon be exhausted." The Western press then drew "the desired conclusion, namely, that Moscow had no other option but to gain access to the Middle East oil fields and that it would certainly use military force to achieve this aim." In addition to this "Soviet threat," the *New Times* continued, the West also claimed to fear the "Palestinian terrorists" who were said to be planning "to attack tankers in order to block the Strait of Hormuz." Taking his cue from Washington, Sultan Qabus then advanced his "plan" for dealing with these fictitious dangers.[106]

"Enthusiastic" support had only been voiced by Egypt—a pro-Western, non-Gulf state—while Israel "expressed readiness to supply U.S. weapons for operations in the Persian Gulf area so that the 'contingency force' now being set up in the United States would not have to bring them from overseas." As for the Gulf states, most had rejected the Omani plan. Saudi Arabia withheld public comment, but the Riyadh press had pointedly expressed "anxiety about the presence of four American warships in the gulf." These considerations led the Soviet publications to conclude that "the proposed bloc," intended to facilitate U.S. interference in the affairs of the Gulf states, "will in all likelihood be no more viable than its predecessors."[107]

Arms Sales. In addition to focusing on Washington's attempts to draw the Gulf countries into military blocs and to secure for itself access to naval and air bases, the Soviets also accused the "imperialist" powers of trying to spread their influence by means of large-scale arms shipments to the various littoral states. Western governments as well as the USSR had long regarded the sale of modern, sophisticated weapons to developing Third World countries as an important and worthwhile pursuit. First, this activity enabled the industrial West to recoup some of the financial losses incurred after the dramatic post-1973 increases in the price of petroleum. (It was, therefore, no coincidence that the Western arms exports to the Middle East increased sharply after 1973.) For the Soviet Union, on the other hand, the weapons sales to its Arab clients became a major source of badly needed hard currency. Second, the initial arms transactions were usually followed by deliveries of spare parts and of maintenance equipment—another source of income for the industrial powers of both the West and the East. Third, service, maintenance, and related training of local technicians were usually performed by specialists supplied by the donor country. In addition to their economic value, the arms sales were also perceived as highly important politically: they contributed to the buyers' dependence on the sellers. In other words, many believed that, in the resulting political climate, it was easier for the industrial patrons to project their influence and to extract concessions from their Third World clients. This view, prevalent not only in the West but also in Moscow, was not generally shared by the recipients of modern military hardware, who regarded such imports, usually paid for in hard cash, as purely commercial transactions. Thus, clients did not view themselves as obligated to the Western powers or the USSR for the goods delivered and the services rendered.

In any event, while the Kremlin usually said very little about its own arms sales to a number of Arab states, it paid a great deal of attention to the activities of the Western powers, especially of the United States. Among the West's "most preferred" customers, the Soviet press singled out Saudi Arabia and prerevolutionary Iran. In early 1976 *Pravda* reported the consummation of a major U.S.-Saudi arms deal. Valued at $1.2 billion, it provided for the delivery to Riyadh of M-60 tanks and armored personnel carriers. Washington also undertook the construction of two Saudi naval bases, in the Gulf and the Red Sea, respectively.[108] In the summer of 1976, in addition to "over $6 billion worth of arms" already purchased from the United States, Saudi Arabia was promised another $5 billion package consisting of coastal patrol boats as well as Sidewinder air-to-air and Maverick air-to-surface missiles for the previously delivered F-5 fighter aircraft.[109] The grand total of the contracts for the sale of U.S. weapons to Riyadh in 1975 and 1976 had exceeded $7 billion; the corresponding figure for the five-year period between 1973 and 1977 was $10 billion.[110] In 1977, at the cost of another $16 billion, the United States was reported to be engaged in construction of a variety of "military installations" in Saudi Arabia.[111] Finally, in early 1978, Washington agreed to comply with Riyadh's request for sixty F-15 fighter planes valued at $1.5 billion.[112]

In the meantime, imperial Iran, Washington's other major Gulf client, was also spending billions of dollars on the acquisition of modern weapons. According to Soviet estimates, by the year 1980, the shah was expected to receive "U.S. arms valued at between" $10 and $15 billion. His purchases included "F-4 and F-5 fighter-bombers, F-14 fighters, the Hawk [surface-to-air] missile system, destroyers, submarines, 500 helicopters, and laser and TV-guided bombs."[113] Agreements, concluded in 1977 alone, provided for the delivery to Iran of seven AWACS planes, 160 F-16 fighters (another 140 were to follow later), and eight nuclear reactors, the latter worth $10 billion.[114]

Soviet publications have long maintained that in selling arms to the developing countries, the Western powers were pursuing military-strategic, political, and economic interests. In scrutinizing the military aspects of Washington's involvement in the affairs of the Gulf, *Pravda* argued that large-scale deliveries of modern weapons enabled the United States to increase its influence in the Persian Gulf.[115] In support of its contention, *Pravda* cited Deputy Assistant Secretary of Defense Amos Jordan, who said that an "expansion of the sphere of our contacts for the purpose of selling arms is of enormous value for maintaining U.S. control in this strategically important region."[116]

In examining the political aspects of Washington's decision to supply large quantities of weapons to its Gulf clients, the Soviet press developed several related themes. First, a regional arms race strengthened America's own position in the area. One commentator quoted an unnamed U.S. diplomat to the effect that the "best means of keeping the Persian Gulf countries in the orbit of U.S. influence lies in establishing there 'ultra-modern' armies, dependent on American weapons and Pentagon specialists."[117] Moreover, advanced military equipment was invariably sent to "reactionary regimes," above all Iran and Saudi Arabia. The reasons for U.S. selectivity, in Moscow's opinion, were quite transparent—in addition to their readiness to "defend Western interests," the "reactionaries" also shared the 'imperialists' " fears of the "national liberation movements" in the developing world. As a result, they were anxious to join "a kind of 'holy alliance' for the struggle against the forces of progress."[118]

Economically, the Soviet analysts argued, large arms transfers to the wealthy Gulf states served two major purposes. First, by tying the oil producers to the West, Washington succeeded in "establishing control" over this important petroleum-producing region. This enabled the Western oil companies to continue reaping enormous profits at the expense of the Gulf states and peoples.[119] Second, the sale of modern weapons made it possible for the United States and its allies to retrieve a "significant part" of money spent on purchasing the Gulf petroleum. "In the process," the West had managed to "deflate considerably the successes scored in recent years by the oil-producing countries in the struggle against the imperialist . . . monopolies."[120] In evaluating "the build-up of U.S. arms supplies to conservative regimes" in the Gulf, Soviet publications described it as "one of the main instruments of [Washington's] imperialist policy."[121]

Among the regional actors, Moscow, even before the Iranian revolution, held Mohammed Reza Shah responsible for the initiation of the Gulf arms race. Ever since the early 1970s, wrote *International Affairs* in 1976, Tehran had received "any [and any amount of] non-nuclear weapons" it requested from the United States. The acquisition of modern arms by Iran had left its neighbors no choice but to do likewise, a decision that, for reasons already described, was heartily endorsed by Washington.[122]

The Soviet Union's own objections to the escalating arms race in the Gulf revolved around several related themes. Domestically, "the colossal sums spent by Iran and Saudi Arabia on modern . . . [weapons]" represented "a serious hindrance to their economic development and the raising of living standards." Regionally, the accumulation of large arsenals was described as a source of instability and tension which could easily result in a major conflict. In the larger arena, "the arms race in the Persian Gulf" was thought to be "the more dangerous because of the persisting tensions in the Middle East, where the consequences of the Israeli aggression have yet to be eliminated." Finally, "the growing U.S. military presence in the Middle East and the U.S.-aided arms build-up in Iran and other countries of the region" ran "counter to the spirit of the times, which are marked by a shift toward détente as a result of the enormous amount of work done to improve the international climate."[123]

Threats to Use Force. In addition to methods discussed previously, the Western powers, and particularly the United States, were also relying on threats of force to protect what they described as their "legitimate interests" in the Gulf, above all, access to the region's petroleum deposits. The fact that intimidation was sometimes directed against regimes which Moscow had labeled as "reactionary" and "subservient to the West" did not present the Soviet analysts with insurmountable theoretical difficulties. Dialectically speaking, it was quite proper for the "capitalist" powers to support their Gulf clients against their "progressive forces" while, at the same time, resisting the "local reaction's" efforts to wrest control of their natural riches from the "clutches of Western monopolies." In fact, similar logic also applied to the USSR's own treatment of the Gulf's conservative governments. While the Soviets opposed their close association with the West as well as their domestic policies aimed at "suppressing the progressive forces," the Kremlin strongly supported the Gulf states' attempts to gain control of their respective oil industries. The reason for this dichotomy was obvious: Moscow condemned the "regressive" tendencies displayed by the conservative Gulf governments while applauding their "objectively progressive" initiatives. The nationalization of the oil resources and industries clearly fell into the latter category—they tended, or so it was argued, to weaken the economic power of the industrial West.

Among the manifestations of Soviet moral backing of the Gulf states were the recurring warnings of possible Western (primarily U.S.) military intervention to stem what was termed the oil-producers' "irreversible march toward economic independence." One of the early comments was a 1976 article in *Pravda*. Quoting *Tariq al-Sha'b*, it accused the West and the "Arab reaction" of total disregard of the "interests of the Arab peoples" in the Gulf and the Arabian peninsula and alerted all concerned to "NATO threats to occupy the oil fields."[124] As usual, Washington was in the forefront of Soviet attention: "Threats have repeatedly come from the United States that force will be used against . . . [the Gulf] states in case of an 'emergency.' "[125]

In February 1978 the Soviet press commented extensively on Secretary Brown's "directive" establishing the Rapid Deployment Force (RDF). *Pravda* described its creation as a direct outgrowth of the Carter administration's decision, adopted in September 1977, to turn the Gulf into an "area of strategic influence of the United States." *Pravda* noted also that this renewed U.S. interest and activity in the Persian Gulf had been condemned by the "official circles in the Arab countries and Arab public opinion" as an "open interference in the affairs of other peoples" and as an "attempt by the USA to take upon itself the function of a policeman in this part of the world."[126] As for the Kremlin, it denounced the creation of the U.S. "mobile fire brigade" as part of a far-flung effort aimed to ensure American "domination of the Persian Gulf." Bound to increase regional tension, the U.S. initiative was "fraught with dangerous consequences" endangering peace in the area and in the Middle East as a whole.[127]

After a temporary lull, the subject resurfaced in early 1979, when Secretaries Brown and Schlesinger reiterated Washington's determination "to secure American military presence in the Persian Gulf zone and to 'apply . . . military might' . . . under the pretext of defending the 'vital interests' of the United States."[128] According to Moscow, these "threatening declarations," prompted by the overthrow of the shah, constituted but another "undisguised claim by the Pentagon to the role of a Middle East policeman." Washington, *Pravda* reported, was fooling no one. Among others, its arguments were rejected by Iraq, Iran, Saudi Arabia, and Kuwait. Sheikh Sabah, in particular, was quoted as saying that the U.S. position "contradicted the UN principles and the right of . . . [any] nation to freedom." He went on to describe the above statements as "unacceptable and irresponsible." The Kremlin concurred.[129]

In examining the reasons for Washington's decision to proceed with the creation of the RDF, Soviet publications singled out the "myth of the 'Soviet threat' " and "possible Palestinian terrorist activity" against the oil tankers traversing the Gulf.[130] In early 1980, the Soviet invasion of Afghanistan was cited as another "factor" in the intensifying U.S.

efforts to establish an American military presence in and near the Gulf. As might have been expected, all three arguments were dismissed by the Kremlin—the USSR was not about to attack anybody, and the Palestinians disclaimed any intention of sabotaging the flow of Gulf oil. As for the Soviet "assistance" to the Babrak Karmal regime in Kabul, it could not possibly have influenced the decision to establish the RDF because plans to acquire such a capability had been advanced well before the April 1978 revolution in Afghanistan.[131]

Soviet Position. Moscow's own position on the Gulf as it evolved in the mid-1970s can be summed up as follows: (1) support of the various producer states in their efforts to nationalize their oil industries; (2) "consolidation of regional peace and security," to be achieved, in part, by eliminating foreign military bases and presence in the Gulf; (3) guaranteed freedom of navigation in the Gulf and the Strait of Hormuz; (4) establishment of regional "trust and cooperation"; and (5) "right of each country to free and independent development."[132]

In mid-1976, echoing the sentiments expressed by Saddam Hussein in 1975, the Kremlin also came out in favor of proclaiming the Indian Ocean a "zone of peace." This formula, which enjoyed the backing of India as well as of most other littoral states, called for "freedom of navigation in accordance with the principles of international law" and for "freedom from all foreign military bases."[133] Subsequently, the "zone of peace" concept was extended to mean a "guarantee of equal security for all interested countries and peoples" and a search of ways "mutually to cut down military activities of the nonlittoral powers in the Indian Ocean." Geographically, the "zone of peace" was said to embrace also "regions directly contiguous" to the Indian Ocean, meaning, in part, the Persian Gulf.[134] Finally, the Kremlin expressed "deep concern" about Washington's efforts to "militaris[e] the Persian Gulf countries." The United States was warned that the "neighboring states, including the Soviet Union, cannot remain indifferent to such action."[135]

Upheavals in Iran and Afghanistan

In 1979–1980 the attention of the Gulf states and of the outside world was once again focused on Tehran, where, by November 1979, power passed into the hands of the fundamentalist Shi'i clergy, led by Ayatollah Rouhollah Khomeini. From then on, all the major foreign and domestic policy decisions were made by the Islamic Republic's aging charismatic leader.

As it happened, Ayatollah Khomeini had long believed that the success of the Islamic revolution in Iran was predicated on settling a
number of scores with the outside world. In addition to his profound
contempt for the West, the East, and the Arab regimes on the western
shore of the Gulf, the Ayatollah bore several specific grudges that influenced the conduct of Tehran's foreign affairs. Thus, the United States,
which had befriended and backed the deposed shah, soon emerged as
the "Great Satan" or "Satan no. 1" in the political lexicon of the Islamic
Republic. After the Soviet invasion of Afghanistan in December 1979,
Persia's ancient northern rival, in its atheistic, communist embodiment, was soon elevated to the status of "Satan no. 2." Among the
Islamic Republic's other neighbors, Iraq attracted and held revolutionary Tehran's early and hostile attention. Ayatollah Khomeini deeply
resented the treatment at the hands of the Baghdad authorities during
his fifteen-year exile in Iraq. In addition, he was doctrinally opposed to
the ruling Ba'th party, which he considered atheist, and believed that
the majority Shi'i segment of Iraq's population should control the affairs of that state.[136]

In view of these circumstances, it came as no surprise that relations
between the Islamic Republic and Iraq deteriorated sharply in 1979 and
1980. As Ayatollah Khomeini and his followers publicly dedicated
themselves to the overthrow of the Ba'thist regime, Iranian moral and
material support was extended to the militant elements in Iraq's Shi'i
community, grouped in and around the underground and militant *al-
Dawah al-Islamiyyah*. Not to be outdone, the Iraqi authorities responded by backing anti-Tehran elements among the ethnic Arab population of Iran's oil-rich province of Khuzistan, which Baghdad referred
to as Arabistan.

Rapidly deteriorating relations led to Saddam Hussein's repudiation
of his 1975 Algiers agreement with the shah and to the intensification
of border clashes between the two states. In June 1979 Iraq accused the
Islamic Republic of reviving the shah's ambition to dominate the Gulf
and, in late October, demanded the return of Abu Musa and the Tunb
islands to their Arab owners. Baghdad also reclaimed sovereignty over
the entire width of the Shatt al-Arab. In Tehran the Revolutionary
Guards retaliated by attacking the Iraqi embassy.[137] In 1980 "thousands
of Iraqis of Iranian origin" were expelled, the propaganda war accelerated, and border clashes intensified. In July, Saddam Hussein promised
to defend the Gulf against "Iranian expansionism."[138] Growing tension
would ordinarily suffice to occupy the attention of both governments.
As it happened, however, this escalating regional conflict was develop-

ing parallel to, and soon became enmeshed with, a series of events that brought onto the Gulf scene both superpowers, intent, as usual, to protect and advance their own respective interests.

On November 4, 1979, a group of Iranian "students" stormed the U.S. embassy in Tehran and seized sixty-three hostages. In 1980 their fate, coupled with American efforts to secure their release, not only preoccupied the Islamic Republic and the United States but was also followed with keen interest by the Kremlin, determined not to let Washington recover from the major blow which its position in the Persian Gulf received as a result of the overthrow of the shah.

Concurrently, in late December 1979, for reasons unrelated to the Gulf and its affairs, the USSR sent its troops into Afghanistan. In retrospect, the move appears to have been dictated by the desire to topple the regime of Hafizullah Amin, whose actions the Kremlin found itself increasingly unable to control. Under more normal circumstances, the Soviet invasion of Afghanistan—moving Moscow closer to the Persian Gulf—and the possibility of a U.S. military intervention in Iran might have served as powerful inducements for Baghdad and Tehran to resolve their differences; both were strongly opposed to the Soviet move into Afghanistan. Given the animosity between Ayatollah Khomeini and Saddam Hussein, however, such was not the case. As a result, the Gulf region was soon exposed to its own stresses and strains, while the superpowers went about securing their own interests and, in the process, often disregarded the wishes of the various Gulf states.

Initially, the regime of Saddam Hussein endeavored to adhere to a basic nonaligned position in its relations with the superpowers while stepping up pressure against Iraq's chief regional rival, the Islamic Republic. This translated itself, in part, into criticism of Tehran's seizure of the American embassy as well as into admonishing Washington not to resort to force and castigating Moscow for the intervention in Afghanistan.

In many respects Iraq's position on the hostage problem paralleled the attitude adopted by the Kremlin and most other states with diplomatic representation in Tehran. Thus, the November 1979 statement by the Iraqi Foreign Ministry condemned the attack on the U.S. embassy and the taking of the hostages as contrary to international law. Baghdad also used this opportunity (as did Moscow) to express "great concern" about what it described as Washington's threats to use force to effect the release of the hostages. The United States was actually accused of using the incident "as a cover and justification for attaining regional political and military objectives which have nothing to do with the rescue of the detainees. . . ."[139]

But if the Soviets had ever hoped that the drama unfolding in Tehran as well as the rapidly deteriorating relations between Iran and Iraq would divert Baghdad's attention from their invasion of Afghanistan, they must have been very disappointed. The Ba'thist regime came out openly in condemnation of Moscow's move. In retrospect, it seems obvious that Iraq could not have done less. Afghanistan, situated in the proximity of the Persian Gulf, was a nonaligned, Muslim state. Silence in this matter would therefore have compromised Iraq's claim to leadership in the nonaligned movement to which Saddam Hussein had been aspiring during the latter 1970s. Moreover, since anti-Moscow sentiments had been on the rise in Baghdad from 1978 on, the decision to condemn the Soviet aggression was not subject to the usual constraints imposed by a close patron-client relationship. Finally, Iraq seemed to have been genuinely worried that "the Soviet Union . . . [intended to] encircle the Middle East and then compel the United States to negotiate spheres of influence in the region."[140] Some hints at Baghdad's apprehension were provided by the Iraqi press. For example, in an editorial entitled "The Path of Independence," *Baghdad Observer* accused the superpowers of vying with each other for the establishment of "their own spheres of influence." To fall under the influence of Washington or Moscow, it was concluded, was "tantamount to abandoning man's eternal struggle for freedom."[141]

In any event, Iraq did respond to the Soviet occupation of Afghanistan and its reaction was both swift and decisive. In his Army Day speech of January 6, 1980, Saddam Hussein termed the invasion "an erroneous and unjustified act that creates anxiety . . . [among] all freedom and independence-loving peoples." The theme was picked up by the Iraqi press. *Al-Thawrah* accused the Kremlin of "flagrant intervention" in the internal affairs of Afghanistan and called on the Soviet Union "to revise its entire Middle East policy . . . 'based [as it was] on converting the region into believing in Marxist ideology.' "[142] A short time later, *al-Thawrah* reiterated that "the Soviet . . . occupation of Afghanistan is a good reason for concern by all those linked with friendship bonds with the Soviets" and censured Moscow for "sneaking into the . . . [Middle East] ideologically and politically." The Ba'th party daily added that the Soviets had previously done so in the PDRY and Ethiopia and were now following those moves by invading Afghanistan.[143] In line with these sentiments, Iraq censured the USSR's intervention in Afghanistan during the January 1980 debates at the United Nations and, in February, voted with the vast majority of UN members to request the withdrawal of Soviet troops from Afghanistan.[144]

Whatever apprehensions Saddam Hussein may have had, however, he had no intention of breaking with the USSR or not remaining "even-handed" in his treatment of the superpowers. In an interview with the Paris-based *al-Watan al-Arabi*, published on January 31, 1980, the Iraqi leader argued that his government perceived the Soviet Union as a great power which had committed "the most outstanding error" by invading Afghanistan. In doing so, Moscow showed itself not to be "a source of doctrinal radiation," an image the USSR had been promoting in the outside world. Nevertheless, Saddam Hussein insisted that Baghdad would continue viewing the Soviets as "friends who have identical attitudes in matters concerning our objectives or the interests of our people."[145]

Iraq was also concerned about Washington's reaction to the hostage crisis and to the Russian move into Afghanistan. In his January 6 speech, Saddam Hussein specifically warned against "exploitation of the foreign intervention in Afghanistan to justify further foreign interventions in this or that country in the [Gulf] region." He restated Baghdad's "firm opposition [to] any attempt . . . at turning the area into an arena of rivalry of the Super Powers . . . and [to] implement[ation of] their strategic schemes at the expense of the sovereignty, independence and security of the countries of the region."[146] He "formally appealed" to the superpowers " 'to stop any aggressive or irresponsible act that threatens the security of the peoples of the area.' " He also "called on the peoples of the region to stand firmly against 'all forms of foreign intervention.' "[147]

On the Gulf diplomatic scene Iraq undertook "urgent consultations" with Saudi Arabia and Kuwait with the view to keeping "the Persian Gulf area free of foreign intervention, from either East or West." As explained by a high Iraqi Ministry of Information official: "Our goal is to see how to avoid international conflict here because in the end we would be the losers." Other Baghdad officials, too, expressed what a *New York Times* report described as "deep apprehension over . . . the danger of confrontation in the region between the United States and the Soviet Union."[148]

The West, too, was shaken by the news of the Soviet invasion of Afghanistan. To forestall the possibility of further Russian advances, President Carter, in his 1980 State of the Union address, promulgated what has since become known as the Carter Doctrine: "An attempt by any outside force to gain control of the Persian Gulf region will be regarded as an assault on the vital interests of the United States. It will be repelled by use of any means necessary, including military force."[149]

Given Saddam Hussein's attitude, Iraq's rejection of the Carter Doctrine should not have come as a surprise. A joint statement, issued by the Revolutionary Command Council and the Regional Command of the Ba'th party in February 1980, declared that "presence of foreign military forces" in the territories of the Arab states was "inadmissible" and called on them to "refuse the establishment in their territories of foreign military bases." The statement warned the Arab governments to abstain from "offering foreign forces any kind of services or privileges under any pretext whatsoever" and concluded that any Arab state refusing to abide by these principles would be subject to "economic and political boycott."[150] Aimed specifically at Egypt and Oman, then engaged in negotiations with Washington concerning the use of some of their military facilities by the RDF, Baghdad's position in these matters corresponded closely to that held by the USSR.

As a result of the consultations with the conservative Arab Gulf states, Saddam Hussein, on February 8, 1980, proposed an eight-point Charter for Pan-Arab Action. Among other things, the draft called for opposition to *any* outside military presence in the Arab world; for avoidance of commitment by the Arab states to either superpower; and, in a major about-face, for an Arab mutual defense pact which, in addition to the outside powers, seemed to be implicitly directed against the Islamic Republic. Moreover, in an effort to dispel long-standing fears of Iraq's own political ambitions, prevalent on the Arab side of the Gulf, Saddam Hussein also proposed prohibition of the use of armed force by one Arab state against another.[151] In view of Riyadh's and Kuwait's well-known apprehensions about Baghdad's own intentions, the charter was well received in those as well as most other Arab capitals,[152] but no action on it has ever been taken.

Thus, the crisis-laden months of late 1979 and early 1980 presented Iraq not only with a number of complex problems but also with unusual opportunities to use its relative military power and its economic wealth to project itself into a leadership position in the Arab world and particularly in the Gulf. In the Arab context, Baghdad benefited from Egypt's estrangement, effected by the signing of the peace treaty with Israel. Moreover, Iraq's enormous oil wealth, which enabled Baghdad to pursue an ambitious "guns and butter" policy, gained Saddam Hussein respect at the expense of his arch-rival President Hafez al-Assad of Syria. In the Gulf, regional destabilization that occurred in the wake of the Iranian revolution and of Ayatollah Khomeini's calls for "Islamic" revolutions in area's conservative Arab states, catapulted Iraq into the position of regional leadership. How Baghdad would have tackled these problems had the Gulf been left to its own devices will never be known. As it happened, the superpowers had no intention of leaving the Middle East alone. Rather, for reasons of their own, they were deeply involved, superimposing themselves on the affairs of this highly volatile and explosive region. Tension in and near the Gulf rose appreciably as a result of the hostage crisis, the Russian invasion of Afghanistan, and the ensuing proclamation by President Carter of Washington's determination to protect the Gulf against possible Soviet encroachments.

Saddam Hussein endeavored to deal with these issues by means of his Charter for Pan-Arab Action. Based on what might be termed "militant nonalignment," it called on the Arabs to maintain equidistance from both superpowers, while reserving for the Arab states the right to criticize "aggressive designs" of the United States as well as the Soviet Union. In line with this approach, Iraq suggested that Washington get out of the Gulf as well as of the Indian Ocean,[153] while the Soviets were told to get out of Afghanistan and to stay out of the Gulf.[154] In late March 1980, Iraq announced that it was mounting an effort to rid the PDRY of "puppet forces and the foreign presence on Yemeni soil."[155] Over and beyond that, the sustained effort to establish Iraq's preeminence in the Gulf placed Baghdad on a collision course with the Islamic Republic. In retrospect, there can be no doubt that the collapse of the Iranian armed forces in the course of the revolution, coupled with the growing military power of Iraq, encouraged Saddam Hussein to pursue an aggressive policy toward the regime of Ayatollah Khomeini.

Once Moscow recognized the extent of the anti-American sentiments prevalent in revolutionary Tehran, the Soviets extended the Islamic Republic their moral as well as material support.[156] This evidenced itself particularly after the storming of the U.S. embassy and the seizure of American hostages. Having its own embassy in Tehran, the USSR, very much like Iraq, was careful not to approve the excesses of the Iranian "students." *Pravda* freely admitted that the latter had indeed been guilty of violating "international convention concerning respect for diplomatic privileges and immunity." In contrast with Baghdad, however, Moscow argued that the events in Tehran had to be viewed in the context of past American interventions in the internal affairs of Iran which "in no way corresponded to legal and moral norms" of international behavior. Moreover, "acceptance of the principle of inviolability of diplomatic missions . . . [could] not serve as a justification, let alone as an excuse, for violating sovereignty of an independent state. . . ." Quoting Brezhnev, *Pravda* warned the United States that the USSR remained opposed to "outside interference in the internal affairs of Iran in any form and under any pretext."[157] This Soviet attitude, which Iraq shared, was maintained throughout 1980.

In addition to moral support, the Kremlin placed the Soviet transportation system at Tehran's disposal to help circumvent an economic embargo, imposed on Iran by the United States and the European Community in April 1980, and otherwise endeavored to improve relations with the Islamic Republic. Nevertheless, these early Soviet efforts at befriending revolutionary Iran came to naught.[158] Paralleling Moscow's setbacks in Tehran, the USSR had run into serious problems in Baghdad. Although all three states were strongly opposed to the concentration of U.S. naval forces in the vicinity of the Persian Gulf, Iraq, as well as the Islamic Republic, were outraged at the Soviet occupation of Afghanistan. In public, the Kremlin ignored these difficulties, concentrating instead on the presumed intentions and actions of the United States. However, Soviet efforts to use the crises in U.S.-Iranian as well as in Iraqi-Iranian relations to divert attention from Moscow's intervention in Kabul failed to achieve the desired results.

Consistent with its previous position, the USSR rejected the Carter Doctrine. In a speech of February 18, 1980, Foreign Minister Gromyko objected to it on the following grounds: (1) the United States was endeavoring "to widen the sphere of its military presence in regions situated many thousands of kilometers from its own territories"; (2) the United States had no right to "somebody else's oil wells"; and (3) the United States had no right "to threaten other countries with the use of force," let alone applying it against those who chose to "dispose of their riches" independent of America's wishes.[159]

In examining the concept of "vital Western interests," Soviet commentators distinguished between the United States and its various allies. Ruben Andreasian noted that the U.S. imports from the Gulf constituted only 12 percent of the country's domestic consumption of oil. In contrast, many members of NATO as well as Japan imported much of their petroleum from that region. For this reason, the Gulf oil could be argued to be of "vital importance" to those nations but not to the United States.[160] Over and beyond that, however, Brezhnev insisted that the Gulf, "as any other region of the world, is a sphere of vital interests of the states situated in it, and not of any . . . [outsider]." For this reason, "nobody from the outside has the right to interfere in . . . [the Gulf's regional] affairs, to step forward in the role of . . . a self-appointed 'guardian of order.'"[161]

On the subject of possible "threats to the flow of Gulf petroleum," the Soviet analysts were not of one mind. While most dismissed such assertions as "absurd arguments, intended to justify the selfish [and] dangerous actions of the U.S.A.,"[162] Andreasian reasoned that if there was any "danger" of cutting oil deliveries to the Western customers, it stemmed primarily from the producers themselves. Such was the case during the 1973 embargo and, likewise, when the Islamic Republic refused to sell petroleum to the United States after the deposed shah was permitted to enter the United States in late 1979. But these were exceptions, Andreasian argued, and there were no reasons to assume that any of the Arab Gulf producers were contemplating to use the "oil weapon" against the Western powers.[163]

What, then, were the real reasons behind the "frantic" U.S. military activity near the Gulf and elsewhere in the Indian Ocean? Although most Soviet commentators continued to insist that Washington was out "to restore direct control over the sources of petroleum" by means of "repelling the national-liberation movement in the region,"[164] Andreasian, once again, struck a more moderate tone. Noting that "What is in question are the positions of U.S. imperialism in the oil-producing countries," he went on to say that Washington merely wanted the producers to pursue economic policies that were amenable to American interests. Among such U.S. interests, Andreasian singled out lower prices, particularly those paid by ARAMCO to Saudi Arabia, as well as increased Saudi production. On a broader scale, the dispatch of warships to the Strait of Hormuz "with the aim of establishing . . . [U.S.] control over supply of Arab and Iranian oil to other countries" was intended to "strengthen . . . [Washington's] position in the capitalist world and [to] gain . . . the upper hand over its rivals." Finally, the invitation issued by the Carter administration to a number of "West European countries and Japan to send their naval ships to the area" of Hormuz was intended to serve a twofold function. By involving them in the U.S.-Iranian conflict, Washington intended "to increase pressure on the Iranians and the Arabs and at the same time foil its competitors' efforts to strengthen their own foothold at the expense of U.S. interests."[165]

In any event, the Soviet press assessed the Carter Doctrine as but "another step on the path of escalation of tension in the regions of the Arabian Sea and the Persian Gulf."[166] It was also a manifestation of Washington's continuing determination to crush the revolutionary regime in Iran. Moscow took issue with the Carter administration's insistence that Ayatollah Khomeini was creating turmoil in the Gulf. It was not the "movement of the . . . masses, believers in Islam" but the United States that was threatening to impose a naval blockade, to mine ports, to land troops in other countries' territory, and to bomb oil-producing areas.[167] Finally, Washington was also said to have contributed to the "destabilization" of the Gulf by veiled warnings to use tactical nuclear weapons in defense of U.S. interests.[168] These threats, backed by the "enormous U.S. naval build-up" in the Arabian Sea, Moscow concluded, were clear indications that the United States had abandoned its "previously announced" efforts at "demilitariz[ing] . . . the Indian Ocean."[169]

According to Soviet commentators, the oil-producing countries recognized that "the U.S. military presence" in or near the Gulf constituted "a direct threat to them. . . ." For this reason, the Carter Doctrine "evoked a negative reaction in Kuwait, Iraq, Abu Dhabi, Jordan, Syria, the United Arab Emirates and other countries of the region."[170] Nevertheless, in June 1980 Washington and Muscat signed an agreement which gave the United States access to some Omani naval and air facilities and permitted "temporary" stationing of American servicemen on Omani territory.[171] As a result, Pravda concluded, Muscat had come to occupy a "special place in Washington's hegemonist plans." The United States was now in a position to "seize control of the Strait of Hormuz" and to exert military pressure on all of the countries of the Gulf. Pravda spoke approvingly of Libya's Colonel Qaddafi's request to expel Oman from the Arab League—its deal with Washington was "correctly seen" by the other Arab states as a "direct interference in their internal affairs" and as an "encroachment on their independence."[172]

Otherwise, since the U.S. initiatives had been explained, in part, in terms of the need to protect the Gulf producers from the "Soviet threat," the Kremlin continued to disclaim any aggressive ambitions. Responding to assertions that Moscow's move into Afghanistan represented a threat to peace and security of the Middle East, Gromyko denounced efforts to equate Moscow's "support [of] the Afghan revolution" with "some dark intentions . . . [in] the oil-producing areas" of the Persian Gulf. Rather, the "Soviet state, from the very first days of its existence, has infringed neither on oil nor on any other riches [belonging to] other states." Gromyko was equally indignant at attempts to explain his government's policy in the Middle East by references to Russia's "drive toward warm-water ports." He dismissed "this fabrication . . . [of the] pre-revolutionary days" by noting that the USSR had "sufficient access to warm as well as cold waters."[173] Brezhnev, too, denied that the Soviet Union was menacing any of its southern neighbors. The outside power with "aggressive designs" on the Middle East was not the Soviet Union but the United States, and Washington was whipping up "anti-Soviet hysteria" to give it a "pretext . . . to expand in Asia." Brezhnev had no trouble seeing through U.S. intentions: "the United States . . . desire[s] to create a network of military bases in the Indian Ocean, in the countries of the Middle East, and in Africa" in order to "subordinate these countries to its hegemony, to drain their natural wealth . . . , and at the same time to use their territory in its strategic designs against peace, socialism, and the national liberation forces. That," Brezhnev concluded, was the "crux of the matter."[174]

In addition, the Kremlin continued to issue stern warnings that it would not stand idly by while events, viewed as harmful to its interests, were unfolding in the vicinity of the Soviet borders. For example, *Pravda* described the "concentration of the U.S. naval power in the Indian Ocean" (occasioned, it will be recalled, by the Iranian hostage crisis) as a "dangerous development" which significantly increased the chances of a "military clash" in the Gulf.[175] Brezhnev concurred in this assessment and went on to add: "We do not claim anybody's lands [and] we do not interfere in anyone's affairs. . . . But we are ready to stand for our rights and legitimate interests." The meaning of Brezhnev's pronouncement was explained in the following manner:

> Those who are planning a further aggravation of tensions in the regions neighboring the Soviet frontiers should clearly be aware that the Soviet Union cannot show indifference to such plans. The USSR has always taken the side, and will continue to do so, of the peoples fighting for liberation from imperialist diktat, for their freedom and independence. It will remain true to its policy in the future as well.[176]

The Brezhnev Plan

In contrasting its own posture with the "aggressiveness" of the United States, the USSR has consistently endeavored to project an image of a friendly power that favored peace, security, and stability and objected to outside interference in the affairs of the Persian Gulf. These and other themes reappeared in the so-called Brezhnev Plan that formed a part of the Soviet president's address to the Indian Parliament on December 10, 1980.

In retrospect, it would appear that there were two major reasons for advancing the Soviet proposals at that particular time and place. First, they were intended to dispel the apprehension in the Gulf capitals as well as in Islamabad about Moscow's intentions in the wake of the Soviet invasion of Afghanistan. Second, the plan constituted the Kremlin's counterproposal to the Carter Doctrine. As such, it was designed to demonstrate that although the United States was pursuing its own selfish goals, the Soviet Union shared the aspirations of the Gulf states and had no intention of infringing on their vital interests.

Brezhnev's New Delhi speech contained new "packaging" but no substantive surprises, however. He attacked the Carter administration for turning the Indian Ocean and the Gulf into "ever more dangerous sources of international tension." He warned the "imperialists" that "we are, of course . . . concerned about what is happening in the region [situated] so close to our borders." He dismissed as "pure invention" Western insistence that the Soviet military presence in Afghanistan presented a threat to national security of any of Kabul's neighbors, above all Pakistan and the petroleum-producing states of the Persian Gulf. Those spreading such rumors, Brezhnev insisted, "know very well that there is no such threat." He went on to repeat that the USSR had "no intention" of attacking anybody or of "encroaching upon either the Middle East oil or its transportation route." Finally, Brezhnev called on "the United States, other Western powers, China, Japan, and all interested states" to join the Soviet Union in promulgating an international "doctrine of peace and security" for the Gulf region. It would rest on the following five principles:

1. No "foreign military bases" would be "established in the Persian Gulf area and on the adjacent islands," and no "nuclear or any other weapons of mass destruction" would be deployed there.

2. The outside powers would undertake "not to use or threaten to use force against the countries of the Persian Gulf region [and] not to interfere in their internal affairs."

3. The outsiders would pledge "to respect the status of nonalignment chosen by the states of the Persian Gulf area by not drawing them into military groupings of which the nuclear powers are members."

4. The outsiders would "respect the inalienable right of the [Gulf] states . . . to their natural resources."

5. The outside powers would agree "not to raise any obstacles or pose threats to normal trade exchanges and to the use of sea lanes linking the states of that region with other countries."[177]

Brezhnev elaborated on the proposal in his February 23, 1981, speech before the Twenty-sixth Congress of the CPSU. He noted that the United

States, by concentrating naval and air power near the Gulf, had created a "military threat" to that region. "A state of stability and calm," he went on to say, could be restored only "by means of a *joint effort*, with due account for the legitimate interests of all sides. The sovereign rights of the [Gulf] states and the security of maritime and other communications connecting the region with the rest of the world can be *guaranteed*," he concluded.[178] Brezhnev clearly implied that the USSR was to be one of the guarantors of the new Gulf order.

The Brezhnev Plan was promptly dismissed by Washington—a "senior State department official" was quoted as saying that the U.S. government "had no quarrel with the broad principles enunciated by Mr. Brezhnev" but "had no interest in enhancing Soviet prestige by reacting positively to Mr. Brezhnev as long as the Soviet Union continued to crush Afghan resistance."[179] More significantly, the plan was also ignored in the Gulf. This was true not only of all but one of the conservative regimes[180] but also of the Islamic Republic and Iraq. Baghdad's failure to comment favorably on Brezhnev's proposal may have surprised some observers of the Gulf scene. After all, in the February 1980 statement by the RCC and the Ba'th party Regional Command, Iraq had rejected the Carter Doctrine, objecting specifically to foreign military bases and to the deployment of foreign troops on the territory of the littoral states—two of Brezhnev's key points. Baghdad was also on record opposing foreign-sponsored military blocs and outside interference in regional affairs. Nevertheless, Iraq and most of its neighbors refused to endorse the Brezhnev Plan. They saw in it but another attempt by the Kremlin to intrude itself into regional affairs at a time when the Gulf governments, in spite of the Kremlin's assurances, remained highly alarmed about Moscow's intentions in view of the continued Soviet military presence in Afghanistan. Even more significantly, the regional actors could not but be painfully aware of the plan's irrelevance in the context of the Iraq-Iran war which, since September 1980, had emerged as the Gulf's most critical regional problem. They were also determined to steer the Gulf clear of the U.S.-Soviet competition. Put differently, most Arab governments as well as Tehran felt that the superpowers were above all concerned not with the problems of the region but with their own global rivalry. For this reason, most of the local actors believed that the best thing the Soviet Union and the United States could do for the Gulf was to leave it alone. Finally, in the case of Iraq, it will be recalled that in 1979 and 1980 Moscow-Baghdad relations had reached a new low. That, in itself, would probably have precluded endorsement of the Brezhnev Plan.[181]

Evaluation

A comparison between the Iraqi and Soviet positions on regional security and stability in the Persian Gulf during the latter 1970s reveals agreement on a number of key issues. Thus, both governments were wary of U.S. intentions and remained committed to declaring the Gulf (as well as the Indian Ocean) a "zone of peace." According to this formula, the great powers would refrain from forging military alliances, from using force, and from competing with each other in the Gulf region. The outsiders would also undertake not to seek the use of bases and other military installations in the territories of the littoral states, not to interfere in their internal affairs, and to respect their nonaligned status. Moreover, and for obvious reasons, the Kremlin supported Iraq's insistence on the oil-producers' right to their "natural resources" as well as on freedom of commercial navigation in and beyond the Gulf.

Yet, Moscow's and Baghdad's positions were not identical. Pertinent Soviet statements (including the Brezhnev Plan) contained no reference to occasional visits to the Gulf by warships of nonlittoral states. Iraq, in contrast, was on record objecting to such visits and extended its injunction not only to Western naval vessels but also, explicitly, to the Soviet navy. Moscow's neglect of a subject which was clearly important to Baghdad illustrates the proposition that although the USSR was attempting to project an image of a peaceful and friendly neighbor intent on promoting the interests of the littoral states, Iraq made no distinction between the outsiders and warned all of them, including the Soviet Union, to stay out of regional affairs. In a similar fashion, while Moscow focused its attention on the activities of the Western powers, above all the United States, Baghdad attached primary importance to the initiatives of the littoral states. For example, Iraq insisted that freedom of navigation in the Gulf be secured by regional means. The Soviets repeatedly endorsed the principle itself but said nothing about how it should be guaranteed. However, their clear preference, as enunciated by Brezhnev in February 1981, was for an international agreement to which the USSR was a party. Moreover, and most importantly, Baghdad saw itself as a leading power in the Gulf: only adoption of its proposals would result in the achievement of regional security and stability. Unmentioned in the Iraqi pronouncements but clearly underlying them was Baghdad's rivalry with Tehran for preeminence in the Gulf area. Dormant after the 1975 Algiers accord, their competition resurfaced in the wake of the Iranian revolution. Although indirectly, the Kremlin did take a stand on this issue. In applauding the ouster of Mohammed Reza

Shah and in seeking to improve relations with the Islamic Republic, the Soviets left no doubt about their refusal to support Iraq in its struggle for regional preeminence. Intended to demonstrate Moscow's displeasure with Baghdad, the Soviet stance also provided another illustration of the Kremlin's preoccupation with its rivalry with the United States—the Iranian revolution removed Washington's staunchest regional ally from the Gulf scene. Iraq's displeasure manifested itself, in part, in unequivocal condemnation of the Soviet move into Afghanistan. Finally, in sharp contrast with Moscow, Baghdad had little to say about the huge amounts of modern weapons flowing into the Gulf arsenals throughout the 1970s. After all, Iraq itself was a recipient of large quantities of Soviet and Western-made arms. Still, the Iraqis were clearly uneasy about the shah's ambitious acquisition program: their own military buildup proceeded apace long after the defeat of the Kurds in 1975.

In short, it might be argued that, in the period between 1975 and 1980, Soviet and Iraqi short-term interests overlapped in that both parties called for noninvolvement by outside powers in the affairs of the Gulf. Even on this issue, however, the USSR and Iraq had found themselves in substantive disagreement: while Baghdad insisted that regional arrangements be worked out and enforced from within the Gulf to the exclusion of *all* outsiders, Moscow, as evidenced by Brezhnev's speech of February 1981, was seeking active participation in formulating and subsequently implementing wider international guarantees. In other words, while Iraq was advocating a Gulf free from superpower rivalry, the USSR endeavored to insert itself into regional affairs. In this sense, even their short-term interests were not the same.

The same conclusion applies to Soviet and Iraqi longer-term interests, as the Kremlin consistently refused to endorse Baghdad's claim to leadership in the Gulf region. During the period under discussion in this chapter, this was evident, in part, in the major pronouncements by the Soviet dignitaries as well as in the joint Soviet-Iraqi communiqués. Thus, Brezhnev's address before the Twenty-fifth Congress of the CPSU, held in February 1976, contained praise for Iraq but did not mention the Gulf or its problems.[182] The joint communiqué, issued at the conclusion of Premier Kosygin's 1976 visit to Baghdad, called for the proclamation of the Indian Ocean as a "zone of peace" but made no reference to the Gulf.[183] Nor was the subject broached in the speeches by Kosygin and Saddam Hussein during the latter's 1977 visit to the USSR or in the joint communiqué.[184] The same was true of official statements occasioned by the Iraqi leader's 1978 trip to Moscow.[185]

Since the public record contains no evidence, one can only wonder whether Brezhnev or Saddam Hussein had ever tried to sway the other party's position on these delicate and important matters. It is, however, likely that if such attempts were made by either one or both, Baghdad and Moscow found themselves unable to "influence" the other side. The issues involved were too sensitive, affecting as they did interests that were no doubt regarded as "vital" by both parties concerned. Under these circumstances, compromise was beyond reach, and any application of pressure would have been counterproductive.

The normalization of Iraqi-Iranian relations, effected in 1975, was one of the early casualties of the Islamic revolution. On September 17, 1980, Saddam Hussein renounced the Algiers treaty, and after five days Iraqi troops invaded Iran. They held the initiative during the first six weeks of the war and captured parts of the oil-rich Khuzistan province. Iran went on a counteroffensive in the spring of 1981, and by June 1982 forced the Iraqis to withdraw from most of the occupied territories. After two years of inconclusive fighting, Iranian forces invaded Iraq in early 1984. They made some inroads into Iraqi territory but failed to capture the city of Basrah—a major strategic and political objective—or to cut the vital Baghdad-Basrah-Kuwait highway. In 1988, the Iraqi army attacked, recovered the territory lost since 1984, and occupied some Iranian territory which it held until 1990. Relative stalemate on the ground was accompanied by intensified air attacks against industrial installations, civilian targets as well as against petroleum shipping in the Gulf. In the last stages of the war, the belligerents also fired Soviet-made Scud missiles at each other's cities.

In the diplomatic arena, Baghdad gradually lowered its demands and, before 1988, was prepared to accept unconditional cease-fire and to negotiate a peaceful settlement of the conflict. The Islamic Republic, in contrast, insisted that it would accept nothing short of the overthrow of the Saddam Hussein regime. Only in the summer of 1988, after it had run out of steam, did Iran accept the UN-sponsored cease-fire.

Early Stages of the Conflict (1980–1981)

Soviet opposition to Iraq's decision to invade Iran became evident on September 21, when RCC member Tariq Aziz arrived in Moscow and conferred with CPSU Central Committee Secretary Boris Ponomarev and First Deputy Foreign Minister Viktor Mal'tsev. The purpose of the visit was to explain to the Kremlin leaders the reasons for Saddam Hussein's decision to invade Iran and to secure Soviet support for the war effort. *Pravda*'s treatment of the Tariq Aziz visit—a short, terse item, appearing on page 4[1]—attested to Moscow's anger with Iraq and, therefore, to the rejection of his requests for Soviet assistance.

Another early indication of the Kremlin's tilt toward the Islamic Republic was provided by the treatment which vice president of the USSR Supreme Soviet Inamadzhan Usmankhodzhaev and Mal'tsev extended to the Iranian ambassador to the Soviet Union. According to Mohammed Mokri's own account, he had asked the USSR to condemn Iraq's aggression and to cut off military assistance to it. The Soviet officials equivocated. They said that Soviet "military aid to Iraq was governed by the 1972 treaty and was intended for use against Israel." They went on to note that the Kremlin regarded the war as "benefitting the imperialists only" and wished it to end "as soon as possible." But, in spite of the clear disapproval of Iraq's decision, the USSR intended to remain neutral in the Tehran-Baghdad conflict. On balance, the Iranian ambassador was pleased: "We are thankful to the Soviet Union because we feel it has adopted a neutral position" in the Gulf conflict.[2]

On September 24 *Pravda* came out with its initial appraisal of the Iran-Iraq war. A commentary by Iurii Glukhov, pointedly entitled "Who Benefits from This?," set the tone for the official Soviet position maintained for the duration of the conflict. Glukhov reminded his readers that the leaders of the 1968 revolution adhered to an "anti-imperialist policy," as evidenced by their espousal of nonalignment and their rejection of the Camp David accords. In Iran the Islamic revolution overthrew the pro-Western shah, depriving Washington of its most important ally in the Persian Gulf. By 1980 both states emerged as the leading anti-Western powers of the Gulf. Because of this, the war between them was welcomed by the "imperialist camp"—by fighting each other, Baghdad and Tehran were destroying their ability to oppose the West. *Pravda* also deplored the Iran-Iraq conflict because Washington regarded it as a "proof" of regional instability. That, in turn, could easily serve as an excuse for American military intervention in the Gulf. For these reasons, Glukhov expressed hope that the belligerents would "demonstrate good will" and would resolve their differences "by means of [direct] negotiations."

But even as the Soviets expressed their opposition to the war, it became obvious that Baghdad was in no hurry to terminate the hostilities. On September 24, *Pravda* published Iraq's conditions for ending the war: the return to Iraqi sovereignty of the three Gulf islands, Iran's recognition of Iraq's right to the entire Shatt al-Arab, and Tehran's respect for territorial integrity and sovereignty of Iraq. According to the same issue of *Pravda*, Iran responded by declaring the Shatt al-Arab a "zone of military operations" and closed the Strait of Hormuz to "strategic goods" being shipped to Iraqi ports.

The degree of Soviet concern with the rapidly deteriorating situation in the Gulf was reflected in the attention which the war received at the Kremlin's highest levels. Speaking at a dinner in honor of Indian President Sanjiva Reddy on September 30, Brezhnev expressed Moscow's regret at the Gulf conflict. He went on to say that the war was not a result of a "simple tragic misunderstanding." Rather, "some people [who] are trying to profiteer from it" bore the responsibility for the Iran-Iraq conflict. Who were these people, Brezhnev asked and answered: "Those who . . . wish to establish their control over Middle Eastern oil, who dream about transforming Iran once again into a military base and into a *gendarme* outpost of imperialism." Turning to the belligerents, the Soviet leader warned that they stood to gain nothing from "mutual destruction, bloodshed, and disruption of each other's economies." Brezhnev returned to these themes eight days later, in a Kremlin speech honoring Syrian President Hafez al-Assad. On that occasion, however, the secretary general went one step further. He "resolutely" warned others: "keep your hands off the unfolding events."[3]

Otherwise, during the early stages of the conflict, the USSR refrained from sending war matériel to either antagonist. According to Secretary of State Edmund S. Muskie, "the Russians appeared to be living up to pledges 'to stand off and away from the conflict in a neutral posture.' "[4] However, although the Kremlin refused to continue supplying weapons to Iraq, it was said to have offered arms to Iran. On October 5 Tehran Radio reported that, in the course of a recent meeting between Prime Minister Ali Rajai and Soviet Ambassador Vladimir M. Vinogradov, the latter had offered Iran "long-term military assistance."[5] The Kremlin denied the report: "No offers to Iran regarding the supply of weapons from the Soviet side have been issued."[6] Nevertheless, it is possible that Vinogradov was exploring Tehran's intentions with the view to committing the USSR to the Islamic Republic. Put differently, in late September to early October 1980, Moscow may have seriously considered abandoning Iraq in favor of Ayatollah Khomeini's Iran. Even if this supposition was correct, however, it soon became obvious that Tehran had no intention of associating itself closely with the USSR. According to Tehran Radio, Rajai rejected Vinogradov's offer.[7]

In November 1980 Tariq Aziz returned to Moscow. The account of his "working visit" in the Soviet press was strikingly similar to that of late September: *Pravda* carried but a short note of his meeting with Ponomarev and Mal'tsev.[8] There can be no doubt that Tariq Aziz returned to Moscow to plead for Soviet arms. Because the Iraqi offensive had by then ground to a halt and Tehran had shown no interest in ending the conflict on Saddam Hussein's terms, it had become imperative for Baghdad to persuade the Kremlin to resume its military assistance program to Iraq. Judging by the coverage of his visit in the Soviet press and by his own subsequent account of the failure of the two missions to the USSR, Tariq Aziz again left Moscow empty-handed.[9]

Seen together, the Kremlin's opposition to the Gulf conflict and its refusal to provide Baghdad with badly needed military equipment[10] served as clear indications of the USSR's profound dissatisfaction with Iraq. At the same time, the unyielding Soviet stance also represented a concerted effort to pressure Saddam Hussein into abandoning war as a means of resolving his differences with Ayatollah Khomeini. Although Moscow held a powerful hand, it failed to achieve the desired results— in 1980 and early 1981, Iraq was not yet in any mood to compromise. Nevertheless, even at this lowest point in their relationship, when, according to Tariq Aziz, "the two countries had narrowly avoided a major blowup,"[11] neither the USSR nor Iraq were prepared to burn all the bridges. Moscow's reluctance to effect a total break was indicated, in part, by the willingness of some members of the Warsaw Pact, particularly Poland, to barter war matériel for Iraqi oil.[12]

Despite Moscow's support of Tehran during the "hostage crisis" with the United States and of the Kremlin's tilt toward the Islamic Republic during the initial phase of the Gulf war, relations between Iran and the USSR were often strained. A major irritant proved to be the Soviet invasion of Afghanistan, an act that Iran condemned decisively. As early as the spring of 1980, Foreign Minister Sadeq Qotbzadeh warned the USSR that refusal to withdraw troops from Afghanistan would cause Iran to extend military assistance to the *mujahideen*.[13] In addition, he accused the Iranian Communist party of harboring Soviet agents. In July 1980, Qotbzadeh ordered the staff of the Soviet embassy in Tehran reduced from three hundred to fifteen and some 1,200 technicians from the USSR and the East European countries expelled from Iran.[14] Moscow attempted to minimize the rift, and none of these occurrences were reported in the Soviet press. However, another incident—the storming of the Soviet embassy in Tehran by a mob of anticommunist Afghans in December 1980—could not be concealed. It badly strained Soviet-Iranian relations but did not lead to a break between the two states.[15]

Brezhnev discussed the subject of Iraqi-Iranian relations in his February 21, 1981, speech before the Twenty-sixth Congress of the CPSU. He praised the Islamic revolution as a "major event in international life of recent years" and went on to say that, "with all of its complexity and contradictions, it is, essentially, an anti-imperialist revolution." For this reason the USSR was "prepared to develop with Iran good relations on the basis of equality and, of course, reciprocity." Turning to the war, Brezhnev branded it as "absolutely senseless from the standpoint of the interests of these states." Since the conflict benefited "imperialism" only, the secretary general repeated the Kremlin's hope that the belligerents would soon negotiate an end to the hostilities. Brezhnev concluded this part of his speech by noting: "We strive to promote this in practice also."[16]

What this "striving to promote" a peaceful settlement in the Iraq-Iran war actually meant was not explained by either Brezhnev or the Soviet media. Judging by his speech and the spring 1981 pronouncements of the Soviet press, however, the Kremlin attempted not only to remain on good terms with Iran but also—in a new departure—to improve relations with Iraq. In retrospect, it would seem that the continuing aloofness of the Islamic Republic was one of the factors which prompted Moscow to seek an improvement in the badly strained relations with Iraq. Another consideration related to the fortunes of war and their impact on the belligerents' respective positions: by early 1981, the Iraqi forces were bogged down in defensive operations and, in May, the Iranians launched their first major counteroffensive. As the Iraqis realized that their blitzkrieg had failed to bring the Islamic Republic to its knees, Baghdad's diplomatic stance began to mellow. Tehran's attitude, in contrast, remained as inflexible as it had been before. In any event, in the spring and summer of 1981 the Gulf war restored partial harmony to Soviet-Iraqi relations, as Baghdad came out in favor of a compromise political settlement—a course of action that Moscow approved of all along—but encountered Ayatollah Khomeini's stubborn opposition to anything less than the removal of Saddam Hussein.

The Iranian Counteroffensive (1981–1982)

In May 1981 Iranian troops mounted their first major counteroffensive. Soon afterward, Israel destroyed the Osirak nuclear reactor, situated near Baghdad, and explained its attack in terms of Iraq's ongoing construction of a nuclear device.[17] One of the unintended consequences of Jerusalem's action (as well as of the changing fortunes of the war and of the deteriorating Soviet-Iranian relations) was the resumption of cooperation between the USSR and Iraq. Before turning to that subject, however, Moscow's relations with Iran will be examined.

Relations with Iran. An important feature of the second phase of the Gulf war was the growing deterioration of Soviet-Iranian relations. One of the issues over which the two states remained at loggerheads was Afghanistan, where some of the outside assistance to the anticommunist *mujahideen* had been channeled through the Islamic Republic. On August 25, 1981, *Pravda* published a lengthy "Statement by the Government of DRA" addressed to Pakistan and Iran. It pleaded for normalization of relations between Afghanistan and its neighbors and called on Islamabad and Tehran to discontinue their support of the antigovernment guerrillas. Kabul's gesture was warmly praised in the Soviet press but was rejected by Iran.[18]

On February 11, 1982, in a marked shift of gears, *Izvestiia* published a highly favorable review of Soviet-Iranian relations. It was written by A. Akhmedzianov and coincided with a visit to Moscow of Energy Minister Hasan Qafuri-Fard. The article disclosed that in the period between 1978 and 1981, the transport of goods to and from Iran through Soviet territory rose from 1 to 3.4 million tons, while the USSR's trade with Iran increased from 671 to 800 million rubles. In addition, in 1981 alone, the Soviets received more than 2.2 million tons of Iranian oil. Akhmedzianov concluded on a highly optimistic note: bilateral cooperation was an "objective necessity stemming not only from geographic proximity of the two countries but also from the fact that it fulfills [their respective] interests. . . ." Given the tone of Akhmedzianov's article, the unfavorable review of Moscow-Tehran relations which appeared in *Pravda* on March 9, 1982, came as a definite surprise. Because of its unusual candor, Pavel Demchenko's exposé deserves to be examined in detail. He began by praising the "positive changes" which the 1979 revolution had effected in Iran's foreign policy—it "broadened the sphere of coincidence in our countries' positions in the international arena and created conditions for developing goodneighborly relations. . . ." Therefore, the USSR had hoped that "great possibilities for development of Soviet-Iranian relations" would be translated into concrete results. They were not.

In terms of economic and trade relations, Demchenko found the figures to be "impressive": after 1979, trade between the two countries had grown appreciably. In addition, the USSR continued to assist Iran in the construction of numerous industrial projects. Tehran, in turn, was on schedule repaying its debts and remained interested in "broadening [its] economic and trade relations with the Soviet Union." Unfortunately, economic cooperation did not extend itself to "other aspects of Soviet-Iranian relations." On the contrary, the Iranian authorities had reduced the number of diplomats, assigned to the Soviet embassy in Tehran, and closed the consulate in Resht. The same thing happened to the offices of the Russo-Iranian Bank, of the Soviet Insurance Company, and of the Soviet-Iranian Cultural Society. These actions were accompanied by "rapidly intensifying anti-Soviet propaganda." To blame were those "forces in the Iranian leadership that oppose goodneighborly relations and cooperation with our country." Demchenko concluded on a conciliatory note: in spite of the existing problems, the USSR remained committed to its "support of the Iranian revolution" and wished to improve bilateral relations "on the basis of genuine equality and mutual interests."

Demchenko's lengthy discourse reflected Moscow's deep disillusionment with the Islamic Republic: the USSR had supported Iran in its confrontation with the United States and it had remained interested in improving bilateral relations. Tehran, in contrast, had made full use of Soviet assistance in its hour of need and then proceeded to show its true anti-Soviet colors. This discovery must have served as an additional impetus for Moscow to improve its relations with Iraq.

Relations with Iraq. A marked shift in Soviet-Iraqi relations occurred after the Israeli destruction of Osirak in June of that year. The Kremlin reacted sharply to what a "TASS Statement" described as a "gangster action," perpetrated in collusion with the United States.[19] While the statement zeroed in on Israel and the United States and said little about the object of the attack, it soon became obvious that the destruction of Osirak provided a major impetus for the resumption of Soviet-Iraqi cooperation.

On June 18, 1981, First Deputy Prime Minister and RCC member Taha Yasin Ramadan arrived in Moscow "at the invitation of the Soviet government." According to *Pravda*, it was an "official visit," the first such event since the beginning of the Gulf war. One of the issues discussed was the "continuing development of relations between the USSR and Iraq on the basis of the [1972] treaty." According to *Pravda*, both sides "expressed readiness to broaden economic ties, trade, and cooperation in other areas [a euphemism for supply of Soviet weapons] on a stable and mutually profitable foundation."[20] Among the outward manifestations of the Ramadan visit were the signings of a bilateral, long-term economic, commercial, and technical cooperation accord in late June and of an Iraq-Comecon agreement in October 1981.[21]

Moscow-Baghdad rapprochement was reflected on the political level as well. In mid-July 1981, a Soviet government delegation arrived in the Iraqi capital to attend the independence day ceremonies. It was pointedly received by Saddam Hussein who used the opportunity to acknowledge the "support and solidarity of the USSR in connection with Israel's bandit attack on the Iraqi nuclear . . . research complex."[22] One of the tangible results of the improvement in Soviet-Iraqi relations was Baghdad's decision to drop its opposition to the Afghan Communist regime and to the Russian invasion of Afghanistan. Moreover, in June 1981, Moscow agreed to lift the arms embargo, instituted in the wake of the Iraqi invasion of Iran. Additional evidence supporting this conclusion was provided by both Ramadan and Tariq Aziz. In interviews with the *Wall Street Journal*, given in April 1982, both officials said that the USSR had "refus[ed] to resupply Iraq with [military] equipment . . . for 10 months after the war started," that is, until July 1981.[23]

Nevertheless, in spite of the outward normalization of Soviet-Iraqi relations and of the continuing deliveries of Russian war matériel (mainly from Eastern Europe) during the second phase of the Gulf conflict, Baghdad remained unhappy with the USSR for at least two important reasons. First, the quantity and perhaps also the quality of Soviet arms received during 1981 were judged inadequate by the Iraqi authorities. Second, Baghdad continued to resent deeply Moscow's refusal to abandon its posture of neutrality and to come out openly in favor of Iraq. As one Iraqi official put it: "The Soviets are straddling the fence, and it's unpardonable."[24]

The War of Attrition (1982–1984)

In the summer of 1982, Iranian troops expelled the Iraqis from most of the territory occupied in the early stages of the conflict and crossed the border in the southern sector of the front. This offensive, *Pravda* regretted to report, was carried out in disregard of the Security Council's resolution calling for "immediate cease-fire, a halt to military operations, and withdrawal of forces to internationally recognized borders."[25] As a result, since mid-1982, Baghdad's and Moscow's positions on the ceasefire and troop withdrawals corresponded closely. This coincidence of interests contributed to the gradual rapprochement between the USSR and Iraq.

In the ensuing months, the Soviet press kept track of the military operations and published occasional analyses of the situation unfolding in the Gulf. These commentaries contained nothing new. It was not until June 1983 that Moscow refocused its attention on the Iraq-Iran conflict: TASS reported that Tehran might finally be interested in ending the war and had made known Iran's conditions for a cease-fire. They included the withdrawal of Iraqi troops to prewar borders and "restitution for material losses." With respect to the disputed frontier areas, Moscow did not seem to care—this was a minor matter that should have been resolved a long time ago. As for restitution, TASS noted that Tariq Aziz had expressed Iraq's readiness to conclude with Iran, under the aegis of the United Nations, an agreement binding both sides not to inflict damage on the civilian population. "The signing of such a document," Tariq Aziz said, "would permit the determination of damage inflicted on Iran's civilian objects." (Tariq Aziz did not say that Iraq would actually pay reparations to Iran, but the notion was clearly implicit in his statement.)[26] However, it soon became obvious that Moscow's optimism had been misplaced.

The Soviet press returned to the subject of peace several months— and two major Iranian offensives (July and October 1983)—later. In a melancholy account, Iurii Glukhov cited the latest figures of the "senseless and cruel bloodletting": some 175,000 dead and 600,000 wounded and more than $2 billion in matériel losses after three years of fighting. Equally disturbing was the belligerents' reaction to the mediation efforts, undertaken by the United Nations and other international organizations. However, while the initial "peace initiatives" had been rebuffed by both belligerents, Iraq, since mid-1982, was willing to accept a peaceful settlement of the conflict. Unfortunately, Glukhov continued, the Iranian leadership refused to reciprocate. Instead, Tehran insisted on "punishing" Iraq, on overthrowing the existing regime, and on receiving "sizeable compensation" for war-related damages. This meant that Iran declined to settle for anything less that "victory," an ambition which Glukhov tied to the rise of a "chauvinist mood" in Tehran.[27]

Relations with Iran. The Islamic Republic's intransigence prompted the USSR to come out openly in support of Iraq, a move that resulted in further deterioration of Moscow-Tehran relations. Specifically, the Soviet media branded Iran's first major thrust into Iraqi territory a violation of the UN Security Council's cease-fire resolution of July 1982. The Kremlin's position, in turn, was interpreted in the Islamic Republic as abandonment of Soviet neutrality in the Gulf conflict. Tehran accused Moscow of resuming large-scale arms shipments to Iraq and publicly upbraided Moscow's policies in Lebanon and especially in Afghanistan.[28]

It was in these circumstances that the Iranian government ordered the crackdown on the Communist People's Party of Iran (PPI), also known as *Tudeh*, which, after the 1979 revolution, had supported the clerical regime. The timing of the campaign—late 1982 and early 1983—suggests that it was directly related to Moscow's position on the Gulf war. In any event, on February 10, 1983, *Pravda* reported the arrest of several PPI leaders, including First Secretary of the Central Committee Nureddin Kiyanuri. Soviet condemnation was not long in coming. In an unsigned article, entitled "Contrary to Iran's National Interests," *Pravda* quoted from a statement by the chief prosecutor, who said that the arrests had been prompted by the party's "espionage activity on behalf of Eastern states." Although the statement did not refer to the USSR specifically, *Pravda* noted that the "recent anti-Soviet campaign [in Iran] leaves no doubt as to who is meant." The article dismissed "accusations, levelled against the leaders of the Tudeh, and attacks on the policy of the Soviet Union" as "groundless [and] slanderous. . . ."[29]

On April 30, 1983, Kiyanuri confessed that he and other PPI members were guilty of "espionage, deceit and treachery." On May 4 Tehran Radio announced that the Tudeh party had been dissolved and that eighteen Soviet diplomats had been expelled.[30] The Kremlin reacted by means of an unsigned article, entitled "Concerning the Anti-Soviet Campaign in Iran," which appeared in *Pravda* on May 6. It denied that the USSR or the PPI had engaged in spying and protested against the expulsion of a group of "Soviet employees" from the Islamic Republic. Nevertheless, *Pravda* concluded, in spite of the "malicious provocations on the part of the enemies of Soviet-Iranian . . . cooperation," the Kremlin would attempt to improve relations with Islamic Republic.[31] The main points of this authoritative article were contained in Gromyko's speech of June 16. However, the foreign minister added, the offer of "normal, friendly relations with Iran" was not unconditional: "Soviet actions will depend on whether Iran will respond by reciprocity and will maintain friendly relations with us, or whether it has some other intentions."[32]

Judging by the subsequent Soviet press comments, Tehran did indeed have "other intentions." For one thing, the Islamic authorities continued persecuting the Tudeh party. In addition, some Iranian officials reportedly attacked economic cooperation between the two states as "ineffective" and "not profitable to Iran." Dismissing such claims as "tendentious" and "incompetent," *Pravda* set out to rectify the record.

Since 1963 the USSR contributed to the development of Iran's "metal-lurgy, machine building, energy, mining, geology, [and] the training of ... cadres." This cooperation resulted in the construction of "close to 160 enterprises ... [that] are the property of the Iranian state." *Pravda* next turned to the problem of Iranian gas, supplied to the USSR since 1970 but discontinued after the revolution. Moscow seemed upset by asser-tions that the Soviet Union had bought the gas "cheaply" and, in so doing, had hurt the Iranian economy. *Pravda* noted that between 1970 and 1980, the USSR had received 72 billion cubic meters of gas in exchange for Soviet equipment and technical services provided in the construction of the Isfahan steel complex, of the machine-building plant in Arak, of the hydroelectrical construction on the Arax River, and of other objects. Since February 1980, when Iran stopped pumping gas to the USSR, more than 40 billion cubic meters of it had been burned. Even in terms of 1979 prices, which Tehran considered low, this amounted to a loss of more than $4 billion. Nevertheless, Moscow remained inter-ested in developing good relations with Iran, provided they were founded on "true equality and mutuality. . . ."[33]

The Islamic Republic refused to accept the Kremlin's olive branch. In December 1983, *Pravda* reported that a group of "patriotic officers" had gone on trial before the Tribunal of the Armed Forces. The article by K. Vital'ev argued that the trial had been organized by the CIA as "part of Reagan's crusade against Communism" and insisted that the "anti-Communist hysteria" in the Islamic Republic was accompanied by an "accelerating anti-Soviet campaign." "The Soviet people expect that the dirty and malicious campaign against the USSR ... will be stopped, ..." Vital'ev concluded, "otherwise, the full burden of responsibility will fall on the ruling circles of that country."[34] The explicit threat failed to sway the Islamic Republic. On January 22, 1984, *Pravda* notified its readers of the end of the Tehran trial: the accused has been found guilty of "anti-Iranian activities and espionage," and thirteen were executed in early February. Although Soviet-Iranian relations had reached a new post-1979 low, no break occurred, however.

Relations with Iraq. As the USSR and Iran were drifting apart, there occurred during the third phase of the Gulf war a corresponding im-provement in relations between the Soviet Union and Iraq. It was re-flected in the texts of the official messages exchanged between the leaders of the two states; in the ongoing high-level contacts between the two governments; in the expanding economic cooperation; and, above all, in the resumption of large-scale arms deliveries to Iraq.

In terms of "atmospherics" the relative warmth of the ceremonial messages could not conceal Saddam Hussein's determination to steer an independent course in Iraq's foreign policy. The tone for his position was set during a revealing interview with *Time* magazine, given in July 1982. Speaking of Moscow's attitude toward the Gulf war, he said, "The Soviet Union says frankly that it is interested in preserving Iraq. . . . At the same time, the Soviets say that what took place in Iran, after the fall of the Shah, has the meaning of a great change in international strategy. . . ." (This was Saddam Hussein's way of saying that the USSR was not interested in destabilizing Iran for fear that such a turn of events might enable Washington to recapture its lost influence in Tehran.) The Kremlin's pursuit of its own interests in the Middle East did not surprise the Iraqi leader. But their professed neutrality in the Gulf war made no sense because Iraq did "not accuse or curse the Soviet Union" although Iran did.[35] Of importance in Saddam Hussein's remarks was his insistence that Baghdad's and Moscow's interests coincided only partially and that Iraq was determined to pursue its foreign policy objectives regardless of Soviet approval.

In the meantime, Deputy Premier Tariq Aziz visited Moscow in June 1982 and discussed "some questions of Soviet-Iraqi relations" with Ponomarev and First Deputy Prime Minister Ivan Arkhipov. It was no coincidence that in July nearly three hundred Communists were released from Iraqi prisons, a gesture that "contributed considerably to an improvement in the atmosphere between the Soviet Union and Iraq."[36] Tariq Aziz and Ramadan returned to Moscow in December. According to *Pravda*, their meetings with the Soviet leaders were conducted in a "business-like, constructive atmosphere" and dealt with "problems of mutual concern and international problems" generally.[37] It may be safely assumed that the Gulf conflict and Soviet military assistance to Iraq were among the more important items on their agenda. In March 1983, a delegation of Iraq's National Council paid an official visit to the USSR at the invitation of the Supreme Soviet.[38] Finally, in November 1983 Tariq Aziz, who in the meanwhile had been appointed foreign minister, returned to Moscow.

The treatment which the Soviet press extended to Tariq Aziz's visit—a lengthy TASS account of his negotiations with Gromyko—left no doubt that relations between Iraq and the USSR had improved significantly: the sides expressed "determination to continue developing relations" on the basis of the 1972 treaty. Moreover, for the first time in years TASS listed several important areas on which the two governments held identical positions: they condemned the foreign policies of the United States and Israel; demanded the withdrawal of Israeli, U.S., and

NATO troops from Lebanon; expressed themselves in favor of Arab solidarity; and supported the PLO as the "legitimate representative of the Palestinian people." With respect to the Gulf, the sides insisted that "no one has the right to interfere in the affairs of the littoral states under any pretext, including the pretext of securing freedom of navigation." Before leaving Moscow, Tariq Aziz announced that the talks were "marked by a spirit of friendship and deep mutual understanding," a formulation which had not been used in public for several years.[39]

Finally, and most important, during the third phase of the war, the USSR resumed large-scale arms shipments to Iraq. In the summer and fall of 1982 the USSR reportedly "resupplied [Iraq] with . . . T-54 tanks, MIG jets and anti-aircraft missiles." The quantities of the various weapons systems were described as "generous."[40] In addition, another "important agreement" on supply of military equipment to Iraq was signed during Tariq Aziz's November 1983 visit to Moscow. Valued at $2.5 billion, the purchase was offset by a $2 billion "package of projects, including hydroelectric generators and a nuclear power plant," which Iraq would receive "on credit."[41]

In retrospect, it seems obvious that the shift in Moscow's attitude toward Iraq was primarily a function of two distinct but interrelated variables: Iran's determination to wage war until the Saddam Hussein regime was eliminated and an "Islamic Republic of Iraq" was set up; and Tehran's unwillingness to respond favorably to Soviet offers of closer relations. In addition, the Kremlin was aware of a gradual thaw in Iraqi-U.S. relations. In 1982 Washington extended credits to Iraq to purchase American agricultural products. In 1983 Donald Rumsfeld, Ronald Reagan's personal envoy, visited Baghdad and conferred with President Saddam Hussein. Later that year, the United States let it be known that it was attempting "to persuade its allies to stop all shipments of arms to Iran."[42] In any event, once the Soviets decided that Iran was not amenable to their wishes and was determined to fight until the "final victory," they resumed large-scale arms deliveries to Baghdad. By mid-1983 Iraq was reported to have received sizeable quantities of T-72 tanks as well as MIG-23, MIG-25, and even some MIG-27 aircraft. As a result, the USSR regained its earlier position as Baghdad's main arms supplier, once again delivering approximately 70 percent of Iraq's requirements.[43] Thus, in 1982 the Kremlin abandoned its position of neutrality in the Gulf war. There can be no doubt that the subsequent crackdown on the Tudeh party and the May 1983 expulsion of Soviet diplomats from Tehran were directly related to the shift in Moscow's policy.

Stalemate (1984–1986)

Commenting on Iran's February 1984 push toward Basrah, *Pravda* again complained that the belligerents, whose "difficult social and economic problems" required immediate attention, were instead inflicting upon each other "enormous human and material losses." The culprit remained the Islamic Republic. In October 1983 the UN Security Council again called on Iran and Iraq to cease military operations. "As is well known, Baghdad greeted this resolution . . . [while] Tehran rejected it." In mid-February 1984 UN Secretary-General Javier Pérez de Cuéllar offered to send a mission to both countries "to collect the latest data on the damage [inflicted by the war] on the civilian sectors" and to ascertain the belligerents' attitude on ending the war. Iraq agreed to receive the UN mission but Iran refused.[44]

In the ensuing months Baghdad endeavored to force Tehran's hand by using poison gas against the attacking Iranian troops, by intensifying air strikes against Iranian cities, and by attacking neutral third-country tankers near Kharg island, Iran's main oil-exporting terminal, as well as the loading facilities on the island itself. These efforts failed to produce the desired results. Instead, Iran retaliated by stepping up artillery, air, and rocket attacks on Iraqi towns and, on occasion, by hitting Saudi and Kuwaiti tankers sailing in the Gulf.

The Soviet media took note of all these developments. However, their coverage of military operations was now marked by an unmistakable pro-Iraqi tilt. The use of poison gas against the Iranian troops was a case in point. When, in April 1984, Tehran complained to the UN Security Council about Iraq's recourse to chemical weapons, the Soviet press reported that the United Nations had considered the issue and that its chairman had expressed concern about their use in the Gulf conflict. Subsequently, the Security Council had "decisively condemned the use of chemical weapons."[45] In short, Iraq was not singled out as the perpetrator of that particular offense.

Although restrained on the subject of chemical weapons, the Kremlin had a great deal to say about the activities of the United States. In February 1984 Iran's President Ali Khamenei warned that oil flow from the Gulf would be cut off if Washington became "directly involved" in the Iraq-Iran war. The statement led to a counterwarning: the United States would "do what is necessary" to keep the Strait of Hormuz open.[46] The exchange produced a strongly-worded TASS Statement which branded the U.S. position a "serious threat to peace and international security" and warned Washington that it would "bear full . . . responsibility for possible future consequences of its policy. . . ."[47]

In contrast, Moscow adopted a restrained attitude toward the "tanker war" which erupted in the Gulf in January 1984. As in the case of chemical weapons, the Kremlin demonstrated clearly which side of the conflict it was now on. Early Iraqi attacks on neutral shipping near Kharg island went unnoticed in the Soviet press and in the TASS Statement of March 1984. Even when the tanker war was intensified significantly in late spring of 1984, with both belligerents attacking neutral shipping, the Kremlin zeroed in on "U.S. determination to use the situation to increase its power in the Gulf region."[48] *Pravda* labeled this "adventurist American policy" as "pregnant with most serious consequences."[49]

Another aspect of the Gulf conflict which initially received little attention in the Soviet press was warfare against the civilian population. In June 1984 Pavel Demchenko wrote that "Iran, having accused the Iraqis of bombing the town of Bane, . . . bombed four Iraqi towns and published a list of seven more . . . that could be subjected to air and artillery attacks." Baghdad published a list of its own: fifteen Iranian towns would be subjected to "powerful response strikes" if Tehran acted on its threat. As in the case of chemical warfare and of the tanker war, the Soviet media refrained from blaming Iraq for initiating attacks against the civilian targets.[50]

After a temporary lull, attacks on nonmilitary targets intensified in early 1985.[51] Commenting on "this new outburst of cruelty," Demchenko described the warfare against the civilian population as "another reminder of the urgent need" to end the conflict. The flareup resulted in another appeal by the UN secretary-general to halt attacks on civilian targets,[52] followed by his visit to Tehran and Baghdad in mid-April 1985. According to *Pravda*, Pérez de Cuéllar found the belligerents' positions "as far away from each other as ever."[53] Another escalation occurred in early summer 1985. Following the late May attempt to assassinate the sheikh of Kuwait, Baghdad resumed air attacks against Iranian cities, against neutral tankers carrying Iranian oil, and against the facilities on Kharg island.[54] Without blaming Iraq for its decision, *Pravda* did not hold out much hope that this latest escalation of hostilities would force Iran to the negotiating table: according to "official sources" in Tehran, peace that was "worse than war" was not acceptable because it would "destroy the glory of the Islamic revolution."[55]

Relations with Iran. In addition to deploring Tehran's insistence on fighting the war, the USSR continued to express concern about what was described as "anticommunism" and "anti-Sovietism" of the Islamic Republic. In January 1984 a military tribunal had found a number of Tudeh members guilty of espionage and other "anti-Iranian activities." In March the PPI Central Committee announced that ten party members had been sentenced to death and executed. The statement was carried by *Pravda* and accused Iran's "oppressive organs" of committing the "gravest crimes"—the sentences and executions constituted violations of the legal statutes of the Islamic Republic and of the "generally recognized norms of international law."[56] Propaganda pressure was intensified in the summer of 1984, when the Tudeh announced impending new trials of "hundreds" of additional party members. This new "wave of oppression" was explained by the authorities' desire to divert public attention from the "deep political and socioeconomic crisis" caused by the regime's insistence on fighting the war.[57]

In addition, the Soviet media continued to attack the Islamic Republic for its support of the Afghan *mujahideen*. In February 1985 Kabul's Ministry of Foreign Affairs issued what *Pravda* called "White Book about Black Deeds." Although directed mainly against Pakistan, the document also cited Iran as a conduit of military support to the antigovernment guerrillas "operating in the northwestern regions" of Afghanistan.[58] In February 1986 Kabul protested against a "secret mission" of an Iranian "religious delegation" and of "representatives of Afghan counterrevolution." Formed on orders of the "highest Iranian clergy," the delegation crossed into Afghanistan for the purpose of creating a "united Islamic front" designed to direct the antigovernment guerrillas.[59]

Finally, the Kremlin remained concerned about Tehran's continuing "anti-Sovietism." An important example was provided by an article "Against National Interests: Concerning the Anti-Soviet Campaign in Iran" by P. Nadezhdin that appeared in *Pravda* on March 6, 1985, and was intended as a response to "official statements" and comments published in the Iranian press. Some pronouncements expressed an interest in strengthening the ties with the USSR. Many others, in contrast, contained "obvious slander" and displayed a "hostile anti-Soviet line." Characteristic of the first category were the statements by the Ministry of Foreign Affairs which noted Tehran's desire to improve relations with the USSR. *Pravda* was very much in favor of these sentiments: acting upon them would indeed correspond to the national interests of both states. Unfortunately, Nadezhdin complained, Tehran did not speak with one voice and, in any event, its friendly words were not matched by its deeds.

Moscow deplored public expressions of opposition to Soviet-Iranian cooperation. For example, *Pravda* objected to a pronouncement by an unnamed Iranian leader who accused the USSR of "hatching various plots directed at the destruction of the Iranian people, its Islamic revolution, and its Islamic state." No sensible person could believe this "invention," Nadezhdin argued. The USSR "greeted the overthrow of the shah" and the Islamic revolution because they paved the way for "positive changes in Iranian policy." The USSR also supported Iran in its confrontation with the United States and helped develop its economy. For these reasons Nadezhdin labeled as "absurd and insulting" a statement by another "high-placed Iranian official" who said that foreign policies of both superpowers were distinguished by a "terrorist bent." Such sentiments were not only false but also harmful: they "enflame[d] unfriendly attitudes toward our country, [including] open anti-Sovietism."

Nadezhdin's article concluded on a conciliatory note: the USSR remained interested in Soviet-Iranian cooperation, provided relations were based "on the principles of equality and mutuality." Of even greater importance, however, was the preceding paragraph which contained a thinly veiled warning:

> The Soviet Union is not indifferent to [Iran's] policy . . . toward Afghanistan which is friendly to us. Neither can we disregard the anti-Soviet attacks in Tehran which have become more frequent. . . . Campaign, hostile to our country, interferes with developing the existing . . . potential for . . . [improving] Soviet-Iranian relations.

On July 8 Prime Minister Mir Hussein Musavi announced that many Russian advisers had left Iran on orders from the Soviet government and blamed their departure for electric power shortages experienced in the country at the time.[60] *Izvestiia* explained that the specialists' withdrawal was caused by the "lack of necessary security precautions" at their places of work.[61] Since the Iranian industry had been subjected to Iraqi air raids for a long time, the Kremlin's explanation rang hollow. Instead, the advisers' recall was a concrete demonstration of Moscow's displeasure with Tehran's policies although the USSR had no intention of breaking with the Islamic Republic. In September 1985 the visiting director of economic affairs at the Iranian Foreign Ministry was received by First Deputy Foreign Minister Georgii Kornienko to discuss "several issues concerning Soviet-Iranian relations," and their talks reportedly resulted in an agreement to expand economic ties.[62]

Relations with Iraq. Tensions in Moscow-Tehran relations were accompanied by continuing rapprochement between the USSR and Iraq. As in the past, this trend manifested itself in the tone of the formal exchanges between the two governments;[63] in the high-level political contacts culminating in Saddam Hussein's visit to Moscow; in the growing economic and technical cooperation; and, above all, in the stepped-up Soviet military assistance to Iraq.

In mid-October 1984 Tariq Aziz returned to Moscow. According to *Pravda*, his meeting with Gromyko was conducted in a "frank [and] friendly atmosphere" and the sides agreed to expand their economic and technical cooperation.[64] Tariq Aziz visited Moscow again in late March 1985. On this occasion he and Gromyko "expressed satisfaction" with the state of Soviet-Iraqi relations and promised "to strengthen them on the basis of the 1972 treaty."[65] But the most important event of this period was Saddam Hussein's December 1985 visit to the USSR, his first since 1978.

The Iraqi president arrived in Moscow on December 16, "at the invitation of the Soviet government," for what *Pravda* described as a "friendly working visit." He was accompanied by Taha Yasin Ramadan, Tariq Aziz, and Minister of State for Military Affairs Abd al-Jabbar Shanshal. Commenting on his arrival, *Pravda* spoke of coincidence of Soviet and Iraqi positions on many important international problems, including the Gulf conflict, and praised Saddam Hussein for "strengthening relations with the Soviet Union."[66]

During a dinner speech Andrei Gromyko, in his new capacity as chairman of the Presidium of the Supreme Soviet, hailed Saddam Hussein's visit as an "important step on the path of . . . perfecting Soviet-Iraqi cooperation." The president's discussions with Secretary General Mikhail Gorbachev had demonstrated that there were "good opportunities to move forward, on a mutually beneficial basis, in the interests of both peoples." Gromyko also used the opportunity to chide Iran's insistence on prolonging the Gulf conflict: "In our opinion, those who, against all logic, call for the continuation of the war 'until victory' . . . are not acting wisely." In his response, Saddam Hussein expressed Iraq's appreciation for Soviet "friendship and cooperation" and noted Baghdad's determination to continue working for improvement of bilateral relations "on the basis of respect for [each other's] sovereignty." Turning to the Gulf war, Saddam Hussein reiterated Baghdad's desire to reestablish "goodneighborly relations" with Tehran and called on "friendly states to apply maximum efforts . . . to achieve a . . . just and comprehensive peace in the Middle East."[67]

Factual cooperation between the two states ranged from the economic and technical support, which Moscow extended Baghdad in exchange for petroleum (at this stage delivered primarily by Saudi Arabia and Kuwait, acting on Iraq's behalf), to deliveries of Soviet weapons. The extent of economic and technical assistance, and, above all, the size of the Iraqi arsenal of Soviet military equipment testified to the vast improvement in Moscow-Baghdad relations. Thus, in March 1984 the two states signed an agreement providing for further development of economic and technical cooperation. In April, Ramadan returned to Moscow and his negotiations with Soviet officials resulted in the signing of yet another agreement.[68] In June 1985 the Iraqi minister of industry and mineral resources visited Moscow. His meetings with Soviet officials dealt with what *Pravda* described as "some questions of the state and of [future] perspectives of Soviet-Iraqi trade and economic cooperation."[69]

Along with the growing economic and technical cooperation between the USSR and Iraq, the Soviet military assistance program was also increased and upgraded during the fourth phase of the Gulf conflict. Based on the agreement of November 1983,[70] the supplies of Soviet weapons resulted in a significant strengthening of Baghdad's armed forces. According to a Senate Foreign Relations Committee report, since the fall of 1983, Iraq had received, "hundreds" of the new Soviet T-72 tanks and "advanced MIG aircraft...."[71] In addition, the USSR also supplied Baghdad with "advanced types of air-to-surface" and surface-to-surface missiles used in attacks against Iranian cities.[72] Tehran reciprocated by firing rockets at Baghdad and other Iraqi towns. They, too, were widely believed to have been Soviet-made Scud missiles, delivered to Iran by Libya.[73] In sum, during the fourth phase of the Gulf war, relations between Moscow and Baghdad continued to improve.

Limited Iranian Successes (1986–1987)

In February 1986 the Iranians captured the port city of Faw and cut off Iraq's access to the Persian Gulf.[74] The fall of Faw brought the Iranians into the vicinity of Kuwait, increasing the apprehension of the members of the Gulf Cooperation Council about Tehran's intentions in the Arabian peninsula. The superpowers, too, seemed purturbed by the Iranian successes. Washington expressed "grave concern" about the spread of the Gulf conflict: it posed new dangers "to both neutral states and U.S. regional interests."[75] *Pravda* reported that the Iraqi government had appealed to the UN Security Council to consider the "grave threat to international peace and security," created by the Iranian occupation of Faw.[76] Pavel Demchenko regretted the escalation of the fighting in the vicinity of Kuwait because it was bound to provide the United States with new excuses for maintaining its naval and air power in the Persian Gulf.[77]

In the ensuing weeks the focus of attention shifted to the political arena. In late February the UN Security Council unanimously called for a cease-fire in the Gulf war. Since the resolution merely "deplored . . . [Iraq's] 'initial' aggression," it was rejected by the Islamic Republic. Tehran continued to insist that Iraq be named explicitly as "the aggressor in the war."[78] In mid-March a UN team of experts upheld Iran's charges of Iraqi recourse to poison gas. As a result, the UN Security Council, on March 21, 1986, "strongly condemned the continued use of chemical weapons by Iraq." But the resolution also objected to the prolongation of the Gulf war and noted Baghdad's willingness to settle it by peaceful means.[79] These additions rendered the resolution unacceptable to Iran.

In the late spring and summer of 1986 the Gulf war heated up again. In May, for the first time in almost a year, Iraqi planes bombed the oil refinery in Tehran[80] while Iraqi troops occupied the Iranian town of Merhan, situated in the central sector of the front. Baghdad also intensified the tanker war in the Gulf.[81] The Iranians recaptured Merhan in July, inflicting heavy losses on the Iraqi forces, a setback that elicited no editorial comment in the Soviet press.[82] Instead, on August 3 *Pravda* reported that President Saddam Hussein had sent an "open message" to the Iranian leaders offering them a "just and honorable peace." On August 4 Gromyko received the visiting deputy foreign minister of Iran and advised him that Tehran would be "wise" to stop the conflict.[83] Ironically, the same issue of *Pravda* reported that President Khamenei had "categorically rejected" Saddam Hussein's offer.

In mid-August, Iraqi planes attacked the oil terminal on Sirri island, situated some three hundred miles south of Kharg; Iran retaliated by firing a Scud-B missile at Baghdad.[84] That outburst of hostilities prompted the UN secretary general to issue another appeal urging the belligerents to refrain from escalating the conflict and to halt attacks on the civilian targets. His initiative was supported by the USSR,[85] but the Islamic Republic remained unmoved. On August 24, Ayatollah Khomeini stated that "Iran must . . . fight until victory and 'finish off' President Saddam Hussein of Iraq."[86]

Efforts at peaceful settlement continued in the fall of 1986. On September 25, in a speech before the UN General Assembly, Tariq Aziz called on the United Nations "to find a way to negotiate an end" to the war. He reiterated Baghdad's assent to "unconditional withdrawal of forces" to international boundaries and urged the United Nations to take Iraq's side "if Iran refuses to withdraw its forces." Speaking two days earlier, Foreign Minister Eduard Shevardnadze, too, expressed himself in favor of stopping "this senseless mutual extermination." A "sincere friend of both peoples," the USSR was using "all the means at its disposal" to convince the belligerents to make peace.[87] In the end, the Security Council adopted yet another resolution; it called for an end to the war but was rejected by Iran.[88]

As the Iraqi air force continued to pound Kharg island and neutral tankers carrying Iranian oil, Tehran, in late 1986 and early 1987, launched a new series of ground attacks. Fighting in the Basrah area lasted several weeks and was particularly heavy. One of the casualties of renewed fighting was the 1985 moratorium on the "war of the cities": in early 1987 the belligerents resumed indiscriminate missile attacks on the enemy's civilian targets.[89] The USSR reacted to the latest carnage by means of a "Soviet Government Statement," published in *Pravda* and *Izvestiia* on January 9, 1987. The statement reiterated that the war had "nothing to do with the interests of the Iraqi and Iranian peoples." It also caused "discord in the ranks of the Arab states" as well as in the nonaligned movement. Hence, "imperialism" remained the main beneficiary of the Iran-Iraq conflict, as evidenced by the vast increase of U.S. military presence in the vicinity of the Persian Gulf. As for the USSR, it had persistently called on the belligerents "to display political will and wisdom" and to arrive at "mutually acceptable agreements that would take into account the legitimate interests" of both countries. The eventual settlement, the statement continued, had to be based on the "principles of mutual respect for the sovereignty, territorial integrity, and noninterference in each other's affairs" as well as on reaffirmation of the prewar frontiers. Moreover, both states had to recognize that "every people has a right to . . . choose its own way of life and to shape its own destiny." Putting an end to the hostilities would "correspond to the interests of the Iraqi and Iranian peoples" and would contribute to a general improvement in the international situation. For these reasons the Soviet government was prepared to support all efforts to end the Iran-Iraq war.

Although it professed Moscow's neutrality in the Gulf conflict, the statement left little doubt that by 1987 the USSR had moved even further away from Tehran and closer to Baghdad: the Kremlin clearly held Iran responsible for the ongoing war and for providing Washington with new opportunities to increase its military presence in the Persian Gulf. In noting that governments had no right to interfere in the internal affairs of other states, the Soviets also specifically rejected Ayatollah Khomeini's argument that the war had to be fought until Saddam Hussein was overthrown. Little wonder, therefore, that Iran chose to ignore the Soviet statement. Iraq, in contrast, immediately expressed readiness "to cooperate with the USSR or any other country" in ending the war and establishing peace.[90]

As the Iranian offensive of the winter of 1986 and 1987 came to an inconclusive halt, the belligerents in mid-February also stopped air and missile attacks on civilian targets. With the land war limited to sporadic fighting, in the spring and summer of 1987 the focus of attention again shifted to the waters of the Persian Gulf. The stage for the new confrontation was set in late November 1986, when Kuwait, after the disclosure of the secret U.S. arms sales to Iran, asked the USSR to lease it three tankers and to escort them in and out of the Gulf under Soviet naval protection.

The Kremlin's decision to accommodate Kuwait led to two parallel but unrelated developments. It intensified Iranian interference with the Soviet maritime traffic in the Gulf: in early May 1987, Iranian gunboats attacked an unescorted Soviet cargo ship heading for Kuwait and, later in the month, a Soviet tanker hit a mine off the sheikhdom's coast.[91] The Kremlin's acquiescence in Kuwait's request also awakened the Reagan administration to the USSR's new role in the Persian Gulf: for the first time, the Soviet navy would be deployed there for an indefinite period of time, serving both political and, potentially, military purposes. Alarmed, Washington attempted to outdo Moscow by offering to "reflag" one half of Kuwait's tanker fleet and to place it under U.S. naval protection.[92]

An elaborate analysis of the developing situation was offered by veteran commentator Pavel Demchenko. Since neither belligerent could win on land, both engaged in indiscriminate attacks on enemy and neutral shipping in the Gulf. The intensification of sea combat was fraught with dangerous consequences—the United States "and, perhaps, some other states" could well be drawn into it. In contrast with official pronouncements, Demchenko admitted that the West had vital interests in the Persian Gulf but argued that the USSR had interests, too, and that they were "not insignificant." In addition to the region's location in the proximity of the Soviet borders, some of Moscow's "trade, economic, [and] political partners" were situated in the Gulf. Demchenko denied the existence of any Soviet threat to the Gulf region. On the contrary, the Kremlin repeatedly expressed its readiness to contribute to the end of the war. And it remained "prepared for collective efforts" to persuade Iran to negotiate an end of the conflict.[93]

While the superpowers were engaged in verbal sparring, the opinion in the Gulf itself on developments precipitated by Kuwait's requests for Soviet and American naval protection was markedly divided. Iraq did not object to its neighbor's initiatives but seemed to doubt that they would effect an end of the war: in early June "high Iraqi officials" were quoted as saying that only "international economic sanctions and a military embargo . . . would bring Tehran to the peace table."[94] Iran's reaction, in contrast, was totally negative. Foreign Minister Ali Akbar Velayati announced during a visit to the UAE that Tehran "will not allow" the United States, the Soviet Union, "or any other forces to interfere in the [Gulf] region."[95]

Relations with Iran. During the fifth phase of the conflict Moscow-Tehran relations remained marred by Iran's insistence on fighting the war, by its crackdown on the "progressive elements" and support of the Afghan *mujahideen,* and by its continued reluctance to improve relations with the USSR.

In March 1986 the *World Marxist Review* reported that "mass reprisals" against the Tudeh, begun three years earlier, continued unabated. As a result, "tens of thousands of fighters" had been executed while "more than 100,000" remained in jail.[96] In mid-summer, the PPI held a "national conference." According to the *Information Bulletin,* its resolutions accused "the reactionary rulers in the Islamic Republic [of] having abandoned the aims of the anti-imperialist . . . revolution. . . ." For this reason the party concluded that

> revolutionary violence is . . . the only possible avenue open to the Popular Front to fight for political power. To bring down the regime one . . . should use all forms of struggle, from demonstrations and general strikes to a mass armed struggle. The PPI sees it as its duty to prime itself and prepare the masses to use various forms of revolutionary violence.[97]

A report on the conference appeared in *Pravda* only on October 1, 1986: it said simply that the PPI had reviewed the course of events and adopted resolutions reflecting "new conditions" prevalent in Iran. Scant attention to the plight of the Tudeh during 1986 indicated that the Kremlin thought it prudent not to attack Tehran at a time when bilateral relations remained strained over the Islamic Republic's determination to fight the war.

In contrast, Afghanistan remained a more visible source of friction: Moscow continued to publicize Kabul's desire to normalize relations with the Islamic Republic[98] and expressed misgivings after Afghanistan's overtures had been turned down by Tehran.[99] The subject of Iranian involvement in Afghanistan came up again during Foreign Minister Velayati's first visit to the USSR. In the course of his February 13, 1987, meeting with President Gromyko, the latter complained that "bands of *dushmans*" (derogatory Russian term for *mujahideen*) were entering the country from the Islamic Republic. Gromyko admonished Tehran that it "would do well to contribute to the resolution of the Afghan situation by political means. . . ."[100] How Velayati reacted to Gromyko's warning, *Pravda* did not report.

It is equally important to note, however, that the USSR remained interested in improving relations with the Islamic Republic. An important step in that direction was taken in February 1986, when First Deputy Foreign Minister Kornienko traveled to Tehran and was received by Khamenei, Speaker Akbar Hashemi-Rafsanjani, Musavi, and Velayati. According to Tehran Radio, Kornienko "urged increased political contacts" between the Islamic Republic and the USSR. A few days later, Rafsanjani expressed "optimism" with respect to cooperation in "technical, military, economic and possibly political" spheres but added that serious problems continued to separate the two countries. He singled out "two major ones: Soviet support for Iraq . . . and the military presence in Afghanistan."[101] On these problems, Rafsanjani clearly implied, no compromise was possible as long as Moscow adhered to its present position.

High-level contacts continued later in 1986. In August, Deputy Foreign Minister Mohammed Javad Larijani arrived in Moscow and was received by Gromyko and Foreign Minister Shevardnadze. He brought with him a message from President Khamenei which, according to *Pravda*, expressed Iran's desire to develop good, neighborly relations with the USSR.[102] A short time later, Minister of Oil Gholam Reza Aqazadeh arrived in Moscow. He and Premier Nikolai Ryzhkov reviewed the state of bilateral relations and concluded that "differences in social systems . . . should not present a barrier to fruitful relations between the two countries."[103] In October, President Gromyko received the Iranian ambassador, who delivered a message from Khamenei. According to *Pravda*, it contained an expression of interest in improving bilateral relations. Gromyko said that this had long been Moscow's desire. He added, however, that the Iranian media continued to fan "anti-Soviet propaganda" and that such activity was not conducive to developing "normal ties" between the two countries. Nevertheless, according to Tehran Radio, Gromyko told the ambassador that Soviet technicians, withdrawn in 1985, would soon return to Iran.[104]

Gradual normalization of Moscow-Tehran relations was one of the temporary victims of the "Irangate" affair. The Kremlin reacted sharply to the news of U.S. arms deliveries to the Islamic Republic. The Soviets used the opportunity to underscore the "deception, hypocrisy, and duplicity" of the American foreign policy. While calling for an end of the Gulf war and assuring one side—Iraq—of its benevolence, Washington was supplying arms to the other. The main purpose of this policy was to weaken both sides in order to facilitate American penetration of the Gulf region.[105] Moscow was particularly upset about former National Security Adviser Robert McFarlane's visit to Tehran. It would have been "unthinkable" had it not "enjoyed support of influential circles" in the Islamic Republic.[106]

Nevertheless, in early December 1986 a high-level Soviet delegation, headed by Chairman of the USSR State Committee for Foreign Economic Relations Konstantin Katushev, arrived in Tehran. It soon became apparent that, although the Islamic Republic remained interested in expanding economic relations, its leaders had been rankled by Moscow's criticism of Iranian arms purchases from the United States. Speaker Rafsanjani used his meeting with Katushev to describe the U.S. arms deal as "a great victory by a third-world country." He went on to say that the Islamic Republic was "fully prepared to improve relations" with the Soviet Union provided the Kremlin reversed its policy in Afghanistan and Iraq.[107]

The continuing divergence of Soviet and Iranian views was aired anew during Foreign Minister Velayati's mid-February 1987 visit to Moscow. The highest Iranian official to visit the USSR after the 1979 revolution, he was received by Gromyko, Ryzhkov, and Shevardnadze. According to *Pravda*, the meetings were marked by a "frank and business-like exchange of opinions on questions concerning Soviet-Iranian relations as well as on international problems of mutual interest." Specifically, the sides continued to diverge on two important issues, Afghanistan and the Iran-Iraq war. According to *Pravda*, Velayati "expressed the well-known position of the Republic of Iran." Gromyko allowed that "our evaluation of this war and your views on it do not coincide" but invoked "common sense" to suggest that "attention ought to be focused not on the past but on the future." Since it was not in Iran's or Iraq's interest to have the killing continue, it was necessary to end the conflict. Nevertheless, in spite of the differences over foreign policy issues, the sides expressed the desire to "strengthen goodneigh-borly relations" between them.[108]

Additional evidence of Moscow's unhappiness with Tehran's position on the Gulf conflict was provided in April 1987 when a delegation of the League of Arab States was received by Gromyko and Shevardnadze.[109] In the course of the meetings both Soviet leaders restated the Kremlin's opposition to the war and Moscow's readiness to contribute to its resolution. Gromyko, in particular, blamed Tehran for the ongoing slaughter: "It is self-evident that the responsibility for the continuation of the war is borne by those forces and those leaders who demon-stratively flout public opinion of virtually the entire world."[110] The Iranian Foreign Ministry responded by denouncing the Soviet policy in the Gulf—the USSR continued to search for opportunities to increase Soviet influence throughout the entire region.[111] It was against this backdrop of mutual recriminations that the Iranians attacked a Soviet freighter sailing to Kuwait.

That action seemed to have been intended as a tangible demonstra-tion of Tehran's annoyance with Moscow's criticism of Iranian policies and with the acceleration of Soviet involvement with Iraq as well as Kuwait. It was also, however, an open challenge of the USSR and its interests that the Kremlin could not afford to ignore. It was probably this realization, coupled with the possibility of superpower cooperation against the Islamic Republic, that prompted its leaders to attempt to defuse the situation. In mid-June 1987, First Deputy Foreign Minister Iulii Vorontsov arrived in Tehran "at the invitation of the Iranian side." During his three-day stay he was received by Khamenei, Rafsanjani, Musavi, Velayati, and the minister of economy and finances—an in-dication of the importance which the Islamic Republic attached to his visit.[112] It was reported in the West that Vorontsov had delivered a strong protest against the Iranian attack, "hinting that the Soviet Union might have to retaliate if Iran attacked another Soviet ship." At the same time, in accepting Tehran's invitation, the Kremlin signaled that it, too, did not wish to break with the Islamic Republic. In short, both sides, for reasons of their own, were leaning toward moderation and showed no inclination to aggravate an already difficult situation.

Relations with Iraq. Cooperation between the USSR and Iraq con-tinued to expand after Saddam Hussein's "summit" meeting with Secretary-General Gorbachev. In April 1986, First Deputy Prime Minis-ter Ramadan, accompanied by Minister of State for Military Affairs Shanshal, returned to Moscow. They were received by Ryzhkov and, according to *Pravda*, discussed with him ways to improve bilateral

cooperation.[113] It may be safely assumed that continuation of the Soviet military assistance program to Iraq was one of the important items
on their agenda.

One month later, the Permanent Soviet-Iraqi Commission for Economic, Scientific, and Technological Cooperation held its sixteenth
session in Baghdad. The Soviet delegation was led by Katushev, and the
Iraqi by Minister of Industry and Mineral Resources Subhi Yasin. In the
course of the negotiations the sides expressed satisfaction with the
state of their cooperation and recorded their wish for its continued
expansion. During his stay in Baghdad, Katushev was received by Saddam Hussein, Ramadan, and Minister of Trade Hassan Ali. Before his
departure the sides signed a new trade agreement and reached an informal accord for continued economic, scientific, and technological cooperation.[114]

In mid-June 1986, Hassan Ali returned to Moscow and was received
by Shevardnadze and Deputy Premier Riabov. The sides discussed "certain aspects of Soviet-Iraqi relations as well as the situation in the
Middle East" and expressed themselves in favor of "further development of mutually beneficial cooperation." On June 13 the USSR and
Iraq formally signed a "long-term trade agreement" for the period between 1986 and 1990.[115] Close contacts continued in the fall and winter
of 1986. In September, Shevardnadze and Tariq Aziz met in New York
and noted their commitment to the development of friendly relations
between the two states.[116] Similar sentiments were expressed during a
December 1986 meeting between Shevardnadze and the Iraqi ambassador to the USSR. The new element was the coincidence of Moscow's
and Baghdad's views on the "Irangate" affair. According to *Pravda*, both
judged the U.S. policy in the Gulf to be "duplicitous." They also agreed
that the Reagan administration's references to the "Soviet threat" were
intended to mask Washington's ambition "to implement its neoglobal-
ist designs" in the Middle East.[117]

On February 19, 1987, Foreign Minister Tariq Aziz returned to Moscow. The timing of his visit, coming as it did on the heels of Foreign
Minister Velayati's stay in the Soviet capital,[118] was intended to demonstrate that, in spite of the Kremlin's commitment to developing friendly
relations with both belligerents, the USSR continued to lean toward
Baghdad. Thus, Tariq Aziz's discussions with Gromyko were conducted
"in a friendly atmosphere," rather than being "frank and businesslike"
during the Gromyko-Velayati meeting. On the subject of Iraqi-Soviet
relations, Tariq Aziz said that his government was "determined to . . .
maintain good, friendly relations with the USSR." He emphasized the

closeness of political ties, which he described as of "decisive importance." Turning to the Gulf war, Tariq Aziz expressed Iraq's readiness "to contribute to [its] immediate end." The problem, he went on to say, lay with Tehran, which refused to terminate the hostilities. Gromyko, too, described Moscow-Baghdad relations as "friendly" and reciprocated Baghdad's intention to work for their continuing improvement. In his comments on the war the president noted that the United Nations as well as "nearly all of the world's states" had expressed themselves in support of peace and chided "those who do not listen to these voices."[119]

Otherwise, the Kremlin used the opportunity provided by the February 1987 visits of the Iranian and Iraqi foreign ministers to register several points. The Soviets restated their continued commitment to peace; lined themselves squarely on the side of the vast majority of the UN members; and expressed a desire to improve relations with both Iran and Iraq. In so doing, the USSR demonstrated to the United States Moscow's "relevance" in the Gulf conflict. Unlike the Arab-Israeli sector, where Washington, by virtue of its intimacy with Israel and a number of key Arab states, held the diplomatic upper hand, in the Persian Gulf it was the Soviet Union that remained on good terms with Iraq and on speaking terms with the Islamic Republic.

Both sides used the fifteenth anniversary of the signing of the 1972 treaty and its automatic renewal to express their commitment to improving bilateral relations. The telegram from the Presidium of the Supreme Soviet and the Council of Ministers to Saddam Hussein was unusually expansive. The treaty provided a "firm foundation for dynamic development of Soviet-Iraqi relations in accordance with the principles of equality, respect for sovereignty, and noninterference in each other's internal affairs." Turning to the future, the telegram expressed "conviction" that the 1972 treaty would help "strengthen the friendship and fruitful cooperation between the USSR and the Iraqi Republic [and would] contribute to efforts directed at the liquidation of the sources of tension . . . in the Middle East and the world generally." In his telegram to Gromyko and Ryzhkov, Saddam Hussein sent "to the Soviet leadership . . . the warmest regards and best wishes." He went on to say that the treaty, "based on the principles of equality, mutual respect, sovereignty, and constructive cooperation, has produced positive results in all spheres of interaction between our countries and . . . remains a firm foundation for further development of bilateral relations."[120]

Moscow-Baghdad cooperation, as well as such current problems as the Iran-Iraq war and the Arab-Israeli conflict, were subjects of the ensuing negotiations between the two states. In April 1987 a delegation headed by Deputy Chairman of the Supreme Soviet Petr Demichev arrived in Baghdad and participated in the celebration of the fifteenth anniversary of the 1972 treaty.[121] In June, after his trip to Tehran, Iulii Vorontsov visited Baghdad and briefed the Iraqis on his negotiations with the Iranian leaders. That occasion, too, was used to emphasize the parties' commitment to "continued strengthening and broadening, in all spheres, of friendly ties between the USSR and Iraq."[122] Finally, according to the data released by the Institute of International and Strategic Studies, in 1985 and 1986 the Soviets continued to supply arms to Iraq. The number of tanks (T-54/-55/-62/-72) remained constant at 2,900. The same was true of interceptor aircraft (40 MIG-19s, 200 MIG-21s, and 25 MIG-25s). There was a small decline in the quantity of MIG-23BM fighter-ground attack planes (from 48 in 1985 to 40 in 1986), while no figures were provided in 1986 for SU-7 and SU-20 aircraft in the same general category (in 1985, the numbers were 75 and 50, respectively).[123] The figures indicate that the USSR did not dramatically increase its weapons exports to Iraq in 1985 and 1986, but it did deliver sufficient quantities to replace the losses resulting from attrition and suffered on the battlefield.

Limited Iraqi Successes (1987–1988)

In mid-1987 the tanker war flared up again. By that time, the USSR had established a modest naval presence in the Persian Gulf—one frigate and three minesweepers were accompanying the three tankers which the Soviets had leased to Kuwait. The United States, too, had strengthened its naval contingent and, in late July, the U.S. navy began accompanying eleven reflagged Kuwaiti tankers. As tension continued to grow, Washington urged the UN Security Council to adopt yet another resolution ordering the belligerents to cease fire. In case of noncompliance, the United Nations would impose an arms embargo on the recalcitrant party or parties. On June 30, General Vernon A. Walters, chief U.S. delegate at the United Nations, arrived in Moscow to seek Soviet support for the American initiative.[124]

It soon became evident, however, that the USSR had its own agenda. On July 3 the Soviet government issued a statement on the situation in the Persian Gulf. It warned that as a result of the increased foreign naval presence, the Iran-Iraq war might well be transformed into an "international crisis situation." To deal with it, Moscow suggested that all warships of the nonlittoral states be withdrawn from the Persian Gulf and that the belligerents, in turn, stop interfering with the freedom of navigation in that region.[125] The call for an end of air and naval attacks on neutral shipping in the Gulf was a novel idea. As was well known at the time, Iraq had dominated that aspect of the war and was determined not to decrease its pressure on Iran until Tehran agreed to a general cease-fire. Conversely, the Islamic Republic was interested in stopping the attacks which, along with technical (i.e., oil well recovery) problems, had severely hampered Tehran's efforts to export its oil. In essence, in early July 1987 the Soviet Union once again shifted its position in the Iran-Iraq equation.

In retrospect, the move seems to have been dictated by considerations of both superpower competition and the USSR's relations with the Gulf belligerents. The common denominator was Moscow's determined opposition to the increase of U.S. naval power and influence in the Persian Gulf, an attitude shared wholeheartedly by Tehran, providing for some common ground and for a degree of cooperation that was totally lacking in U.S.-Iranian relations. In any case, the Kremlin appears to have felt that continued Iraqi attacks on Iranian shipping left Tehran no alternative but to strike the Kuwaiti, Saudi, and other neutral tankers. That, in turn, was responsible for the vast increase in U.S. naval power in the Persian Gulf and the concurrent likelihood of a military showdown between the Islamic Republic and the United States. Therefore, in mid-1987, Baghdad bore the responsibility for escalating the naval warfare in the Gulf, and Moscow seems to have felt that the Iraqis had simply gone too far.

On July 20, 1987, the UN Security Council unanimously adopted a resolution ordering an immediate cease-fire in the Iran-Iraq war. It also called for the withdrawal of all forces to "internationally recognized boundaries," an exchange of the prisoners of war, and "the establishment of a body to determine which side was responsible for starting the war." Known as Resolution 598, the document contained no enforcement provisions, but its language was stronger than that contained in the earlier Security Council resolutions. Moreover, it was widely believed at the time that noncompliance with 598 would lead to the adoption of another resolution, "to be considered within two months," imposing an arms embargo against the recalcitrant party or parties.[126] Iraq accepted Resolution 598 on condition that Iran did likewise. Since the Islamic Republic refused to do so, Baghdad rejected Tehran's and Moscow's suggestion that the belligerents discontinue attacks on the Gulf shipping.[127]

On July 24 one of the reflagged Kuwaiti tankers struck a mine in the vicinity of the Iranian island of Farsi. On the same day, Rafsanjani warned that Tehran would strike at the "economic centers of Iraq's regional allies" if Baghdad's air force continued to attack Iran's economic objects.[128] The rise in tension coincided with large-scale violence which had occurred in Mecca, where thousands of Iranian pilgrims rioted and had to be subdued by the Saudi police and the military. Hundreds of Iranians were killed, leading the Islamic Republic to call for the "uprooting of the Saudi royalty." In this dispute the United States came down squarely on the side of Saudi Arabia.[129] In contrast, *Pravda*'s account of the Mecca disturbances exhibited a slight but discernable pro-Iranian slant. According to *Pravda*, President Khamenei called on the Muslim countries to condemn "the barbarian massacre of peaceful pilgrims" and placed the responsibility for Saudi excesses on the United States and its policy.[130]

It was under these circumstances that Deputy Foreign Minister Vorontsov returned to Baghdad and Tehran in late July-early August 1987. According to *Pravda*, he and Tariq Aziz met in a "warm [and] friendly atmosphere." Both expressed their approval of Resolution 598 and support of the forthcoming diplomatic efforts by Secretary-General Pérez de Cuéllar. The account of Vorontsov's stay in Tehran was couched in more neutral terms. This was particularly true of the cardinal issue of the continuation of the war. As noted by *Pravda*, "the Soviet side stated its ... principled position for ending the war and reaching a just political settlement." Nothing was said about the Iranian reaction. Nor did the public account of the Vorontsov visit to Tehran contain any reference to Resolution 598. But the sides did agree on the desirability of withdrawal of foreign warships and on the halt of naval and air attacks on shipping in the Persian Gulf.[131]

The seemingly contradictory tones in the Soviet coverage of events taking place in the Gulf in mid-1987 were but a reflection of a certain ambiguity inherent in the Soviet policy as the Kremlin simultaneously pursued two objectives—the end of the war and the elimination (or, at least, weakening) of the American military presence and influence in the Gulf. To achieve the first objective, Iran had to be persuaded to drop its opposition to the peaceful settlement of the conflict. Since Tehran made no secret of its determination to continue the war, it had to be pressured to change its stance. In this respect, the Soviet and American interests coincided to a remarkable degree. But acting on this premise meant not only cooperation with the United States but also accepting and supporting the American initiative—the proposed arms embargo— to effect the end of the war. Since, in doing so, Moscow would be assisting Washington to achieve its goals (which included keeping the USSR out of the Persian Gulf), the Soviets backed off. Instead, the Kremlin continued to emphasize the importance of a "collective" approach to the solution of the Iran-Iraq problems.

At the same time, Moscow was determined to prevent the expansion of the U.S. military power and influence generally in the Persian Gulf region. In this respect, the Soviet Union and the Islamic Republic were pursuing the same goal. However, opposition to American naval presence—introduced into the Gulf to protect Kuwait and Saudi Arabia—brought the USSR into a political conflict not only with those GCC states but also with Iraq. Baghdad's aggravation was reinforced by the Kremlin's support of Tehran's demand for a halt of military operations in the Gulf, where Iraq had the upper hand, but not on land, where Iran still had an advantage.

Moscow's position brought the USSR into a thinly veiled conflict with Iraq which, along with the United States, had been urging the Security Council to pressure Iran to accept the cease-fire. On August 27, the Iraqi UN delegate announced that Baghdad refused to "accept . . . [Tehran's] procrastination . . . [and] fully reserve[d] . . . its right to conduct any kind of operations against Iran as long as Iran does not comply with the resolution of the Security Council."[132] Two days later, Iraq broke the informal six-week cease-fire in the Gulf by attacking Iranian offshore oil installations. Tehran retaliated and, by early September, twenty ships were reported damaged over the span of six days.[133]

The United States reacted to the renewal of hostilities by calling on the Security Council "to impose a global arms embargo on Iran."[134] Instead, on September 3, Pérez de Cuéllar announced his intention to travel to the Gulf for another round of exploratory talks. His decision caused Washington to postpone temporarily its call for the arms embargo.[135] The USSR, too, expressed grave concern about the recent developments in the Persian Gulf. On September 8, visiting Deputy Foreign Minister Larijani was received by Ryzhkov and Shevardnadze. Both Soviet officials expressed themselves in favor of an "immediate halt of the Iran-Iraq war," noted that the basis for a political settlement of the conflict had been provided by Resolution 598, and urged the Islamic Republic to cooperate with the UN secretary-general.[136]

It soon became obvious that Pérez de Cuéllar had failed in persuading Tehran to accept Resolution 598.[137] Some observers concluded that the United States would use this opportunity to try to persuade the Security Council to impose a universal arms embargo on the Islamic Republic. However, they also anticipated that Washington's initiative would run into opposition from some permanent members of the UN Security Council, above all the USSR and the PRC. Iraq was visibly irritated with Beijing's and Moscow's foot-dragging. On September 14, an editorial in *al-Thawrah* said, in part: "The international community is requested now more than any time before to practice collective pressure against the Tehran regime. . . ." In addition, "senior Iraqi officials" let it be known that "diplomatic relations might suffer unless unnamed 'major powers' adopted pro-Iraqi positions concerning the UN cease-fire call."[138]

On September 23, Shevardnadze addressed the UN General Assembly. He described the state of affairs in the Persian Gulf as "critically dangerous" and reiterated Moscow's insistence that all foreign military presence should be withdrawn from it. To take its place, Shevardnadze recommended the creation of a UN naval force. It would be composed of warships of the member states and would fly a United Nations flag. Turning to the Iran-Iraq war, Shevardnadze said that the investigation into the origins of the war should begin "concurrently and immediately" with the halt in military operations and should be concluded by a "precisely determined" date.[139] Since the question of an investigation of the responsibility for the war had been an Iranian notion in which Iraq was not the least bit interested, Shevardnadze's insistence on tying the idea to the cease-fire was clearly an attempt to please Tehran.

Moscow's tactical tilt toward Iran infuriated Baghdad. At a press conference, held in New York on October 2, Tariq Aziz said that he had immediately objected to Shevardnadze's latest proposal.[140] Instead, Iraq demanded a "strict interpretation" of Resolution 598 which ordered immediate cease-fire and the withdrawal of troops. Only then would an impartial body be established to study the origins of the war. Apparent concern about Arab criticism prompted the Kremlin to react even before Tariq Aziz's press conference. In late September the Soviet embassy in Beirut issued a statement assuring the Arabs that "Moscow's efforts to maintain neighborly relations with Tehran would not be made at the expense of Iraq or other Arab countries." Baghdad was not convinced. As an unnamed Iraqi official put it: "There is a mini-crisis in our relations with the Soviet Union."[141]

In the fall of 1987 the belligerents stepped up air and missile attacks against enemy targets. Tension rose also as a result of President Khamenei's statement that Tehran would close the Strait of Hormuz in the event of an imposition of a general embargo on the Islamic Republic.[142] It was in those circumstances that Deputy Foreign Minister Vorontsov returned to the Gulf. The visit to Tehran did not produce positive results. On November 2, one day after his departure from the Islamic Republic, both belligerents sent messages to Pérez de Cuéllar "stiffening their positions on how to implement" Resolution 598. Iran continued to insist that an informal cease-fire and the creation of an impartial commission to study the origin of the war occur simultaneously. A formal cease-fire would then be announced together with a condemnation of Iraq for having started the conflict. These demands had been advanced before. However, on this particular occasion, Tehran also linked withdrawal from Iraqi territory to the payment of reparations for war damages suffered by Iran. It also insisted on redrawing the international boundary, saying that this was necessary because Baghdad had abrogated the treaty of 1975. The stiffening of the Iranian attitude reflected optimism prevalent in Tehran; it was hoped that the major winter offensive being readied at the time would result in the fall of Basrah and, subsequently, of Saddam Hussein. Iraq's position, too, had grown firm and inflexible; it now demanded that formal cease-fire and withdrawal of Iranian troops from the occupied territory precede the discussion of other topics, including the creation of a commission to investigate the causes of the war.[143]

In early December 1987, Larijani came to New York for another round of negotiations with Pérez de Cuéllar. It soon became apparent that the Islamic Republic had no intention of softening its position on ending the war: Larijani made it clear that Tehran would agree to the implementation of Resolution 598 only after Iraq had been branded aggressor and had paid Iran reparations for the losses suffered during the war.[144] Iran's refusal to cooperate with the UN Security Council strengthened Washington's argument in favor of a universal arms embargo against the Islamic Republic. It also made it more difficult for Moscow to resist the growing sentiment for the application of sanctions. In fact, the Arab— and particularly Iraqi—suspicions that the USSR refused to support the arms embargo because the Soviets wished to befriend the Islamic Republic infuriated Baghdad. Therefore, it came as no surprise when, on November 30, Foreign Minister Tariq Aziz labeled the USSR "an obstacle to UN peace efforts."[145]

An opportunity to deflect growing Arab criticism presented itself in early December, when President Gromyko received Iranian ambassador Nasser Khayrani-Nobari. Turning to what he described as the "main" topic, the Soviet president chided the Islamic Republic for continuing the war despite repeated assurances that Tehran wished the hostilities to end: "In practice, Iran is not working toward ending the war. For this reason, no solution to this question has been found." Gromyko concluded his remarks on the war with a thinly veiled warning. He reiterated the urgency of implementing Resolution 598 and went on to say that, should it not be carried into effect, "the question of taking further steps . . . could [well] be placed on the current [Security Council] agenda." This course of action, Gromyko added, was provided for in Resolution 598.[146]

In mid-December the USSR refined its position on the Gulf war. During the consultations among the members of the UN Security Council, the Soviets agreed "to *consider* an arms embargo against Iran, provided it was enforced by a naval blockade under a United Nations flag." Although nothing was known initially about the composition of the proposed UN fleet and other related matters, Washington's reaction was negative. According to Assistant Secretary of State Richard W. Murphy, "these Soviet positions reflect continuous efforts to play this issue both ways: avoiding actions in the UN which would sour Soviet-Iranian relations while doing just enough to blunt the increasing criticism of the Arab states directed at Moscow."[147]

For a while it appeared that the relentless U.S. and Arab pressure for a follow-up resolution had paid off. On December 24, the Security Council reached a unanimous decision "to consider sanctions to force Iran to comply" with Resolution 598.[148] In the next three weeks, its permanent members met three times but failed to draft a resolution acceptable to all because of "Soviet insistence on creating a United Nations naval force in the Persian Gulf, which the United States has opposed." By mid-January 1988, Secretary of State George Shultz complained publicly that the USSR had shown no inclination to proceed with the drafting of the arms embargo resolution.[149]

Another opportunity to discuss the Iran-Iraq impasse presented itself in early February, when Tariq Aziz returned to Moscow and was received by Ryzhkov and Shevardnadze. Since it was reported, in late January, that Baghdad had become exasperated with the USSR and had, in fact, warned the Soviets that their delaying tactics in the Security Council's deliberations of the arms embargo were "unacceptable,"[150] it may be assumed that Tariq Aziz was sent to Moscow to pressure the Kremlin to stop shielding the Islamic Republic. But the USSR, too, had an ax to grind—it strongly resented Iraq's approval of the continued, large-scale U.S. naval presence in the Persian Gulf. Given their clashing viewpoints, no constructive outcome could be expected from the Moscow meetings. The Soviet account of them supported this conclusion.[151] A slight change in the Soviet position occurred on February 18,

1988, when Moscow agreed that the five permanent members of the Security Council should enlarge the forum debating arms embargo against Iran by bringing into the informal discussions all of the council's remaining members. Although the USSR insisted that its decision did not imply acceptance of the embargo resolution, the Western powers chose to interpret Moscow's acquiescence to a larger forum as "a significant step forward."[152]

In this upbeat atmosphere Secretary of State Shultz traveled to Moscow for negotiations with Foreign Minister Shevardnadze. The American press reported prior to his February 21 arrival that the secretary's agenda placed "an unusually heavy emphasis on regional disputes." The Soviet officials did not seem to mind, assuring all concerned that the Kremlin, too, was eager "to accomplish something in these areas." It soon became apparent, however, that, in the context of regional conflicts, Washington and Moscow were in disagreement not only over the means of achieving peace but also over some of the ends.[153] At his press conference held after the conclusion of the talks, Shevardnadze was asked whether the superpowers had succeeded in narrowing their differences on the imposition of sanctions against Iran. He replied that Resolution 598 had been a product of "collective efforts" of all of the council members and added that future steps, too, would have to be arrived at in a similar fashion.[154]

In late February 1988, after the Iraqi air force attacked an oil refinery situated in a Tehran suburb, Iran retaliated by firing three Soviet-made Scud-B missiles into Baghdad. Iraq reciprocated in kind, launching the so-called al-Hussein rockets against a number of Iranian targets.[155] In these exchanges the Iraqis had the upper hand. As reported by *Pravda*, during the first week of the 1988 "war of the cities," nineteen Iranian rockets exploded in Baghdad, while 376 Iraqi missiles struck Tehran and three struck Qum.[156]

One of the early consequences of this escalation of the war was a sharp deterioration in relations between the Islamic Republic and the USSR. As some Iranian officials accused the USSR of providing Iraq with longer-range missiles, Moscow endeavored to distance itself from Baghdad. In private conversations, Soviet officials reportedly criticized the rocket attacks on the Iranian cities. Publicly, Foreign Ministry spokesman Gennadii Gerasimov admitted that the USSR had provided missiles to Iraq but went on to say that they were of a short-range variety and therefore could not have reached Tehran. Gerasimov added that the rockets had been delivered "on the condition that they not be 'modernized' in any way."[157]

In the meantime, the level of violence continued to rise. The Iraqis kept firing missiles at Tehran and other cities, while Iranian troops captured two Iraqi border towns despite the use of chemical weapons by the retreating enemy forces. This phase of the war culminated in a major poison gas attack on the town of Halabjah where, according to the Iranian UN delegate, some five thousand Kurdish inhabitants had been killed.[158] The large-scale recourse to poison gas caused "deep concern" in the USSR. On March 29, Gerasimov said that the reported "massive use of chemical weapons" represented a violation of the 1925 Geneva protocol and should therefore be condemned "decisively" by the international community. He added that this conclusion applied to both belligerents.[159]

Before the "war of the cities" came to an end on April 20, Iran suffered two serious setbacks. On April 18, after an American frigate had been damaged by a mine, U.S. naval vessels destroyed two Iranian oil rigs in the Persian Gulf. On the same day, the Iraqis recaptured the Faw peninsula.[160] Given its balancing act in the Iran-Iraq conflict, Moscow had little to say about the reconquest of Faw; the news was reported, but no editorial comment was made.[161] The same was not true of the other happenings in the Gulf, however. "Serious concern," which the Kremlin felt about the "recent U.S. military actions against Iran," was conveyed by Shevardnadze to Shultz, who arrived in the USSR a few days after the Gulf incident. According to the Soviet account, the foreign minister admonished the secretary that American engagement of the Iranian forces postponed the "peaceful resolution of the Iran-Iraq conflict," interfered with the peacemaking mission of the UN secretary-general, and could result in an "uncontrolled escalation of tension in the Persian Gulf area."[162]

In late May the Iraqis drove the Iranians from the border town of Shalamchah and, some four weeks later, from the Majnun oil fields northeast of Basrah.[163] Although some territory in Iraqi Kurdistan remained under Iranian control, it was clear that the Islamic Republic had lost the war. On July 18, 1988, the Iranian government accepted Resolution 598. The Kremlin was elated; at a Foreign Ministry briefing on July 19, Gerasimov reminded all concerned that the USSR had repeatedly expressed itself "in favor of Iran's acceptance of Resolution 598 and . . . [was] delighted that Iran has taken this important step. . . ."[164]

On July 20, Tariq Aziz dispatched a letter to Pérez de Cuéllar outlining Baghdad's plan for ending the war. It envisaged a meeting between the representatives of the warring states to mark the beginning of "direct, official negotiations concerning the implementation of Resolution

598." Tariq Aziz suggested also the inclusion in the agenda of the "questions of freedom of navigation in the Shatt al-Arab river and in the Persian Gulf" and called on Tehran to halt the attacks on neutral tankers. Upon discussing Baghdad's plan with the members of the Security Council, Pérez de Cuéllar announced that "military experts of the UN" would soon be dispatched to Iran and Iraq to begin the implementation of Resolution 598.[165] After almost eight years of war, peace finally seemed to be at hand.

Baghdad stuck to its position when the foreign ministers of Iran and Iraq began their respective discussions with Pérez de Cuéllar: Tariq Aziz insisted that the first step in the peace process should be Iran's acquiescence to "immediate face-to-face negotiations" with Iraq. Tehran demurred. On July 28, its UN representative argued that under the United Nations charter, Resolution 598 was "a mandatory one . . . and as such . . . [was] binding on Iraq, which thus has no right to impose any preconditions."[166]

By early August 1988 it was becoming clear that international pressure was building to get Baghdad to modify its intractable position. The *New York Times* reported that the United States had urged Iraq to accept the cease-fire without preconditions.[167] There was no direct evidence of Soviet diplomatic pressure on Iraq, but judging by the pronouncements of Moscow's press, there can be little doubt that the USSR, too, attempted to exert its influence in Baghdad on behalf of an early and unconditional acceptance of the cease-fire. For example, in an article entitled "It Is Time to Stop," Pavel Demchenko suggested that the preconditions for ending the war had been met when Iran accepted Resolution 598. Nevertheless, no progress was achieved because Baghdad and Tehran adhered to "different concepts of reaching a settlement."[168] Although Demchenko's article addressed both belligerents, even a cursory reading of the text left no doubt about who the real culprit in the stalled peace process was: Iran had finally and unconditionally accepted Resolution 598 while Iraq was blocking the implementation of the cease-fire.

On August 20, 1988, as stipulated by Pérez de Cuéllar, the cease-fire went into effect. Five days later, direct negotiations between Iraq and Iran opened in Geneva.[169] As envisaged by the secretary-general, the purpose of the opening round was to reach an agreement on "a timetable for carrying out the various stages of" Resolution 598.[170] The Soviet reaction to these events was predictably positive but cautious. *Pravda* noted Tariq Aziz's statement to the effect that Iraq was genuinely interested in restoring peace and hoped that Iran would respond in kind.

Velayati, too, expressed willingness to cooperate in the achievement of "comprehensive, just, honorable, and durable" peace. In spite of these encouraging signs, *Pravda* warned, the negotiations about to begin in Geneva were bound to be difficult. More than 1 million casualties as well as "enormous destruction and material losses . . . [had] widened the chasm of mutual suspicion and hostility."[171]

Relations with Iran. In mid-1987 the Soviet position in the Gulf conflict underwent yet another subtle change. Before that time, and going back to 1982 and 1983, Moscow had supported Baghdad. The Kremlin's stance was conditioned mainly by Tehran's intransigence and refusal to end the war. In the summer of 1987 Iran had not yet retracted from its insistence on defeating Iraq, but the situation in the Gulf had changed dramatically in ways that alarmed and annoyed the Kremlin. For example, the Soviets were concerned with the projected rise of U.S. naval presence and political influence in the Persian Gulf. Because Iran also shared these sentiments, an area of overlapping interests between the two states was established, paving the way for some rapprochement and renewed attempts at cooperation.

One of the early indications of improving relations was provided in mid-July 1987, when Deputy Foreign Minister Larijani arrived in Moscow and was received by President Gromyko. According to a lengthy account in *Pravda*, Gromyko insisted that the USSR had "always . . . stood and continues to stand for goodneighborly relations with Iran." It also adhered to the principles of "equality, mutual respect, and noninterference in each other's internal affairs." Gromyko believed that the two neighbors "must always live in peace and friendship" and urged Tehran to "build its relations with us on such a reliable and just basis." For his part, Larijani assured his host that the "Iranian leadership was striving to . . . strengthen good relations with the Soviet Union" and expressed himself in favor of implementing "new projects in the sphere of economic cooperation."[172] Another indication of a pro-Iranian slant in Moscow's position was provided by the coverage of the Mecca disturbances in late July and early August 1987.[173]

In early August, Vorontsov returned to Tehran. The Soviet account of his talks with the Iranian leaders referred to a "detailed exchange of views on matters concerning [long-term development of] Soviet-Iranian relations. . . ." The sides "favored the implementation of large-scale projects . . . [designed to promote] mutually profitable economic cooperation."[174] Tehran's version of the negotiations was more specific. According to the Iranian News Agency, the sides "discussed the building of oil pipelines, expansion of cooperation in the area of power and steel, oil refining, preliminary progress in joint shipping in the Caspian Sea and plans to build a railroad linking the Soviet border with the Persian Gulf."[175] Taken at its face value, this account of Vorontsov's discussions in Tehran could have been interpreted as a major Soviet breakthrough in Iran. Yet, widespread Western apprehension that the USSR had registered a major gain in the Islamic Republic turned out to be premature. The flurry of diplomatic activity undertaken in July and August 1987 produced an apparent rapprochement between the Soviet Union and the Islamic Republic, but it did not result in a strategic realignment in the region.

In September, Larijani returned to Moscow and conferred with Ryzhkov and Shevardnadze about the situation in the Gulf and the state of bilateral relations. According to the deputy foreign minister, the Islamic Republic continued to attach "great importance to the development of relations with the Soviet Union" and was determined to take "appropriate practical action" to foster them, although the Soviet press did not specify what some of these actions might be. Similar sentiments were expressed by the Soviet officials as well.[176] In mid-October, the Iranian oil minister came to Moscow. Western accounts of his visit demonstrated how little had been accomplished despite earlier Iranian optimism concerning the expansion of economic cooperation between the two states. The minister said that the sides "would probably conclude a natural gas sales agreement and discuss two other projects." These were identified as "a possible oil pipeline . . . and a new rail link." Judging by subsequent developments, or the lack of them, no breakthrough had been achieved. The only visible signs of a return to relative normalcy were the appointment of a new Soviet ambassador to the Islamic Republic and the resumption of Aeroflot's flights between Moscow and Tehran after a break of two years.[177] Finally, in late 1987 an agreement was reached to establish a joint Soviet-Iranian shipping line in the Caspian Sea.[178]

In the meantime, it had become obvious that Moscow's pressure on Iran to accept Resolution 598 failed to produce the desired results. In early December 1987, Larijani arrived at the UN headquarters in New York and reiterated Tehran's demand that Iraq be branded aggressor and agree to pay reparations before Iran accepted a cease-fire. Gromyko's reception of the Iranian ambassador to the USSR must be seen in the light of these developments. On that occasion Khayrani-Nobari delivered to the Soviet president a message from the leadership of the Islamic Republic and went on to explain that the "spirit of the document" reflected Tehran's desire to broaden cooperation with the Soviet Union.

The message thanked the USSR for its "firm position in the Security Council" and expressed hope that it would remain unchanged. The ambassador noted also that Iran was ready "to cooperate closely with the Soviet Union so that all naval vessels of nonlittoral states, which are presently deployed in the Persian Gulf and are creating an explosive situation there, be withdrawn."[179] Coming at the time of strong Soviet pressure on Iran to accept Resolution 598, Tehran's diplomatic gambit reflected its determination to stay the course while appealing to Moscow not to change its stance on the embargo resolution, advocated by the United States. In short, subjected to sustained Soviet political and, it would also seem, economic pressure, Tehran chose not to alter its basic position but to apply pressure of its own.

In early 1988 Soviet-Iranian relations took a sharp turn for the worse. At that time the "war of the cities" was resumed and Tehran became one of its major casualties. The incoming missiles were a modified version of the Soviet-made Scud-Bs, and it was not immediately clear whether the changes which enabled the rockets to reach Tehran had been effected with Soviet assistance. The Iranians believed in Moscow's involvement, however. On March 1, Vladimir Gudev, the new Soviet ambassador, was summoned to the Ministry of Foreign Affairs and handed a protest against the supply of Soviet missiles to Iraq.[180]

On March 6 the Soviet embassy and the consulate in Isfahan were attacked by demonstrators who accused the USSR of supplying Iraq with long-range missiles. According to *Pravda*, these events were preceded by "inciting reports in some Iranian media which attempted to ascribe to the Soviet Union the responsibility for the current Iraqi missile attacks on Tehran and other Iranian cities." Alarmed, the Ministry of Foreign Affairs summoned the Iranian chargé d'affaires and conveyed to him "serious concern of the Soviet leadership" about the events in Tehran and Isfahan. The Kremlin regarded these occurrences as "totally unacceptable" and warned the chargé that his government had to take the "most urgent, immediate measures" to protect the Soviet institutions in Iran. Moscow also rejected "all fabrications concerning the USSR's complicity in missile strikes" against the Iranian cities.[181]

In addition to the Iran-Iraq war, Moscow and Tehran remained at odds about the situation in Afghanistan and about the crackdown on Iran's "democratic organizations." On December 27 a group of "Afghan counterrevolutionaries, based in Iran" stormed the Soviet consulate in Isfahan. In an official protest Moscow demanded that the Tehran authorities take "all necessary measures to guarantee full safety of all the [Soviet] institutions and citizens in Iran." The Iranian Ministry of Foreign Affairs expressed regrets and gave assurances that the government would not tolerate such attacks in the future.[182]

In 1988 the Kremlin continued preparations for the troop pullout from Afghanistan, scheduled for early 1989. Its successful completion as well as some assurance that the communist regime in Kabul would remain in power after the Soviets had left depended on Pakistan's and Iran's willingness to curb the activities of the *mujahideen* operating in their respective territories. However, neither Islamabad nor Tehran had shown any willingness to assist the withdrawal by cooperating with the communist regime in Kabul. Their attitude prompted First Secretary Najibullah as well as Gorbachev to urge Iran "not [to] stand aside from political settlement."[183] Their words fell on deaf ears.

Another issue troubling Moscow was the continuing persecution of the pro-Soviet Tudeh and Fedayeen e-Khalq parties by the Iranian authorities. Although in the late 1980s the fate of the two Marxist organizations was of little importance to Moscow, some of their leaders had found refuge in the Soviet Union or in Eastern Europe. They reappeared from time to time at official party gatherings, delivered speeches, issued proclamations, and otherwise disseminated their propaganda. Occasionally, the pages of the main Soviet publications were made available for their pronouncements but more often than not these were relegated to *Problemy mira i sotsializma* (*World Marxist Review*) and its *Information Bulletin*. In this sense the fate of the Iranian Marxist organizations remained a problem affecting Moscow-Tehran relations, although only in a negligible way.

On July 20, 1988, two days after the Islamic Republic had accepted the cease-fire in the Gulf conflict, Vorontsov arrived in Tehran. In addition to the war and Afghanistan, his discussions with Khamenei, Velayati, and Larijani dealt also with the state of Soviet-Iranian relations. TASS reported that the "sides expressed mutual interest in developing goodneighborly relations . . . , in continuing regular political contacts . . . , [and] in expanding . . . trade [and] economic cooperation on a long-term basis. . . ." Similar sentiments were expressed during Larijani's subsequent visit to Moscow.[184] In short, not a great deal had changed on the substantive level even after the cease-fire had gone into effect. This point was driven home a few months later when Ayatollah Khomeini, in line with his consistent stand, declared that the Islamic Republic refused to rely either on the "world-devouring" United States or on the "criminal" Soviet Union[185]—yet another allusion to the Kremlin's involvement in Afghanistan.

Relations with Iraq. As in the past, ongoing contacts with Tehran ran parallel to attempts at close association with Baghdad. This was not surprising. The Ba'thist regime had long been in favor of ending the war with Iran and of resolving the outstanding problems by political means. This coincided with the Soviet position and accounted for close military cooperation between the two states. On a more general level, Iraq was an important Soviet client in the Middle East, and the prospect of Saddam Hussein's overthrow by the fundamentalist Islamic Republic disturbed Moscow for regional reasons as well as for the broader considerations of superpower rivalry.

In any event, in July 1987, at a time when Soviet-Iranian relations were on one of their occasional upswings, Deputy Premier Ramadan arrived in Moscow at the head of an official Iraqi delegation. He was received by President Gromyko on July 2, one day before the Soviet government issued its official statement on the situation in the Persian Gulf.[186] As Gromyko outlined, Moscow's position encompassed the following provisions: the hostilities were to come to an end without delay; the sides were to initiate a peaceful dialogue; "lawful interests" of both parties were to be respected; and the United Nations was to play an important part in ending the conflict. Ramadan endorsed the Soviet stance, noting that "Iraq follow[ed] closely on the work of the Security Council . . . and wish[ed] that the [proposed] resolution would contribute to peace." In an important formulation, Gromyko and Ramadan also "objected to any attempts to use the tension in the Persian Gulf zone as a pretext for interference in the internal affairs of the [littoral] states. . . ." In retrospect, this rather innocuous statement reflected Soviet pressure on Iraq to condemn the U.S. naval presence in the Gulf. Because the Western navies in the Gulf were helping Baghdad's cause, however, it made no sense for Iraq to oppose them. Hence, the sides compromised, objecting to Western "interference in the internal affairs" of the Persian Gulf states but not to the naval presence itself. Finally, Gromyko and Ramadan examined the state of Soviet-Iraqi relations and expressed their customary satisfaction with it. They concluded that "further strengthening" of bilateral ties "correspond[ed] with the interests of both peoples" and made a "positive contribution to the cause of . . . peace and stability in the Middle East." Defense Minister Dmitrii Iazov participated in the discussions between Gromyko and Ramadan—a clear indication that the question of Soviet arms supplies to Iraq was included in the meeting's agenda. Upon his return to Baghdad, Ramadan described the negotiations as "frank and constructive" and said that Iraq was satisfied with the cooperation between the two states.[187]

Nevertheless, by mid- and late August 1987 relations between the USSR and Iraq began to deteriorate. The major source of friction was the Kremlin's stand on the Gulf conflict. It will be recalled that the Soviets let it be known early on that they were opposed to the application of sanctions against Iran. In addition, the Kremlin was perturbed about the drastic increase in the Western (and particularly U.S.) naval presence in the Persian Gulf. For this reason Moscow's determination to reduce, if not totally eliminate, it became one of the major objectives of its regional policy. This stance was in harmony with the Iranian position but ran into determined Iraqi opposition, adding to the growing strains in Moscow-Baghdad relations.

The clash between the Soviet and Iraqi positions came out into the open in late August, when two editorials in *al-Thawrah* attacked Moscow's policy in the Persian Gulf. The USSR was not mentioned by name, but the reference to the "shortsighted superpower opposing the imposition of sanctions against Iran" left no doubt about the meaning. The other editorial assailed unnamed governments which had called for the unconditional removal of foreign fleets from the Persian Gulf. Iran would be the only beneficiary of such a turn of events, *al-Thawrah* argued, because it would be left free to carry out its "terrorist operations" in the Gulf region.[188]

The differences between the Soviet and Iraqi approaches to the war resurfaced in early October. In his UN General Assembly speech, Shevardnadze suggested that an impartial committee, charged with investigating the causes of the war, should be set up "concurrently and immediately" with the cease-fire, a proposal that Tariq Aziz publicly and indignantly rejected. As tension grew, an unnamed Iraqi official asserted that there was, in fact, "a mini-crisis in our relations with the Soviet Union. . . . What we don't know is whether this is something that will pass or whether this is a permanent condition."[189]

Given Iraq's insistence on airing its differences with the USSR, high Soviet officials went out of their way attempting to reassure their unruly client. For example, Deputy Foreign Minister Vladimir Petrovskii argued that the USSR and Iraq were tied by the treaty of friendship and cooperation "which we follow very strictly, but we also want good relations with Iran, our neighbor." According to Petrovskii, there were no contradictions in Moscow's respective approaches to the Gulf belligerents: "We don't make relations with one country at the expense of another."[190]

Nevertheless, as long as the war dragged on and Iran refused to bow to the will of the UN Security Council, Baghdad perceived Moscow as shielding Tehran. It will be recalled that, in late January 1988, Iraq publicly described the USSR's stance as "unacceptable." Shortly thereafter, in yet another effort to overcome the difficulties which the Gulf war had created in their relations, Tariq Aziz returned to Moscow and conducted far-reaching discussions with Ryzhkov and Shevardnadze. In addition to the Persian Gulf problems, the officials discussed Afghanistan, the Arab-Israeli conflict, and bilateral relations between the two states. Specifically, Tariq Aziz "greeted the Soviet Union's determination to move its military contingent out of Afghanistan." Similar harmony prevailed with respect to the Arab-Israeli problem. Finally, the parties gave "high marks to the state of bilateral relations which are developing successfully on the firm foundation of the Treaty of Friendship and Cooperation" and discussed the "prospects for developing cooperation" in a number of unspecified areas.[191]

Given the Iraqi censure of Soviet policy in the Persian Gulf in 1987 and early 1988 as well as the seeming inability to bridge their differences on several war-related issues, the harmony of the statements dealing with bilateral relations and the "high marks" which Iraq conferred upon the USSR's efforts to broaden bilateral cooperation came as something of a surprise. In retrospect, it would seem that the apparent desire that both sides exhibited to improve relations despite disagreements on various aspects of the Gulf war was dictated by the parties' perception of their respective basic interests. Specifically, Iraq understood that the Soviets were likely to remain involved in the politics of the Persian Gulf region and that they would, therefore, play a role in the eventual resolution of the differences separating Baghdad and Tehran. The USSR would do so both as a permanent member of the UN Security Council and as a powerful northern neighbor of the Islamic Republic. Moreover, as noted repeatedly, the Soviet Union remained the major arms supplier of Iraq. The Kremlin, for its part, was under no illusion that its ability to conduct an effective policy in the Persian Gulf as well as in the Arab world generally depended on maintaining close relations with Iraq. Thus, although disagreeing on many tactical, short-term matters, Moscow and Baghdad needed each other for the implementation and success of their respective longer-range policies. In the final analysis this awareness could not prevent the occurrence of occasionally serious strains in the relationship, but it did preclude an open break between the superpower patron and its important Third World client. Indeed, in mid-July 1988, a few days before Iran's surprise acceptance of Resolution 598, an official delegation headed by RCC member and Chairman of the National Council Sa'dun Hammadi arrived in Moscow. His meeting with Gromyko was conducted in a "warm [and] benevolent" atmosphere, a marked improvement over the standard "frank," "business-like," or even "friendly."[192]

Finally, a few words should be said about the outlawed Iraqi Communist party and its activities during the Gulf conflict. To begin with, the fortunes of the country's Marxist, pro-Soviet organization were of relatively little concern to Moscow. The Iraqi party continued to exist, but its leaders had been exiled and whatever remained of its once sizable membership had been imprisoned or driven underground. Living abroad and enjoying a measure of Soviet organizational and financial backing, the top echelon of the party were left relatively free to write much as they pleased. Like the Tudeh, the ICP remained opposed to the Iran-Iraq war and expressed its sentiments regularly in the *World Marxist Review* and the *Information Bulletin*. By and large, the main Soviet press organs avoided references to such articles, yet another indication of the lack of Moscow's interest in the Iranian and Iraqi Marxist organizations.

Mikhail Gorbachev's advent to power in 1985 resulted in yet another major reappraisal of the Soviet approach to the Third World. Driven by the inexorable reality of Soviet economic stagnation, Gorbachev in the latter 1980s introduced momentous changes in the foreign policy of the USSR. As a result, the Kremlin has disavowed the concept of worldwide competition between the "socialist" and "capitalist" systems; ideological underpinnings have all but disappeared from major Soviet pronouncements as well as from actual policies. In comparison with his predecessors, Gorbachev has embarked upon a course of a truly remarkable retrenchment: withdrawal of Soviet troops from Afghanistan and the dissolution of the East European empire have been accompanied by less dramatic but nonetheless important curtailment of Soviet commitment and assistance to such formerly invaluable clients as Vietnam, Ethiopia, the PDRY, and Cuba. In addition, the Kremlin has earnestly attempted to contribute to peaceful resolution of such conflicts as the Kampuchean and Angolan civil wars, the Arab-Israeli imbroglio, and the war between Iraq and Iran.

Nevertheless, although Gorbachev's Kremlin has sought to defuse the various international conflicts, some—particularly the Iran-Iraq war—have attracted a livelier Soviet interest than others. In retrospect, this was not surprising because the geographic location of the belligerents in the Persian Gulf, the proximity and the regional importance of Iraq, the direct border with Iran (with all the problems attendant to it), and the eventual involvement of the superpowers had rendered the Iraq-Iran conflict a highly explosive and, to the Kremlin, dangerous situation. In short, Gorbachev's foreign policy has openly discarded communist ideology as one of its motivating factors and is now governed exclusively by pragmatic pursuit of the USSR's perceived national interests.

Evaluation

Judging by its public declarations as well as by its actions, the USSR consistently opposed the Iran-Iraq war. Brezhnev stated in his December 1980 speech before the Indian Parliament that the Gulf conflict was "tragic in its senselessness," and the Kremlin has adhered to this view ever since. According to its own pronouncements, Moscow adopted this position for a number of reasons. The Soviets expressed dismay with the two leading "anti-imperialist" powers of the Gulf which were squandering their human and material resources in a useless conflict instead of centering their attention on the United States and its regional "machinations." In addition, the Iran-Iraq war split the Arab world and diverted attention from the Arab-Israeli conflict, thus benefiting the Israeli "aggressors" and their American patrons. Moreover, the war destabilized the entire Gulf region and interfered with the flow of petroleum, providing Washington with new opportunities to increase the U.S. military presence in the Gulf and with potential excuses for direct military intervention.

In view of these considerations the USSR deplored the Iran-Iraq war as well as the regional instability associated with it; urged the belligerents to cease fire and to resolve their differences through negotiations; and endorsed various international efforts to end the conflict. Concurrently, Moscow denied allegations that it intended either to attack Iran or to disrupt the oil traffic in the Gulf and "resolutely" warned "others," that is, the United States, not to intervene in the war. In addition, in an apparent attempt to dispel the notion that the Kremlin was merely talking, Brezhnev, in his February 1981 speech before the Twenty-sixth Congress of the CPSU, said that the Soviet Union was trying to promote peace in the Persian Gulf "in practice also." Similar sentiments were also expressed by Gromyko in his October 1982 speech before the UN General Assembly. Since both Soviet leaders claimed that Moscow was pursuing an *active* policy in the quest for peace in the Persian Gulf and since this issue is of direct relevance to the question of Soviet influence in Baghdad as well as in Tehran, the implications of Brezhnev's and Gromyko's assertions deserve to be analyzed more closely.

Evidence provided earlier in the chapter supports the conclusion that the Soviets did in fact apply pressure on both belligerents to end the war and to settle their differences by peaceful means. Moscow did so publicly (in the form of official pronouncements, UN votes, and support of mediation efforts by international organizations) and privately during bilateral negotiations with representatives of the Iraqi and Iranian governments. Pressure was also applied verbally as well as by direct and indirect action. Specifically, it is a well-known fact that after the outbreak of the war, the USSR cut off arms deliveries to Iraq. This extreme measure, taken in violation of existing contracts, signified the Kremlin's censure of Saddam Hussein's decision to invade Iran and was no doubt intended to pressure Baghdad into abandoning its bellicosity. In 1981 and 1982, however, Moscow resumed arms deliveries to Iraq, an about-face that does not seem to have been directed at Baghdad. Rather, it was an expression of growing Soviet displeasure with the Islamic Republic. It will be recalled that in 1981, Tehran not only insisted on carrying on the war against Iraq—a stand that the Kremlin argued benefitted "U.S. imperialism" only—but also embarked upon a number of policies which the USSR had found extremely repugnant, such as "anticommunism," "anti-Sovietism," and support of the Afghan *mujahideen*.

In short, in its efforts to help end the Gulf war, Moscow, in addition to diplomatic efforts, also played the major trump card at its disposal—the supply of weapons to Iraq—as a means of attempting to persuade first Baghdad and then Tehran to end the hostilities. For seven years, these attempts at exerting pressure on both belligerents failed to produce the desired results: Iraq was able to continue fighting despite the Soviet arms cut-off, and Iran, until 1988, did not waver in its determination to win the war even after the USSR resumed its weapons supplies to the Saddam Hussein regime in 1981 and 1982. Because the term "applying pressure" in this context is synonymous with "exerting influence," it is obvious that the Soviets used all the means at their disposal short of direct application of military power and came up empty. In this sense, the Iran-Iraq war provided another important illustration of the limitations of the proposition that great powers have the ability to exert pressure on (or exercise influence over) a much weaker client whose interests dictate a course of action at variance with the wishes of the patron.

Soviet experiences in Iran offer additional insights into the problem of patron-client relationship in the multipolar political system. As argued earlier, in 1979 and 1980 Moscow made a determined effort to befriend the Islamic Republic. It did so, among other things, by lending Tehran important political and economic support during the hostage crisis with the United States and by tilting toward Iran after the Iraqi attack of September 1980. The Kremlin also expressed itself against the war—thus indirectly condemning Saddam Hussein for starting it—and, for a while, suspended arms deliveries to Baghdad. It is impossible to ascertain now what benefits the USSR expected to gain as a result of its anti-Iraqi stance during the initial stages of the war. It may well be that the Kremlin wished to dump Baghdad and to align itself with Tehran in the manner of the Somalia-Ethiopia switch executed in the mid-1970s. Whatever hopes the Soviets may have harbored, however, they had little to show for their efforts. In spite of occasional warnings and even threats, the Islamic Republic persevered in the war effort and in its "anticommunist" and "anti-Soviet" activities. It also continued to support the anti-Russian *mujahideen* in Afghanistan. Put differently, Moscow's efforts to exert pressure on Tehran by "carrot" (i.e., offers of friendship and cooperation, withholding arms from Iraq) and by "stick" (resumption of weapons deliveries to Baghdad) both failed to produce the desired results. The same conclusion applies to the Iranian efforts to drive a wedge between the USSR and Iraq. In sum, what Moscow and Tehran have had in common is their opposition to the U.S. presence in the Persian Gulf. This shared determination to undercut Washington's positions has prevented a complete break between the Soviet Union and the Islamic Republic and accounts for a degree of cooperation between them. At the same time their very real differences have precluded a close relationship and have severely inhibited their respective ability to exert pressure on, and exercise influence over, the other party.

In a similar vein, the Kremlin's decision to resume arms shipments to Iraq and to expand trade as well as economic and technical cooperation between the two states could be interpreted not only as evidence of Soviet frustration with Ayatollah Khomeini, but also as acknowledgment that earlier efforts at exerting influence on Baghdad by withholding war matériel had been futile. In any event, Saddam Hussein must have recognized that Moscow's renewed attempts at improving relations were a direct outgrowth of the difficulties which the USSR had experienced in Tehran. Nevertheless, these considerations did not pre-vent the hard-pressed Iraqi leader from accepting (and, in fact, from actively seeking) Soviet assistance. In short, although, after 1981, the USSR and Iraq were in agreement on the need to end the war and to resolve the outstanding problems by political means, Baghdad had strong misgivings about Moscow's determination to maintain a bal-anced relationship with both belligerents. In the latter stages of the Gulf conflict, in particular, the Iraqis endeavored to prevail upon the Kremlin to modify its posture on the war. This became evident, above all, in Baghdad's insistence that the USSR support an arms embargo against the Islamic Republic. Iraq's efforts at influencing Moscow were no more successful than those exerted by Tehran's clerical leaders. Conversely, the Kremlin could not prevail upon Baghdad to stop the escalation of aerial attacks on the Iranian and neutral shipping in the Gulf. Tehran responded in kind, and its activity led ultimately to the vast increase of the U.S. naval presence in the region. Saddam Hussein has had no illusions about the nature of Iraq's relationship with the USSR: it continues to be based on a coincidence of national interests as well as on mutual profit and on no other considerations. For this reason, he has felt obliged periodically to remind the Kremlin leaders that they must "respect the will of the Iraqi people," another way of saying that Moscow's ability to influence Baghdad's behavior has remained limited in the extreme.

■ Conclusion: The Lessons of the Soviet Quest for Influence in Iraq

The USSR first showed an interest in post-World War II Iraq in 1958, when Colonel Abd al-Kerim Kassem overthrew the pro-Western monarchy and took his country out of the Baghdad Pact. The next ten years comprised a period of great instability in Baghdad, marked by a series of coups d'état which led eventually to the emergence of the Iraqi Ba'th as the stable ruling party and finally to the accession of Saddam Hussein as a virtual dictator (chapter 1). Throughout this period of internal volatility and despite occasional vissicitudes in relations between the two states, the link between Iraq and the Soviet Union rested on what both regimes perceived to be the mutuality of their interests.

Specifically, Baghdad's interest in courting the Kremlin's goodwill and assistance was based on the need for a powerful patron in its efforts to shed all the remnants of Western colonialism and to establish Iraq as an autonomous member of the world order of nation states. It is important to recognize, however, that this goal never accommodated the notion of replacing one form of domination with another. For their part, the Soviet leaders were only too happy to assist any nation or movement intent on "throwing off the yoke of imperialism," for this was the heyday of the cold war and of Moscow's quest for recognition of its status as a global superpower. In the ebullient era of Khrushchevian expansionism, the leaders of the USSR were apparently convinced that any diminution of Western influence represented a gain for Soviet interests. (Whether there was much thought given in the Kremlin to the specific goals and the mechanisms for their achievement attendant to supplanting the Western powers is inevitably a matter for inconclusive speculation.)

In the late 1960s and early 1970s the Soviet Union and Iraq developed what, from the typical Western perspective, was seen as a very strong patron-client relationship, culminating with the signing in 1972 of the Treaty of Friendship and Cooperation. This period was characterized by substantial Soviet aid to Iraq (chapter 1), a pattern of practice which the Kremlin leaders apparently rationalized as an investment. Very shortly thereafter, however, the nationalization of the Iraqi oil industry and the subsequent astronomical rise in the world price for petroleum transformed Iraq from its former status as a putatively grateful aid recipient into a cash-paying, fully autonomous trading partner. Indeed, even in the earlier era of apparent dependence, Baghdad's ruling elite had shown stubborn resistance toward anything which could be regarded as an intrusion into the country's internal affairs or as an infringement upon Iraq's sovereignty over its international policies. Thus, the case studies which have comprised the bulk of this volume amply demonstrate that Soviet influence in Iraq, even in the era of its apparent zenith, was often limited indeed.

As the events that led to the nationalization of the Iraq Petroleum Company unfolded (chapter 2), a classic case of what was earlier labeled *constructive facilitative influence* emerged. Iraq was pursuing its own goals and objectives, and the Soviet Union, through the provision of resources at moderate cost and risk, saw the opportunity to reach for some of its own aims. This was made possible by the fact that although the long-term goals of each were quite different, the specific objective (i.e., nationalization of the Iraq Petroleum Company) which each perceived as likely to serve their respective ends was the same. Even here, however, as the case study makes clear, the two governments differed over the questions of timing and tactics.

The Kremlin leaders may well have understood that Baghdad would not struggle for the real and symbolic autonomy which eviction of its "Western oppressors" would bring and then quietly accept a Soviet understudy in the same role. However, they could not have predicted what the oil shock of the mid-1970s would do for Iraq's resource base and thus probably counted on a period of relative resource dependence by the Ba'th to assure its leaders' malleability.

From the Kremlin view, the 1972 nationalization of the oil company, in prospect, would likely provide Iraq with sufficient revenue to help foot the bill for the modernization of its military and economic infrastructure, thus rendering Baghdad a discount cash customer instead of a regular aid recipient. Much direct Soviet assistance, favorable trading terms, and economic as well as political "guidance" would ostensibly still be needed from Soviet benefactors. (Having alienated the major Western powers by the very act of nationalization, Baghdad would have few other patrons save the USSR and its allies to whom to turn for that assistance.] After a period of years of the evolution of their relationship, Iraq would be bound to the Soviet Union through many strands of functional interdependence (such as trading partner, and military, economic, and technical aid recipient). As a result, Moscow's position in Baghdad would have solidified significantly. This would, from the happiest of Soviet perspectives, perhaps even give the USSR its long-sought foothold in the Persian Gulf.

Therefore, the Kremlin leaders must have viewed as cruel irony the realities which ultimately shattered their pleasant vision. Specifically, having used the Kremlin's assistance to position itself for the nationalization of the IPC, Baghdad took advantage of the explosive increase in oil profits which resulted from the restructuring of the world petroleum market in the mid-1970s, and, in short order, proved itself to be an autonomous trading partner rather than a compliant client. Any hope of a Soviet foothold in the Gulf was soundly dashed as Iraq provided one of the loudest voices in the international chorus calling for exclusion of the superpowers from the region.

While the June 1, 1972, decree nationalizing the oil industry brought to a dramatic conclusion one of the long-pending issues on the Iraqi agenda, the very event exacerbated another of the long-range problems of mutual concern to Moscow and Baghdad. Specifically, the issue of how to deal with the quest by Iraq's Kurdish minority for an autonomous regional homeland was made more salient by the act of nationalization, for the region in which the Kurds comprised a population majority included the important oil-producing area of northern Iraq. This area became even more valuable to the central government after the nationalization decree, rendering the autonomy issue even less subject to negotiation by the Ba'th.

Chapter 3 has presented a detailed analysis of the zigzag path of shifting Soviet support for one side and then the other in the Ba'th-Kurdish dispute. Although the struggle by Iraq's Kurds for independence or autonomy in a predominantly Arab society goes back dozens of years, the more recent conflict between the Kurdish nationalists led by Mulla Mustafa (at one time an apparent Soviet protegé) and the various regimes which have ruled post-monarchical Iraq constituted a continuing thorny issue for the USSR.

During periods of Moscow's displeasure with Baghdad, the Kremlin leaders tended to reassert their support for Kurdish autonomy. But even when they refrained from directly backing the Kurds, the Soviets continued to urge a political resolution of the conflict. Moscow apparently saw the maintenance of creative tension between the Ba'th and Mulla Mustafa's Kurds as a potential source of leverage for Soviet involvement in Iraqi affairs.

At the same time, each of the indigenous contending factions tried to use Moscow's support to strengthen its own position in Iraq. In the end, the Kremlin's preferred balancing act collapsed, and the USSR was forced to side with the Ba'th despite awareness that Baghdad's eventual triumph would only lessen its dependence on Moscow. Soviet interest in the Kurdish problem had been essentially a tactical matter, while for Baghdad it involved what the Ba'thi government defined as a vital national interest. Thus, the Soviet Union in the long run had no hope of controlling the relevant events, and the Kremlin wound up lamely endorsing Baghdad's imposed solution.

Soviet involvement in this entire episode can be seen as an instance of *protective facilitative influence*, one in which the USSR provided resources to the central government in Baghdad sufficient to prevent Kurdish secession. The major policy initiatives clearly came from Baghdad, and that meant that the Iraqis inevitably exercised primary control over events. The specific benefits which Moscow may have hoped to gain from its involvement in the process are not clear. Indeed, given the details of the situation as well as the mind-set of the ruling circles in the Kremlin at the time, it seems likely that Soviet involvement was but one link in a hoped-for chain called "influence" with which the USSR wished to bind Iraq to itself as a client state in its superpower contest with the United States. The crowning irony in the entire affair is the fact that it was not the actions of either superpower nor even the direct actions of the Iraqi or Kurdish forces which eventually settled the issue. Rather, it was the decision by the shah to cut off support to the rebels as a part of his 1975 rapprochement with Iraq which finally tipped the scales in Baghdad's favor.

With the Kurdish question ostensibly settled, the Ba'th was able to turn after 1975 to the final necessary step in consolidating its internal control over Iraq, the complete subordination of the Iraqi Communist party (chapter 4). In the early years of Soviet patronage the Ba'th did not allow the ICP anything approximating equal status but made a show of moderate power-sharing, and, at one point, even accepted some communist functionaries into the national cabinet. In retrospect, however, it seems clear that the Ba'th always saw these concessions as temporary, tactical expedients only necessary until full national autonomy was gained by the consolidation of power internally and the building of a resource base.

Predictably, the monetary bonanza provided Baghdad by the transformation of the world's oil economy in the mid-1970s, followed by the settlement of the Kurdish question, brought the opportunity for quashing the ICP earlier than the Ba'thi leadership might have anticipated originally. The Ba'th, unwavering in its goal of complete domination over the Iraqi political process, lost little time in following through, executing many members of the ICP. The Kremlin protested vigorously, but, in the final crunch, the Soviets had only two options: they could support their ideological compatriots (probably to no avail) thus alienating the Ba'th or they could swallow hard and leave the members of the Iraqi Communist party to their fate. Having invested so much time and resources in wooing the Ba'th, Moscow made the obvious latter choice.

Thus, in this instance the USSR briefly engaged in the attempt to exercise what was earlier labeled *coercive instigative influence*, but, in the end, the effort was a crushing failure. The equilibrium in Soviet-Iraqi relations had apparently shifted by 1975, so that the extent of the USSR's investment in the relationship, ironically, had become a source of leverage for Iraq. In the case of the ICP, the Kremlin either had to acquiesce in Baghdad's decision or sever the relationship, which it was unwilling to do. The entire episode demonstrated once again the limits of great power influence, especially with respect to the internal affairs of putative clients.

Since the very concept of national sovereignty can be interpreted to entail an inevitable resistance to external efforts to influence domestic political issues, chapters 5 and 6 have dealt separately with Soviet attempts to affect the international affairs of Iraq in two successive periods, through 1975 and after 1975. In other words, one can argue that it is unrealistic to expect many overt signs of one nation's influence in the internal affairs of another state. The international arena, in contrast, can be said to provide the purer cases for the analysis of inter-state influence.

Certainly, the Soviet Union made little secret of its interest in influencing the foreign policy of Iraq during the period under review. Great Britain's 1968 announcement of its intention to withdraw its forces from East of Suez as of late 1971 set the pot to boiling in both Moscow and Washington, as well as in all the capitals of the Gulf region. Russian interest in the Persian Gulf has a long history, but in the face of entrenched British hegemony few policy initiatives had seemed inviting. Be that as it may, the prospect of a full-scale British withdrawal stirred enthusiasm in both Baghdad and Moscow, but the two governments differed substantially from the beginning on the preferred mechanisms needed to assure a continuation of "useful" order and stability in the region.

Although some Western observers have long contended that the Kremlin preferred instability for its own sake, perhaps as a prelude to an overt attempt to occupy the area militarily or at least disrupt oil supplies to the West by means of economic or political domination, the Soviet response to more recent events such as the Iranian revolution and the war between Iraq and Iran make that a highly arguable view. Indeed, the USSR's activities in helping damp down the Iraqi-Kuwaiti conflict in 1973 provide an earlier example suggesting that Moscow understood even then the benefits of keeping Gulf conflicts under control.

From the beginning of the post-British era, Baghdad asserted the need for exclusively intra-regional arrangements to guarantee peace and security in the Gulf. Given their long-standing rivalry with Iran, the Iraqis preferred a regional defense system comprised exclusively of the littoral Arab states. In such a system, by virtue of Iraq's size, population, and other resources, Baghdad was bound to play a dominant role. The Soviet Union would probably have liked simply to replace Great Britain as the external warrantor of regional security but, fully aware of the unacceptability of such an arrangement to both the riparian states and the Western powers, the Kremlin favored a system of regional defense which embraced all of the Gulf countries, including Iran. Moscow's position brought it into a direct conflict with Baghdad which, in the period between 1968 and 1975, refused to accept Iran's participation in any regional defense system. Soviet-Iraqi difficulties were further exacerbated by the Kremlin's attempts to improve relations with the shah. In brief, while the Soviets found the idea of Iranian hegemony in the Gulf virtually as unappetizing as did the Ba'th, they saw Iraqi dominance over the region as equally distasteful. Moreover, Moscow realistically viewed as doomed to failure any effort to exclude Tehran from a stable regional security system. Hence, the Soviet Union was consigned to yet another balancing act on this important issue. It endorsed a regional defense system probably as a way to ensure that the Americans would not simply replace the British as the hegemonistic power in the Persian Gulf, but it disagreed with its Iraqi "clients" about the framework of that system, particularly with respect to the Iranian role.

Another link in the chain of events set into motion by the announcement of the impending British withdrawal from the region also showed how superficial was the bond between "the fraternal peoples of the USSR and Iraq." The two governments disagreed over the formation of a confederation of the small sheikhdoms of the lower Gulf. Initially, the Kremlin was highly suspicious of such an entity, feeling that it would be a de facto Western puppet, while the Ba'th endorsed the idea of another Arab state in the Gulf region. However, Baghdad eventually reversed itself and refused to recognize the United Arab Emirates (UAE) when it was formed in December 1971 because the Ba'th had strenuously objected to the sheikhdoms' tacit acceptance of Iran's occupation of the Gulf islands of Abu Musa and the Tunbs in November of that year.

In contrast, Moscow promptly accorded diplomatic recognition to the United Arab Emirates. The Kremlin apparently felt that the disputed islands were of little significance and did not wish to offend the shah over such a matter. Moreover, most of the other Arab Gulf states were supportive of the new federation and the USSR was in the process of attempting to improve its relations with these countries during this period. Finally, the UAE had rapidly shown itself to be more independent of its Western "sponsors" than the Kremlin had originally feared. Under these circumstances the Soviet Union apparently thought it best to endorse a development that it perceived to be essentially benign and that it could not, in any case, prevent.

From 1968 through 1975, the Kremlin does appear to have successfully exercised some direct influence over one episode in Iraq's foreign affairs (chapter 5). Specifically, in the March 1973 incursion into Kuwaiti territory designed to "reclaim" some border lands over which Iraq had claimed sovereignty, the USSR overtly opposed Baghdad's action and appears to have helped to pressure Iraq into withdrawing its forces.

It is, of course, impossible to disaggregate the specific impact of Soviet pressure in this episode since virtually the entire international community, including a singularly united Arab League, was pushing for an Iraqi withdrawal and an end to the conflict. In this instance, then, while the Soviet Union can be said to have successfully exercised *coercive instigative influence*, it is doubtful whether the Kremlin could have done so without an almost unanimously supportive international community behind it. Moreover, the sense of betrayal felt by the Ba'th over this failure of Russian support for Iraq's first major foreign policy initiative after the signing of the Treaty of Friendship and Cooperation must have been acute. It no doubt engendered mistrust and even bitterness toward the Kremlin among some Ba'thi leaders and impressed upon all of them the undesirability of allowing Iraq to become further dependent on the USSR. Thus, even this brief "success" for Soviet influence left a costly legacy.

Of all the ironies attendant to a relationship which bristles with them, none was more striking than that which confronted the Kremlin in 1975, when, without Soviet advice or intercession, Saddam Hussein negotiated a broad-based rapprochement with the shah. Having preached reconciliation and cooperation between the two for many years, Moscow was suddenly confronted with independently executed acquiescence to its earlier advice. Paradoxically, this particular "success" failed to strengthen the Soviet position (although it did take the USSR temporarily out of the verbal cross fire between Iran and Iraq), for it made a truly regional solution to the Gulf security problem seem feasible at last.

Moscow had for several years endorsed the concept, long favored by Baghdad, of the Gulf as a "zone of peace" (chapter 6). However, upon closer examination it seems clear that the two governments meant quite different things by that term. The Iraqi version envisioned a region from which all the great powers would be excluded militarily and one in which the littoral powers would determine their own fate. In contrast, the preferred Soviet scenario would have accommodated visits by Russian warships to Gulf ports and would have rested on international agreements to which the USSR would have been an important party. The Kremlin was highly suspicious of American intentions in the Persian Gulf and contended that the regional states lacked the resources to thwart a concerted effort by Washington and its allies to dominate the region.

Moreover, Brezhnev and his colleagues also apparently (and correctly) viewed as only temporary the "resolution" of the long-standing conflict between Iraq and Iran. This meant that any exclusively regional solution to the Gulf security problem would have to rest on some sort of external buffering of the seemingly inevitable rivalry between these two contestants for dominance within the region.

In sum, throughout the second half of the 1970s the acknowledged general goals for the Gulf region of Iraq and the Soviet Union were the same, but their real policy objectives were quite different. Thus, the two discreetly ignored their substantive disagreements and gave public lip service to the commonality of their cause. This meant that the leaders of the USSR had come to recognize the severe limits of their influence in Baghdad (especially in light of their impotence in attempting to intervene on behalf of the Iraqi Communist party). Conversely, Saddam

Hussein, given his ambitions in the Gulf and hence his need for ongoing Soviet resupply of his armed forces, saw the utility of maintaining "correct" relations with his patron.

Even this thin veneer of civility crumbled in 1979 with the Soviet invasion of Afghanistan. Repaying the symbolic debt incurred in 1973, when the Kremlin joined the chorus urging Baghdad's withdrawal from Kuwaiti territory, Iraq became one of the early and loudest voices condemning the Soviet military intervention in Afghanistan. Finally, in September 1980, in a conclusive demonstration of the long-term failure of the Kremlin's quest for influence in Iraq, Saddam Hussein, without so much as a perfunctory consultation or even any prior notification to Moscow, staged his invasion of Iran.

His actions produced both shock and dismay in the Kremlin (chapter 7). Indeed, the ensuing months should be seen as the nadir of Soviet-Iraqi relations during the last thirty years. The USSR, in an obvious attempt to keep Saddam Hussein from pressing his initial military advantage, peremptorily cut off all shipments of military supplies to Iraq, even those designed to fulfill existing contracts. While Baghdad may not have expected so dramatic a Soviet response, its planners had apparently stockpiled sufficient war matériel to continue the hostilities for at least a year. Eventually, however, when the expected Iranian collapse did not occur, those supplies began to dwindle and the tide of battle began to turn in favor of Tehran.

At that point, Brezhnev faced another dilemma. His interim efforts at currying favor with Khomeini had enjoyed virtually no success; Tehran continued its hard-line anticommunist and anti-Soviet rhetoric, its persecution of the Tudeh, and its support of the Afghan *mujahideen*. Thus, the prospect of an Iranian military victory over Iraq was totally unacceptable to the Soviet leaders. At the same time, Saddam Hussein had proven himself a singularly unreliable ally. Choosing the lesser of two evils, the Kremlin grudgingly resumed its shipments of military equipment and supplies to Baghdad on a scale designed to forestall a conclusive victory by either side. One can only wonder whether Soviet analysts imagined that the ensuing stalemate would last for six long years.

Indeed, the Scud-B missiles used in the rocket attacks on Iranian cities—which finally led to Khomeini's acceptance of the necessity to drink metaphorical poison and, thus, to the end of military hostilities—were provided by the Soviet Union (whatever its role in modifying the missiles' range). Therefore, the only important tangible forms of influence successfully exercised throughout the wartime period by the

USSR were the two we have labeled *facilitative*, at first *protective* (to prevent an Iraqi defeat in 1982) and later *constructive* (to induce an Iranian agreement for a cease-fire in 1988). In no instance was the Kremlin able successfully to exert direct *instigative* influence over either Iraq or Iran.

Viewed over time, the Soviet-Iraqi relationship represents a fine exemplar of the inherent instability of such relations and, thus, of the processes which we earlier (following Emerson) called "balancing operations." Indeed, all the ways and means alluded to in the Introduction eventually became part of the unfolding dynamic. For example, the revolutionary changes in the world oil market serendipitously reduced Baghdad's economic dependence on the Kremlin in the mid-1970s and gave it independent access to other suppliers. Thus, the exclusivity of crucial resource control by the USSR diminished dramatically.

A second although later example of such a balancing operation is evident in Baghdad's actions during the long war with Iran. In retrospect, it seems clear that Saddam Hussein massively miscalculated the impact of postrevolutionary internal upheaval on the Iranian will to resist Iraqi aggression. He apparently assumed that the disarray in Tehran would permit him to achieve such a swift and decisive military victory that Khomeini would have to sue for peace on terms that would satisfy Iraq's long-standing territorial ambitions in the Gulf. As the war unfolded and it became evident that a quick victory was unattainable and that the USSR was unwilling, even after the resumption of military shipments to Iraq, to supply Saddam Hussein with the level and kind of military assistance necessary to achieve a conclusive victory, he prudently scaled down his original objective. In the end, he contented himself with a settlement which allowed Iraq to emerge essentially intact in its prewar territorial form.

Even in the prewar era, especially after the signing of the Treaty of Friendship and Cooperation, the Kremlin had begun to experience the ultimate irony of the shifting balance in the natural history of such relationships. Specifically, as time passed and various Iraqi "needs" were met, Soviet leverage inevitably declined; Moscow was caught in what we earlier called the "dialectical contradiction" of the influence-seeking process, one in which success breeds failure. Concomitantly, the Kremlin leaders' own sense of a vested interest in maintaining the relationship (in order to justify the history of their expenditures to their constituents and themselves) increased. Even the disruption in the relationship induced by the Iraqi attack on Iran was not allowed to completely rupture Moscow's ties to Baghdad. Given this relative Soviet constancy in nurturing their relationship with Iraq despite periodic provocations, it seems reasonable to examine objectively what kind of return the Kremlin leaders have earned on their investment.

Militarily, the Moscow-Baghdad relationship has failed to produce the sorts of tangible benefits (e.g., bases or dependable access to resupply or repair facilities) to which Soviet military planners no doubt originally aspired. Moreover, although it is hard to wean strategic analysts from their traditional assumptions, the circumstances of the nuclear age should cause them to assign a very low priority to the acquisition of buffer states, especially when they are likely to prove so unreliable as allies as has modern Iraq.

Economically, Soviet returns might be most accurately described as rapidly diminishing. That is, while Baghdad has been a sizeable cash-paying customer for some Soviet goods since the mid-seventies, it has exhibited a growing preference for Western goods when the relevant items were available in both Eastern and Western markets and a declining patience with the shoddiness of many Soviet Bloc products. Only in the purchase of military parts and supplies, constrained as such purchases are by the nature of one's original equipment, has the Soviet source remained dominant. Even that balance has shifted some more since the USSR's cutoff of military shipments from 1980 through 1982.

Politically, since the sixties, the Iraqis more commonly sided with the Soviet Union than with the United States and its allies in international disputes, both formally (e.g., in the United Nations) and informally (e.g., in the content disseminated by its propaganda organs), but so have most of the other former colonial territories that gained their independence in the post-World War II era. In other words, Iraq is a natural constituent of the bloc of Third World nations with which the USSR has generally aligned itself by dint of its litany of anticolonial, anti-imperialist rhetoric. Thus, it seems likely that many of the political benefits ostensibly gained by the Soviet investment in Iraq would have accrued to the Kremlin as a result of larger international forces and processes without such extensive direct involvement. Despite the substantial magnitude of that investment, Baghdad has always maintained its right to express its opinions independently in the international arena, as its leading role in the chorus of condemnation of the Russian invasion of Afghanistan so amply demonstrated.

In sum, whether providing Iraq with some of the means required to make it yet another thorn in the side of the Western powers has been worth the resource expenditures undertaken seems highly unlikely since Baghdad would almost certainly have played that role in due course anyway with much more restrained Soviet support. Certainly, the direct benefits to Moscow have been few and far between. In the final analysis, it is often unclear just who is the knight and who is the pawn in any given episode.

Two additional questions implicit in the analytical framework established in the Introduction remain: (1) to what extent and/or in what way may the Soviet-Iraqi relationship be a generalizable exemplar of the nature of influence relationships between great and lesser powers; and (2) what major lessons can be learned from this specific example?

First, it is important to acknowledge one important constraint on the generalizability of insights gained from this analysis of the Soviet-Iraqi relationship to other great-lesser power linkages. Specifically, anyone familiar with diverse examples of such relations can readily see the significance of the presence or absence of a credible threat of the use of military force by the great power to enforce its preferred policies on the lesser power. The first implicit priority of any government is the protection of whatever autonomy it enjoys. Therefore, those governments which must operate under the cloud of potential military interventions must act differently with respect to the wishes of those who control that military power from those governments that have no such threat hanging over them.

Iraq, in the period under discussion, has enjoyed a freedom of action not characteristic of nations operating under such a threat. Although Iraq lies not far from the Soviet border, the Kremlin has long known that it could not count on Western acquiescence to any attempt to impose its will on Iraq by military means. The strategic importance of Middle Eastern oil and Western sensitivity to any Soviet action that would threaten the flow of that oil have made any direct Russian military intervention in the area far too risky. The Iraqis fully understand this fact, and the Ba'th has used it to full advantage. Thus, any lessons to be drawn from the Moscow-Baghdad relationship can only be applied to other similarly noninterventionist situations.

Second, the main theme which emerges from a summary assessment of the case studies comprising the bulk of this volume is the long-term failure or the transitoriness of any apparent successes by the USSR in its efforts to achieve what we have called *instigative* influence. Indeed, in the only instance when Baghdad clearly changed its course of action in the direction being urged by Moscow—the withdrawal of its troops from Kuwaiti territory in 1973—Soviet pressure was bolstered by similar calls for action by a united Arab League and most of the rest of the nations of the world. It seems doubtful that solitary Soviet pressure would have achieved the same result.

It appears, then, that inter-state relations of the type exemplified by the modern Soviet-Iraqi relationship (i.e., the relationship between a great and lesser power, absent the credible threat of the direct use of military force by the great power) will inevitably be affected by idiosyncratic factors, both historical and contextual. However, the primary lesson to be drawn is that the quest by great powers for influence over less powerful states will be most fruitful when it focuses upon the search for areas of mutual interest or upon the effort to convince putative clients of the mutual benefits of courses of action desired by the patron state. Any great power that undertakes the cultivation of such a relationship with more grandiose expectations is likely to be sadly disappointed.

■ Notes

Introduction

1. See Alvin Z. Rubinstein, ed., *Soviet and Chinese Influence in the Third World* (New York: Praeger, 1975), *Red Star on the Nile: The Soviet-Egyptian Influence Relationship since the June War* (Princeton: Princeton University Press, 1977), and *Soviet Policy Toward Turkey, Iran, and Afghanistan: The Dynamics of Influence* (New York: Praeger, 1982).

2. Rubinstein, *Soviet and Chinese Influence in the Third World*, p. 10; see also Rubinstein, *Red Star*, p. xiv, emphasis added.

3. Center for Defense Information, Washington, D.C., "Soviet Geopolitical Momentum: Myth or Menace? Trends of Soviet Influence Around the World From 1945 to 1986," *Defense Monitor* 15, no. 5 (1986): 2. The principal analysts were David T. Johnson and Stephen D. Goose.

4. Richard M. Emerson, "Power-Dependence Relations," *American Sociological Review* 27 (February 1962): 31–41.

5. Emerson, "Power-Dependence Relations," p. 32.

6. For the enumeration of the kinds of balancing or cost-reduction processes which flow from such unstable situations we are indebted to Emerson; the specific applications to international relations are those of the authors.

7. See the discussion of perceived and objective national interests in Bettie Smolansky, Oles M. Smolansky, and George Ginsburgs, "A National-Interest Framework: The United States and the Soviet Union in the Eastern Mediterranean," in Carl F. Pinkele and Adamantia Pollis, eds., *The Contemporary Mediterranean World* (New York: Praeger, 1983), pp. 3–16.

8. Center for Defense Information, "Soviet Geopolitical Momentum," p. 2.

9. The negative case is generally easier to see than the positive. Thus, a declining presence probably does signal a decline in influence although it is difficult for the external observer to know whether the decline has been voluntarily effected by the patron because the latter perceives itself to be wasting its efforts or has been precipitated by a client's request for some retrenchment. Ironically, successful influence building is often too subtle for ready measurement.

10. Rubinstein, *Red Star*, p. xvii.

11. Ibid., p. xxii.

12 The relationship with Syria since the late fifties has also required the Kremlin to travel a rocky road. The Soviet-Syrian connection is thus another great-lesser power influence relationship deserving a separate full-scale analysis.

13 For the sake of simplicity, the Persian/Arabian Gulf will herein be referred to as the Persian Gulf.

1 Soviet-Iraqi Relations, 1958–80

1 See Majid Khadduri, *Independent Iraq, 1932–1958: A Study in Iraqi Politics* (London: Oxford University Press, 1960), p. 252, and Ivison Macadam, ed., *The Annual Register of World Events, 1955* (cited hereinafter as *AR*) (London: Longmans, Green, 1956), p. 293.

2 See Oles M. Smolansky, *The Soviet Union and the Arab East Under Khrushchev* (Lewisburg, Pa.: Bucknell University Press, 1974), ch. 5.

3 Smolansky, *The Soviet Union*, pp. 119–20, 157.

4 Ibid., pp. 157–73. For a thorough discussion of the confrontation between Kassem and the Iraqi Communist party, see Uriel Dann, *Iraq Under Qassem: A Political History, 1958–1963* (Jerusalem: Israel Universities Press, 1969), chs. 8–9, 14–18, and 21.

5 For details, see Smolansky, *The Soviet Union*, pp. 173–74, 185–86.

6 For background on the Iraqi Ba'th, see R. D. McLaurin, Don Peretz, and Lewis W. Snider, *Middle East Foreign Policy: Issues and Processes* (New York: Praeger, 1982), pp. 89–95; Edmund Ghareeb, "Iraq: Emergent Gulf Power," in Hossein Amirsadeghi, ed., *The Security of the Persian Gulf* (New York: St. Martin's Press, 1981), pp. 201–3; and Phebe Marr, *The Modern History of Iraq* (Boulder: Westview Press, 1985), pp. 184–90, 206–8.

7 For some details, see Smolansky, *The Soviet Union*, pp. 227–40.

8 Details in Majid Khadduri, *Socialist Iraq: A Study in Iraqi Politics since 1968* (Washington, D.C.: Middle East Institute, 1978), pp. 144–45.

9 Text in Khadduri, *Socialist Iraq.*, pp. 241–43.

10 Roger F. Pajak, "Soviet Military Aid to Iraq and Syria," *Strategic Review* 4 (Winter 1976): 52.

11 Pajak, "Soviet Military Aid," p. 53. According to *The Military Balance, 1975–1976* (London: International Institute for Strategic Studies, 1976), p. 90, the Soviets initially agreed to deliver forty MIG-23s.

12 *Arab Report and Record* (London, cited hereinafter as *ARR*), 1972, p. 426; *AR*, 1973, p. 216; for some details of Soviet-Iraqi economic relations before 1972, see pp. 47–48.

13 As quoted by Juan de Onis, *New York Times*, March 19, 1975.

14 "Uncle Sam and Ivan in Iraq," ibid., April 2, 1975.

15 Edith Penrose and E. F. Penrose, *Iraq: International Relations and National Development* (Boulder: Westview Press, 1978), p. 434.

16 See Marshall I. Goldmann, *New York Times*, January 20, 1975.

17 *Arab World* (Beirut), October 12, 1974, as quoted in *ARR*, 1974, p. 424.

18 Goldmann, *New York Times*.

19 An accusation made by the New China News Agency on December 23, 1973, and picked up, among others, by Kuwait's *al-Rai al-Amm*, as quoted in *ARR*, 1973, p. 581.

20 Goldmann, *New York Times*.

21   *ARR*, 1974, p. 424.
22   Ibid., 1974, pp. 104, 195, 218.
23   Ibid., 1974, p. 481; for some details, see *Pravda*, November 6, 1974, March 5, 1975.
24   *ARR*, 1972, p. 426; 1973, p. 155; 1974, p. 347; 1975, p. 336.
25   Ibid., 1972, pp. 426, 531; 1975, pp. 76, 336. See B. Orekhov, *Pravda*, January 9, 1973, on Lake Tharthar canal; ibid., August 31, 1973, on the Euphrates irrigation system.
26   *ARR*, 1972, p. 426.
27   Ibid., 1974, pp. 251, 512–13; 1975, p. 336.
28   Ibid., 1972, p. 426; 1974, pp. 171, 512.
29   Ibid., 1975, p. 497.
30   Ibid., 1973, p. 295.
31   Ibid., 1975, p. 360.
32   Ibid., pp. 192, 336.
33   Ministerstvo vneshnei torgovli, *Vneshniaia torgovlia SSSR v 1976 g.* (Moscow: Statistika, 1977), p. 228.
34   *ARR*, 1975, pp. 108, 520.
35   *Vneshniaia torgovlia SSSR v 1976 g.*, pp. 225, 228.
36   *ARR*, 1975, p. 386.
37   Ibid., 1972, pp. 278, 303.
38   Ibid., pp. 303, 111.
39   For some details, see p. 50 of this volume.
40   Over the next two years additional oil purchase contracts were signed with Spain (*ARR*, 1973, p. 6), India (ibid., p. 366; 1974, p. 103), Brazil (ibid., 1973, p. 509), and Portugal (ibid., 1974, p. 512).
41   Ibid., 1973, pp. 411, 449–50.
42   The decision to build a pipeline through Turkey was prompted by the desire to avoid the possibility of the closure of the outlets in Syria and Lebanon due to periodic difficulties in Baghdad's relations with Damascus.
43   Ibid., 1975, p. 42; 1974, p. 544.
44   It was to be repaid by 100 million tons of petroleum over a ten-year period beginning in 1976 and 30 million tons of liquified gas over a fifteen-year period. Ibid., 1973, p. 389.
45   Repayment was in 160 million tons of crude, to be supplied over a ten-year period. Ibid., 1974, p. 347.
46   Ibid., 1975, p. 526.
47   Ibid., 1974, p. 298.
48   Ibid., 1973, p. 156. The import program was affected by the drop of Iraq's oil production from 84 million metric tons in 1971 to 70.2 million metric tons in 1972. The comparable figure for 1969 was 74.7 million metric tons and, for 1973, 93.2 million. Ibid., 1974, p. 512.
49   Ibid., 1973, p. 156.
50   *AR*, 1974, p. 218.
51   For details, see *ARR*, 1974, pp. 82, 369, 424, 481, 544; ibid., 1975, p. 108.
52   Ibid., p. 164; the agreement was signed in November 1975, for details, see ibid., pp. 496, 631.
53   Ibid., p. 496.
54   Juan de Onis, *New York Times*, March 19, 1975.

55 Francis Fukuyama, *The Soviet Union and Iraq Since 1968* (Santa Monica: Rand Corporation, 1980), p. 46.

56 As quoted in *ARR*, 1977, p. 675. For more details, see J. M. Abdulghani, *Iraq and Iran: The Years of Crisis* (Baltimore: Johns Hopkins University Press, 1984), pp. 162–63. Iraq's hostility to Ethiopia was prompted by Addis Ababa's close ties to Israel.

57 Bill Lee, "The Crunch in Eritrea," *ARR*, 1978, p. 535; John K. Cooley, "Conflict Within the Iraqi Left," *Problems of Communism* 29 (January–February 1980): 89. See, in particular, Saddam Hussein's interview with Arnaud de Borchgrave, *Newsweek*, July 17, 1978, p. 50.

58 As quoted in *New York Times*, May 27, 1978.

59 See pp. 202–3 of this volume. For background and details, see Stephen Page, *The Soviet Union and the Yemens: Influence in Asymmetrical Relationships* (New York: Praeger, 1985), chs. 3, 4, and 7. See also Anthony H. Cordesman, *The Gulf and the Search for Strategic Stability: Saudi Arabia, the Military Balance in the Gulf, and Trends in the Arab-Israeli Military Balance* (Boulder: Westview Press, 1984), pp. 446–49, and Mark N. Katz, *Russia and Arabia: Soviet Foreign Policy toward the Arabian Peninsula* (Baltimore: Johns Hopkins University Press, 1986), pp. 90–93.

60 As quoted in *ARR*, 1978, p. 403.

61 *The Military Balance, 1977–1978*, p. 97.

62 Ibid., *1978–1979*, p. 105. At that time the IL-76 aircraft had not been made available not only to other Third World clients but also, according to U.S. intelligence sources, to such East European satellites as Poland and Czechoslovakia. *ARR*, 1977, p. 973.

63 *The Military Balance, 1980–1981*, p. 102. All systems were scheduled for 1979–1980 delivery.

64 U.S. Arms Control and Disarmament Agency, *World Military Expenditures and Arms Transfers, 1963–1973* (Washington, D.C.: U.S. Government Printing Office, 1975), pp. 67–71.

65 Ibid., p. 70.

66 *World Military Expenditures, 1969–1978*, p. 160.

67 See *SIPRI Yearbook, 1975* (Cambridge: MIT Press, 1975), p. 23, and *Military Aviation News*, September 1974, p. 16, both quoted by Pajak, "Soviet Military Aid," p. 54; *The Military Balance, 1975–1976*, p. 90.

68 *The Military Balance, 1977–1978*, p. 97, *1978–1979*, p. 105.

69 See ibid., *1979–1980*, p. 104, *1980–1981*, p. 102.

70 See *Arab Report* (London), May 23, 1979, p. 22; *AR*, 1979, p. 194.

71 *New York Times*, January 5, 1980; 1981 was listed as the scheduled delivery date, *The Military Balance, 1980–1981*, p. 102.

72 Pajak, "Soviet Military Aid," p. 54. To support this contention, he cited a statement by Saddam Hussein to the effect that "If national conditions dictate that we should diversify in this field, we shall do so. . . . We have a free will." *Washington Post*, April 25, 1975.

73 For some details, including the 1973 $2,000 million deal between Iran and the United States, see *SIPRI, The Arms Trade with the Third World* (New York: Holmes and Meier, 1975), pp. 221–23.

74 During his December 1978 visit to Moscow, Saddam Hussein was in fact reported to have expressed dissatisfaction with Soviet arms supplies. See *AR*, 1978, p. 185. There had been precedents among the Arab states for breaking excessive dependence on

Soviet military supplies and turning to France in search of military assistance. Both steps had been taken by Algeria in the late 1960s. See SIPRI, *The Arms Trade*, p. 226.

75 *New York Times*, January 27, 1980.

76 The above information is based on *The Military Balance, 1980–1981*, p. 43.

77 Ibid., pp. 43, 42.

78 International Monetary Fund (IMF), *Direction of Trade Yearbook, 1980* (Washington, D.C.: International Monetary Fund, 1980), p. 208.

79 Ihsan A. Hijazi, *New York Times*, June 11, 1978.

80 *ARR*, 1976, pp. 507–8, 595, 627; *Pravda*, January 3, 1976.

81 Ibid., August 26, 1976; *ARR*, 1976, p. 723.

82 Ibid., p. 113; 1977, p. 722.

83 Ibid., 1976, pp. 215–16; 1977, p. 77.

84 Ibid., 1978, p. 882.

85 Figures compiled from table 3.

2 Nationalization of the Oil Industry

1 See table 3 in Michael E. Brown, "The Nationalization of the Iraqi Petroleum Company," *International Journal of Middle East Studies* 10 (February 1979): 114.

2 Fear of a Western boycott of the Iraqi oil and lack of technical and managerial expertise precluded outright nationalization of the IPC in 1961. Brown, "The Nationalization of the Iraqi Petroleum Company," p. 109; for background and details, see ibid., pp. 107–9; Majid Khadduri, *Republican 'Iraq: A Study in 'Iraqi Politics Since the Revolution of 1958* (London: Oxford University Press, 1969), pp. 160–66; Edith Penrose and E. F. Penrose, *Iraq: International Relations and National Development* (Boulder: Westview Press, 1978), pp. 257–69.

3 Penrose and Penrose, *Iraq*, p. 269.

4 The Iraq National Oil Company (INOC) was formed in 1964. For details, see Khadduri, *Republican 'Iraq*, p. 291, and Ivison Macadam, ed., *The Annual Register of World Events, 1964* (cited hereinafter as *AR*) (New York: St. Martin's Press, 1965), p. 306.

5 Ibid., 1967, p. 297.

6 *Arab Report and Record* (London, cited hereinafter as ARR), 1968, p. 3.

7 Khadduri, *Republican 'Iraq*, p. 293.

8 *ARR*, 1968, p. 32; Penrose and Penrose, *Iraq*, pp. 424–26. For a discussion of subsequent difficulties between Baghdad and ERAP, see ibid., pp. 431–33. Abd al-Rahman Aref succeeded his brother, Abd al-Salam Aref, who was killed in a helicopter crash on April 13, 1966.

9 *AR*, 1967, p. 298; *ARR*, 1967, p. 387. See also ibid., 1969, p. 257. For some details, see Penrose and Penrose, *Iraq*, pp. 426–27, and O. Gerasimov, *Irakskaia neft'* (Moscow: Nauka, 1969), pp. 160–65.

10 *ARR*, 1968, p. 88; Khadduri, *Republican 'Iraq*, pp. 293–94.

11 Ibid., p. 294; for more details on the French and Soviet deals, see Penrose and Penrose, *Iraq*, pp. 394–97, 423–27.

12 R. Andreasyan, "New Aspects of Middle East Countries' Oil Policy," *International Affairs*, no. 9 (September 1968): 28, 29.

13 Andreasyan, "New Aspects," p. 28.

14 Ibid., p. 29.

15 R. Andreasyan and D. Penzin, "Oil and the Anti-Imperialist Struggle," *International Affairs*, no. 8 (August 1971): 55.

16 Andreasyan, "New Aspects," p. 29.

17 Ibid.

18 The existence of "independent" Western companies (among them Italian, French, Japanese, and West German) and their determination to outbid the Seven Sisters (the major Western oil companies) to capture a share of the Middle Eastern oil market was cited as another factor enabling the producers "to overcome the resistance of the cartel" to their assertive policies. Andreasyan and Penzin, "Oil and the Anti-Imperialist Struggle," p. 55.

19 Andreasyan, "New Aspects," p. 30.

20 Ibid., p. 31; Andreasyan and Penzin, "Oil and the Anti-Imperialist Struggle," pp. 55–56.

21 Andreasyan, "New Aspects," pp. 31, 30.

22 Ibid., p. 31; Andreasyan and Penzin, "Oil and the Anti-Imperialist Struggle," p. 56.

23 Andreasyan, "New Aspects," p. 32.

24 Ibid., p. 33.

25 Gerasimov, *Irakskaia neft'*, p. 90.

26 Ibid., p. 91. For a detailed discussion of the situation preceding the passage of Law 80, see R. N. Andreasian and A. Ia. El'ianov, *Blizhnii Vostok: neft' i nezavisimost'* (Moscow: Izdatel'stvo vostochnoi literatury, 1961), pp. 246–56.

27 Gerasimov, *Irakskaia neft'*, p. 93. For more details on Law 80, see S. A. Losoev and Iu. K. Tyssovskii, *Blizhnevostochnyi krizis: neft' i politika* (Moscow: Mezhdunarodnye otnosheniia, 1980), pp. 44–46.

28 Dmitry Volsky, "Iraqi Oil," *New Times*, no. 2 (January 14, 1968): 19. For a discussion of the government's negotiations with the IPC in the period between 1963 and 1965 and 1965 and 1967, see Gerasimov, *Irakskaia neft'*, pp. 109–27, 133–45. For the impact of the 1967 war, see ibid., pp. 145–48.

29 Ibid., pp. 148–52.

30 Ibid., pp. 152–53.

31 Ibid., pp. 154–55.

32 See p. 38 of this volume.

33 Volsky, "Iraqi Oil," p. 19. For more details, see Gerasimov, *Irakskaia neft'*, pp. 155–60; and Losoev and Tyssovskii, *Blizhnevostochnyi krizis*, pp. 46–48. The ERAP agreement was criticized by the Iraqi Communist party on the ground that the exploitation of the country's oil resources should be conducted by INOC "with the broad technical and financial assistance of the countries of the socialist camp." Gerasimov, *Irakskaia neft'*, p. 164.

34 December 28, 1967, as quoted by Andreasyan, "New Aspects," p. 33, n. 18.

35 Volsky, "Iraqi Oil," p. 20. See also L. Medvedko, *Pravda*, January 24, 1968.

36 K. Vishnevetskii, ibid., February 4, 1968.

37 I. Pogodina, ibid., April 13, 1968.

38 ARR, 1968, p. 204.

39 Ibid., p. 324; see also President Ahmad Hasan al-Bakr's speech opening the seventeenth conference of OPEC, p. 349.

40 Majid Khadduri, *Socialist Iraq: A Study in Iraqi Politics since 1968* (Washington, D.C.: Middle East Institute, 1978), p. 125. These points were made, among others, by Bakr and Vice-President Salih Mahdi Ammash in July 1970. ARR, 1970, pp. 410, 382.

41 Ammash threatened the withdrawal of concessions (ibid., p. 381), while Bakr hinted darkly that "the revolutionary government will spare no effort to obtain Iraqi rights . . . and will brook no temporising tactics to avoid restitution of these rights" (ibid., p. 410). See also editorial in *al-Thawrah*, November 24, 1970, warning the oil companies to expect "a battle" if they refused the government's demands; and the government statement of January 27, 1971, as quoted in *ARR*, 1971, p. 56.

42 Ibid., 1970, p. 579.

43 For details of OPEC's negotiations with the Western oil companies, see Penrose and Penrose, *Iraq*, pp. 383–87.

44 Khadduri, *Socialist Iraq*, p. 125.

45 *ARR*, 1971, p. 288.

46 *Financial Times* (London), April 30, 1971. For Iraqi reaction, see the statement by Oil Minister Sa'dun Hammadi, as quoted in *ARR*, 1971, p. 165, and editorial in *al-Thawrah*, April 29, 1971.

47 *Al-Kifah* (Beirut), July 23, 1970, as quoted in *ARR*, 1970, p. 411. "The original concession to the IPC in 1925 contained a clause allowing up to 20 percent Iraqi participation in the company if it ever made a public issue of [its] shares. So far it has not done this." Ibid., 1971, p. 288.

48 Ibid., 1972, p. 139.

49 Ibid., pp. 111, 179.

50 See ibid., p. 232, for the Iraqi government's statement of May 14, 1972.

51 Ibid., p. 253; Brown, "The Nationalization of the Iraqi Petroleum Company," pp. 111–12.

52 For more details, see Khadduri, *Socialist Iraq*, pp. 126–27.

53 As quoted in *ARR*, 1971, p. 261.

54 The North Rumailah deal "was part of a general Soviet aid agreement which included assistance to the Euphrates Dam project and the recently formed National Minerals Company," ibid., 1969, pp. 280. For details, see p. 256.

55 Ibid., 1970, p. 442.

56 Ibid., pp. 470, 550; 1971, pp. 108, 261, 321.

57 These two projects were part of a major agreement, reached in April 1971. The USSR lent Iraq 200 million rubles (£92 million) to help finance the construction of the projects as well as of "two hydroelectric power stations in northern Iraq, a phosphates mine and a fertilizer plant." See ibid., 1971, p. 188. For supplementary agreements, signed in May and June 1971, see ibid., pp. 261, 321. The agreement on the Mosul refinery was finalized during Premier Kosygin's April 1972 visit to Iraq. See ibid., 1972, pp. 179, 207.

58 Baghdad Radio, January 8, 1972.

59 *ARR*, 1970, pp. 293, 608; 1971, p. 322.

60 *Financial Times*, November 25, 1969. See also L. Z. Zevin, *Economic Cooperation of Socialist and Developing Countries: New Trends* (Moscow: Nauka, 1976), pp. 148–49.

61 The protocol was signed in late 1969 and the agreement in April 1970. See *ARR*, 1969, p. 508; and 1970, p. 206. For agreement on repayment in Iraqi crude, see ibid., pp. 516–17.

62 Ibid., 1969, p. 533; 1971, p. 137.

63 For agreements with Hungary, see ibid., 1969, p. 432, and *AR*, 1971, p. 209; with Bulgaria, *ARR*, 1970, pp. 550, 686; ibid., 1971, p. 600; ibid., 1972, p. 179; with

Rumania, ibid., 1971, p. 552; 1972, p. 55; East Germany, ibid., pp. 55, 207; with Yugoslavia, ibid., p. 207. For additional information on Iraq's economic relations with Poland, see ibid., 1970, p. 145; 1972, p. 7; with Hungary, ibid., pp. 238, 292; with Czechoslovakia, ibid., 1972, p. 111; with North Korea, ibid., 1971, p. 553. Moreover, in 1972, Iraq and the PRC signed a trade agreement which provided for the purchase of Iraqi sulphur by Beijing. See ibid., 1972, p. 7. For a summary of oil-related projects between Iraq and the states of Eastern Europe, see Zevin, *Economic Cooperation*, pp. 144–45, 156.

64 *ARR*, 1970, p. 116.

65 Ibid., 1972, pp. 178–79, 209.

66 Ibid., 1970, pp. 292, 383.

67 Although, in February 1971, ERAP agreed to relinquish 65 percent of the concessionary area negotiated in 1968, negotiations continued and were reported to have "reached a state of complete deadlock" in November. Ibid., 1971, pp. 84, 600.

68 Ibid., 1970, p. 292. For more details, see ibid., p. 354, and 1971, p. 261.

69 Ibid., 1970, p. 634; 1972, p. 111.

70 Ibid., 1971, p. 648.

71 Iraq was a founding member of OPEC, formed in September 1960, Penrose and Penrose, *Iraq*, p. 259. OAPEC was founded by Saudi Arabia, Kuwait, and Libya in 1968. Iraq was admitted in late 1971, although formal acceptance was delayed until March 4, 1972. *ARR*, 1971, p. 625; 1972, p. 111.

72 Ibid., p. 278. For details of Iraq's diplomatic efforts in OPEC and OAPEC, see Penrose and Penrose, pp. 398–412.

73 The government's concern is illustrated by the following figures: in November 1970, the State Planning Council had allocated ID 45 million to enable INOC to finance its 1970 through 1974 development plan. In February 1971 this amount was increased to ID 70 million, and in December 1971, the RCC approved the allocation of additional ID 489 million for the implementation of INOC's investment program over a ten-year period. See *ARR*, 1970, p. 608; 1971, pp. 84, 648.

74 Khadduri, *Socialist Iraq*, p. 127. For details, see *ARR*, 1972, p. 303.

75 Khadduri, *Socialist Iraq*, p. 127. See also Penrose and Penrose, *Iraq*, p. 411.

76 For details, see Khadduri, *Socialist Iraq*, pp. 127–28; *AR*, 1973, p. 216; *ARR*, 1973, pp. 82–83; Penrose and Penrose, *Iraq*, p. 414.

77 *Official Gazette* (Baghdad), October 21, 1973, as quoted by Khadduri, *Socialist Iraq*, p. 128; see also *ARR*, 1973, pp. 449, 492, 580.

78 *New York Times*, December 9, 1975. Text of the law in the *Official Gazette*, December 8, 1975, as quoted in Khadduri, *Socialist Iraq*, p. 128.

79 Text of the joint communiqué in *Pravda*, July 6, 1969. See also A. Usvatov, "North Rumaila Oil," *New Times*, no. 17 (April 1972): 27, and Zevin, *Economic Cooperation*, p. 144.

80 B. Rachkov, *Izvestiia*, July 12, 1969.

81 Evgenii Primakov, *Pravda*, September 21, 1969.

82 B. Rachkov, *Izvestiia*, July 12, 1969.

83 *Pravda*, November 5, 1971.

84 For details, see R. Petrov, ibid., July 14, 1971.

85 See the text of the joint communiqué in ibid., August 13, 1970.

86 Ibid., February 12, 1972.

87 Khadduri, *Socialist Iraq*, p. 126.

88 Text in *Pravda*, February 18, 1972.

89 Usvatov, "North Rumaila Oil," p. 26.

90 Ibid., p. 27; R. Petrov, *Pravda*, April 5, 1972.

91 As quoted in Usvatov, "North Rumaila Oil," p. 27.

92 Text in *Pravda*, April 11, 1972.

93 A. Vasil'ev, ibid., March 27, 1970.

94 I. Pogodina, ibid., October 31, 1970.

95 B. Rachkov, "The Future of Arab Oil," *International Affairs*, no. 8 (August 1970): 37.

96 "Ultimatum to Oil Monopolies," *New Times*, no. 22 (May 1972): 9, 11. For a detailed analysis of events leading to the nationalization, see D. Penzin, "Oil and Independence," *International Affairs*, no. 10 (October 1972): 34–35.

97 I. Pogodina, *Pravda*, May 24, 1972.

98 Text in ibid., June 8, 1972.

99 "A Blow at Oil Monopolies," *New Times*, no. 24 (June 1972): 17; B. Orekhov and A. Matiushin, *Pravda*, June 3, 1972.

100 P. Demchenko, ibid., June 4, 1972; see also his articles, ibid., July 14, 1972, and "Arab Oil for the Arabs," *New Times*, no. 25 (June 1972): 10–11; B. Orekhov, *Pravda*, June 18, 1972.

101 Penzin, "Oil and Independence," p. 34. On this point, see also P. Demchenko, "Arab Oil for the Arabs," *New Times*, no. 25 (June 1972), p. 10; V. Nekrasov and B. Orekhov, *Pravda*, November 14, 1972; E. Primakov, ibid., March 10, 1973.

102 Penzin, "Oil and Independence," p. 34.

103 Ibid., pp. 34, 36.

104 V. Nekrasov and B. Orekhov, *Pravda*, November 14, 1972.

105 See B. Orekhov and G. Marunin, ibid., January 1, 1973; E. Primakov, March 10, 1973.

106 Penzin, "Oil and Independence," pp. 36–37. For additional comments, see *Pravda*, June 20, 1972; *Izvestiia*, June 21, 1972; "France and Iraqi Oil," *New Times*, no. 26 (June 1972): 9; and B. Orekhov and G. Marunin, *Pravda*, January 1, 1973.

107 Penzin, "Oil and Independence," pp. 37, 36.

108 B. Orekhov and A. Matiushin, *Pravda*, July 12, 1972. See also P. Demchenko, ibid., July 14, 1972; Yuri Kornilov, "Iraq's Progress," *New Times*, no. 38 (September 1972): 25; and B. Orekhov and G. Marunin, *Pravda*, January 1, 1973.

109 "A Blow at Oil Monopolies," *New Times*, no. 24 (June 1972): 17. See also P. Demchenko, "Arab Oil for the Arabs," ibid., no. 25 (June 1972): 11.

110 B. Orekhov and A. Matiushin, *Pravda*, June 4, 1972.

111 See, for example, Kosygin's message to the International Conference of Solidarity with the Iraqi People, held in Baghdad in mid-August 1972, as quoted by D. Volsky, "Iraq's Battle for Her Oil," *New Times*, no. 35 (August 1972): 8. Similar sentiments were expressed in the joint communiqué, following President Bakr's visit to the USSR. Text in *Pravda*, September 20, 1972. For a subsequent evaluation, see Losoev and Tyssovskii, *Blizhnevostochnyi krizis*, p. 48.

112 I. Pogodina, *Pravda*, October 30, 1972.

113 "Iraq Wins Battle of Oil," *New Times*, no. 10 (March 1973): 7; B. Orekhov, *Pravda*, March 5, 1973.

114 E. Primakov, ibid., March 10, 1973; Ruben Andreasyan, "The Energy Crisis and Mid-East Oil," *New Times*, no. 16 (April 1973): 23–26.

115 Text in *Pravda*, March 23, 1973. See also B. Orekhov and G. Marunin, ibid., April 9,

1973; "Soviet-Iraqi Friendship," *New Times,* no. 15 (April 1973): 16–17; and E. Primakov, *Pravda,* July 12, 1973.

116 Ibid., March 23, 1973.

117 Saddam Hussein's press conference of July 20, 1973, as quoted in ibid., July 21, 1973. See also the Iraqi government's statement on occasion of the first anniversary of the nationalization of the IPC, as quoted in ibid., June 1, 1973.

118 Ruben Andreasyan, "Middle East: The Oil Factor," *New Times,* ns. 45–46 (November 1973): 20; *Pravda,* October 23, 1973.

119 Ibid., December 3, 1973.

120 Ibid., December 11, 1975.

121 "Iraq Completes Oil Nationalization," *New Times,* no. 51 (December 1975): 11.

3   The Kurdish Question

1 For the Kurdistan section of the Treaty of Sèvres, see J. C. Hurewitz, *Diplomacy in the Near and Middle East: A Documentary Record: 1914–1956* (New York: Van Nostrand, 1956), vol. 2, p. 82. The text of the Treaty of Lausanne is on pp. 119–27.

2 Of the approximately six to seven million Kurds, one-half presently reside in Turkey; the remainder is divided between Iran and Iraq (1.5 to 2 million each), Syria (more than 300,000), and the Soviet Union (approximately 80,000). However, estimates vary widely. See Stephen C. Pelletiere, *The Kurds: An Unstable Element in the Gulf* (Boulder: Westview Press, 1984), p. 15.

3 *Arab Report and Record* (London, cited hereinafter as ARR), 1970, p. 144.

4 Edmund Ghareeb, *The Kurdish Question in Iraq* (Syracuse: Syracuse University Press, 1981), pp. 35–37.

5 For details, see Majid Khadduri, *Republican 'Iraq: A Study in 'Iraqi Politics Since the Revolution of 1958* (London: Oxford University Press, 1969), pp. 173–81.

6 Ibid., pp. 268–72.

7 Ibid., pp. 272–73.

8 Ibid., pp. 273–78.

9 As quoted in Aziz al-Hajj, "Support the Just Struggle of the Kurdish People," *World Marxist Review* 9 (April 1966): 79. The North American edition of the *World Marxist Review,* as well as of its supplement, the *Information Bulletin,* was published in Toronto by Peace and Socialism Publishers.

10 Al-Hajj, "Support the Just Struggle," p. 79; for subsequent reiteration of the ICP's position, see *World Marxist Review* 11 (April 1968): 83. For Soviet support of the Kurds in 1963, see Edgar O'Ballance, *The Kurdish Revolt: 1961–1970* (Hamden: Archon Books, 1973), pp. 101–2 and passim.

11 Dmitry Volsky, "Arabs and Kurds," *New Times,* no. 3 (January 24, 1968): 13–14. Talabani, who kept feuding with Mulla Mustafa, was expelled from the KDP in 1964. The rivalry enabled Baghdad to promote its own interests in Kurdistan. O'Ballance, *The Kurdish Revolt,* p. 142 and passim.

12 Volsky, "Arabs and Kurds," p. 14.

13 *Pravda,* September 1, 1968; for an earlier comment, see L. Medvedko, ibid., January 24, 1968.

14 Nina Nikolayeva, "Iraq: Arabs and Kurds," *New Times,* no. 12 (March 24, 1970): 27.

15 Text in ARR, 1968, p. 204.

16   Majid Khadduri, *Socialist Iraq: A Study in Iraqi Politics since 1968* (Washington, D.C.: Middle East Institute, 1978), pp. 25–26; *ARR*, 1968, p. 219.

17   *Middle East Journal* (Washington, D.C.), 23, no. 4 (1969): 513; A. F. Fedchenko, *Irak v bor'be za nezavisimost'* (Moscow: Nauka, 1970), p. 296.

18   *ARR*, 1969, p. 507; 1970, p. 36.

19   R. Andreasian, "Irak v 1968 g.," *Mezhdunarodnyi ezhegodnik, 1969g.* (Moscow: Politizdat, 1969), p. 260.

20   *ARR*, 1968, pp. 203, 220, 238.

21   Ibid., pp. 300, 371.

22   Ibid., 1969, pp. 299, 431.

23   Ibid., p. 532; 1970, p. 60. For more details, see O'Ballance, *The Kurdish Revolt*, pp. 148–59; Sa'ad Jawad, *Iraq and the Kurdish Question, 1958–1970* (London: Ithaca Press, 1981), ch. 8.

24   *Pravda*, August 7, 1968; G. Mirsky, "Developments in Iraq," *New Times*, no. 33 (August 21, 1968): 13. See also Nikolayeva, "Iraq," p. 27; Andreasian, "Irak v 1968," p. 260.

25   Fedchenko, *Irak v bor'be*, p. 293; Andreasian, "Irak v 1968," p. 260.

26   Fedchenko, *Irak v bor'be*, pp. 293–94.

27   *Pravda*, October 3, 1968. See also September 9, 20, 1968.

28   Ibid., September 21, 1969.

29   Ibid., January 29, 1970.

30   *ARR*, 1970, p. 144.

31   For details, see ibid.; see also *Pravda*, March 13, 1970. For a summary of the manifesto's main points, see Khadduri, *Socialist Iraq*, pp. 103–5, full text in Appendix C.

32   *ARR*, 1972, p. 139.

33   Ibid., 1970, pp. 173, 174. For some details of Mulla Mustafa's statement, see *Pravda*, March 15, 1970.

34   *ARR*, 1970, p. 381; 1971, p. 137.

35   Ibid., 1970, pp. 173–74; *Middle East Journal* 23, no. 3 (1970): 361.

36   *ARR*, 1970, pp. 174, 238.

37   Ibid, pp. 174, 265.

38   Ibid., 1971, p. 107; Ghareeb, *The Kurdish Question*, pp. 98–101.

39   *ARR*, 1970, p. 410.

40   Ibid., 1971, pp. 57, 107.

41   Keith McLachlan, "Iraq: Problems of Regional Development," in Abbas Kelidar, ed., *The Integration of Modern Iraq* (New York: St. Martin's Press, 1979), p. 139.

42   *ARR*, 1970, p. 685.

43   As reported by *al-Ahram* (Cairo), August 19, 1970, and quoted in ibid., p. 468.

44   As quoted in ibid., p. 491.

45   *Le Monde* (Paris), July 15, 1970, as quoted in ibid., pp. 381–82.

46   Ibid., 1971, p. 260.

47   Ibid.

48   *Pravda*, January 29, 1970.

49   Ibid., April 5, 1970.

50   A. Vasil'ev, ibid., March 14, 1970.

51   Text in ibid., March 18, 1970.

52   A. Vasil'ev, ibid., March 14, 1970. See also the text of the speech by Kirill Mazurov,

member of the Politburo and first deputy premier, at a Kremlin breakfast honoring Saddam Hussein during his first visit to the USSR; text in ibid., August 6, 1970.

53 Ibid., March 11, 1971; for more details, see I. Beliaev and E. Primakov, ibid., April 5, 1970.

54 A. Vasil'ev, ibid., March 11, 1971.

55 As quoted by I. Beliaev and E. Primakov, ibid., April 5, 1970. Similar sentiments were later expressed also by Mulla Mustafa. See ibid., July 30, 1970.

56 A. Vasil'ev, ibid., March 14, 1970, March 11, 1971. Similar sentiments were also expressed by Saddam Hussein, as quoted in ibid., August 6, 1970.

57 I. Pogodina, ibid., March 13, 1970.

58 A. Vasil'ev, ibid., March 14, 1970; I. Beliaev and E. Primakov, ibid., April 5, 1970.

59 A. Vasil'ev, ibid., March 14, 1970.

60 Ibid., March 31, July 19, October 29, 1970.

61 A. Vasil'ev, ibid., March 11, 1971; P. Demchenko, ibid., August 16, 1971.

62 Ibid., July 3, 4, 8, and 17, 1970.

63 Ibid., August 16, 19, 1971.

64 Text in ibid., August 16, 1971.

65 A. Vasil'ev, ibid., March 11, 1971.

66 ARR, 1971, pp. 509, 527–28.

67 Ibid., p. 600; Middle-East Intelligence Survey (Tel Aviv), 1, no. 8 (1973): 58 and no. 10 (1973): 80.

68 See p. 117 of this volume.

69 Pravda, November 5, 1971.

70 Ibid.

71 Ibid.

72 Ibid.; for more details, see ibid., November 17, 1971; P. Demchenko, ibid., November 21, 1971; ibid., December 4, 1971; and R. Petrov, "Iraq: New Horizons," New Times, no. 49 (December 1971): 20–21.

73 See, for example, Bakr's interview with al-Jumhuriyyah, published on March 11, 1972, as quoted in ARR, 1972, p. 110.

74 Ibid., p. 231.

75 Ibid., pp. 351, 374; for other KDP communications, see ibid., pp. 531, 578.

76 Sa'ad Jawad, "Recent Developments in the Kurdish Issue," in Tim Niblock, ed., Iraq: The Contemporary State (New York: St. Martin's Press, 1982), pp. 51–53.

77 As quoted in ARR, 1972, p. 531.

78 For some details on Iran, see Ghareeb, The Kurdish Question, pp. 43, 77–78, 84, and passim; on Israel, pp. 140, 142–45; and on the United States, pp. 131–34, 138–42. See also J. M. Abdulghani, Iraq and Iran: The Years of Crisis (Baltimore: Johns Hopkins University Press, 1984), pp. 139–47.

79 Washington Post, June 23, 1973, as quoted in ARR, 1973, p. 271.

80 Ibid., p. 318; Niblock, ed., Iraq, pp. 53–54.

81 Texts of Kosygin's speeches in Pravda, February 12 and April 8; Podgorny's speech in ibid., September 15, 1972.

82 Text in ibid., September 20, 1972.

83 See, for example, a report on the visit to Moscow of a high-level KDP delegation and on its reception in the CPSU Central Committee in Izvestiia, August 26, 1972. See also Viktor Kudriavtsev, "Gory i gordost'," Aziia i Afrika segodnia (hereinafter cited as AiAS), no. 1 (January 1973): 24.

84 Kerim Ahmed (member of the Politburo, ICP), "Against Bourgeois Nationalism and Chauvinism," *World Marxist Review* 15, no. 10 (October 1972): 107; Kudriavtsev, "Gory i gordost',"p. 24; Malamud Ata Alla, *Arab Struggle for Economic Independence* (Moscow: Progress Publications, 1974), p. 104.

85 V. Nekrasov and B. Orekhov, *Pravda*, October 31, 1972; E. Primakov, ibid., March 10, 1973.

86 Ahmed, "Against Bourgeois Nationalism," p. 106.

87 *Izvestiia*, August 26, 1972; Kudriavtsev, "Gory i gordost'." For expressions of similar sentiments by Mulla Mustafa and other Kurdish leaders, see E. Primakov, *Pravda*, March 10, 1973.

88 Ibid., July 12, 1973.

89 For details, see p. 117 of this volume.

90 See, for example, the account of the meeting of the KDP and CPSU officials in *Izvestiia*, August 26, 1972; Kudriavtsev, "Gory i gordost',"p. 25; Primakov, *Pravda*, July 12, 1973.

91 As quoted in ARR, 1973, p. 365.

92 As quoted in ibid., pp. 388–89.

93 As quoted in ibid., p. 449.

94 Ibid., p. 538; see also Jean Riollot, "Moscow Worries About Political Stability in Iraq," *Radio Liberty Dispatch*, January 23, 1974, p. 2.

95 *Financial Times*, August 15, 1972.

96 See p. 79 of this volume.

97 *Izvestiia*, August 26, 1972.

98 E. Primakov, *Pravda*, July 12, 1973.

99 Ibid., November 16, 1973; Vladimir Shmarov, "The Baghdad Dialogue," *New Times*, no. 5 (February 1974): 11.

100 *Pravda*, December 3, 1973; February 28, 1974.

101 Shmarov, "The Baghdad Dialogue," p. 10. Moscow Radio acknowledged the outbreak of hostilities on January 4, 1974. It assessed no blame and called on both sides to reconcile their differences. See Riollot, "Moscow Worries," p. 3.

102 H. V. Hodson, ed., *The Annual Register of World Events, 1974* (cited hereinafter as AR) (New York: St. Martin's Press, 1975), p. 217; *Middle-East Intelligence Survey* 2, no. 3 (1974): 23. The text of the March 11, 1974, decree is in ARR, 1974, pp. 162–64, 214.

103 Ibid., pp. 102–3; *Middle-East Intelligence Survey* 1, no. 24 (1974): 191–92; 2, no. 3 (1974): 126–27. For the statement of KDP's position, see ARR, 1974, pp. 126–27.

104 Ghareeb, *The Kurdish Question*, pp. 154–56.

105 *Middle-East Intelligence Survey*, 2, no. 3 (1974): 23; ARR, 1974, p. 148.

106 *Middle-East Intelligence Survey*, 2, no. 10 (1974): 80; ARR, 1974, p. 322.

107 Ibid., pp. 423, 481; *Middle-East Intelligence Survey*, 2, no. 3 (1974): 23; 2, no. 10 (1974): 80.

108 ARR, 1975, p. 76; Phebe Marr, *The Modern History of Iraq* (Boulder: Westview Press, 1985), pp. 234–35.

109 For some details of the fighting, see Ghareeb, *The Kurdish Question*, pp. 160–65, 169–70.

110 P. Demchenko, *Pravda*, March 14, 1974; see also the text of an ICP statement, ibid., March 28, 1974. For a comprehensive Soviet analysis of the reasons for the breakdown of the Iraqi-Kurdish negotiations, see P. Nadezhdin, ibid., May 14, 1974, and A. Vavilov, "Irak: uspekhi progressivnogo antiimperialisticheskogo kursa," *Mezh-*

dunarodnyi ezhegodnik, 1975g. (Moscow: Politizdat, 1975), pp. 250–54. See also P. Demchenko and A. Lukovets, *Pravda*, May 24, 1975.

111 Ibid., April 26, 1974; the ICP concurred. Ibid., April 27, 1974.

112 *ARR*, 1974, p. 127.

113 As quoted in ibid., p. 170.

114 Alexander Ignatov, "Iraq Today," *New Times*, no. 21 (May 1974): 23.

115 P. Nadezhdin, *Pravda*, May 14, 1974.

116 Ignatov, "Iraq Today"; for more details about the "subversive" activities of the "right wing" of the KDP, see pp. 23–24 and P. Nadezhdin, *Pravda*, May 14, 1974.

117 Broadcast of May 27, 1974, as quoted in *ARR*, 1974, p. 194.

118 Broadcast of June 25, 1974, as quoted in ibid., p. 250. Similar sentiments were expressed also in the resolutions adopted in late June by the plenary session of the Central Committee of the ICP (*Pravda*, June 25, 1974) and in articles by V. Korionov and B. Orekhov, ibid., July 17, August 21, 1974.

119 *ARR*, 1974, p. 103.

120 *Pravda*, March 27, 1974.

121 *Washington Post*, February 2, 1975, as quoted in Roger F. Pajak, "Soviet Military Aid to Iraq and Syria," *Strategic Review* 4 (Winter 1976): 53.

122 Pajak, "Soviet Military Aid," pp. 53–54: Richard Jones, *Financial Times*, September 11; Michael Getler, *International Herald-Tribune* (Paris), October 7, 1974. For an earlier reference, see *The Times*, June 19, 1974.

123 November 16, as quoted in *ARR*, 1974, p. 511.

124 B. Orekhov, *Pravda*, November 26, 1974.

125 Ibid.; see also B. Orekhov, ibid., October 8, 1974; Vavilov, "Irak."

126 *AR*, 1975, pp. 188–89; *ARR*, 1975, pp. 163–64; Ghareeb, *The Kurdish Question*, pp. 171–76.

127 For an evaluation, see p. 190 of this volume.

128 "Joint Soviet-Iraqi Communiqué," issued during Saddam Hussein's April 1975 visit to Moscow; text in *Pravda*, April 17, 1975.

129 Text in ibid., April 15, 1975.

130 *ARR*, 1975, pp. 277, 308.

131 Ibid., pp. 248, 630–31.

132 Ibid., 1976, p. 627; Ghareeb, *The Kurdish Question*, pp. 176–78.

133 *ARR*, 1975, pp. 164, 191–92, 248, 277, 308; 1976, pp. 506, 627; 1977, p. 974.

134 Ibid., 1976, p. 148; 1977, p. 154. For more details on the late 1970s and early 1980s, see Ghareeb, *The Kurdish Question*, pp. 178–81.

135 *ARR*, 1975, pp. 385–86. For an early report of Syrian support of Kurdish dissidents, see *Financial Times*, June 23, 1975.

136 Lenore G. Martin, *The Unstable Gulf: Threats from Within* (Lexington, Mass.: Lexington Books, 1984), p. 89.

137 *Financial Times*, March 3, 1976.

138 *ARR*, 1976, pp. 379, 478; *The Times*, July 27, 1976.

139 *ARR*, 1977, p. 247.

140 Ibid., pp. 298, 899; Marr, *Modern History of Iraq*, pp. 235–36.

141 V. Shmarov, *Izvestiia*, May 16, 1975; P. Demchenko and A. Lukovets, *Pravda*, May 24, 1975; ibid., August 29, 1976; A. Vavilov, "Irak: po puti nezavisimosti i progressa," *Mezhdunarodnyi ezhegodnik, 1977g.* (Moscow: Politizdat, 1977), p. 251.

142 *Pravda,* October 16, 1975; Iu. Glukhov, "Gorizonty Iraka," *Aziia i Afrika segodnia* (cited hereinafter as *AiAS*) no. 4 (April 1978): 16.

143 *Pravda,* October 16, 1975; Y. Troitsky, "Socialist-Oriented Countries: The National Question," *International Affairs,* no. 4 (April 1977): 38.

144 *Pravda,* June 23, October 16, 1975. See also Troitsky, "Socialist-Oriented Countries"; Vavilov, *Mezhdunarodnyi ezhegodnik, 1977g.,* p. 251; Glukhov, "Gorizonty Iraka," p. 16.

145 *Pravda,* December 5, 1976; Glukhov, "Gorizonty Iraka," p. 16.

146 *Pravda,* May 9, 21, 1976; see also ibid., December 26, 1977.

147 K. Geivandov and O. Skalkin, ibid., September 1, 1976; Troitsky, "Socialist-Oriented Countries," pp. 33–41; A. Repin, "Towards the Future," *New Times,* no. 20 (May 1977): 22–23; Glukhov, "Gorizonty Iraka," pp. 14–17; and P. Pak, "Irak: zalog uspekhov—v edinstve," *AiAS,* no. 7 (July 1978): 9–11.

148 Akademiia nauk SSSR. Institut vostokovedeniia, *Noveishaia istoriia arabskikh stran Azii, 1917–1985* (Moscow: Nauka, 1988), p. 322.

149 Ibid., pp. 325, 329, 331.

150 Ibid., p. 332.

151 Iu. Georgiev and Iu. Dakhab, *Argumenty i fakty,* no. 21 (May 16–June 1, 1990), pp. 6–7.

152 Khadduri, *Socialist Iraq,* pp. 102–3.

153 Ibid., pp. 105–6.

4 The Iraqi Communist Party

1 "Iraqi Communist Party," *World Marxist Review* 16 (October 1973): 130.

2 Majid Khadduri, *Republican 'Iraq: A Study in 'Iraqi Politics since the Revolution of 1958* (London: Oxford University Press, 1969), p. 117. For an exceptional in-depth study of the history of the ICP, see Hanna Batatu, *The Old Social Classes and the Revolutionary Movements of Iraq* (Princeton: Princeton University Press, 1978), chs. 11–41.

3 Batatu, *The Old Social Classes,* chs. 41–52.

4 Ibid., chs. 53–55. See also Uriel Dann, "The Communist Movement in Iraq since 1963," in Michael Confino and Shimon Shamir, eds., *The U.S.S.R. and the Middle East* (New York: John Wiley and Sons, 1973), pp. 377–78.

5 Dann, "The Communist Movement in Iraq," pp. 378–83; Batatu, *The Old Social Classes,* chs. 56–57; and A. R. Kelidar, "Aziz al-Haj: A Communist Radical," in *The Integration of Modern Iraq* (New York: St. Martin's Press, 1979), ch. 11.

6 Oles M. Smolansky, *The Soviet Union and the Arab East Under Khrushchev* (Lewisburg, Pa.: Bucknell University Press, 1974), pp. 227–39.

7 For details on the Ba'thi coup, see Batatu, *The Old Social Classes,* ch. 58.

8 *Information Bulletin,* no. 19 (1968): 16, full text on pp. 16–19.

9 Ibid., pp. 16–17.

10 Ibid., p. 17.

11 *Arab Report and Record* (London, cited hereinafter as *ARR*), 1968, pp. 219, 323; see also *Pravda,* August 26, September 7, 1968.

12 Text in *Information Bulletin,* no. 10 (1969): 48–49.

13 *ARR,* 1970, pp. 410, 381.

14 See John K. Cooley, "The Shifting Sands of Arab Communism," *Problems of Communism* 24 (March–April 1975): 34; *ARR,* 1969, p. 280; 1970, p. 173.

15　Ibid., 1970, p. 238; Ara Kachadoor, "Who Profits from Execution of Communists in Iraq," *World Marxist Review* 14 (April 1971): 147.

16　"Second Congress of the Iraqi Communist Party," *Information Bulletin*, no. 19 (1970): 20. For additional information on arrests of the Communists, see ARR, 1970, p. 607, and Kachadoor, "Who Profits from Execution," pp. 146–47. See also "Conference of the Communist Parties of Jordan, Syria, Iraq and Lebanon," *Information Bulletin*, ns. 3–4 (1971): 75.

17　As quoted in ARR, 1971, p. 237.

18　A. F. Fedchenko, *Irak v bor'be za nezavisimost'* (Moscow : Nauka, 1970), p. 292. For a Soviet account of ICP's attitude toward "united fronts" in the 1963–1968 period, see R. Andreasian, "Irak v 1968g," *Mezhdunarodnyi ezhegodnik, 1969g.* (Moscow: Politizdat, 1969), p. 258.

19　Dann, "The Communist Movement," p. 383.

20　Fedchenko, *Irak v bor'be*, p. 293.

21　Ibid., p. 295. For details of ICP position, see E. Primakov, *Pravda*, August 18, 1969.

22　In an interview with *al-Sayyad*, a Beirut weekly, as quoted in ARR, 1969, pp. 407–8.

23　For details of ICP's backing of Mulla Mustafa's KDP in 1968 and 1969, see Edmund Ghareeb, *The Kurdish Question in Iraq* (Syracuse: Syracuse University Press, 1980), pp. 77–78. In 1970 the ICP, along with the Soviet Union, endorsed the March Manifesto. Ibid., p. 90.

24　*Al-Thawrah*, July 10, 1970, as quoted in ARR, 1970, p. 381.

25　*Information Bulletin*, no. 19 (1970): 19.

26　Ibid., p. 20.

27　Ibid., pp. 20–21.

28　See, for example, the statement by the Jordanian, Syrian, Lebanese, and Iraqi Communist parties of January 13, 1971, and a statement by Saddam Hussein to the effect that the ICP would be denied participation in a proposed legislative body until it joined the National Front on conditions laid down by the Ba'th. As quoted in ARR, 1971, p. 137.

29　*Pravda*, August 12, 1968.

30　Ibid.

31　Ibid., August 26, 1968.

32　Andreasian, *Mezhdunarodnyi ezhegodnik, 1969g.*, p. 260.

33　For additional comments, see E. Primakov, *Pravda*, August 18, 1969.

34　Ibid., September 18, 1969.

35　Ibid.

36　Similar sentiments, combined with warnings to beware of the "reactionary forces," were also expressed by Primakov in ibid., January 29, 1970.

37　As quoted in ARR, 1970, p. 173; 1971, p. 84.

38　E. Primakov and I. Beliaev, *Pravda*, April 5, 1970.

39　The statement appeared in the Lebanese Communist party daily *al-Nid'a* on April 6, 1970, see ARR, 1970, p. 238.

40　*Information Bulletin*, no. 19 (1970): 19–25; ns. 3–4 (1971): 71–76.

41　*World Marxist Review* 14 (April 1971): 148.

42　*Pravda*, May 7, 1971.

43　For example, see R. Petrov, ibid., July 14, 1971; R. Ulyanovsky, "The 'Third World'—Problems of Socialist Orientation," *International Affairs*, no. 9 (September 1971): 26–35; P. Demchenko, *Pravda*, August 16, November 5, 1971.

44 Ivison Macadam, ed., *The Annual Register of World Events*, 1971 (cited hereinafter as *AR*) (New York: St. Martin's Press, 1972), p. 207.

45 *ARR*, 1971, p. 575; R. Petrov, "Iraq: New Horizons," *New Times*, no. 49 (December 1971): 20. Full text of the Charter in Majid Khadduri, *Socialist Iraq: A Study in Iraqi Politics since 1968* (Washington, D.C.: Middle East Institute, 1978), appendix B, pp. 199–229.

46 As quoted in *ARR*, 1971, p. 599.

47 "Statement of the Political Bureau, Iraqi Communist Party," *Information Bulletin*, ns. 1–2 (1972): 52.

48 Ibid., pp. 53–54.

49 Khadduri, *Socialist Iraq*, pp. 98–99.

50 "Statement of the Iraqi Communist Party on Participation in Government," *Information Bulletin*, no. 12 (1972): 39.

51 *ARR*, 1972, p. 231.

52 *Al-Thawrah*, May 16, 1972; "Statement of the Iraqi Communist Party," p. 40; *World Marxist Review* 15 (July 1972): 158.

53 For ICP position, see Ara Khachadoor, "A Blow at Oil Monopolies," ibid., 15 (August 1972): 121; "Statement of the Iraqi Communist Party on the Nationalization of the Iraq Petroleum Company," *Information Bulletin*, no. 12 (1972): 41–42.

54 "Plenary Meeting of the Central Committee, Iraqi Communist Party," ibid., ns. 11–12 (1973): 39–40.

55 Ibid., p. 44.

56 *ARR*, 1973, p. 318. The initial agreement to cooperate was reached in May 1973. Malamud Ata Alla, *Arab Struggle for Economic Independence* (Moscow: Progress Publications, 1976), p. 104.

57 *Baghdad Observer*, July 18, 1973, and *al-Thawrah*, August 2, 1973, as quoted in Cooley, "The Shifting Sands," p. 37.

58 *Pravda*, November 21, 1971; see also R. Petrov, "Iraq: New Horizons," *New Times*, no. 49 (December 1971): 20–21; V. Rumyantsev, "Rebirth on the Euphrates," ibid., no. 9 (March 1973): 22–23; P. Demchenko, *Pravda*, March 11, 1973.

59 Petrov, "Iraq: New Horizons," p. 20.

60 Ibid.

61 See pp. 111–12 of this volume.

62 *ARR*, 1972, p. 231; John K. Cooley, *Christian Science Monitor*, May 17, 1972.

63 I. Pogodina, *Pravda*, May 24, 1972; see also ibid., May 17, 1972; P. Demchenko, ibid., July 14, 1972; and V. Rumiantsev, "Irak: po puti ukrepleniia nezavisimosti," *Mezhdunarodnyi ezhegodnik: politika i ekonomika, 1973g.* (Moscow: Politizdat, 1973), p. 254.

64 *Izvestiia*, June 8, 1972, emphasis added.

65 R. Ulyanovsky, "Arab East: Problems of a United Progressive Front," *New Times*, no. 41 (October 1972): 20.

66 *Pravda*, October 21, 1972; V. Nekrasov and B. Orekhov, ibid., October 31, 1972; P. Demchenko, ibid., February 3, 1973.

67 See ibid., March 23, 25, 1973. The same pattern was followed during Saddam Hussein's April 1975 and February 1977 visits to Moscow.

68 As quoted in *ARR*, 1973, p. 365.

69 Ibid., p. 411; 1974, pp. 103, 194.

70 *Pravda*, September 17, 1973. For the text of its first editorial, see *World Marxist Review* 16 (November 1973): 142–43.

71 See p. 83 of this volume.

72 "Plenary Meeting of the CC Iraqi CP," *Information Bulletin*, ns. 5–6 (1974): 22.

73 "Plenary Meeting," pp. 22–23.

74 Ibid., pp. 23–24. For a later, relatively upbeat assessment of the Front, see excerpts from a speech by Aziz Mohammed, ibid., ns. 7–8 (1974): 84–87.

75 *ARR*, 1974, p. 103.

76 Adel Haba, "Promising First Steps," *World Marxist Review* 17 (June 1974): 114. For a detailed exposition of ICP's position, see Aziz Mohammed, "The Socialist Community Is Our Dependable Ally," ibid., 18 (January 1975): 53–61. See also statements by Aziz Mohammed during his October–November 1974 visit to the USSR, as quoted in *Pravda*, October 30 and November 14, 1974.

77 Rahim Adjina is quoted by Alexander Ignatov, "Iraq Today," *New Times*, no. 21 (May 1974): 24 and Amir Abdallah by B. Orekhov, *Pravda*, November 26, 1974.

78 See "Communique on Meeting of Communist and Workers' Parties of Arab Countries," *Information Bulletin*, no. 8 (1975): 11.

79 "Revolutionary Democrats and the Socialist Orientation," *World Marxist Review* 18 (November 1975): 32.

80 "Revolutionary Democrats," p. 33.

81 Ibid., p. 35.

82 Ibid., p. 36.

83 Ibid., pp. 36–37, 43–44.

84 See Aziz Mohammed's speeches before the Twenty-fifth Congress of the CPSU and at a meeting commemorating the forty-second anniversary of the founding of the Iraqi Communist party. Texts in *Pravda*, March 2, April 1, 1976, emphasis added.

85 Speech by Saddam Hussein before the plenary session of the National Front, ibid., June 10, 1975; see also speeches by Zayd Haydar, Ba'th's delegate to the Twenty-fifth Congress of the CPSU, and Naim Haddad at the anniversary of the ICP, ibid., March 2, April 1, 1976, as well as excerpts of the Ba'th's telegram to the Third Congress of the ICP, ibid., May 8, 1976.

86 "Third Congress of the Iraqi Communist Party," *Information Bulletin*, no. 11 (1976): 12–20.

87 "Third Congress," pp. 17–18.

88 Ibid., pp. 18–19; Aziz Mukhammed, "Za konsolidatsiiu patrioticheskikh sil," *Aziia i Afrika segodnia* (hereinafter cited as *AiAS*), no. 6 (June 1976), p. 9.

89 *AR*, 1976, p. 191.

90 "Third Congress," pp. 19–20.

91 As quoted in *Pravda*, February 23, 1977; see also Thabit Habib al-Ani, *al-Fikr al-Jadid* (Baghdad), as quoted in *Pravda*, March 6, 1977.

92 B. Orekhov, ibid., July 28, 1973; for initial Soviet reaction, see "Vazhnyi akt," ibid., July 19, 1973; "Towards Unity," *New Times*, no. 30 (July 1973): 16–17; the texts of the CPSU Central Committee's congratulatory telegrams to "Comrades" Hasan al-Bakr and Aziz Mohammed and their replies, *Pravda*, August 15 and 30, 1973; B. Orekhov, ibid., August 21, 1973.

93 *ARR*, 1974, pp. 103, 480.

94 See text and P. Demchenko, *Pravda*, March 31, 1974; the text of the CPSU telegram,

congratulating Aziz Mohammed on his fiftieth birthday and G. Nedelin's article on Iraq, ibid., July 1, 1974.

95 Ibid., November 14, 1974; for details on the ICP visit, see ibid., October 30, 1974.

96 B. Orekhov, ibid., November 26, 1974; see also Kosygin's dinner speech in honor of Saddam Hussein, text in ibid., April 15, 1975.

97 As quoted in ibid., June 10, 1975.

98 K. Geivandov, ibid., July 16, July 18, 1975.

99 As quoted in ibid., May 12, 1976. Similar sentiments were expressed in the new party program, ibid., May 18, 1976. See also A. Vavilov, "Irak: po puti nezavisimosti i progressa," *Mezhdunarodnyi ezhegodnik, 1977g.* (Moscow: Politizdat, 1977), p. 250.

100 Text in *Pravda*, March 2, 1976; see also the statement by Naim Haddad representing the National Front.

101 A. Vasil'ev, ibid., May 26, 1976.

102 Khadduri, *Socialist Iraq*, pp. 68–69.

103 *ARR*, 1977, p. 114; *Pravda*, February 23, 1977. Similarly critical sentiments were expressed later in the year in the ICP statement condemning President Sadat's visit to Jerusalem; text in *Tariq al-Sha'b*, December 4, 1977.

104 See, for example, Kosygin's June 1, 1976 speech delivered on Iraqi television during the premier's visit to Baghdad; text in *Pravda*, June 2, 1976. See also his speech in honor of Saddam Hussein, ibid., February 2, 1977.

105 For a good example, see the text of the CPSU Central Committee telegram to the Third Congress of the ICP, ibid., May 8, 1976.

106 Ibid., June 22, December 13, 1975; *New Times*, no. 43 (October 1976): 2; *Pravda*, December 30, 1977.

107 Ibid., June 2, 1976. See also the telegram by the CPSU Central Committee, the Presidium of the Supreme Soviet, and the Soviet government to President Bakr, ibid., July 17, 1976; K. Geivandov and O. Skalkin, ibid., September 1, 1976; and ibid., January 20, 1977.

108 Texts in ibid., February 2, 1977, emphasis added.

109 *Tariq al-Sha'b*, November 21, 1978.

110 See ICP Program of April 1978, as quoted in Dilip Hiro, *Inside the Middle East* (New York: McGraw-Hill, 1982), p. 172 and Aziz Mukhammed, "Internatsionalizm, edinstvo, sotrudnichestvo," *AiAS*, no. 1 (January 1977): 24–25.

111 *Tariq al-Sha'b*, March 14, 1978. For additional details, see Amanda Cuthbert, "Iraq: Communists Under Pressure," *Arab Report*, April 25, 1979, pp. 11–12.

112 As quoted in *ARR*, 1978, p. 327 and Cuthbert, "Iraq," p. 12; for more details, see Edward Mortimer, *The Times*, June 1, 1978.

113 As quoted in *ARR*, 1978, p. 363.

114 Ibid.; *Arab Report*, March 14, 1979, p. 22.

115 As quoted in *Information Bulletin*, ns. 18–19 (1978): 66–67.

116 Ibid., pp. 68–69.

117 Ibid., p. 71.

118 As quoted in *ARR*, 1978, p. 402. It may be reasonably assumed that the number of Communists executed by May 1978 far exceeded twenty-one. See John K. Cooley, "Conflict Within the Iraqi Left," *Problems of Communism* 29 (January–February 1980): 89.

119 *ARR*, 1978, p. 919; *Arab Report*, January 31, 1979, p. 21.

120 Ibid., February 28, 1979, p. 21; March 14, 1979, p. 22.
121 "Stop the Repressions and Persecution," *World Marxist Review* 22 (March 1979): 142–43.
122 For details, see statement by Saad Ahmad, member of the ICP Central Committee, in *al-Safir* (a Beirut leftist daily), March 14, 1979, as quoted in *Arab Report*, March 28, 1979, p. 22 and Cuthbert, "Iraq," p. 11. Among the ICP leaders who left for the Soviet Union were Aziz Mohammed and Amir Abdallah, *Arab Report*, April 25, 1979, p. 22. After his departure the latter was stripped of his ministerial position. Ibid., May 9, 1979, p. 22.
123 Ibid., April 25, 1979, p. 22.
124 Ibid., May 9, 1979, p. 22.
125 Ibid., May 23, 1979, p. 22.
126 Ibid., June 20, 1979, p. 22.
127 Ibid., August 1, 1979, p. 22.
128 For full text, see "End the Dictatorship and Establish a Democratic Regime in Iraq," *Information Bulletin*, ns. 1–2 (1980): 54–65.
129 "End the Dictatorship," p. 54.
130 Ibid., pp. 54–56.
131 Ibid., pp. 59–61.
132 Ibid., pp. 63, 65.
133 Ibid., pp. 64–65.
134 *Pravda*, February 23, 1977. Similar sentiments were also expressed by ICP Politburo member Thabit Habib al-Ani, writing in the party weekly *al-Fikr al-Jadid*. His views, too, were reproduced in ibid. on March 6, 1977.
135 Ibid., May 7, 11, 1977; Aziz Mukhammed, "Strana Oktiabria—maiak svobody," *AiAS*, no. 8 (August 1977): 7–8; Abdul Razak al-Safi, "For Stronger Alliance with the Socialist System," *World Marxist Review* 20 (September 1977): 24–26.
136 *Pravda*, June 18, 20, 1977; V. Konstantinov, "Iraq," *International Affairs*, no. 6 (June 1977): 148.
137 *Pravda*, October 14, November 4, 13, and 14, 1977.
138 Ibid., March 16, 1978.
139 See p. 128 of this volume.
140 See p. 128 of this volume.
141 *ARR*, 1978, p. 403.
142 Ibid., emphasis added.
143 Interview with *al-Nahar* (Beirut), June 21, 1978, as quoted in *ARR*, 1978, p. 438.
144 *Pravda*, July 14, 1978.
145 Ibid., July 18, 1978.
146 P. Pak, "Irak: zalog uspekhov—v edinstve," *AiAS*, no. 7 (July 1978): 11.
147 Ibid., pp. 10–11.
148 Texts in *Pravda*, July 22, 1978.
149 *Newsweek*, July 17, 1978, p. 50.
150 Baghdad Radio, July 21, 1978, as quoted in Cooley, "Conflict," p. 90.
151 See p. 129 of this volume.
152 Baghdad Radio, October 17, 1978, as quoted in Cooley, "Conflict," p. 90.
153 For Khayrallah's visit, see *Pravda*, November 22, 1978. It may be safely assumed that Soviet military aid to Iraq figured prominently on the agenda of Khayrallah's discussions with the Soviet leaders.

154   Text in ibid., December 13, 1978.

155   As quoted in *Arab Report*, January 31, 1979, p. 21. The warning was probably prompted by the reported execution of thirteen additional Communist members of Iraq's armed forces. See James M. Markham, *New York Times*, January 29, 1979.

156   *Pravda*, February 16, 1979.

157   Text in ibid., March 31, 1979.

158   See also "Conference of Communist and Workers' Parties of Arab Countries. Statement," *Information Bulletin*, no. 4 (1979), especially pp. 12–13; A. Muhammed, "Relationship Between Socialism and the National-Liberation Movement," *World Marxist Review* 22 (March 1979): 13–16; Naziha Duleimi, "Stop the Repressions and Persecution," ibid., pp. 142–43. After March 1979, see "End the Dictatorship and Establish a Democratic Regime in Iraq," *Information Bulletin*, ns. 1–2 (1980): 54–65; and "Joint Communique," ibid., no. 9 (1980): 22–27.

159   Nazihah Dulaymi, then ICP representative on the *World Marxist Review*, wrote in early 1979: "We are confident that the fraternal Communist and workers' parties . . . will upgrade the solidarity campaign, demanding an immediate end to the repressions against Communists and their friends in Iraq." "Stop the Repressions and Persecution," *World Marxist Review* 22 (March 1979): 143.

160   Iu. Georgiev and Iu. Dakhab, *Argumenty i fakty*, no. 21 (May 16–June 1, 1990), pp. 6–7.

161   This point is made forcefully by Georgiev and Dakhab.

5   The Persian Gulf, 1968–75: Problems of Security and Stability

1   Shahram Chubin and Sepehr Zabih, *The Foreign Relations of Iran: A Developing State in a Zone of Great-Power Conflict* (Berkeley: University of California Press, 1974), p. 215.

2   Ivison Macadam, ed., *The Annual Register of World Events, 1968* (cited hereinafter as AR) (New York: St. Martin's Press, 1969), p. 2; for background information, see Jacob Abadi, *Britain's Withdrawal from the Middle East, 1947–1971: The Economic and Strategic Imperatives* (Princeton: Kingston Press, 1982), ch. 7.

3   *Arab Report and Record* (London, cited hereinafter as ARR), 1968, p. 2. According to other reports, Iraq was to be included as well; see Chubin and Zabih, *Foreign Relations of Iran*, pp. 236–37, n. 4.

4   *Ettelaat* (Tehran), January 8, 1968, as quoted in Chubin and Zabih, *Foreign Relations of Iran*, p. 236.

5   As quoted in ibid., p. 237.

6   Ibid.

7   See statement by Prime Minister Amir Abbas Hoveida, as quoted in "Zaiavlenie TASS," *Pravda*, March 4, 1968.

8   For a detailed account and a conservative critique of the British policy, see J. B. Kelly, *Arabia, the Gulf and the West* (New York: Basic Books, 1980), ch. 2.

9   Broadcast of December 16, 1969, as quoted in ARR, 1969, p. 530.

10   Ibid., 1971, pp. 28, 137; see also statements by Bakr, as quoted in ibid., 1970, pp. 353, 410.

11   Broadcast of December 12, 1970, as quoted in ibid., pp. 662–63, emphasis added.

12   Ibid., 1969, p. 2; 1970, p. 379; Kuwait concurred, see ibid., 1972, p. 553.

13   Ibid., 1971, p. 239.

14   Statement, made in November 1970, by Iran's ambassador to Great Britain, ibid., 1970, p. 605.

15   Message to several Gulf states and principalities, as quoted in ibid., 1968, p. 238. See also statement by Minister of Defense Hardan al-Takriti, *al-Siyassah* (Kuwait), November 7, 1968, as quoted in ibid., p. 349.

16   Statement issued by the Seventh Congress of the Iraqi Ba'th in February 1969, as quoted in ibid., 1969, p. 50; statement by the Pan-Arab Command of the Iraqi Ba'th, as quoted in *The Times*, April 28, 1970; and statements by Salah Mahdi Ammash and Hardan al-Takriti, ARR, 1970, p. 265.

17   Ibid., 1969, p. 2.

18   Ibid., 1970, p. 379, emphasis added.

19   Ibid., p. 410, emphasis added.

20   Ibid., pp. 411, 412.

21   Baghdad Radio, December 12, 1970, as quoted in ARR, 1970, p. 663.

22   Broadcast of January 10, 1971, as quoted in ibid., 1971, p. 28.

23   Ibid., p. 135; see also Zahedi's statement of May 12, as quoted in ibid., p. 236.

24   Statement by Iraqi Foreign Ministry, issued on March 3, 1971, as quoted in ibid., p. 137.

25   "Provocative Imperialist Bustle in the Persian Gulf," *International Affairs*, no. 3 (March 1968): 76.

26   "Zaiavlenie TASS."

27   Ibid.

28   Such sentiments were expressed, among others, by Iran's Foreign Minister Zahedi, see *The Guardian* (London), March 12, 1968.

29   K. Vishnevetskii, *Pravda*, March 7, 1968; for a later comment, see L. Medvedko, ibid., October 17, 1969.

30   O. Orestov, ibid., January 27, 1968; G. Drambiants, "Misfire in Abu Dhabi," *International Affairs*, no. 12 (December 1969): 75; S. Kozlov, "British Political Manoevring 'East of Suez,'" ibid., ns. 2–3 (February–March 1970): 72–77; and G. Drambyantz, "The Persian Gulf: Twixt the Past and Future," ibid., no. 10 (October 1970): 67.

31   Drambyantz, "The Persian Gulf," p. 67.

32   P. Demchenko, *Pravda*, August 19, 1971.

33   G. Drambyantz, "Persian Gulf States," *International Affairs*, no. 1 (January 1972): 102.

34   "Provocative Imperialist Bustle," pp. 75–76.

35   G. Drambyantz, "The Persian Gulf," p. 68.

36   Ibid.

37   As quoted by L. Medvedko, *Pravda*, March 20, 1968.

38   Ibid.; ARR, 1968, pp. 71, 163; AR, 1968, pp. 295, 299.

39   Ibid., pp. 301, 309, 310; ARR, 1969, p. 2.

40   Hardan al-Takriti's interview with *al-Siyassah*, as quoted in ibid., 1968, p. 349.

41   Ibid., and 1969, p. 140.

42   Ibid., p. 360; 1970, p. 265; 1969, p. 205.

43   AR, 1968, p. 309.

44   *The Times*, April 28, 1970.

45   See p. 146 of this volume.

46 Interview with Algiers Radio, broadcast on May 9, 1970, as quoted in *ARR,* 1970, p. 265; see also Bakr's statement of June 21, as quoted in ibid., p. 353.

47 As quoted in ibid., 1971, p. 622.

48 L. Medvedko, *Pravda,* March 20, 1968.

49 Ibid. For a discussion of the importance of Saudi Arabia to the establishment of the federation, see ibid., June 27, 1968.

50 L. Medvedko, ibid., July 17, 1968; ibid., July 4, 1968.

51 L. Medvedko, ibid., July 17, 1968.

52 V. Bodianskii, "V Persidskom zalive nespokoino," *Aziia i Afrika segodnia* (hereinafter cited as *AiAS,* no. 7 (July 1968): 10; see also L. Medvedko, *Pravda,* October 17, 1969.

53 "New Stage in the Liberation Struggle," *International Affairs,* no. 4 (April 1969): 89; why Kuwait was excluded was left unexplained.

54 Drambyantz, "The Persian Gulf," p. 69.

55 Ibid., pp. 69–70.

56 Ibid.

57 Ibid., pp. 70–71.

58 G. Drambyants, "The Thorny Path of Federation," *International Affairs,* no. 10 (October 1971): 96–97. For a general evaluation of the events of the past four years, see also Drambyants, "Persian Gulf States," pp. 100–102.

59 Ibid., p. 102; V. Ozoling, "Ob'edinenie arabskikh emiratov," *AiAS,* no. 3 (March 1972): 43.

60 A. Vasil'ev, *Pravda,* January 9, 1972; for an extended discussion, see L. I. Medvedko, *Vetry peremen v Persidskom zalive* (Moscow: Nauka, 1973), chs. 5 and 6.

61 Text in *Pravda,* February 12, 1972.

62 As quoted in *ARR,* 1969, p. 2. For a discussion of Iran's position, see Chubin and Zabih, *The Foreign Relations of Iran,* pp. 214–21, and Rouhollah K. Ramazani, *The Persian Gulf: Iran's Role* (Charlottesville: University Press of Virginia, 1972), pp. 45–46.

63 As quoted in *ARR,* 1969, p. 234.

64 See p. 145 of this volume.

65 *ARR,* 1969, pp. 50, 140.

66 Baghdad Radio, February 11, 1970, as quoted in ibid., 1970, p. 88.

67 Ibid., p. 262.

68 *AR,* 1970, p. 192.

69 See pp. 150–51 of this volume.

70 *AR,* 1970, pp. 334, 219.

71 For Iraq's position, see *ARR,* 1970, p. 352.

72 *AR,* 1970, p. 208.

73 *Kayhan International* (Tehran), November 9, 1970, as quoted in *ARR,* 1970, p. 605. See also statements by the shah, as quoted in ibid., 1971, pp. 106, 320, 502, and 550.

74 Chubin and Zabih, *The Foreign Relations of Iran,* p. 222; Kelly, *Arabia, the Gulf,* pp. 87–88.

75 *ARR,* 1971, p. 291. The validity of the strategic argument has been questioned by some scholars; see Kelly, *Arabia, the Gulf,* p. 89 and Robert Litwak, *Security in the Persian Gulf: Sources of Inter-State Conflict* (London: International Institute for Strategic Studies, 1981), p. 57.

76 *ARR,* 1971, pp. 287, 574.

77 Ibid., pp. 320, 574.

78 Ibid., p. 321.

79 Ibid., p. 598; David E. Long, *The Persian Gulf: An Introduction to Its Peoples, Politics, and Economics* (Boulder: Westview Press, 1976), p. 49.

80 *AR*, 1971, p. 197.

81 *ARR*, 1971, pp. 599, 623. On December 9 the Security Council "agreed to defer consideration of the matter while third-party mediation by States friendly to Iran and Iraq was taking place." *AR*, 1971, p. 336.

82 Statement by Ali Ghannam, member of the Ba'th Party National Command, as quoted in *ARR*, 1971, p. 648. For a detailed discussion of the islands dispute, see Ramazani, *The Persian Gulf*, pp. 56–68.

83 Drambyantz, "The Persian Gulf," pp. 70–71.

84 P. Demchenko, *Pravda*, August 19, 1971.

85 *ARR*, 1968, pp. 47, 164; 1970, pp. 578–79.

86 Ibid., 1969, pp. 161, 300; Majid Khadduri, *Socialist Iraq: A Study in Iraqi Politics since 1968* (Washington, D.C.: The Middle East Institute, 1978), pp. 148–49.

87 Ibid., p. 148. On the background of the dispute, see Peter Huensler, "The Historical Antecedents of the Shatt al-Arab Dispute" in M. S. El Azhary, ed., *The Iran-Iraq War: An Historical, Economic and Political Analysis* (New York: St. Martin's Press, 1984), pp. 8–19; J. M. Abdulghani, *Iraq and Iran: The Years of Crisis* (Baltimore: Johns Hopkins University Press, 1984), ch. 5; and G. D. Alibeili, *Iran i sopredel'nye strany Vostoka, 1946–1978* (Moscow: Nauka, 1989), pp. 99–113. See also Tareq Y. Ismael, *Iraq and Iran: Roots of Conflict* (Syracuse: Syracuse University Press, 1982).

88 *ARR*, 1968, p. 392.

89 Ibid., 1969, p. 160.

90 Ibid., pp. 166, 180, 201, 236, 280, 432.

91 Ibid., pp. 180, 200, 236.

92 Ibid., 1970, p. 60.

93 Ibid., pp. 88, 116, 410, 549.

94 Ibid., 1971, p. 647; 1972, pp. 6, 30, 55, 231.

95 For more details on the border clashes, see ibid., pp. 178, 206, 232, 279; on the United Nations, see ibid., pp. 206, 231. See also Rouhollah K. Ramazani, *Iran's Foreign Policy, 1941–1973: A Study of Foreign Policy in Modernizing Nations* (Charlottesville: University Press of Virginia, 1975), pp. 408–27, 435–38.

96 *ARR*, 1972, pp. 304, 351.

97 Ibid., 1973, pp. 6, 82, 128, 155, 202.

98 Ibid., p. 449; 1974, pp. 45, 82, 103, 148, 170, 194.

99 Ibid., p. 369; 1975, p. 75.

100 Ibid., 1974, pp. 346, 369, 398, 452, 481, 576; 1975, pp. 41, 107.

101 Ibid., 1974, pp. 576, 423, 514.

102 Ibid., 1975, p. 75.

103 Ibid., pp. 163, 192.

104 See Shahram Chubin, "Soviet Policy Towards Iran and the Gulf," in Charles Tripp, ed., *Regional Security in the Middle East* (New York: St. Martin's Press, 1984), p. 151, and Abdulghani, *Iraq and Iran*, p. 158.

105 *ARR*, 1975, pp. 335, 358–59. For details and evaluation, see Abdulghani, *Iraq and Iran*, pp. 152–57, and S. H. Amin, *Political and Strategic Issues in the Persian-Arabian Gulf* (Glasgow: Royston Limited, 1984), pp. 67–69.

106   "Zaiavlenie TASS," *Pravda,* March 4, 1968.

107   Drambyantz, "The Persian Gulf," p. 70; for additional press comments on tensions between Iraq and Iran, see *Pravda,* April 24 and 26, 1969, April 16, 1972; *Izvestiia,* January 24, 1970.

108   For more details on Soviet-Iranian relations, see Ramazani, *Iran's Foreign Policy,* chs. 13 and 14 and Chubin and Zabih, *The Foreign Relations of Iran,* pp. 69–85, 262–66. For an evaluation, see Alvin Z. Rubinstein, "Soviet Policy Toward South and Southwest Asia: Strategic and Political Aspects," in Rubinstein, ed., *The Great Game: Rivalry in the Persian Gulf and South Asia* (New York: Praeger, 1983), pp. 90–91. For some contemporary Soviet comments, see "Real Equality in Cooperation," *International Affairs,* no. 6 (June 1968): 66–67; A. Bashkirov, "Iran i strany SEV," *AiAS,* no. 12 (December 1968): 12–13; P. Yaminsky, "USSR-Iran: Way of Friendship and Cooperation," *International Affairs,* no. 1 (January 1971): 70; M. Krutikhin, "Soviet Union-Iran: Good-Neighbour Relations," ibid., no. 6 (June 1973): 111–12; and A. Sychuzhnikov, "Soviet-Iranian Economic Cooperation," ibid., no. 6 (June 1974): 111–12.

109   Aryeh Y. Yodfat, *The Soviet Union and Revolutionary Iran* (New York: St. Martin's Press, 1984), p. 33.

110   For texts of the dinner speeches and of the joint communiqué of the Kosygin visit, see *Pravda,* April 3 and 8, 1968. Texts of the speeches by the shah and Podgorny as well as of the official statement (no joint communiqué was issued on that occasion, possibly in deference to international opinion in the wake of the Soviet occupation of Czechoslovakia) in ibid., September 25 and October 5, 1968. Texts of speeches by Podgorny and the shah and of the joint communiqué in ibid., March 27 and April 1, 1970.

111   Text in ibid., March 27, 1969.

112   Text in ibid., August 13, 1970. A similar formulation was also found in the joint communiqué of June 1971, issued at the conclusion of a visit to Iraq of a CPSU and government delegation, headed by a member of the Central Committee and Deputy Premier V. Novikov. Text in ibid., June 26, 1971.

113   Ibid., February 12 and 18, 1972.

114   The next paragraph is based on Bettie M. and Oles M. Smolansky, "Soviet and Chinese Influence in the Persian Gulf," in Alvin Z. Rubinstein, ed., *Soviet and Chinese Influence in the Third World* (New York: Praeger, 1975), pp. 148–49.

115   *Pravda,* April 10 and 11, 1972.

116   Ibid., September 15 and 19, 1972.

117   Ibid., October 22, 1972, emphasis added. A fifteen-year Treaty on the Development of Economic and Technical Cooperation between the USSR and Iran was signed on this occasion. Hussein Sirriyeh, *US Policy in the Gulf, 1968–1977: Aftermath of the British Withdrawal* (London: Ithaca Press, 1984), p. 218.

118   *Pravda,* October 22, 1972, emphasis added.

119   In 1973 and 1974 the Soviet leaders "privately warned" Tehran against accelerating arms purchases from the United States. See Chubin, "Soviet Policy Towards Iran," p. 136.

120   *Pravda,* March 16 and 18, 1973.

121   Ibid., August 7 and 13, 1973.

122   Ibid., March 23 and 25, 1973, February 28, 1974. It is noteworthy that no joint communiqués were issued during either visit. The third produced a "statement"—a

deliberate downgrading of the proceedings—and the fourth not even that. Ibid., December 3, 1973.

123 For brief factual references to Iraqi-Iranian relations, see ibid., October 9 and 10, 1973, February 12, 1974.

124 Text in ibid., November 19, 1974.

125 Ibid.

126 Ibid., November 21, 1974. In late 1974 and early 1975 the Soviet press commentaries on the Iraqi-Iranian border incidents, although brief as usual, were marked by a subtle shift in favor of Baghdad's position. See, for example, ibid., December 19, 1974, January 21, 1975, and February 11, 1975.

127 Ibid., April 15 and 17, 1975. For the initial announcement of the accord, ibid., March 8, 1975; for details, ibid., April 22, 1975. See also "Iran-Iraq Agreement," *New Times*, no. 11 (March 1975): 9 and "Iran-Iraq Talks," ibid., no. 12 (March 1975): 7–8.

128 V. Shmarov, "Iran-Iraq: Constructive Dialogue," ibid., no. 13 (March 1975): 10.

129 V. Shmarov, "On a Firm Foundation," ibid., no. 15 (April 1975): 6; see also "Agreements Ratified," ibid., no. 27 (July 1976): 11.

130 Oles M. Smolansky, *The Soviet Union and the Arab East Under Khrushchev* (Lewisburg, Pa.: Bucknell University Press, 1974), pp. 175–76.

131 *AR*, 1968, p. 299; *ARR*, 1968, pp. 47, 163, 349; 1969, p. 506; 1970, pp. 118, 262, 294, 384, 471, 581, 636–37, 666; 1971, pp. 27, 135.

132 Ibid., 1970, p. 384.

133 Ibid., p. 294; 1971, p. 320.

134 *AR*, 1971, p. 214.

135 *ARR*, 1972, p. 556.

136 For some details of economic cooperation and trade, see ibid., 1968, pp. 4, 71, 413; 1970, pp. 118, 294, 663; 1971, pp. 108, 111, 408; 1972, p. 600; and *AR*, 1972, p. 217.

137 *ARR*, 1970, pp. 384–85; 1972, p. 110.

138 Ibid., 1973, p. 130.

139 In an interview with *al-Rai al-Amm* (Kuwait), published on January 9, 1968, as quoted in ibid., 1968, p. 4.

140 For details, see Khadduri, *Socialist Iraq*, p. 155.

141 Interview published in *al-Siyassah* on October 17, 1971, as quoted in *ARR*, 1971, p. 552.

142 *AR*, 1972, p. 210.

143 *ARR*, 1972, pp. 598, 600; 1973, pp. 82, 102, 127, 130; *AR*, 1973, p. 221.

144 *ARR*, 1973, pp. 127–28.

145 As quoted in ibid.

146 For more details, see Anne M. Kelly, "The Soviet Naval Presence During the Iraq-Kuwait Border Dispute," in Michael MccGwire, Ken Booth, John McDonnell, eds., *Soviet Naval Policy: Objectives and Constraints* (New York: Praeger, 1975), pp. 287–89.

147 Litwak, *Security in the Persian Gulf*, p. 31.

148 As quoted in *ARR*, 1973, pp. 154–55, 157.

149 Ibid., p. 154.

150 An interview with *al-Sayyad*, published on April 12, as quoted in ibid., p. 157.

151 For a detailed discussion of the episode, see Khadduri, *Socialist Iraq*, pp. 153–59.

152 *Pravda*, March 21, 1973.

153 See pp. 163–68 of this volume.

154 *Pravda,* March 22, 1973.

155 Texts in ibid., March 23, 1973.

156 Ibid., March 24, 25, 1973.

157 Ibid., March 23, 1973.

158 Article 7 calls for "regular consultations . . . on all important international issues affecting the interests of the two countries. . . ." As quoted in Khadduri, *Socialist Iraq,* p. 242.

159 *Pravda,* March 14, 1973.

160 For a positive analysis of Kuwait's foreign and domestic policies, see A. Vasil'ev, ibid., October 10, 1972.

161 On Kosygin's trip to Iran, see p. 168 of this volume.

162 Text in ibid., March 25, 1973.

163 "Border Incident," *New Times,* no. 14 (April 1973): 7.

164 Gorshkov's impending "friendship visit" was announced by TASS on March 30, see Kelly, "Soviet Naval Presence," p. 290. On April 5, *Pravda* reported that the admiral had been received by President Bakr.

165 "Border Incident," p. 7.

166 Ibid.; *Pravda,* April 2, 1973.

167 V. Zelenin, "Britain's Manoeuvres East of Suez," *International Affairs,* no. 11 (November 1972): 48–49.

168 G. Dymov, "Persian Gulf Countries at the Cross-Roads," ibid., no. 3 (March 1973): 54.

169 Dymov, "Persian Gulf Countries," p. 55.

170 Ibid. For an earlier discussion of Bahrain's importance to the United States, see "Zaiavlenie TASS"; for subsequent discussion, see I. Lebedev, *Pravda,* April 13, 1972; A. Vasil'ev, ibid., August 13, 1972, May 31, 1974.

171 A. Vasil'ev, ibid., January 9, 1972.

172 A. Vasil'ev, ibid., August 13, 1972; see also I. Lebedev, ibid., August 24, 1972.

173 Dymov, "Persian Gulf Countries," p. 57

174 A. Maslennikov, *Pravda,* June 15, 1973.

175 A. Vasil'ev, ibid., August 13, 1972. See also Dymov, "Persian Gulf Countries," pp. 58–59; A. Vasil'ev, *Pravda,* June 10, 1973; and V. Peresada, ibid., June 21, 1973.

176 Dymov, "Persian Gulf Countries," p. 58.

177 A. Vasil'ev, *Pravda,* May 31, 1974; for later comments, see ibid., February 12, 13, 25, 1975.

178 L. Medvedko, ibid., March 1, 1975.

179 Ibid., January 22, 1975.

180 O. Skalkin, ibid., January 24, 1975; V. Shurygin, ibid., December 29, 1974.

181 See *al-Siyassah,* March 19 and 27, 1974, as quoted in Melhem Chaoul, *La securité dans le Golfe Arabo-Persique* (Paris: Fondation pour les Etudes de Défense Nationale, 1978), p. 93.

182 *ARR,* 1972, pp. 123–24, 231.

183 Ibid., pp. 428, 556.

184 Ibid., p. 231.

185 As quoted in ibid., pp. 584, 583; for an excellent discussion of Saudi-Iranian relations, see G. D. Alibeili, *Iran i sopredel'nye strany Vostoka, 1946–1978* (Moscow: Nauka, 1989), pp. 46–59.

186 *International Herald-Tribune,* October 6, 1974, as quoted in *ARR,* 1974, p. 419.

187   As quoted in ibid., p. 507.

188   *Kayhan International*, February 26, 1975, as quoted in ARR, 1975, p. 131.

189   See p. 162 of this volume.

190   Ibid., p. 41.

191   Interview published on February 21 and 22, 1975, as quoted in ibid., p. 135.

192   Ibid., p. 41.

6   The Persian Gulf, 1975–80: Problems of Security and Stability

1   *Arab Report and Record* (London, cited hereinafter as ARR), 1975, p. 192.

2   Ibid., p. 248.

3   See pp. 162–63 of this volume.

4   ARR, 1975, p. 438.

5   Ibid., pp. 464, 686; 1976, p. 7.

6   Ibid., p. 25.

7   *L'Orient-Le Jour*, April 5, 1976, as quoted in ibid., p. 215.

8   Ibid., pp. 379, 446.

9   As quoted in ibid., 1977, p. 6; for details of other high-level visits, see ibid., pp. 154, 198, 297, 298, 676, 973, 830, 899.

10   Ibid., p. 198.

11   Ibid., 1977, pp. 534, 900.

12   Ibid., 1978, pp. 127, 159, 725.

13   Ibid., p. 328. For some details on continuing high-level visits, see ibid., pp. 87, 159, 284, 725, 850.

14   In a speech honoring the visiting foreign minister of Kuwait; text in *Pravda*, December 3, 1975.

15   See, for example, Soviet comments on the five-year trade agreement, signed on October 18, 1976, which provided for near doubling of the volume of trade between the two countries. *New Times*, no. 44 (October 1976): 16.

16   The Liberation Front of the Persian Gulf Region of the late 1960s was renamed the Popular Front for the Liberation of Oman and the Arabian Gulf (PFLOAG) in the early 1970s and the Popular Front for the Liberation of Oman (PFLO) in 1974. For reasons and circumstances, see Bettie M. Smolansky and Oles M. Smolansky, "Sino-Soviet Interaction in the Middle East," in Herbert J. Ellison, ed., *The Sino-Soviet Conflict: A Global Perspective* (Seattle: University of Washington Press, 1982), pp. 254–65, and Mark N. Katz, *Russia and Arabia: Soviet Foreign Policy Toward the Arabian Peninsula* (Baltimore: Johns Hopkins University Press, 1986), pp. 108–16.

17   Broadcast of July 12, 1975, as quoted in ARR, 1975, p. 393.

18   See p. 163 of this volume.

19   As quoted in ARR, 1975, p. 445.

20   Ibid., p. 503.

21   ARR, 1976, p. 40; H. V. Hodson, ed., *The Annual Register of World Events, 1976* (cited hereinafter as AR) (New York: St. Martin's Press, 1977), p. 191.

22   Broadcast of June 24, 1976, as quoted in ARR, 1976, p. 388.

23   For example, Minister of Information Tariq Aziz insisted that Iraq continued to support the PFLO, *Washington Post*, July 26, 1976.

24   As quoted in ARR, 1975, p. 550.

25   Ibid., pp. 604, 600.

26 See pp. 153 and 167 of this volume.

27 For more details, see Smolansky and Smolansky, "Sino-Soviet Interaction," pp. 257–60.

28 This paragraph is based on ibid., pp. 260–62.

29 *Pravda*, October 23, 1975.

30 Ibid., December 6, 1975, emphasis added.

31 As quoted in ibid., May 12, 1976.

32 S. Aleksandrov, "Oman: bor'ba prodolzhaetsia," *Aziia i Afrika segodnia* (hereinafter cited as *AiAS*), no. 6 (June 1978), pp. 20–21.

33 *Pravda*, December 9, 1977; B. Shkol'nikov, "Pakt protivorechashchii interesam narodov," *AiAS*, no. 2 (February 1978): 50–51; and *Pravda*, July 18, August 18, 1978.

34 Ibid., June 6, June 26, 1978.

35 Moscow Radio, April 21, 1976, as quoted in *ARR*, 1976, p. 244.

36 Shahram Chubin, *Security in the Persian Gulf: The Role of the Outside Powers* (Montclair, N.J.: Allanheld, Osmun, 1982), p. 152.

37 *Washington Post*, April 25, 1975, emphasis added.

38 As quoted in *ARR*, 1975, p. 411.

39 Shahram Chubin in Charles Tripp, ed., *Regional Security in the Middle East* (New York: St. Martin's Press, 1984), p. 147; see also J. M. Abdulghani, *Iraq and Iran: The Years of Crisis* (Baltimore: Johns Hopkins University Press, 1984), p. 170.

40 *ARR*, 1975, p. 411.

41 Ibid., p. 452.

42 *Al-Dustur*, August 28, 1975, as quoted in ibid., p. 463.

43 Ibid., 1976, p. 446.

44 For some details of developing relations with Bahrain, see ibid., 1975, pp. 308, 359; 1976, pp. 182, 249. For Qatar, see ibid., 1975, pp. 316, 359, 393; 1976, pp. 147, 249. For the UAE, see ibid., 1975, pp. 359, 658, 686, 703; 1976, p. 364. On the Iraqi-Kuwaiti understanding settling the dispute over the contested islands near Umm Qasr, see *AR*, 1975, p. 189; for other contacts, see *ARR*, 1975, p. 359; 1976, p. 249.

45 *Middle East Journal* 29 (Summer 1975): 336–37; *ARR*, 1975, p. 394. For more details, see Edmund Ghareeb, "Iraq in the Gulf," in Frederick W. Axelgard, ed., *Iraq in Transition: A Political, Economic, and Strategic Perspective* (Boulder: Westview Press, 1986), p. 70.

46 *ARR*, 1976, p. 214.

47 Ibid., 1975, p. 394.

48 Ibid.; see also David Holden and Richard Johns, *The House of Saud: The Rise and Rule of the Most Powerful Dynasty in the Arab World* (New York: Holt, Rinehart & Winston, 1981), p. 424.

49 *Washington Post*, July 26, 1976.

50 *ARR*, 1975, p. 394; see also the UAE-Iranian communiqué of December 1975, p. 672.

51 *Daily News* (Kuwait), September 20, 1975, as quoted in ibid., p. 527.

52 For a reference to the secret meetings, see Khalatbari's press conference of March 17, 1976, as quoted in ibid., 1976, p. 201. Iraq's nonparticipation is mentioned in *AR*, 1976, p. 192.

53 The preceding paragraph is based on *ARR*, 1976, pp. 689 and 710.

54 Ibid., p. 710.

55 *Gulf Weekly Mirror*, November 28, 1976, as quoted in ibid., p. 690.

56 *Kuwait Times*, February 6, 1977, as quoted in *ARR*, 1977, p. 70.

57 For an elaboration of Kuwait's position, see the article in *al-Siyassah* by its editor Ahmad Jarallah which appeared on November 24, 1976, and was thought to reflect the view of the government. Among other things, it denied "the need for a security alliance of states in the Gulf region" and urged them to "resolve inter-Gulf conflicts first." For more details, see ARR, 1976, p. 692.

58 As quoted in ibid., 1977, pp. 70–71, emphasis added.

59 See his interview with *al-Siyassah*, published on April 24, 1977, as quoted in ibid., 1977, p. 321, emphasis added.

60 AR, 1976, p. 192. For more details on continuing tension, see ARR, 1976, pp. 537, 722–24; 1977, pp. 76, 296, 301, 343, 485, 534, 538. A border agreement was finally reached in July 1977, ibid., p. 590.

61 In addition to Saudi Arabia, Kuwait, Qatar, and the UAE, the participants also included Egypt, Syria, Jordan, and the PLO, ibid., p. 16.

62 Ibid., pp. 5–6, 15–16.

63 Ibid., p. 99.

64 *Al-Iraq* (Baghdad), March 12, 1977, as quoted in Y. Tyunkov, "Sheikh Kamal and Others," *New Times*, no. 16 (April 1977): 21.

65 Qatar News Agency report of April 23, 1977, as quoted in ARR, 1977, p. 296. For more information on the tour, see ibid., pp. 313, 321, 342, 359–60.

66 As quoted in ibid., p. 876. For some details on Iraq's improved relations with the Arab Gulf states, see Naomi Sakr, "Economic Relations Between Iraq and Other Arab Gulf States," in Tim Niblock, ed., *Iraq: The Contemporary State* (New York: St. Martin's Press, 1982), pp. 150–67.

67 As quoted in ARR, 1977, p. 297, emphasis added.

68 See his interview with *al-Siyassah*, published on April 24, 1977, as quoted in ibid., p. 321.

69 Inter-Press Service, September 21, 1977, and Iraq News Agency, as quoted in ibid., p. 774.

70 As quoted by Iu. Glukhov, *Pravda*, February 14, 1978.

71 As quoted in ARR, 1977, p. 774.

72 As quoted in ibid., 1978, p. 283.

73 As quoted in ibid., p. 438.

74 AR, 1978, p. 189; Stephen Page, *The Soviet Union and the Yemens: Influence in Asymmetrical Relationships* (New York: Praeger, 1985), pp. 181–82.

75 Page, *The Soviet Union and the Yemens*, p. 77.

76 *Al-Siyassah*, July 8, 1978, as quoted in ARR, 1978, p. 501.

77 AR, 1979, pp. 198–99; Page, *The Soviet Union and the Yemens*, pp. 184–85.

78 As quoted in R. D. McLaurin, Don Peretz, and Lewis W. Snider, *Middle East Foreign Policy: Issues and Processes* (New York: Praeger, 1982), p. 119.

79 As quoted in *Arab Report*, May 9, 1979, p. 22; for additional information on deteriorating relations between Baghdad and Aden, see ibid., June 20, 1979, p. 2.

80 Interview with *al-Nahar*, published on September 9, 1978, as quoted in ARR, 1978, p. 636.

81 *Arab Times* (Kuwait), as quoted in *Arab Report*, February 14, 1979, p. 22.

82 Kuwait News Agency report, as quoted in ibid.

83 The preceding paragraph is based on ibid., February 28, 1979, p. 17.

84 *Pravda*, September 24, 1979; AR, 1979, p. 203.

85 *Pravda*, September 24, 1979.

86 Iu. Glukhov, ibid., October 6, 1979.

87 Ibid., September 24, 1979.

88 Ibid.

89 As quoted in A. Stepanov, "New Fit of Pactomania," *New Times*, no. 42 (October 1979): 12.

90 As quoted in *Pravda*, September 24, 1979.

91 A. Filippov, ibid., October 2, 1975.

92 A. Chernyshov, "Peace and Security for the Indian Ocean," *International Affairs*, no. 12 (December 1976): 42. See also *Pravda*, June 26, 1975; Iu. Mikhailov, ibid., August 8, 1976; and D. Kasatkin, "Indiiskii okean v planakh imperialistov," *AiAS*, no. 5 (May 1977): 28.

93 Filippov, *Pravda*, October 2, 1975.

94 Kasatkin, "Indiiskii okean," p. 28.

95 Iu. Glukhov, *Pravda*, February 12, 1977.

96 Kasatkin, "Indiiskii okean," p. 28; see also L. Mironov, "Indiiskii okean: problemy bezopasnosti i sotrudnichestva," *AiAS*, no. 6 (June 1978): 3.

97 *Pravda*, July 27, 1976.

98 Ibid., May 25, 1976.

99 See pp. oo–oo of this volume.

100 L. Medvedko, *Pravda*, July 9, 1977; for a subsequent similar assessment of the Muscat conference, see Iu. Glukhov, ibid., May 19, 1978.

101 Ibid., May 19, July 18, 1978.

102 Ibid., September 24, 1979.

103 Ibid., September 25, 1979.

104 Iu. Glukhov, ibid., October 6, 1979.

105 N. Simoniia, "Imperializm i osvobodivshiesia strany," *AiAS*, no. 1 (January 1980): 6–7.

106 Stepanov, "New Fit of Pactomania."

107 Ibid.; for more details, see V. Peresada, *Pravda*, September 28, 1979; Iu. Glukhov, ibid., October 6, 1979; and I. Tarutin, ibid., February 19, 1980.

108 Ibid., February 20, 1976.

109 For details, see ibid., July 24, July 30, August 28, 1976; for a summary, see Chernyshov, "Peace and Security," p. 44; Kasatkin, "Indiiskii okean," p. 29.

110 L. Medvedko, *Pravda*, July 9, 1977, and ibid., January 7, 1978.

111 L. Medvedko, ibid., July 9, 1977.

112 Ibid., January 7; L. Medvedko, ibid., March 6, 1978; for Saudi purchases of French military equipment, see ibid., August 16, 1977, May 31, 1978.

113 Chernyshov, "Peace and Security," p. 43; Kasatkin, "Indiiskii okean," p. 29; *Pravda*, February 20, 1976, January 12, 1977.

114 On AWACS and F-16s, see Kasatkin, "Indiiskii okean," and *Pravda*, November 10, 1977; on nuclear reactors, see ibid., August 12, 1977. Iran was also buying British arms, ibid., August 11, 1976.

115 Ibid., August 28, 1976.

116 As quoted in ibid., June 26, 1975; see also ibid., October 27, 1977, and Tyunkov, "Sheik Kamal," p. 21. For a discussion of the Nixon Doctrine and the resulting arms sales to Iran, see G. D. Alibeili, *Iran i sopredel'nye strany Vostoka, 1946–1978* (Moscow: Nauka, 1989), pp. 39–40.

117 Mironov, "Indiiskii okean," p. 3; see also A. Chernyshov, "Peace and Security," p. 43.

118 A. Maslennikov, *Pravda*, June 4, 1978; see also ibid., May 31, 1978; A. Vasil'ev, ibid., June 15, 1978; and A. Feokistov, "Saudi Arabia and the Arab World," *International Affairs*, no. 7 (July 1977): 101.

119 Iu. Mikhailov, *Pravda*, August 8, 1976.

120 B. Shkol'nikov, "Pakt protivorechashchii interesam narodov," *AiAS*, no. 2 (February 1978): 51.

121 Chernyshov, "Peace and Security," p. 43.

122 Ibid.

123 Ibid., p. 44. It was noted later that the U.S. arms and military presence in the Gulf also violated President Carter's earlier promises to limit both. *Pravda*, June 25, 1977.

124 Ibid., May 25, 1976.

125 Chernyshov, "Peace and Security," p. 43.

126 Iu. Glukhov, *Pravda*, February 14, 1978.

127 Ibid., May 19, 1978.

128 Ibid., February 28, 1979; for more details on the RDF, see E. Rusakov, ibid., April 28, 1979, and V. Bol'shakov, ibid., June 28, 1979.

129 Ibid., February 28, 1979; G. Kashoyan, "Seeking a Way Out of the Impasse," *New Times*, no. 11 (March 1979): 9.

130 E. Rusakov, *Pravda*, April 28, 1979; V. Peresada, ibid., July 28, 1979.

131 E. Rusakov, ibid., April 28, 1979; V. Korionov, ibid., February 7, 1980.

132 These items were the main points of Gromyko's speech at a dinner honoring the foreign minister of Kuwait; text in ibid., December 3, 1975.

133 Joint Soviet-Iraqi communiqué; text in ibid., June 1, 1976.

134 Mironov, "Indiiskii okean," p. 4.

135 Chernyshov, "Peace and Security," p. 44.

136 For an excellent analysis of Ayatollah Khomeini's impact on Iran's foreign policy, see Richard Cottam, "Iran: Motives Behind Its Foreign Policy," *Survival* (London), November–December 1986, pp. 483–94; and R. K. Ramazani, *Revolutionary Iran: Challenge and Response in the Middle East* (Baltimore: Johns Hopkins University Press, 1986), ch. 2.

137 *AR*, 1979, p. 194.

138 Ibid., 1980, pp. 196–97.

139 *Baghdad Observer*, November 28, 1979.

140 As reported by Marvine Howe, *New York Times*, January 27, 1980.

141 *Baghdad Observer*, February 2, 1980.

142 As quoted by Marvine Howe, *New York Times*, January 18, 1980.

143 Ibid., January 27, 1980; see also *Baghdad Observer*, January 21, 1980.

144 Ibid., January 17, 1980, and Claudia Wright, *New York Times*, February 8, 1980. Iraq also "vehemently" condemned the invasion at the Muslim foreign ministers' conference, held in Islamabad (Pakistan), in January 1980. See Youssef M. Ibrahim, ibid., April 13, 1980.

145 As quoted in *Baghdad Observer*, February 1, 1980. It is also noteworthy that Soviet deputy minister of the oil and gas industry arrived in Baghdad on January 12, 1980, to discuss with the Iraqi oil officials "aspects of bilateral cooperation." Ibid., January 14, 1980.

146 As quoted in *Iraq Today*, January 1–15, 1980, p. 2.

147 As quoted by Marvine Howe, *New York Times*, January 18, 1980.

148 Ibid.

149 As quoted in *AR*, 1980, p. 63. For a detailed analysis of the background, including evaluation of the "Soviet Threat to Southwest Asia," see Maxwell Orme Johnson, *The Military as an Instrument of U.S. Policy in Southwest Asia: The Rapid Deployment Joint Task Force, 1979–1982* (Boulder: Westview Press, 1983), pp. 5–15; and Harold H. Saunders, "The Iran-Iraq War: Implications for US Policy," in Thomas Naff, ed., *Gulf Security and the Iran–Iraq War* (Washington, D.C.: National Defense University Press, 1985), pp. 64–71. For an insider's evaluation, see Zbigniew Brzezinski, *Power and Principle: Memoirs of the National Security Adviser, 1977–1981* (New York: Farrar, Straus & Giroux, 1983), ch. 12.

150 As quoted in *Pravda*, February 10, 1980; see also the statement by Foreign Minister Hammadi, as quoted by T. Kolesnichenko, ibid., April 15, 1980.

151 Text in *Iraq Today*, February 1–15, 1980, pp. 2–3.

152 See Youssef M. Ibrahim, *New York Times*, April 13, 1980.

153 In addition to material cited, see also Mohammed K. Nasser in *Baghdad Observer*, February 4, 1980.

154 See, for example, Foreign Minister Hammadi's interview with Helsinki's *Helsingen Sanomat*, published on April 14, 1980, as quoted by Christopher S. Wren in *New York Times* of the next day. On Afghanistan, see also joint Iraqi-Guinean communiqué of March 2, 1980, text in *Iraq Today*, March 1–15, 1980, pp. 3–6.

155 As quoted in *New York Times*, March 30, 1980.

156 For more details on Soviet reaction to the Iranian revolution, see Aryeh Y. Yodfat, *The Soviet Union and Revolutionary Iran* (New York: St. Martin's Press, 1984), chs. 4–6.

157 A. Petrov, *Pravda*, December 5, 1979; for a subsequent analysis, see P. Demchenko, ibid., January 19, 1981; for Brezhnev's initial warning, see ibid., November 19, 1978.

158 For a subsequent Soviet account, see pp. 235–36 of this volume.

159 Text in ibid., February 19, 1980. For more details, see Yuri Gudkov, "Old New Doctrine," *New Times*, no. 5 (February 1980): 5–6; for variations on these themes, see S. Vishnevskii, *Pravda*, March 14, 1980; Iu. Glukhov, ibid., September 22, 1980; and L. Medvedko, "The Persian Gulf: A Revival of Gunboat Diplomacy," *International Affairs*, no. 12 (December 1980): 23–29.

160 Ruben Andreasyan, "The 'Vital Interests' of Oil Imperialism," *New Times*, no. 14 (April 1980): 21.

161 Text of Brezhnev's speech in *Pravda*, October 9, 1980; see also text of joint Soviet-Syrian communiqué, ibid., October 11, 1980.

162 A. Vasil'ev, ibid., June 23, 1980.

163 Andreasyan, "The 'Vital Interests,'" p. 21.

164 A. Vasil'ev, *Pravda*, June 23, 1980.

165 Andreasyan, "The 'Vital Interests,'" pp. 21–22.

166 V. Bol'shakov, *Pravda*, February 14, 1980.

167 A. Vasil'ev, ibid., June 23, 1980.

168 R. Moseev, ibid., March 4, 1980.

169 Gudkov, "Old New Doctrine," p. 6. For more details, see Boris Pyadyshev, "Ill-Starred Doctrines," *New Times*, no. 12 (March 1980): 6, and A. Mirov, "Amerikanskii imperializm: stavka na silu," *AiAS*, no. 3 (March 1980): 19–20.

170 Gudkov, "Old New Doctrine," p. 7; for more details on the Arab reaction, see T.

Kolesnichenko, *Pravda*, April 15, 1980; and Iu. Glukhov, ibid., September 22, 1980, and March 27, 1981.

171   V. Peresada, ibid., June 7, 1980.

172   R. Moseev, ibid., June 14, 1980; for a detailed account of U.S. "penetration" of Oman, see V. Mikhin, ibid., July 26, 1980. See also B. Kotov, ibid., September 7, 1980; and M. Zenailov, "Net—imperialisticheskomu vmeshatel'stvu v Persidskom zalive," *AiAS*, no. 1 (January 1981): 21.

173   Text in *Pravda*, February 19, 1980.

174   Text of Brezhnev's speech in ibid., February 23, 1980; for variations on this theme, see A. Petrov, ibid., March 24, 1980; and N. Vasin, "Iran and US Imperialism," *International Affairs*, no. 5 (May 1980): 77.

175   P. Demchenko, *Pravda*, March 16, 1980.

176   As quoted in Medvedko, "The Persian Gulf," p. 29.

177   Text in *Pravda*, December 11, 1980.

178   Text in ibid., February 24, 1981, emphasis added.

179   As quoted by Bernard Gwertzman, *New York Times*, December 12, 1980; for an American analysis of the Brezhnev plan, see Herbert L. Sawyer, *Soviet Perceptions of the Oil Factor in U.S. Foreign Policy: The Middle East-Gulf Region* (Boulder: Westview Press, 1983), pp. 126–27.

180   Even Kuwait endorsed it implicitly, and only in April 1981. See the text of the Soviet-Kuwaiti communiqué issued during a visit to Moscow of Kuwait's minister of foreign affairs, *Pravda*, April 26, 1981. Of the other Arab states, only Libya and the PDRY expressed themselves in favor of the Brezhnev plan. See G. Kuznetsov, "The Persian Gulf: Real Paths to Peace," *International Affairs*, no. 7 (July 1981): 104.

181   For an excellent discussion of the background and ramifications of the Brezhnev plan, see Roy Allison, *The Soviet Union and the Strategy of Non-Alignment in the Third World* (New York: Cambridge University Press, 1988), pp. 147–57.

182   Text in *Pravda*, February 25, 1976.

183   Text in ibid., June 1, 1976.

184   Ibid., February 2, 4, 1977.

185   Ibid., December 13, 14, 1978.

7   The Iran-Iraq War

1   *Pravda*, September 23, 1980.

2   TASS in English, September 23, 1980, in Foreign Broadcast Information Service, *Daily Report*, Soviet Union, September 24, 1980, p. H3; *New York Times*, September 24, 1980.

3   Texts in *Pravda*, October 1, 9, 1980.

4   As quoted by Bernard Gwertzman, *New York Times*, October 3, 1980.

5   See Henry Tanner, ibid., October 6, 1980, and Bernard Gwertzman, ibid., October 11, 1980.

6   *Izvestiia*, October 10, 1980.

7   As quoted by Henry Tanner, *New York Times*, October 6, 1980.

8   *Pravda*, November 12, 1980.

9   For details, see Tariq Aziz's candid interview with David B. Ottaway, *Washington Post*, April 21, 1981.

10 For formal denials of Soviet military assistance to Iraq, see *Pravda*, November 4, 1980, and January 11, 1981.

11 *Washington Post*, April 21, 1981.

12 "Defending the Gulf: A Survey," *Economist*, June 6, 1981, p. 16.

13 Ibid., May 24, 1980, p. 50.

14 Amir Taheri, *The Sunday Times* (London), September 19, 1982.

15 *Pravda*, December 28, 29, 1980, and January 13, 1981.

16 Text in ibid., February 24, 1981.

17 For the background of the attack, see John R. Emshwiller, *Wall Street Journal*, June 9, 1981.

18 P. Demchenko, *Pravda*, August 30, 1981; for Iranian attitude, see ibid., November 16, 1981.

19 Text in ibid., June 10, 1981.

20 Ibid., June 19, 1981, pp. 4, 2.

21 John Yemma, *Christian Science Monitor*, August 26, 1981; *Pravda*, October 30, 1981.

22 *Izvestiia*, July 15, 19, 1981.

23 Karen Elliot House, *Wall Steet Journal*, April 29, 1982.

24 As quoted in *U.S. News and World Report*, May 3, 1982, p. 29.

25 *Pravda*, June 22, July 15, 1982.

26 Ibid., June 4, 1983.

27 Ibid., November 14, 1983.

28 On Lebanon, see Robert Rand, "Soviet Policy Towards Lebanon: The View from the Arab World and Iran," *Radio Liberty Research Notes*, RL 288/82, July 15, 1982; the rest of the paragraph is based on Claude van England, *Christian Science Monitor*, March 28, 1983.

29 *Pravda*, February 19, 1983.

30 Sallie Wise, "Soviet-Iranian Tensions on the Rise," *Radio Liberty Research Notes*, RL 182/83, May 5, 1983, p. 1.

31 *Pravda*, May 6, 1983.

32 Text in ibid., June 17, 1983.

33 N. Iakubov, ibid., August 5, 1983.

34 Ibid., December 31, 1983.

35 *Time*, July 19, 1982, p. 46.

36 *Pravda*, June 5, 1982; Aryeh Yodfat, *The Soviet Union and Revolutionary Iran* (New York: St. Martin's Press, 1984), p. 135.

37 *Pravda*, December 11, 1982.

38 Ibid., March 19, 1983.

39 Ibid., November 22, 23, 1983.

40 *Economist*, October 16, 1982, p. 62, October 9, 1982, p. 41.

41 Jean Gueyras, "Iraq and the Gulf War," *Le Monde* (Paris) as reproduced in *Manchester Guardian Weekly*, April 29, 1984; John Kifner, *New York Times*, July 17, 1984.

42 Milton Viorst, "Iraq at War," *Foreign Affairs* 65 (Winter 1986–87): 362.

43 Drew Middleton, *New York Times*, July 18, 1983.

44 Iurii Kharlanov, *Pravda*, February 26, 1984.

45 Ibid., April 3, 1984.

46 *New York Times*, February 11, 22, 1984.

47 Text in *Pravda*, March 8, 1984.

48   Ibid., May 18, and Pavel Demchenko, ibid., May 19, 1984.
49   Ibid., May 20, 1984.
50   Ibid., June 9, 1984.
51   Ibid., February 3, 17, and March 11, 12, 1985.
52   Pavel Demchenko, ibid., March 15, 1985.
53   Ibid., April 11, 1985.
54   *Economist*, September 14, 1985, p. 43, November 2, 1985, p. 36.
55   Pavel Demchenko, *Pravda*, June 6, 1985.
56   Text in ibid., March 7, 1984.
57   Text in ibid., May 30, 1984; see also ibid., October 6, November 15, 1984.
58   V. Okulov, ibid., February 20, 1985.
59   Ibid., February 12, 1986.
60   As quoted in *Middle East Journal* 39 (Autumn 1985): 810.
61   V. Zotov, *Izvestiia*, July 17, 1985.
62   Ibid., July 20, September 14, 1985.
63   See, for example, the texts of telegrams exchanged by Saddam Hussein and Presidium of the Supreme Soviet on occasion of the fourteenth anniversary of the signing of the 1972 treaty. *Pravda*, April 9, 1984.
64   Ibid., October 19, 26, 1984.
65   Ibid., March 30, 1985.
66   Ibid., December 17, 1985.
67   Texts in ibid.
68   Ibid., March 20, April 27, 1984.
69   Ibid., June 18, 1985.
70   See above, p. 242 of this volume.
71   As quoted by Bernard Gwertzman, *New York Times*, August 28, 1984.
72   Judith Miller, ibid., June 8, 1984.
73   John Kifner, ibid., July 17, 1984; Bernard Gwertzman, ibid., March 20, 1985.
74   *Economist*, February 15, 1986, pp. 32–33.
75   Jim Muir, *Christian Science Monitor*, February 14, 1986.
76   *Pravda*, February 12, 1986; Iu. Glukhov, ibid., February 14, 1986.
77   P. Demchenko, ibid., February 14, 1986.
78   *New York Times*, February 26, 1986.
79   Ibid., March 15, 22, 1986.
80   Gerald F. Seib, *Wall Street Journal*, May 8, 1986.
81   See Iu. Glukhov, *Pravda*, May 16, 1986; Paul Lewis, *New York Times*, May 18, 1986.
82   John Kifner, *New York Times*, July 3, 1986.
83   *Pravda*, August 5, 1986.
84   Iran was said to have twenty to thirty such missiles, reportedly provided by Syria and Libya, *New York Times*, August 13, 1986.
85   *Pravda*, August 16 and 20, 1986.
86   As quoted in *New York Times*, August 25, 1986.
87   As quoted in ibid., September 26, and *Pravda*, September 24, 1986.
88   Ibid., October 9, 11, 1986.
89   *Economist*, January 3, 1987, pp. 26–28, January 17, 1987, pp. 36–37.
90   *Pravda*, January 11, 1987.
91   See Bernard E. Trainor, *New York Times*, January 20, 1987, I. Kuznetsov, *Pravda*, May 21, 1987.

92 John H. Cushman, *New York Times*, March 24, 1987.

93 P. Demchenko, *Pravda*, June 12, 1987.

94 As quoted in *New York Times*, June 4, 1987.

95 As quoted by John Kifner, ibid., June 3, 1987.

96 *World Marxist Review* 29 (March 1986): 93–94.

97 *Information Bulletin*, ns. 17–18 (1986): 31, 33.

98 See the report on the Plenary Session of the People's Democratic Party of Afghanistan (PDPA) in *Pravda*, July 12, 1986.

99 Ibid., July 11, 1986; M. Kozhevnikov, *Izvestiia*, December 2, 1986.

100 *Pravda*, February 14, 1987.

101 *New York Times*, February 3, 10, 1986.

102 *Pravda*, August 5, 1986.

103 Ibid., August 20, 1986.

104 Ibid., October 9, 1986, and Reuters of the same date, as quoted in Bohdan Nahaylo, "Moscow and Tehran: Cultivating Mutual Interests without Budging on Political Differences," *Radio Liberty Research*, RL 47/87, February 3, 1987, p. 3.

105 V. Korionov, *Pravda*, December 2, 1986; "Observer," ibid., November 9, 1986.

106 "Observer," ibid., November 9, 1986.

107 Information based on *New York Times*, December 10, 1986; Elaine Sciolino, ibid., January 8, 1987; Nahaylo, "Moscow and Tehran," p. 6.

108 *Pravda*, February 14, 1987.

109 As quoted in ibid., April 7, 1987.

110 Ibid., April 30, 1987; for the account of Shevardnadze's meeting, see ibid., April 29, 1987.

111 UPI, May 1, 1987, as quoted in Bohdan Nahaylo, "A New Crisis in Soviet-Iranian Relations," *Radio Liberty Research*, RL 178/87, May 11, 1987, p. 3.

112 *Pravda*, June 16, 1987.

113 Ibid., April 20, 1986.

114 Ibid., May 20, 22, 1986.

115 Ibid., June 13, 14, 1986.

116 Ibid., September 27, 1986.

117 Ibid., December 10, 1986.

118 See pp. 254–55 of this volume.

119 *Pravda*, February 21, 1987.

120 Texts in ibid., April 9, 1987.

121 Ibid., April 9, 10, 11, 1987.

122 Ibid., June 19, 1987.

123 International Institute for Strategic Studies, *The Military Balance, 1985–1986* (London, 1986), p. 76; *1986–1987* (London, 1987), p. 97.

124 Elaine Sciolino, *New York Times*, July 2, 3, 1987.

125 Text in *Pravda*, July 4, 1987.

126 The preceding paragraph is based on Neil A. Lewis, *New York Times*, July 21, 1987. Text of Resolution 598 in ibid.

127 Warren Richey, *Christian Science Monitor*, July 22, 1987.

128 Alan Cowell, *New York Times*, July 26, 1987; *Pravda*, July 25, 1987.

129 John Kifner and Elaine Sciolino, respectively, in *New York Times*, August 3, 1987.

130 *Pravda*, August 4, 1987.

131 Ibid., August 1, 5, 1987.

132   As quoted by Marian Houk, *Christian Science Monitor*, August 28, 1987.

133   John Kifner, *New York Times*, August 30, September 4, 1987.

134   Francis X. Clines, ibid., September 2, 1987.

135   Paul Lewis, ibid., September 4, 1987.

136   TASS statement on the meeting between Ryzhkov and Larijani, *Pravda*, September 9, 1987.

137   Ibid., September 15, 1987.

138   Warren Richey, *Christian Science Monitor*, September 15, 1987.

139   Text in *Pravda*, September 25, 1987.

140   As quoted by Elaine Sciolino, *New York Times*, October 3, 1987.

141   Ibid., September 29; Elaine Sciolino, ibid., October 3, 1987.

142   *Pravda*, October 29, 1987.

143   Elaine Sciolino, *New York Times*, November 8, 1987.

144   As quoted by Paul Lewis, ibid., December 4, 1987.

145   As quoted by Warren Richey, *Christian Science Monitor*, December 4, 1987.

146   *Pravda*, December 5, 1987.

147   David K. Shipler, *New York Times*, December 17, 1987, emphasis added.

148   E. A. Wayne, *Christian Science Monitor*, January 4, 1988.

149   David K. Shipler, *New York Times*, January 16, 1988.

150   Alan Cowell, ibid., January 26, 1988.

151   Accounts of meetings between Tariq Aziz and Soviet officials in *Pravda*, February 3, 1988.

152   Paul Lewis, *New York Times*, February 21, 1988.

153   David K. Shipler, ibid., February 21, 1988.

154   Text in *Pravda*, February 24, 1988.

155   Alan Cowell, *New York Times*, March 23, 1988. Most analysts agreed that the al-Hussein rockets were modified Scud-Bs. Some felt that their range was doubled by halving the weight of the one-ton rocket warhead. Others argued that the extended range had been achieved by means of strap-on boosters developed with West European, Soviet, Chinese, or Brazilian assistance. John H. Cushman, Jr., ibid., March 2, 1988; Kenneth R. Timmerman, *Wall Street Journal*, March 31, 1988.

156   *Pravda*, March 7, 1988.

157   Paul Quinn-Judge, *Christian Science Monitor*, March 10, 1988; for Iranian accusations, see Claude van England, ibid., March 9, 1988.

158   *New York Times*, March 18, 1988; on Halabjah massacre, see Alan Cowell, ibid., March 22, 1988.

159   *Pravda*, March 30, 1988.

160   *New York Times*, April 19, 1988.

161   *Pravda*, April 19, 1988.

162   Ibid., April 23, 1988.

163   Bernard E. Trainor, *New York Times*, May 26, 1988; Youssef M. Ibrahim, ibid., June 26, 1988.

164   *Pravda*, July 20, 1988.

165   Ibid., July 21, 1988.

166   Paul Lewis, *New York Times*, July 29, 1988.

167   Robert Pear, ibid., August 5, 1988.

168   Pavel Demchenko, *Pravda*, August 6, 1988.

169   Ibid., August 26, 1988.

170 Paul Lewis, *New York Times*, August 26, 1988.

171 Arkadii Maslennikov, *Pravda*, August 28, 1988.

172 Ibid., July 18, 1987.

173 See p. 260 of this volume; *Pravda*, August 2, 3, 4, 1987.

174 *Izvestiia*, August 5, 1987.

175 As quoted by Philip Taubman, *New York Times*, August 5, 1987.

176 Statements on Larijani's negotiations with Ryzhkov and Shevardnadze in *Pravda*, September 9, 1987.

177 E. A. Wayne, *Christian Science Monitor*, October 19, 1987.

178 *Pravda*, November 2, 1987; Warren Richey, *Christian Science Monitor*, December 4, 1987.

179 *Pravda*, December 5, 1987.

180 John H. Cushman, Jr., *New York Times*, March 2, 1988.

181 *Pravda*, March 7, 1988.

182 Ibid., December 28, 1987.

183 Texts of statements in ibid., February 9, 1988.

184 Ibid., July 23, August 4, 1988.

185 As quoted by Elaine Sciolino, *New York Times*, October 5, 1988.

186 See pp. 258–59 of this volume.

187 *Pravda*, July 3, 7, 1987.

188 As quoted in *New York Times*, August 22, 1987.

189 As quoted by Elaine Sciolino, ibid., October 3, 1987.

190 As quoted in ibid.; see also Shevardnadze's press conference, text in *Pravda*, October 25, 1987.

191 Ibid., February 3, 1988.

192 Ibid., July 14, 1988.

Bibliography

I. Newspapers and Periodicals

Al-Ahram (Cairo); *Al-Dustur* (Beirut); *Al-Fikr al-Jadid* (Baghdad); *Al-Iraq* (Baghdad); *Al-Jazirah* (Riyadh); *Al-Jumhuriyyah* (Baghdad); *Al-Kifah* (Beirut); *Al-Nahar* (Beirut); *Al-Nid'a* (Beirut); *Al-Nur* (Baghdad); *Al-Rasid* (Baghdad); *Al-Rai al-Amm* (Kuwait); *Al-Safir* (Beirut); *Al-Sayyad* (Beirut); *Al-Siyassah* (Kuwait); *Al-Ta'khi* (Baghdad); *Al-Thawrah* (Baghdad); *Al-Watan* (Kuwait); *Al-Watan al-Arabi* (Paris); *American Sociological Review*; *Arab Report* (London); *Arab Report and Record* (London); *Arab Times (Kuwait)*; *Arab World* (Beirut); *Argumenty i fakty* (Moscow); *Aziia i Afrika segodnia* (Moscow); *Baghdad Observer*; *Christian Science Monitor*; *Daily News* (Kuwait); *Defense Monitor* (Washington); *Economist* (London); *Ettelaat* (Tehran); *Financial Times* (London); *Foreign Affairs* (New York); Foreign Broadcast Information Service, *Daily Report* (Washington); *Foreign Policy* (Washington); *Guardian Weekly* (Manchester); *Gulf Weekly Mirror* (Beirut); *Information Bulletin* (supplement to *World Marxist Review*, Toronto); *International Affairs* (London); *International Affairs* (Moscow); *International Herald-Tribune* (Paris); *International Journal of Middle East Studies* (New York); *Iraq Today* (Baghdad); *Izvestiia* (Moscow); *Kayhan International* (Tehran); *Krasnaia zvezda* (Moscow); *Kuwait Times* (Kuwait); *Le Monde* (Paris); *L'Orient-Le Jour* (Beirut); *Middle East Economic Digest* (London); *Middle-East Intelligence Survey* (Tel Aviv); *Middle East Journal* (Washington, D.C.); *Mirovaia ekonomika i mezhdunarodnye otnosheniia* (Moscow); *Narody Azii i Afriki* (Moscow); *Newsweek*; *New Times* (Moscow); *New York Times*; *Official Gazette* (Baghdad); *Orbis* (Philadelphia); *Pravda* (Moscow); *Problems of Communism* (Washington, D.C.); *Radio Liberty Dispatch* (Munich); *Radio Liberty Research Notes* (Munich); *Soviet Union and the Middle East* (Jerusalem); *Strategic Review* (Cambridge, Mass.); *Sunday Times* (London); *Survival* (London); *Tariq al-Sha'b* (Baghdad); *The Times* (London); *U.S. News and World Report*; *Voprosy ekonomiki* (Moscow); *Wall Street Journal*; *Washington Post*; *World Marxist Review* (Toronto)

II. Books and Surveys

Abadi, Jacob. *Britain's Withdrawal from the Middle East, 1947–1971: The Economic and Strategic Imperatives*. Princeton: Kingston Press, 1982.

Abdulghani, J. M. *Iraq and Iran: The Years of Crisis*. Baltimore: Johns Hopkins University Press, 1984.

Abir, Mordechai. *Oil, Power and Politics: Conflict in Arabia, the Red Sea and the Gulf*. London: Frank Cass, 1974.

Abu Jaber, K. S. *The Arab Ba'th Socialist Party: History, Ideology, and Organization*. Syracuse: Syracuse University Press, 1966.

Adamson, David. *The Kurdish War*. New York: Praeger, 1965.

Agwani, M. S. *Politics in the Gulf*. New Delhi: Vikas Publishing House, 1978.

Akademiia nauk SSSR. Institut mirovoi ekonomiki i mezhdunarodnykh otnoshenii. *Mezhdunarodnyi ezhegodnik: politika i ekonomika*. 1968–1987. Moscow: Izdatel'stvo politicheskoi literatury.

Akademiia nauk SSSR. Institut vostokovedeniia. *Iranskaia revoliutsiia, 1978–1979: prichiny i uroki*. Moscow: Nauka, 1989.

———. *Neftedollary i sotsial'no-ekonomicheskoe razvitie stran Blizhnego i Srednego Vostoka*. Moscow: Nauka, 1979.

———. *Noveishaia istoriia arabskikh stran Azii, 1917–1985*. Moscow: Nauka, 1988.

Albaharna, Husain M. *The Legal Status of the Arabian Gulf States: A Study of Their Treaty Relations and Their International Problems*. Manchester: Manchester University Press, 1968.

Alibeili, G. D. *Iran i sopredel'nye strany Vostoka, 1946–1978*. Moscow: Nauka, 1989.

Allison, Roy. *The Soviet Union and the Strategy of Non-Alignment in the Third World*. Cambridge: Cambridge University Press, 1988.

Al-Sowayegh, Abdulaziz. *Arab Petropolitics*. New York: St. Martin's Press, 1984.

Amin, S. H. *Political and Strategic Issues in the Persian-Arabian Gulf*. Glasgow: Royston Limited, 1984.

Amirie, Abbas, ed. *The Persian Gulf and Indian Ocean in International Politics*. Tehran: Institute for International Political and Economic Studies, 1975.

Amirsadeghi, Hossein, ed. *The Security of the Persian Gulf*. New York: St. Martin's Press, 1981.

Andreasian, R. N., El'ianov, A. Ia. *Blizhnii Vostok: neft' i nezavisimost'*. Moscow: Izdatel'stvo vostochnoi literatury, 1961.

Anthony, John Duke. *Arab States of the Lower Gulf: People, Politics, Petroleum*. Washington, D. C.: Middle East Institute, 1975.

Ata Alla, Malamud. *Arab Struggle for Economic Independence*. Moscow: Progress Publications, 1974.

Axelgard, Frederick W., ed. *Iraq in Transition: A Political, Economic, and Strategic Perspective*. Boulder: Westview Press, 1986.

Bakhash, Shaul. *The Reign of the Ayatollahs: Iran and the Islamic Revolution*. New York: Basic Books, 1984.

Batatu, Hanna. *The Old Social Classes and the Revolutionary Movements of Iraq*. Princeton: Princeton University Press, 1978.

Bissell, Richard E. *South Africa and the United States: The Erosion of an Influence Relationship*. New York: Praeger, 1982.

Bradley, C. Paul. *Recent United States Policy in the Persian Gulf (1971–82)*. Grantham, N. H.: Tompson and Rutter, 1982.

Braun, Aurel, ed. *The Middle East in Global Strategy*. Boulder: Westview Press, 1987.

Brown, James, and William P. Snyder. *The Regionalization of Warfare: The Falkland/ Malvinas Islands, Lebanon, and the Iran-Iraq Conflict*. New Brunswick, N.J.: Transaction Books, 1985.

Brzezinski, Zbigniew. *Power and Principle: Memoirs of the National Security Adviser, 1977–1981*. New York: Farrar, Straus & Giroux, 1983.

Burrell, R. M., and Alvin J. Cottrell. *Iran, the Arabian Peninsula, and the Indian Ocean*. New York: National Strategy Information Center, 1973.

Carter, Jimmy. *Keeping Faith: Memoirs of a President*. New York: Bantam Books, 1982.

Central Intelligence Agency. *Communist Aid Activities in Non-Communist Less Developed Countries*. 1978, 1979, and 1954–79. Washington, D.C.

———. *Communist Aid to Less Developed Countries of the Free World*. 1975, 1976, 1977. Washington, D.C.

Chaoul, Melhem. *La sécurité dans le Golfe Arabo-Persique*. Paris: Fondation pour les Etudes de Défense Nationale, 1978.

Chubin, Shahram. *Security in the Persian Gulf: The Role of the Outside Powers*. Montclair, N.J.: Allanheld, Osmun, 1982.

———, ed. *Security in the Persian Gulf: Domestic Political Factors*. Montclair, N.J.: Allanheld, Osmun, 1981.

Chubin, Shahram, and Sepehr Zabih. *The Foreign Relations of Iran: A Developing State in a Zone of Great-Power Conflict*. Berkeley: University of California Press, 1974.

Committee Against Repression and for Democratic Rights in Iraq (CARDRI). *Saddam's Iraq: Revolution or Reaction?* London: ZED Books, 1986.

Confino, Michael, and Shimon Shamir, eds. *The U.S.S.R. and the Middle East*. New York: John Wiley and Sons, 1973.

Cordesman, Anthony H. *The Gulf and the Search for Strategic Stability: Saudi Arabia, the Military Balance in the Gulf, and Trends in the Arab-Israeli Military Balance*. Boulder: Westview Press, 1984.

———. *The Gulf and the West: Strategic Relations and Military Realities*. Boulder: Westview Press, 1988.

Cottrell, Alvin J., and Michael L. Moodie. *The United States and the Persian Gulf: Past Mistakes, Present Needs*. New York: National Strategy Information Center, 1984.

Dann, Uriel. *Iraq Under Qassem: A Political History, 1958–1963*. Jerusalem: Israel Universities Press, 1969.

Darius, Robert G., John W. Amos, II, and Ralph H. Magnus, eds. *Gulf Security into the 1980s: Perceptual and Strategic Dimensions*. Stanford: Hoover Institution Press, 1984.

Day, Alan J., ed. *The Annual Register: A Report of World Events, 1988*. Burnt Mill, U.K.: Longman, 1989.

Duncan, W. Raymond. *The Soviet Union and Cuba: Interests and Influence*. New York: Praeger, 1985.

Duncan, W. Raymond, and Carolyn McGiffert Ekedahl. *Moscow and the Third World under Gorbachev*. Boulder: Westview Press, 1990.

El Azhary, M. S., ed. *The Iran-Iraq War: An Historical, Economic and Political Analysis*. New York: St. Martin's Press, 1984.

Ellison, Herbert J., ed. *The Sino-Soviet Conflict: A Global Perspective*. Seattle: University of Washington Press, 1982.

Farid, Abdel Majid, ed. *Oil and Security in the Arabian Gulf*. New York: St. Martin's Press, 1981.

Fedchenko, A. F. *Irak v bor'be za nezavisimost'*. Moscow: Nauka, 1970.

Freedman, Robert O. *Soviet Policy Toward the Middle East since 1970*. 3d ed. New York: Praeger, 1982.

Fukuyama, Francis. *The Soviet Union and Iraq since 1968*. Santa Monica: Rand Corporation, 1980.

Ganev, Ivan. *sev i 'tretii mir.'* Moscow: Ekonomika, 1976.

Garthoff, Raymond L. *Détente and Confrontation: American-Soviet Relations from Nixon to Reagan*. Washington, D.C.: Brookings Institution, 1985.

Gerasimov, O. *Irakskaia neft'*. Moscow: Nauka, 1969.

Ghareeb, Edmund. *The Kurdish Question in Iraq*. Syracuse: Syracuse University Press, 1981.

Gogitidze, I. V. *Britanskaia politika 'k vostoku of Suetsa': 70-e-pervaia polovina 80-kh godov*. Moscow: Nauka, 1989.

Golan, Galia. *The Soviet Union and National Liberation Movements in the Third World*. Boston: Unwin Hyman, 1988.

Gordon, Murray. *Conflict in the Persian Gulf*. New York: Facts on File, 1981.

Goshev, V. Iu. *SSSR i strany Persidskogo zaliva*. Moscow: Mezhdunarodnye otnosheniia, 1988.

Grayson, George W. *The United States and Mexico: Patterns of Influence*. New York: Praeger, 1984.

Grimmet, Richard F. *Trends in Conventional Arms Transfers to the Third World by Major Supplier, 1977–1984*. Washington: Congressional Research Service, 1985. Report No. 85-86F.

Grummon, Stephen R. *The Iran-Iraq War: Islam Embattled*. The Washington Papers, no. 92. New York: Praeger, 1982.

Halliday, Fred. *Soviet Policy in the Arc of Crisis*. Washington, D.C.: The Institute for Policy Studies, 1981.

Hameed, Mazher A. *Arabia Imperilled: The Security Imperatives of the Arab Gulf States*. Washington, D.C.: Middle East Assessments Group, 1986.

Heller, Mark, ed., Dov Tamari, and Zeev Eytan. *The Middle East Military Balance 1984*. Tel Aviv: Tel Aviv University, 1984.

Helms, Christine Moss. *Iraq: Eastern Flank of the Arab World*. Washington, D.C.: Brookings Institution, 1984.

Hiro, Dilip. *Inside the Middle East*. New York: McGraw-Hill, 1982.

———. *Iran under the Ayatollahs*. 2d ed. London: Routledge and Kegan Paul, 1987.

Hodson, H. V., ed. *The Annual Register of World Events*. 1973–87. New York: St. Martin's Press (1973–78); Detroit: Gale Research (1979–83); Burnt Mill, U.K.: Longman (1984–87).

Holden, David, and Richard Johns. *The House of Saud: The Rise and Rule of the Most Powerful Dynasty in the Arab World*. New York: Holt, Rinehart and Winston, 1981.

Horn, Robert C. *Soviet-Indian Relations: Issues and Influence*. New York: Praeger, 1982.

Hough, Jerry F. *The Struggle for the Third World: Soviet Debates and American Options*. Washington, D. C.: Brookings Institution, 1986.

Hurewitz, J. C. *Diplomacy in the Near and Middle East. A Documentary Record: 1914–1956*. Vol. 2. New York: Van Nostrand, 1956.

———. *The Persian Gulf: After Iran's Revolution*. Headline Series 244. New York: Foreign Policy Association, 1979.

International Monetary Fund (IMF). *Direction of Trade Yearbook*. 1968—. Washington.

Ismael, Tareq Y. *Iraq and Iran: Roots of Conflict*. Syracuse: Syracuse University Press, 1982.

Jawad, Sa'ad. *Iraq and the Kurdish Question, 1958–1970*. London: Ithaca Press, 1981.

Johnson, Maxwell Orme. *The Military as an Instrument of U.S. Policy in Southwest Asia: The Rapid Deployment Joint Task Force, 1979–1982*. Boulder: Westview Press, 1983.

Jones, Christopher D. *Soviet Influence in Eastern Europe: Political Autonomy and the Warsaw Pact*. New York: Praeger, 1981.

Katz, Mark N. *Russia and Arabia: Soviet Foreign Policy toward the Arabian Peninsula*. Baltimore: Johns Hopkins University Press, 1986.

Kauppi, Mark V., and R. Craig Nation. *The Soviet Union and the Middle East in the 1980s: Opportunities, Constraints, and Dilemmas*. Lexington, Mass.: Lexington Books, 1983.

Kelidar, Abbas, ed. *The Integration of Modern Iraq*. New York: St. Martin's Press, 1979.

Kelly, J. B. *Arabia, the Gulf and the West*. New York: Basic Books, 1980.

Khadduri, Majid. *Independent Iraq, 1932–1958: A Study in Iraqi Politics*. London: Oxford University Press, 1960.

———. *Republican 'Iraq: A Study in 'Iraqi Politics since the Revolution of 1958*. London: Oxford University Press, 1969.

———. *Socialist Iraq: A Study in Iraqi Politics since 1968*. Washington, D.C.: Middle East Institute, 1978.

Khalizdad, Zalmay, Timothy George, Robert Litwak, and Shahram Chubin. *Security in Southern Asia*. New York: St. Martin's Press, 1984.

Kimball, Lorenzo Kent. *The Changing Pattern of Political Power in Iraq, 1958–1971*. New York: Speller, 1972.

Kissinger, Henry. *White House Years*. Boston: Little, Brown, 1979.

———. *Years of Upheaval*. Boston: Little, Brown, 1982.

Klare, Michael T. *American Arms Supermarket*. Austin: University of Texas Press, 1984.

Klinghoffer, Arthur Jay. *The Soviet Union and International Oil Politics*. New York: Columbia University Press, 1977.

Korany, Bahgat, and Ali E. Hillal Dessouki, eds. *The Foreign Policies of Arab States*. Boulder: Westview Press, 1984.

Koury, Enver M., and Charles G. MacDonald, eds. *Revolution in Iran: A Reappraisal*. Hyattsville, Md.: Institute of Middle Eastern and North African Affairs, 1982.

Kutschera, Chris. *Le mouvement national kurde*. Paris: Flammarion, 1979.

Landau, Jacob, ed. *Man, State, and Society in the Contemporary Middle East*. New York: Praeger, 1972.

Lee, Chae-Jin, and Hideo Sato. *U.S. Policy Toward Japan and Korea: A Changing Influence Relationship*. New York: Praeger, 1982.

Litwak, Robert. *Security in the Persian Gulf: Sources of Inter-State Conflict*. London: International Institute for Strategic Studies, 1981.

Long, David E. *The Persian Gulf: An Introduction to Its Peoples, Politics, and Economics*. Boulder: Westview Press, 1976.

Losoev, S. A., and Iu. K. Tyssovskii. *Blizhnevostochnyi krizis: neft' i politika*. Moscow: Mezhdunarodnye otnosheniia, 1980.

Macadam, Ivison, ed. *The Annual Register of World Events*. 1968–1972. New York: St. Martin's Press.

MccGwire, Michael, Ken Booth, and John McDonnell, eds. *Soviet Naval Policy: Objectives and Constraints*. New York: Praeger, 1975.

McLaurin, R. D., Don Peretz, and Lewis W. Snider. *Middle East Foreign Policy: Issues and Processes.* New York: Praeger, 1982.

McNaugher, Thomas L. *Arms and Oil: U.S. Military Strategy and the Persian Gulf.* Washington, D.C.: Brookings Institution, 1985.

Malik, Hafeez, ed. *International Security in Southwest Asia.* New York: Praeger, 1984.

Markarian, R. V. *Zona Persidskogo zaliva: problemy, perspektivy.* Moscow: Nauka, 1986.

Marr, Phebe. *The Modern History of Iraq.* Boulder: Westview Press, 1985.

Martin, Lenore G. *The Unstable Gulf: Threats from Within.* Lexington, Mass.: Lexington Books, 1984.

Matar, Fuad. *Saddam Hussein: The Man, the Cause and the Future.* Beirut: Third World Centre, 1981.

Medvedko, L. I. *Vetry peremen v Persidskom zalive.* Moscow: Nauka, 1973.

Menon, Rajan. *Soviet Power and the Third World.* New Haven: Yale University Press, 1986.

Ministerstvo vneshnei torgovli. *Vneshniaia torgovlia SSSR.* 1968—. Moscow: Statistika, 1969—.

Mirskii, G. I. *Armiia i politika v stranakh Azii i Afriki.* Moscow: Nauka, 1970.

Monroe, Elizabeth. *The Changing Balance of Power in the Persian Gulf.* New York: American Universities Field Staff, 1972.

Mottale, Morris M. *The Arms Buildup in the Persian Gulf.* Lanham, Md.: University Press of America, 1986.

Mughisuddin, Mohammed, ed. *Conflict and Cooperation in the Persian Gulf.* New York: Praeger, 1977.

Naff, Thomas, ed. *Gulf Security and the Iran-Iraq War.* Washington, D.C.: National Defense University Press, 1985.

Nakhleh, Emile A. *Arab-American Relations in the Persian Gulf.* Washington, D.C.: American Enterprise Institute, 1975.

Niblock, Tim, ed. *Iraq: The Contemporary State.* New York: St. Martin's Press, 1982.

Nixon, Richard. *The Real War.* New York: Warner Books, 1980.

Noyes, James H. *The Clouded Lens: Persian Gulf Secuirty and U.S. Policy.* 2d ed. Stanford: Hoover Institution Press, 1982.

O'Ballance, Edgar. *The Kurdish Revolt: 1961–1970.* Hamden: Archon Books, 1973.

Oganesian, N. O. *Otnosheniia Irakskoi Respubliki so stranami Arabskogo Vostoka.* Erevan: Izdatel'stvo Akademii nauk Armianskoi SSR, 1985.

Olson, Wm. J., ed. *US Strategic Interests in the Gulf Region.* Boulder: Westview Press, 1987.

Osipov, A. Iu. *Ekonomicheskaia ekspansiia SShA v arabskikh stranakh.* Moscow: Nauka, 1980.

Ottaway, Marina. *Soviet and American Influence in the Horn of Africa.* New York: Praeger, 1982.

Page, Stephen. *The Soviet Union and the Yemens: Influence in Asymmetrical Relationships.* New York: Praeger, 1985.

Pajak, Roger F. *Nuclear Proliferation in the Middle East: Implications for the Superpowers.* Monograph Series no. 82-1. Washington, D.C.: National Defense University, 1982.

Pelletiere, Stephen C. *The Kurds: An Unstable Element in the Gulf.* Boulder: Westview Press, 1984.

Penrose, Edith, and E. F. Penrose. *Iraq: International Relations and National Development*. Boulder: Westview Press, 1978.

Peterson, J. E., ed. *The Politics of Middle Eastern Oil*. Washington, D.C.: Middle East Institute, 1983.

Pinkele, Carl F., and Adamantia Pollis, eds. *The Contemporary Mediterranean World*. New York: Praeger, 1983.

Plascov, Avi. *Security in the Persian Gulf: Modernization, Political Development and Stability*. Montclair, N.J.: Allanheld, Osmun, 1982.

Porter, Bruce D. *The USSR in Third World Conflicts*. Cambridge: Cambridge University Press, 1984.

Pridham, B. R., ed. *The Arab Gulf and the West*. New York: St. Martin's Press, 1985.

Ramazani, Rouhollah K. *Iran's Foreign Policy, 1941–1973: A Study of Foreign Policy in Modernizing Nations*. Charlottesville: University Press of Virginia, 1975.

———. *Revolutionary Iran: Challenge and Response in the Middle East*. Baltimore: Johns Hopkins University Press, 1986.

———. *The Foreign Policy of Iran: A Developing Nation in World Affairs, 1500–1941*. Charlottesville: University Press of Virginia, 1966.

———. *The Persian Gulf and the Strait of Hormuz*. Alphen an den Rijn, The Netherlands: Sijthoff and Noordhoff, 1979.

———. *The Persian Gulf: Iran's Role*. Charlottesville: University Press of Virgina, 1972.

———. *The United States and Iran: The Patterns of Influence*. New York: Praeger, 1982.

Reich, Bernard. *The United States and Israel: Influence in the Special Relationship*. New York: Praeger, 1984.

Ro'i, Yaacov, ed. *The USSR and the Muslim World: Issues in Domestic and Foreign Policy*. London: Geoge Allen and Unwin, 1984.

Rosenau, James N., ed. *International Politics and Foreign Policy: A Reader in Research and Theory*. New York: Free Press, 1969.

Rubinstein, Alvin Z. *Moscow's Third World Strategy*. Princeton: Princeton University Press, 1989.

———. *Red Star on the Nile: The Soviet-Egyptian Influence Relationship since the June War*. Princeton: Princeton University Press, 1977.

———, ed. *Soviet and Chinese Influence in the Third World*. New York Praeger, 1975.

———. *Soviet Policy Toward Turkey, Iran, and Afghanistan: The Dynamics of Influence*. New York: Praeger, 1982.

———, ed. *The Great Game: Rivalry in the Persian Gulf and South Asia*. New York: Praeger, 1983.

Saivetz, Carol R. *The Soviet Union and the Gulf in the 1980s*. Boulder: Westview Press, 1989.

Saivetz, Carol R., and Sylvia Woodby. *Soviet-Third World Relations*. Boulder: Westview Press, 1985.

Sawyer, Herbert L. *Soviet Perceptions of the Oil Factor in U.S. Foreign Policy: The Middle East-Gulf Region*. Boulder: Westview Press, 1983.

Schmidt, Dana Adams. *Journey Among Brave Men*. Boston: Little, Brown, 1964.

Sirriyeh, Hussein. *US Policy in the Gulf, 1968–1977: Aftermath of the British Withdrawal*. London: Ithaca Press, 1984.

Smolansky, Oles M. *The Soviet Union and the Arab East under Khrushchev*. Lewisburg, Pa.: Bucknell University Press, 1974.

Stockholm International Peace Research Institute (SIPRI). *The Arms Trade with the Third World.* New York: Holmes and Meier, 1975.

———. *Yearbook, 1975.* Cambridge, Mass.: MIT Press, 1975.

Tahir-Kheli, Shirin. *The United States and Pakistan: The Evolution of an Influence Relationship.* New York: Praeger, 1982.

Tahir-Kheli, Shirin, and Shaheen Ayubi, eds. *The Iran-Iraq War: New Weapons, Old Conflicts.* New York: Praeger, 1983.

The International Institute for Strategic Studies. *Strategic Survey.* 1968, 1969—. Dorking: Bartholomew Press, 1969—.

———. *The Military Balance.* 1968–1969—. Dorking: Bartholomew Press, 1968—.

Tripp, Charles, ed. *Regional Security in the Middle East.* New York: St. Martin's Press, 1984.

United Nations. Department of International Economic and Social Affairs. Statistical Office. *Yearbook of International Trade Statistics, 1968—.* New York, United Nations, 1970—.

U.S. Arms Control and Disarmament Agency. *World Military Expenditures and Arms Trade, 1963–1973.* Washington, D.C.: U. S. Government Printing Office, 1975.

U.S. Department of State. Bureau of Public Affairs. *Communist States and Developing Countries: Aid and Trade in 1972.* Washington, D.C., 1973.

———. *Conventional Arms Transfers in the Third World, 1972–81.* Special Report No. 102. Washington, D.C., 1982.

———. Bureau of Intelligence and Research. *Soviet and East European Aid to the Third World, 1981.* Washington, D.C., 1983.

———. *Warsaw Pact Economic Aid to Non-Communist LDCs.* 1984, 1985, 1986. Washington, D.C.

Valkenier, Elizabeth K. *The Soviet Union and the Third World: An Economic Bind.* New York: Praeger, 1983.

Vanly, Ismet Cheriff. *Le Kurdistan Irakien, Entité Nationale: Etude de la Révolution de 1961.* Neuchâtel (Switzerland): Editions de la Baconnière, 1970.

Vasil'ev, Aleksei. *Persidskii zaliv v epitsentre buri.* Moscow: Izdatel'stvo politicheskoi literatury, 1983.

Wessen, Robert. *The United States and Brazil: Limits of Influence.* New York: Praeger, 1981.

Wharton Econometric Forecasting Associates. *Soviet Arms Trade with the Non-Communist Third World in the 1970s and 1980s: Special Report.* Washington, D.C., 1983.

Whelan, Joseph G., and Michael J. Dixon. *The Soviet Union in the Third World: Threat to World Peace?* New York: Pergamon-Brassey's, 1986.

Yodfat, Aryeh Y. *The Soviet Union and Revolutionary Iran.* New York: St. Martin's Press, 1984.

Yodfat A., and M. Abir. *In the Direction of the Persian Gulf: The Soviet Union and the Persian Gulf.* London: Frank Cass, 1977.

Zabih, Sepehr. *Iran since the Revolution.* Baltimore: Johns Hopkins University Press, 1982.

———. *The Communist Movement in Iran.* Berkeley: University of California Press, 1966.

Zevin L. S. *Economic Cooperation of Socialist and Developing Countries: New Trends.* Moscow: Nauka, 1976.

■ Index

Abdallah, Amir, 112, 124
Abu Musa, 151, 155, 157, 159, 167, 171, 182, 215, 286
Afghanistan, 27, 214, 217, 288
Ahmad, Ibrahim, 63
Akhmedzianov, A., 235
Algiers agreement of March 1975, 86, 163, 169, 188–89, 195, 196, 215, 230
Ali, Hasan, 256
Ali, Salim Rubayyi, 202
Amin, Hafizullah, 216
Ammash, Salih Mahdi, 151
Amuzegar, Jamshid, 188
Andreasian, Ruben, 39, 40, 41, 42, 221–22, 322 n.60
Anglo-American Kuwait Petroleum Company, 181
Anglo-Iranian Oil Company, 57
al-Ani, Thabit Habib, 102
Aqazadeh, Gholam Reza, 253
Arabian Gulf News Agency, 189
Arab-Israeli sector, 11
Arab-Israeli war of 1967, 64
Arab-Israeli war of 1973, 180
Arabistan Popular Front, 161
Arab principalities: formation, 143; Gulf arms race, 209–14; Iranian claim to Abu Musa, 157; Muscat conference, 198; National Liberation movements, 190–94; recognition by USSR, 286; regional security, 194–98, 205–7; United Arab Emirates, 144, 149, 150, 152, 154, 155, 182, 197–98, 286; U.S. arms, 209–14
ARAMCO, 222

Aref, Abd al-Rahman, 9, 16, 38, 44, 65, 100
Aref, Abd al-Salam, 64
Arkhipov, Ivan, 241
Arms: diversification, 30; from France, 28; Gulf arms race, 209–14; for the Kurds, 79; from the USSR, 19, 25, 28–31, 89, 97, 237, 238, 243, 258, 288, 290; from the USSR cut off, 277, 288; from the West, 209–10
Al-Assad, Hafez, 219, 232
al-Aysami, Shibli, 156
Aziz, Tariq: appeal to UN, 250; civilian protection, 238; communist release, 241; cooperation with ICP, 125; Iran invasion, 231; peace plan, 257, 266, 267; Resolution 598, 262; USSR relations, 233, 242, 247, 256

Ba'th: Afghanistan, 217; Algiers agreement, 188; Charter for National Action, 111–17; coup (1968), 66; CPSU, 18; deteriorating relations with ICP, 101–11, 127–40; deteriorating relations with KDP, 76–84; economic policy, 45, 49; ICP, 10, 25, 33, 99–102, 108, 109, 111–15, 123, 128–31, 132–33; Israel, 18; Kurdish autonomy, 67, 68, 94–98, 283, 284; Kurdish war (1974–75), 85–90, 138, 283–84; Kuwait, 175, 291; March manifesto, 70–74; nationalization (see Oil), 17, 59; Oman, relations, 194; PNPF, formation, 114; strategic importance, 291; USSR, relations, 61, 90, 107–11, 127, 133–34, 164, 291
Baghdad Pact, 15

About the Authors

Oles M. Smolansky is University Professor of International Relations at Lehigh University in Bethlehem, Pa. A native of Ukraine, he received his Ph.D. from Columbia University in 1959 and has served on the faculties at UCLA and Lehigh University. He has held senior research fellowships from the Rockefeller Foundation, the Ford Foundation, and Columbia University. His previous work includes *The Soviet Union and the Arab East Under Khrushchev*, numerous book chapters, and articles in professional journals.

Bettie M. Smolansky, a Professor of Sociology at Moravian College in Bethlehem, Pa., earned her Ph.D. at the Pennsylvania State University. She has collaborated with her husband on numerous chapters and articles.

Library of Congress Cataloging-in-Publication Data
Smolansky, Oles M.
The USSR and Iraq : the Soviet quest for influence / Oles M. Smolansky with Bettie M. Smolansky.
Includes bibliographical references and index.
ISBN 0-8223-1103-8. — ISBN 0-8223-1116-x (pbk.)
1. Soviet Union—Foreign relations—Iraq. 2. Iraq—Foreign relations—Soviet Union. 3. Soviet Union—Foreign relations—1953–1975. 4. Soviet Union—Foreign relations—1975–1985. 5. Soviet Union—Foreign relations—1985–
I. Smolansky, Bettie M. (Bettie Moretz), 1940–
II. Title.
DK68.7.I7S56 1991
327.470567—dc20   90-48597 CIP